T0323493

Growth and Inequality

Inequality is today a global concern, both for its social and human consequences, and for its impact on the pace and pattern of economic growth. In middle-income countries such as India and Brazil, this issue has received increasing attention in recent years. In Brazil, inequality grew until the 1980s, when it reached extreme levels, but has since been declining, especially after the turn of the century. In India, inequality showed little change up to the 1980s, but has since been rising. These differences result from a variety of economic, social and political factors, which are examined in depth in this comparative study.

Growth and Inequality: The Contrasting Trajectories of India and Brazil is a long-term historical study of the patterns of growth in both countries and their consequences for inequality, along with an analysis of labour market structures, wages and employment. It examines both the overall distributions of income and expenditure, and disparities across gender, region, caste, race, and access to education. It compares the experience of the two countries, and draws conclusions on the policies that might lead to a more equitable development path.

The book provides much material of value to policy-makers and other social actors concerned with development, labour and social policy. It will also be helpful for researchers, teachers and students of development economics, sociology and history.

Alexandre de Freitas Barbosa is Professor of Economic History and International Economics at the Institute of Brazilian Studies of the University of São Paulo, and Senior Researcher at the Brazilian Center for Analysis and Planning (CEBRAP). His research is concerned with inequality and the labour market in Brazil, the role of developmentalism in Brazilian economic history, and Brazil's pattern of international economic integration.

Maria Cristina Cacciamali is Professor of Latin American Political Economy, Public Policy and Labour Studies at the University of São Paulo, where she is Coordinator of the Research Group on International Studies and Comparative Policies. A Senior Researcher of the Brazilian National Research Council, her work covers political economy and comparative studies of labour markets, institutions, income distribution, and informal economy.

Gerry Rodgers is Visiting Professor at the Institute for Human Development, New Delhi. He was Director of the International Institute for Labour Studies at the International Labour Organization and headed several other research programmes at ILO. He works on poverty, inequality, inclusive development, labour and employment, especially in India and in Latin America.

Growth and Inequality

The Contrasting Trajectories of India and Brazil

Alexandre de Freitas Barbosa
Maria Cristina Cacciamali
Gerry Rodgers

With contributions from
Taniya Chakrabarty
Magda Chang
Eduardo Cury
Nandita Gupta
Janine Rodgers
Ian Prates
Fabio Tatei
Vidhya Soundararajan

INSTITUTE FOR
HUMAN DEVELOPMENT

CAMBRIDGE
UNIVERSITY PRESS

CAMBRIDGE
UNIVERSITY PRESS

University Printing House, Cambridge CB2 8BS, United Kingdom

One Liberty Plaza, 20th Floor, New York, NY 10006, USA

477 Williamstown Road, Port Melbourne, vic 3207, Australia

314 to 321, 3rd Floor, Plot No.3, Splendor Forum, Jasola District Centre, New Delhi 110025, India

79 Anson Road, #06–04/06, Singapore 079906

Cambridge University Press is part of the University of Cambridge.

It furthers the University's mission by disseminating knowledge in the pursuit of education, learning and research at the highest international levels of excellence.

www.cambridge.org
Information on this title: www.cambridge.org/9781108416191

© Alexandre de Freitas Barbosa, Maria Cristina Cacciamali and Gerry Rodgers 2017

First published 2017

Printed in India by Shree Maitrey Printech Pvt. Ltd., Noida

A catalogue record for this publication is available from the British Library

Library of Congress Cataloging-in-Publication Data

Names: Barbosa, Alexandre de Freitas, author. | Cacciamali, Maria Cristina, author. | Rodgers, Gerry, author.
Title: Growth and inequality : the contrasting trajectories of India and Brazil / Alexandre de Freitas Barbosa, Maria Cristina Cacciamali, Gerry Rodgers.
Description: New York : Cambridge University Press, [2017] | Includes bibliographical references and index.
Identifiers: LCCN 2017034625 | ISBN 9781108416191 (hardback : alk. paper)
Subjects: LCSH: India--Economic conditions--21st century. | Brazil--Economic conditions--21st century. | Economic development--India. | Economic development--Brazil. | Equality--India. | Equality--Brazil.
Classification: LCC HC435.3 .B363 2017 | DDC 338.954--dc23 LC record available at https://lccn.loc.gov/2017034625

ISBN 978-1-108-41619-1 Hardback

Contents

List of Tables

List of Graphs and Maps

Preface and Acknowledgements

This book presents the main results of a research project that was undertaken at the Brazilian Centre for Analysis and Planning, São Paulo, Brazil (CEBRAP) and at the Institute for Human Development, New Delhi, India (IHD), with the financial support of the International Development Research Centre, Canada (IDRC, grant 106919). The project aimed to better understand the factors shaping labour market inequality in India and Brazil, on the basis of a comparison of the experiences of the two countries, and to inform policies that might lead to its reduction. It also aimed to contribute to the development of methods of comparative research on labour market issues, drawing on the intellectual traditions in the two countries, and to strengthen research collaboration across countries of the South.

This is a long term study of a subject that is always in the political spotlight. As we write, both countries are undergoing substantial change, as new governments reverse earlier policies and introduce new initiatives. We take note of some recent developments in the last chapter, but this is a never-ending story. We do not have a crystal ball and do not try to second-guess the outcomes of current debates. Our argument is rather that positions and actions today have to be understood in historical context. Economic structures and social institutions change slowly, and the patterns observed in the past provide lessons for the future, and help build a critical perspective on political claims and arguments.

Further results from this research can be found in publications listed in the references at the end of the book. These include papers on data sources and research approaches in the two countries, policy papers on minimum wages and on training systems, lectures, presentations, and more detailed quantitative papers and monographs. While this book is a comparative study of Brazil and India, the research was also based on more detailed studies of each country.

This was a team effort in which many people made important contributions. Among the IHD team, Vidhya Soundararajan undertook much of the processing of survey data from the Indian National Sample Survey and other sources, including basic information on patterns of inequality and employment, inequality decompositions, and other econometric work; Taniya Chakrabarty worked on labour market structure and labour institutions in India, and on inequalities across social groups, and provided research support on several other issues; Nandita Gupta wrote on social policy, education, and training in India; and Janine Rodgers wrote the section on gender inequality in the two countries, prepared analyses of output and employment trends in manufacturing and services, and commented extensively on other sections. Among the CEBRAP team, Fabio Tatei undertook much of the quantitative work, including basic information on patterns of inequality and employment, inequality decompositions, and other econometric work, and also contributed to different chapters of the book. Magda Chang, Eduardo Cury, and Ian Prates, the other members of the Brazilian team, compiled and organized macroeconomic and/or labour market data and provided crucial inputs to their analysis. Rogerio Barbosa shared with the group his knowledge on different Brazilian databases. Murilo Marschner Alves and Priscila Vieira also participated in different parts of the research process. André Gambier Campos and Ricardo Luiz Chagas Amorim were close partners, providing methodological insights on how to cope with the scarcity of data for some periods. This book could not have been completed without these substantial contributions.

In the early stages of the project, J. Krishnamurty prepared a paper on patterns of inequality in the colonial period in India and the decades after independence, and helped in the analysis, notably of the Indian growth regime before 1980. Ashok Pankaj, who was a member of the IHD team for some months, made contributions on social policy, caste inequality, and other topics, and provided helpful comments on drafts of this manuscript. In India, two external advisers participated in discussions and made a variety of valuable comments and suggestions – Jayati Ghosh from Jawaharlal Nehru University, and T. S. Papola from the Institute for Studies in Industrial Development. We all greatly regretted Professor Papola's untimely death in November 2015. Jean Drèze gave helpful comments on the analysis of social policy. Colleagues at IHD participated in workshops and made a variety of valuable comments in the course of the work, and we would like to in particular thank the Director of IHD, Alakh Sharma, for his steadfast support for this work, as well as the secretarial and administrative staff of IHD for their unfailing help. The International Labour Office's Delhi office also provided support, and we are particularly grateful to Sher Verick for his comments and assistance.

On the Brazilian side, we would like to thank CEBRAP research staff who participated in the workshops held in Brazil and also CEBRAP administrative staff who provided support throughout the whole project. Comments by Adalberto Cardoso, Kjeld Jakobsen, Marcos da Costa Lima, Anne Posthuma and Rafael Osorio in advisory meetings held in São Paulo were strategic for refining the methodology and the approaches used in this book. We would like to thank Laís Abramo and Anne Posthuma, who kindly helped in the organization of policy dialogues in Brasília at the ILO office, during which representatives of civil society, academia, and the government, as well as ILO staff, attended and shared with the research team their reactions and insights.

We would like to acknowledge the unfailing support of the IDRC, and in particular that of Edgard Rodriguez, who managed the IDRC grant to this project, and who provided help and encouragement, and participated in substantive discussions in the course of this project. We would also like to thank the Cambridge University Press team in New Delhi, and in particular Anwesha Rana and Anurupa Sen, for their sustained support and assistance in the finalization of this book.

Last but not least, the mirror image metaphor, which we use in the book to compare Brazil and India, also helped to shape our own perceptions and interactions. Coming from different theoretical backgrounds and working trajectories, all the members of the two teams shared experiences that seemed quite far apart in the beginning, only to find out that sometimes what initially seems strange belongs to a hidden and heretofore unknown side of our souls. The most important outcome of a cooperative endeavour is about friendship. By understanding and sharing with others, we enrich ourselves.

List of Abbreviations

Abbreviation	Expansion	Expansion in Portuguese
AITUC	All India Trade Union Congress	
ANMs	Auxiliary Nurses and Midwives	
ASDP	Ajeevika Skill Development Programme	
BCE	Before Common Era	
BJP	Bharatiya Janata Party	
BNDES	Brazilian Bank for Economic and Social Development	*Banco Nacional de Desenvolvimento Econômico e Social*
BPC	Continuous Cash Benefit Programme	*Benefício de Prestação Continuada*
BPL	Below Poverty Line	
BRICS	Brazil, Russia, India, China and South Africa	
CDS	Current Daily Status	
CEBRAP	Brazilian Center for Analysis and Planning	*Centro Brasileiro de Análise e Planejamento*
CNSS	National Council for Social Service	*Conselho Nacional de Serviço Social*
CPF	Personal Register System	*Cadastro de Pessoas Físicas*
CPI	Communist Party of India	

Abbreviation	Expansion	Expansion in Portuguese
CPI	Consumer Price Index	
CSO	Central Statistical Office	
CUT	United Workers Confederation,	*Central Única dos Trabalhadores*
DIEESE	The Inter-union Department of Statistics and Socio-economic Studies	*Departamento Intersindical de Estatística e Estudos Socioeconômicos*
ECE	Early Childhood Education	
ENEM	National High School Examination	*Exame Nacional do Ensino Médio*
EPF	Employee's Provident Fund	
ESI	Employees' State Insurance	
EU	European Union	
FAT	Workers' Support Fund	*Fundo de Amparo ao Trabalhador*
FDI	Foreign Direct Investment	
FGTS	Severance Pay Fund	*Fundo de Garantia do Tempo de Serviço*
FIESP	Federation of Industries of the State of São Paulo	*Federação das Indústrias do Estado de São Paulo*
FIPE	The Institute of Economic Research Foundation	*Fundação Instituto de Pesquisas Econômicas*
FS	Union Power	*Força Sindical*
FUNRURAL	Fund for Social Assistance and Social Security of Rural Workers	*Fundo de Assistência Social e Previdência do Trabalhador Rural*
GDCF	Gross Domestic Capital Formation	
GDP	Gross Domestic Product	

Abbreviation	Expansion	Expansion in Portuguese
GFCF	Gross Fixed Capital Formation	
GNI	Gross National Income	
HDI	Human Development Index	
IBGE	Brazilian Institute of Geography and Statistics	*Instituto Brasileiro de Geografia e Estatística*
ICDS	Integrated Child Development Scheme	
IHD	Institute for Human Development	
ILO	International Labour Organization	
INEP	National Institute of Educational Studies and Research	*Instituto Nacional de Estudos e Pesquisas Educacionais*
INPS	National Social Security Institute	*Instituto Nacional de Previdência Social*
INTUC	Indian National Trade Union Congress	
IPCA/IBGE	National Consumer Price Index of IBGE	*Índice Nacional de Preços ao Consumidor Amplo*
IPEA	Brazil Institute of Applied Economic Research	*Instituto de Pesquisa Econômica Aplicada*
IRDP	Integrated Rural Development Programme	
JK	Juscelino Kubitschek	
KILM	Key Indicators of the Labour Market	
LDB	Law with Guidelines for National Education	*Lei de Diretrizes e Bases da Educação Nacional*
MGNREGA	Mahatma Gandhi National Rural Employment Guarantee Act	

Abbreviation	Expansion	Expansion in Portuguese
MNC	Multinational Companies	
MoRD	Ministry of Rural Development	
MOSPI	Ministry of Statistics and Programme Implementation	
MST	Landless Workers' Movement	*Movimento dos Trabalhadores Sem Terra*
NCAER	National Council of Applied Economic Research	
NCEUS	National Commission for Enterprises in the Unorganised Sector	
NGO	Nongovernmental Organizations	
NNI	Net National Income	
NREGA	See MGNREGA	
NREGS	National Rural Employment Guarantee Scheme	
NSDP	Net State Domestic Product	
NSS	National Sample Survey	
NSSO	National Sample Survey Organisation	
OBC	Other Backward Classes	
OECD	Organisation for Economic Co-Operation and Development	
PBF	Family Allowance Programme	*Programa Bolsa Familia*
PDE	Education Development Plan	*Plano de Desenvolvimento da Educação*
PDS	Public Distribution System	

Abbreviation	Expansion	Expansion in Portuguese
PETI	Programme for the Eradication of Child Labour	*Programa de Erradicação do Trabalho Infantil*
PMDB	Brazilian Democratic Movement Party	*Partido do Movimento Democrático Brasileiro*
PNAD	National Sample Household Survey	*Pesquisa Nacional por Amostra de Domicílios*
PNE	National Education Plan	*Plano Nacional de Educação*
POF	Family Expenditures Survey	*Pesquisa de Orçamentos Familiares*
PPP	Purchasing Power Parity	
PROGER	Programme for Employment and Income Generation	*Programa Geração de Emprego e Renda*
PRONATEC	National Programme of Access to Technical Education and Employment	*Programa Nacional de Acesso ao Ensino Técnico e Emprego*
ProUni	University for All Programme	*Programa Universidade Para Todos*
PSDB	Brazilian Social Democracy Party	*Partido da Social Democracia Brasileira*
PT	Workers' Party	*Partido dos Trabalhadores*
RBI	Reserve Bank of India	
RMV	Monthly Basic Income	*Renda Mensal Vitalícia*
SC	Scheduled Caste	
SELIC Rate	Brazilian Basic Interest Rate	*Sistema Especial de Liquidação e Custodia*
SEPPIR	Secretariat for the Promotion of Racial Equality	*Secretaria Para a Promoção da Igualdade Racial*

Abbreviation	Expansion	Expansion in Portuguese
SEWA	Self-Employed Women's Association	
SINAPIR	National System for the Promotion of Racial Equality	*Sistema Nacional Para a Promoção da Igualdade Racial*
SINE	Brazilian National Employment Service	*Serviço Nacional de Emprego*
ST	Scheduled Tribe	
SUAS	Integrated Social Assistance System	*Sistema Único da Assistência Social*
SUDENE	Superintendency for the Development of the Northeast	*Superintendência de Desenvolvimento do Nordeste*
SUS	Integrated Health System	*Sistema Único de Saúde*
TFR	Total Fertility Rate	
TNCs	Transnational Corporations	
UGT	General Union of Workers	*União Geral dos Trabalhadores*
UNDP	United Nations Development Programme	
UPA	United Progressive Alliance	
UPSS	Usual Principal and Subsidiary Status	
VET	Vocational Education and Training	
WIEGO	Women in Informal Employment: Globalizing and Organizing	
WIID	World Income Inequality Database	

1

Brazil and India
A Mirror Image of Each Other?

Concern about inequality is nothing new, but in recent years it has become a central part of the debate on growth and development. There are many reasons. One is that economic inequality has been growing in many parts of the world, raising doubts about the fairness and inclusiveness of prevailing development paths. Another is that globalization has changed the pattern of winners and losers and excluded many from the benefits of global growth. There is also increasing recognition that high levels of inequality may adversely affect not only the nature of growth, but also its pace and sustainability. Political reactions to inequality include a sense that there must be limits to how far wealth and income should be concentrated among a small fraction of the world's population.

The political debate draws on the growing academic literature on inequality, in which an important landmark was Kuznets' pioneering empirical work in the 1950s (Kuznets, 1955). This was followed by a substantial expansion of research into the nature and sources of economic inequality (Atkinson, 1973, 1983; Sen, 1982). In the last decade or so a number of influential publications (including Atkinson and Piketty, 2010; Stiglitz, 2012; Piketty, 2014; Atkinson, 2015; Milanovic, 2016) have documented the extent of inequality of income and wealth and its consequences. These authors show that inequality is a fundamental dimension of both national and global economies, and one that needs to be more effectively addressed by public policy.

That is the point of departure of the present book, which is built on the view that economic inequality can only be understood, and policies to reduce it can only be effective, when the historical process through which particular patterns of inequality arise both within and between countries is taken into consideration.

This calls for an analysis of social and political forces, their development over time, and how they interact with capital accumulation and growth.

The debate on inequality runs parallel to the emergence, in recent decades, of a large number of middle-income countries as influential participants in the global economy. That is the genesis of the BRICS group of Brazil, Russia, India, China, and South Africa. But, beyond the political grouping, the history of these countries can provide insights into how patterns of distribution have been embedded in their growth and development, and into the ways economic, social, and political structures have interacted.

These five countries are too different to learn much from trying to compare them all, but a comparison of two of these countries can provide a basis for improving the understanding of each. That is why this book examines the issue of inequality through a comparison of India and Brazil, two countries which differ in many ways – so that sometimes they seem to be the mirror image of each other – but which also have some relationships and patterns in common.

India and Brazil are today the third and seventh largest economies of the world, and together they account for almost 10 per cent of world GDP.[1] Both countries had similar rates of economic growth during the 1950 to 2010 period as a whole (4.9 per cent per year in India, and 4.6 per cent per year in Brazil). However, the distribution of this growth has been quite different over time (Graph 1.1). From 1950 to 1980, Brazil's economy grew at almost 7 per cent per year, while India's growth was slow. After 1980, the trend was reversed, and India's GDP started growing at a much faster rate than Brazil's. But, despite this difference in growth over more than three decades, per capita GDP in Brazil, expressed in dollars at purchasing power parity (PPP), is still almost three times that of India.

Together, the two countries account for one-fifth of the world's population. India is the second most populous country in the world, with a population of over 1.2 billion, whereas Brazil ranks fifth, with close to 200 million inhabitants in 2010. Over the period from 1960 to 2010, population in both countries has grown at a similar average rate, of about 2 per cent per annum. But the rate of growth, higher in Brazil in the 1960s and 1970s, has since been declining more rapidly than in India, as Brazil has entered the last stage of demographic transition before India (Graph 1.2).

---

[1] Calculated in purchasing power parity (PPP) terms. They are seventh and ninth in nominal terms.

Graph 1.1. Annual Rates of GDP Growth (%), Brazil and India, 1950–2010

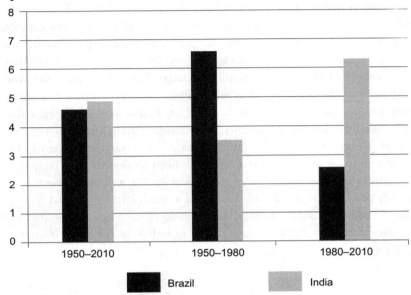

Source: Maddison database (2013); World Bank, *World Development Indicators*.

Graph 1.2. Annual Rates of Population Growth (%), Brazil and India, 1960–2010

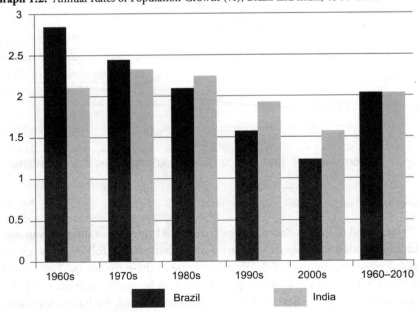

Source: World Bank, *World Development Indicators*.

The economic differences between the two countries do not concern only the rate of growth – there is also a large difference in terms of urbanization production and social structures. From the 1950s until 2000, Brazil urbanized rapidly (Graph 1.3), and today over 85 per cent of the population is urban. In India, urbanization started from a much lower level, and has been slow. Almost 70 per cent of India's population is still rural today. This is reflected in the pattern of production and employment – half of India's workers are still employed in agriculture, against only an eighth in Brazil. In Brazil, most of the agricultural land is used for large-scale commercial farming, although around two-thirds of rural workers are found on family farms. India's agrarian system is more subsistence-based, small-scale, and informal. Both economies have large service sectors, but India's has been growing faster than Brazil's, and the Indian economy is widely described as service-led. Brazil had a much larger industrial base than India in 1980, but its share in GDP has been declining and – if we consider the secondary sector as a whole – is now similar to India's, at just over a quarter.

Graph 1.3. Urbanization (%), Brazil and India, 1950–2010

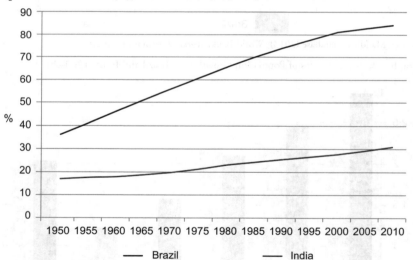

Source: United Nations Population Division (2014).

The period of high economic growth in Brazil brought not only urbanization and industrialization. Social and economic change was followed by greater inequality, so that by the 1980s, Brazil was one of the most unequal societies in the world. Graph 1.4 shows the long-term trends in inequality in India and Brazil, as measured by the Gini coefficient. In the case of Brazil, we have a long series measuring inequality of individual labour income; while for India, inequality of household expenditure per capita is the main measure provided by the existing data. These measures for Brazil and India are different, but when we discuss them in more detail (Section 4.2), we argue that their pattern of change over time can be compared.

What we see is almost a mirror image. Inequality rose in Brazil from the 1960s to the 1980s, but then peaked and started to fall, especially after 2000. In India, inequality showed little change until the 1990s. Then, and especially from the end of the 1990s, it started to rise.

Graph 1.4.A. Inequality over Time: Brazil – Gini Coefficient of Labour Income

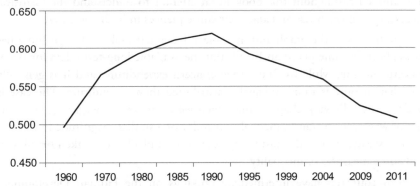

Source: 1985 onwards, computed from Brazilian National Household Sample Survey data (PNAD; IBGE, various dates). Earlier years, Census data (1960, 1970, 1980).

Graph 1.4.B. Inequality over Time: India – Gini Coefficient of Household Expenditure Per Capita

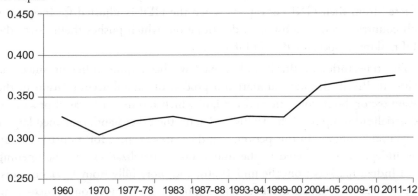

Source: Mainly based on data from the National Sample Survey (NSS)(Government of India, National Sample Survey Office/Organization, various years). For earlier years, UNU-WIDER, World Income Inequality Database.

This difference between the two countries in the time path of inequality calls for an explanation. The steepest rise in inequality in Brazil was during the high-growth period before 1980. In India also inequality started to rise after the growth rate accelerated in the 1990s. But the story is more complicated than a simple positive correlation between growth rates and inequality might suggest. Inequality in Brazil stayed high during a period of slow growth in the 1980s, and declined during a period of moderate growth after 2000. In India, inequality rose more slowly after 2004, when growth rates were highest, than between 1999 and 2004. It is not just the pace, but also the nature of growth, which will be examined throughout this book in an attempt to understand the historical succession of growth regimes and their consequences in both countries.

The figures in the graph and in Table 1.1 make it look as though India has always been less unequal than Brazil. But the available long-term data for Brazil concern income, while for India they concern expenditure, and it is generally true that income is more unequally distributed than expenditure. The case is made in the following chapters that when we compare like with like, as in the case of wages, for instance, inequality is today of a similar magnitude in the two countries; indeed, over the past thirty years or so, India has overtaken Brazil in at least some measures of inequality.

Both countries have intermediate rankings on the Human Development Index (HDI), but are some way apart, Brazil at the 75th position and India 130th (UNDP, 2015). These rankings are close to – slightly lower than – their Gross National Income (GNI) per capita rankings. For both countries, this is because their education indicators (average years of schooling) are worse than would be expected from their GNI per capita. When the HDI is adjusted for inequality, both countries show a substantial deterioration, which pushes them down the HDI rankings, especially Brazil (Table 1.1).

The trajectories of Brazil and India have been quite different since the 1940s. In Brazil, the state supported a process of capital accumulation in the private sector, both domestic and foreign, which resulted in a rapid process of industrialization up until the 1970s. India, on the other hand, remained largely an agrarian economy in this period, and the state-led drive for industrialization after independence faltered in the mid-1960s. Liberalization and the opening up of Indian markets from the mid-1980s, and more fully from 1991 onwards, were associated with an acceleration of growth, built more on services than manufacturing. During the same period, Brazil's pattern of integration with the world economy changed, but the liberalization policies applied in the 1990s did not bring about a resumption of economic growth. Growth recovered in the 2000s, reflecting commodity exports as well as the expanding internal market, but the rate of growth in Brazil was only half of that of India even during the high-growth period from 2004 to 2008, and the gap has widened since.

Table 1.1. Selected Economic and Social Indicators – Brazil and India (1980–2014)

	Brazil				India			
	1980	1990	2005	2014	1980	1990	2005	2014
Per capita GNI in PPP (current international $)		6475	10560	15630		1174	2966	5610
HDI	0.545	0.612	0.705	0.755	0.369	0.431	0.527	0.609
Inequality-adjusted HDI (IHDI)				0.557				0.435
Overall loss in HDI due to inequality (%)				26.3				28.6
Population below poverty line (%)	24.0*	20.6	9.6	4.9§	~54**	45.3#	37.2	21.9##
Gini coefficient of household income per capita (Brazil), expenditure (India)	0.597**	0.602#	0.565	0.527##	0.326**	0.326#	0.363	0.375##

Source: GNI per capita and poverty data for Brazil from the World Bank Database; HDI data and IHDI from the UNDP Database.

Note: Poverty line for Brazil, $1.90 per day at 2011 PPP. For India, Tendulkar estimates (Table 4.2.8). * 1981; ** 1983; # 1993 or 1993-94; ## 2011 or 2011-12; § 2013.

These are both capitalist growth paths, in the sense that in the end they rely on private accumulation, even if the state still plays an important role. One way to interpret these differences is to suggest that the two countries have produced their own varieties of capitalism, as they experience specific patterns of integration in the world economy with very different social and institutional underpinnings. The nature of economic and social goals in each country, and the degrees of success in meeting them, also differ substantially.

But there are also many parallels. In both countries, the state has been a central actor, and the development strategy was initially built around industrialization. In both countries, the process of industrialization has been regionally unbalanced. In the case of Brazil, it was concentrated mainly in São Paulo and in the Southeast, increasing economic and social differences with other regions; in India, industry has developed fastest in the West and the South of the country, while the eastern region remained relatively backward. There are parallels in terms of inequalities between social groups as well, as in the case of historical social divisions of caste and race respectively in India and Brazil, which have different meanings but underpin inequalities and discriminations in each. Tribes living in many geographical pockets are particularly deprived in both countries. Gender inequality is important in both, more prominently so in India. Both countries have a significant workforce that is informal or unprotected, though the sizes and economic roles of this informal 'sector' are different.

Both countries have initiated welfare policies to address the issues of poverty, deprivation and distribution with different purposes, motivations and scope. In Brazil, measures to combat poverty were strengthened after the 1990s, and the goal in the 2000s was to 'end extreme poverty' (measured by the government poverty line of a quarter of the minimum wage per family member). In India, anti-poverty programmes have been implemented since independence and more so since the 1970s, and poverty has fallen (Table 1.1), but rural poverty continues to be widespread and there has been some movement of rural poverty to urban areas. Just to give an idea, the Indian population below the World Bank poverty line of $1.90 per day still exceeds 250 million, that is, considerably in excess of the total population of Brazil.

Attitudes to inequality, on the other hand, have been divergent. In Brazil, the adverse economic and social consequences of high inequality have been acknowledged and policies to address this issue have been prominent, especially during the 2000s. In India, the primary focus of policy has been on reducing poverty rather than inequality. Nevertheless, some important problems that the country faces, including the persistence of social unrest and conflict around issues of identity and opportunity, are rooted more in inequality than in poverty.

In Brazil, the fall of inequality since the mid-1990s cannot be explained by a single factor, but it can be said that government redistribution policy was more coherent after 2003. Declining inequality has reflected a set of different social and economic policies that were mutually reinforcing. A rising minimum wage, labour market dynamism and improvement in the social security and cash transfer mechanisms were some of these factors, combined with a resumption of economic growth.

In India, rising inequality after the mid-1990s was widely seen as a result of the liberalization process. There has been some flattening of the rising trend in inequality since the mid-2000s, and this may at least in part reflect social policy innovations, of which the most visible is the Mahatma Gandhi National Rural Employment Guarantee Act (MGNREGA). However, the expansion of social policy has not been on the scale of the more comprehensive policies implemented in Brazil.

These divergent patterns raise important questions for both analysis and policy. What are the sources of these differences in inequality between the two countries? Do they lie in economic structures and growth paths, in embedded social inequalities, in policy choices, in the functioning of markets? Do they reflect patterns of integration in the global economy or are they home-grown? How important is the labour market, the types of jobs that are created and the distribution of employment opportunities? What is the importance in overall inequality of differences in remuneration between different groups of workers, as compared with the distribution of income between capital and labour? What impacts may the changing social structure have on patterns of inequality? In particular, what is the importance and impact of gender inequality, and of inequalities between social groups? What structures, historical processes, and new forces (such as the changing patterns of integration in the global economy) are affecting India's and Brazil's ability to take advantage of growth to achieve social ends? Which aspects of inequality are deeply embedded and call for structural economic and social changes, and which aspects respond to redistributive policies? The following chapters explore some of these issues.

The next chapter presents the methodological framework that has been used for the comparative analysis. In reality, we have combined two different approaches to inequality. The first is historical and qualitative, and attempts to show how inequality has been an inherent feature of the process of growth and development in each country. This requires an analysis of social institutions, economic structures and political forces, and how they have interacted over time. The second is focused on particular dimensions of inequality, their nature, their importance and how they connect with each other and with the broader economic and social framework.

Chapters 3 and 4 then pursue the historical and structural analysis, the first up to 1980, the second since that date and up to 2014. In both countries, 1980, or the 1980s, forms a natural dividing line, though for different reasons.

We consider how different 'growth regimes' have led to particular patterns of inequality. We examine macroeconomic patterns and their interconnections with key factors such as labour markets and labour market institutions, and discuss the role of the state in social policies and their success or failure in reducing inequalities.

Chapter 5 explores how these broader forces are intertwined with major social cleavages, in terms of inequality between sexes, social groups – race, caste, and community – and regions. It also considers whether education has also been a factor of differentiation. It addresses the significance of each of these dimensions of inequality, how they have changed since the 1980s, how far they overlap and how they interact with the broader forces discussed in the preceding two chapters.

Chapter 6 synthesizes the main findings, sets the changing pattern of inequality in a wider historical, economic, and social context and presents the main challenges for inclusive growth in both countries.

Finally, Chapter 7 considers some of the new economic and political uncertainties that have come to the fore, especially in Brazil, which is facing one of the deepest crises in its history (not only economic, but also affecting its democratic institutions). Although India is not experiencing the same kind of crisis, the contradictions of its growth regime have also grown. So in the concluding section, we reflect on these new social, economic and political realities and their implications for inequality in the light of the past and present growth regimes in both countries.

2

Approach and Method

Why compare Brazil and India? Can this duo provide a meaningful comparison that will help to explain the patterns and trends of inequality within each country?

Brazil and India have different social structures and histories, the urban/rural divide is expressed in quite different ways, and their labour markets have different shapes – for instance, in the nature of segmentation and in the importance and role of informal work. Moreover, the patterns of international economic integration are dissimilar, as well as some of the drivers of economic growth and how these have changed over time.

However, there are common elements too. Both countries underwent a process of industrialization on the periphery of the world economy, led by the state, which not only modified their position in the international division of labour, but also brought about deep social changes and ruptures. Both countries had break points at similar dates in their development process – first in the 1930s (Brazil) or the 1940s (India), and then in the 1980s for both. After the 1980s, both economies liberalized, at different speeds and in different ways, while maintaining an important economic role of the state. This changed the dynamics of the economy and the labour market, especially after 2000, when the comparison is particularly interesting, because the main outcomes in terms of inequality diverged, although both economies increased their engagement with the global economy.

Even though different political settings prevailed after the 1980s, Brazil and India were both stable democracies during this period,[1] with more or less solid institutions, allowing for a public debate over their development strategies. The role of the state, the size of the internal market, a significant position in the global

---

[1] We discuss recent developments in the last chapter.

economy, and a vibrant and fast-changing civil society demanding redistribution are some other points they have in common. This combination is not generally found in other developing countries.

For a comparison to be productive, the differences need to be understood as well as the similarities, and care is required in interpreting apparently similar patterns that may in fact have different origins and natures. Also the framework of analysis needs to be the same for both cases. But comparative analysis of this type provides additional degrees of freedom and a perspective on social and economic relationships that is relative rather than absolute.[2]

The literature on comparative development is large, and a wide variety of methodologies have been applied. Many studies consider countries as observations, collect information on a large number of them and examine patterns on the basis of selected variables defined at the country level. With respect to inequality, for instance, the tradition goes back to Kuznets (1955), Paukert (1973), and many others. More recently, publications by Milanovitch (e.g., 2005) provide a good example of this type of work. Some authors apply this sort of approach at the regional level, as in Cornia's (2014) work on Latin America.

While such studies often produce important and influential findings (witness the continuing influence of Kuznets' inverted U-shaped pattern of inequality with development), it is also clear that they are limited by their inability to reflect the institutional and historical specificities of each country. They capture some parts of the picture, assuming that the rest is devoid of movement.

Other studies select a group of countries where similar factors or relationships can be identified (for instance OECD (2010) and Ravallion (2011)). Much comparative policy analysis is of this type, examining the impact of particular economic and social policy instruments in different countries and drawing conclusions on their effectiveness. Such studies can treat country characteristics and institutions as explanatory variables, but they tend to be narrowly defined, as they are limited to analysing the impact of the chosen policies taken as independent variables.

In our view, inequality is too broad and complex to be addressed in this way. Inequality itself has many dimensions, and its origins and determinants are rooted in a wide variety of economic and social structures and relationships. This has led us to attempt a more holistic approach, which takes as its point of departure how inequality is embedded in national institutions and histories.

---

[2] Concepts, methods and data sets for making Brazil-India comparisons have been discussed in detail in Barbosa, Cacciamali et al. (2014a, 2014b).

This method requires an investigation of the dynamics of social and economic change, which makes it less precise – because of the number of 'variables' and interactions involved – than more focused studies. So this approach is essentially qualitative in nature.

An example of comparative work in a holistic perspective, as applied to the process of development and change, can be found in the attempt by Pomeranz (2000) to contrast Europe and China and their different development paths in the nineteeth century. A significant feature of this method is the demise of the idea of a universal pattern of development. Comparison should be 'reciprocal', in the sense that it explores how actual paths and patterns deviate from one another. Deviations are looked at not as something that does not follow the norm but as something 'seen through the expectations of the other' (Pomeranz, 2000). If 'contingencies and conjunctures' differ, their totalities are composed of a variety of relations not necessarily found in the other case. This strategy allows for the identification of important driving forces that – absent in their counterpart – underpin the divergent paths. According to this 'reciprocal comparative method', the paths and trajectories observed in each country are considered a result of interacting and conflicting forces that can be historically unveiled. So there are no independent variables as such, but a set of factors that work out in each economy or society, bringing about contrasting patterns through their interactions in the historical context.

Another example of the holistic approach is Evans' examination (1995) of the role of states in the periphery that seek to change their relations within the wider global economy. Evans presupposes the existence of a cohesive bureaucracy embedded in civil society, supporting the process of industrialization and technological catch-up. On the basis of these premises, he addresses some country-specific realities in order to investigate the forms of state intervention and the patterns of relationship with the society. There is no universal norm. Japan and South Korea would be the ideal types of 'developmental state' and the former Zaire the best example of a 'predatory state'. Brazil and India are situated in between.

Following these earlier traditions, our comparative approach is grounded in a specific, although not exclusive, theoretical framework. We draw on the work of the 'Regulation school', adopted here as a frame of reference, not as a straitjacket. The basic insight of the Regulation approach, as expressed in the work of Aglietta (1982), Boyer (1990) and others, is that a set of mutually interacting institutions underpins a particular path of growth, capital accumulation, and distribution. We term such a path a 'regime of accumulation' or 'growth regime'. These institutions shape the balance between the interests of different groups within the political economy, and potentially pave the way for a 'mode of regulation' that can stabilize the growth path. But there is no universal law. Moreover, institutional forms change over time or external factors (including the way the global economy operates) may change, and ultimately contradictions arise, bringing the growth regime to a stalemate. These changes can lead to economic or political crisis and a shift in the growth regime, in which institutional forms are rearranged or modified and eventually a new mode of regulation emerges.

The classic application of the Regulation approach was to the 'Golden Age' of growth in Western Europe in the post-war period up to the oil shocks of the 1970s (Marglin and Schor, 1990), but the approach is of more general application. For instance, Boyer (1994) shows how specific growth regimes arise in different spaces within the wider global economy.

Growth regimes comprise a variety of economic and social relations, usually grouped under five institutional forms in the analysis of industrialized countries: monetary/fiscal regime; wage labour relations; the competition regime; type of integration in the international economy; and the role of the state. In India and Brazil, we found it desirable to add a sixth, the agrarian system, since this is a major component of the national economy in both countries, not fully captured by wage labour relations. All these institutional forms do not have the same importance, as some dominate others, but the hierarchy varies across time and geography. Nor are they independent, for within a growth regime there is a dynamic process of mutual adaptation among institutions.

This approach has elements in common with the 'varieties of capitalism' literature (Albert, 1993; Boyer and Hollingsworth, 1997; Crouch and Streeck, 1997; Hall and Soskice, 2001; Amable, 2005), which has arisen more recently. This literature builds on the basic understanding of capitalist societies found in Polanyi's (1944) work; that is, institutional arrangements other than the market are needed in order to contain its explosive nature. Actually, the market could not exist without them. The recent literature contests the idea that globalization leads to one single model, as resilient institutions are a prerequisite for the continuing dynamism of capitalism, and this tends to increase the divergence between nations (Boyer and Hollingsworth, 1997). At the same time, 'pure' models – however they are defined – may turn into more hybrid versions (Crouch and Streeck, 1997).

In this literature, some of the main assumptions of the Regulation school, such as institutional complementarity – institutions are embedded in historical and social contexts, so it is not possible to export isolated institutions from one situation to another – and institutional hierarchy are maintained. Some authors deal with institutional sectors, instead of the institutional forms (Amable, 2005), which could be easily translated to the Regulation school's theoretical framework. The advantage of this latter framework – and the reason we use it – is that its main concepts are in more widespread use than those of the varieties of capitalism literature, which is largely confined to developed countries.[3]

Our approach departs from much analysis of social and economic phenomena such as inequality, which usually takes national settings and institutions as given. This is also its main challenge, as in principle almost nothing is left out of the picture. In practice, it must bypass some complex issues, but it nevertheless seeks to cast the net wide. When combined with an international perspective on development processes in different spaces of the world economy, this also helps to remove national blinkers. The observed national patterns of development are seen as just one of the possibilities, rather than an inevitable outcome.

Another advantage of a wider systemic approach is that it permits us to examine some of the assumptions that are otherwise taken for granted, and shows how notionally culture-free theory is in fact grounded in particular historical situations. So our effort differs from, for example, the dualistic view of extractive versus inclusive institutions adopted by Acemoglu and Robinson (2012), in which history is mostly reduced to 'path dependence'. As Gerschenkron (1962) pointed out more than fifty years ago, it is meaningless to track 'the' origin of a set of events, if the causal chain throughout history, complex as it may be, is not unveiled by some overall theoretical framework.

So the basic idea is to try, insofar as it is possible, to compare totalities – the growth regime, the institutions that underpin it, the different dimensions of inequality that result – in different periods of time for each country. But of course, the 'totality' can never be complete. Even the most comprehensive approach is necessarily partial, and is constructed on the basis of knowledge of specific relationships. We have therefore tried to complement the broader approach, and strengthen its foundation, by also examining, separately, some of the important cleavages and divides in the labour and social spheres of the two countries. Within the overall growth regime, there are some embedded social and economic disparities, which may take different forms as the overall framework

---

[3] One interesting exception can be found in Nölke (2012), in which the author tries to address the specificities of the varieties of capitalism in BRICS countries.

evolves, and then feed back on the character of the growth regime itself. These are different in each country, but often parallels can be found.

The most basic such divide lies in the segmentation of the labour market itself, and the structural inequalities in employment opportunities and wages that result. In both countries, labour status is a central factor in labour market inequality. In India, there is a gap between casual and regular wage workers, and in Brazil, between workers who have a signed labour card, establishing their rights, and those who do not. The existence, persistence, and impact of these differences constitute an important element in the growth regime of both countries.

But there are also a number of other dimensions of inequality that are embedded in different ways, and which we try to explore individually. One of the most pervasive is gender inequality, which conditions the pattern of opportunity in any growth regime. A second dimension, which is particularly important in large countries like Brazil and India, is regional inequality. The regional pattern of growth is part of the growth regime too, and can be an important source of polarization, which is persistent over time, although not static. A third dimension concerns the differentiation and discrimination between social groups. In India, caste, tribe and community are powerful forces, as they condition labour market outcomes and inequalities. In Brazil, the key historical divide is race. The nature and origins of these categories, all socially constructed, are very different in the two countries, but the mechanisms through which they operate can be compared. A fourth, and slightly different dimension is education, often analysed in terms of investment in human capital. But because there are differences in access to education, which are transmitted across generations, this too is a structural dimension of inequality.

There is a considerable literature on all these factors, which we cannot review here. The factors are analysed in terms of their importance and impact, using household survey data, with particular stress on their relative importance and how their impact has changed over time. In practice, the resistance to change of these differentiations and discriminations is an important reason for the persistence of inequality, working as a source of hysteresis within the growth regime. Comparable surveys since the 1980s in the two countries make it possible to connect these specific inequalities with the growth regimes, at least during the period of economic liberalization of the past three decades.

In sum, inequality is analysed not only as a statistical result, but as part of a complex of economic, political, and social forces that are historically intertwined. There are several steps in this method. It starts with an overview and comparison of the process of growth and distribution in the two countries – identifying the principal components of the regimes of growth and capital accumulation, including the role of the state and other institutions and their implications for inequality. Two comprehensive charts in Chapters 3 and 4 summarize the basic institutions and corresponding growth regimes and modes of regulation over the long run. The remainder of the book examines the social and economic elements of this framework and how they have changed in recent decades, comparing the patterns between the two countries.

This analysis is both synchronic (between countries in a given period of time) and diachronic (how countries change over time), for growth regimes are dynamic concepts. The shifts witnessed in the two countries reflect both internal and external forces, and the dynamics of change is not the same. Some similar patterns can be seen in both India and Brazil, but earlier in one than in the other, reflecting the shape of institutions or the differing strength of external factors. But these patterns need to be interpreted in historical context, rather than comparing isolated trends that occurred in different periods of time.

Finally, a word is required on the concept of inequality itself. We use the word as if its meaning is self-evident, but it is not, as is apparent from the literature on the subject (notably Sen (1982) and Atkinson (1983)). Among economists, the most frequent practice is to consider inequality in terms of the distribution of household income/expenditure or household income/expenditure per capita. We have restricted ourselves mainly to an economic concept of inequality, choosing a practical approach. At various points in this book, we consider inequality in terms of the distribution of household income and expenditure, assets, or wages; disparities between social groups in these measures; disparities in access to employment or education; and, more generally, structural differences in opportunities and options for different categories of the population. We have used the measures of inequality that are most frequent in the literature. Moreover, the statistical traditions in the two countries often provide different measurements. For instance, in India, data on household expenditure are much more abundant than data on income, while in Brazil the situation is the reverse. These factors add to the complexity of comparison, and make it less precise, without making it less interesting.

At this point, we may come back to the initial question: why Brazil and India? The first answer is methodological. There is a range of common factors, of diverse nature – actual and potential productive capacity; large and heterogeneous labour markets; democratic institutions; relevance of social movements; and an important role in the industrial semi-periphery of the global economy – which makes a comparison between India and Brazil more interesting than, say India and Indonesia or Brazil and Argentina.

The second answer is rather pragmatic. The increasing importance of the BRICS in the global economy, and the fact that these large middle-income countries are subject to somewhat similar challenges, naturally raises the question of their similarity or difference. Each comparison can provide its own insights, especially when we look beyond short term politics to longer term patterns. Brazil and India, two prominent globalizing capitalist economies, have shown diverging trends in inequality, which naturally raises the question – why? In a world where inequality is increasingly on the political agenda, the reasons for these different outcomes are of considerable interest, even more so if these countries are considered important players in the changing geopolitical game. So, a search for factors that transcend the specifics of each country has the potential to deliver high returns.

3

Brazil and India in the Decades before 1980

Chapters 3 and 4 review the patterns and trends of economic and social inequality in Brazil and India since the middle of the twentieth century. As noted above, 1980, or the early 1980s, is an important dividing line in both countries (as it was in much of the world), albeit for different reasons, and we therefore separate the discussion into two parts, treating the period up to 1980 in Chapter 3 and the period after 1980 in Chapter 4.

In both chapters, the first section presents the broad picture – the political and social environment, the nature of growth and capital accumulation, the underlying social and economic institutions, and how these different elements of the growth regime emerged, changed and underpinned a historically specific pattern of inequality. The following three sections in each chapter examine particular dimensions of the growth regime. We first discuss the macroeconomics of the growth regime, in terms of the pace of growth and of capital accumulation, sectoral patterns of final demand, output and employment, and the resulting level of inequality and poverty in the economy as a whole. The next section examines labour institutions and labour markets. A central focus of this study is the nature and extent of labour market inequality, and how it relates to broader aspects of distribution. Key factors include the type of labour market segmentation and its relationship with heterogeneity in the production system, wage differentiation and wage shares, the regulatory framework and other labour market interventions such as the minimum wage, and the organization of labour. The final section considers more specifically the role of the state, and how state policy has impacted on inequality, through the pattern of government expenditure, through direct redistribution and through social policies. In many of these areas, more can be said for the period after 1980, when data sources are usually more extensive.

With such a broad compass it is not possible to examine all of these issues in depth – the aim has been to present the overall picture, sometimes at the cost of loss of detail. But in Chapter 5 we complement the systemic approach of Chapters 3 and 4 with a more detailed discussion of some pervasive dimensions of inequality – gender, region, caste, race and education – using analytical categories and measures that can be compared between the two countries.

3.1 Political Context, Social Environment, and Growth Regimes

3.1.1 The point of departure

In both India and Brazil, the foundations of many of today's institutions were laid in the 1930s and 1940s. However, the two countries had very different economic and social structures at that time. In 1940, while a majority of Brazil's population of 40 million people was still rural, 31 per cent already lived in urban areas (a figure only reached by India in 2011), and the economy was increasingly driven by the industrial powerhouse of the city of São Paulo and its surrounding region. India, on the other hand, was a populous agrarian economy dominated by subsistence agriculture, with limited industrial capacity and weak international linkages.

Brazil's colonial past was behind it, but the country remained dependent on the dominant global forces, both economically and politically. In political terms, the slavery-based monarchy of the nineteenth century had been replaced by an oligarchic republic (1889–1930), run by a political elite in the capital, Rio de Janeiro, and backed up by regional clientelistic arrangements. The nationalist leader Getúlio Vargas, who came to power in 1930 backed by urban social groups and by rural oligarchies of some states, aimed to do away with this fragmented economy and polity.

India achieved independence only in 1947, and its economy was to a significant degree shaped by the interests of the colonial rulers. But it was embarking on an explicitly socialist development path in a democratic parliamentary framework. A great deal of political influence was exerted by a national elite that reflected the prevailing social hierarchy and the pattern of economic power in the agrarian system and in industry. However, the struggle for independence had thrown up a socially committed leadership with a vision that aimed to go beyond class interests.

These different starting points condition our analysis of accumulation and growth. We will compare the two countries during the same time period, but some challenges were faced by India later than Brazil, or took different forms because of the dissimilar political and social contexts.

Despite these differences, the two countries had some elements in common in the middle of the twentieth century. Both were large enough to have substantial domestic economies, with a significant industrial sector. Both had a long history of discrimination and exclusion. In Brazil, the legacy of slavery was still felt in its embryonic labour market and in the extremely different opportunities for black and white populations. The former slaves and their descendants had not been integrated as wage workers in a labour market that was still concentrated in São Paulo and Rio de Janeiro. In India, the caste system had also structured the labour market and the opportunities for different groups, in ways which seemed more rigid and difficult to change. Within both countries, there were large regional differences in resources and production structures, which helped to concentrate the benefits of economic growth. In addition, both countries could by 1950 be described as 'developmental states', in the sense that their governments saw their mission as one of promoting industrialization and economic growth.[1]

3.1.2 Political context and economic strategy

In Brazil, the political configuration of this period was quite unstable, starting with the 1930 Revolution, led by Getúlio Vargas, who claimed to have lost the presidential election due to fraud. After taking office by force in November 1930, his main goal was to centralize power, promote national integration, and intensify the role of the state in economic and social matters. Indirectly elected by the parliament in 1934, and once again ruling the country as a dictator from 1937 to 1945, he took advantage of a wide political support base to modernize the Brazilian economy. This went much beyond the old oligarchies (to which in reality he belonged) to include new groups – industrialists, segments of the middle classes, and the state-controlled trade unions (Ianni, 1971). The main political events of the period are summarized in Table 3.1.1.

Two major political projects competed with each other throughout the period up to the 1960s (Ferreira, 2005). On one side, the 'national-statist' project sought to advance the country's industrialization by means of social reforms, fiscal subsidies, and public investment – without adopting an autarkic posture, as it was believed that industrialization would change the external relations of the economy. Foreign capital should not be barred, but regulated. On the other side

---

[1] See the discussion of Evans' (1995) work in Chapter 2. In fact, he labels both countries 'intermediate states', and considers South Korea the archetypal 'developmental state'.

was the 'liberal-conservative' project, which unified segments of the oligarchies and portions of the business and middle classes. Though not opposed to the industrializing drive, it sought to open up entry for foreign capital, and to restrict state intervention to high risk activities.

The second, now democratically elected Vargas administration (1951–1954), created the economic institutions to underpin industrialization – the oil company Petrobras, the Brazilian Development Bank (BNDE from Portuguese *Banco Nacional de Desenvolvimento Econômico*), state-led energy sector projects, and the first attempts at regional intervention, among many others. Nevertheless, it was the administration of Juscelino Kubitschek (JK) (1956–1960) that consolidated the process of industrialization by opening the national market to investment by transnational companies. Using the state machinery developed in the previous government, the JK government launched the Plano de Metas (Goals Plan). This involved a partnership between the government and private companies (both national and transnational), the latter responsible for the dynamic sectors of capital and durable goods in manufacturing. Growth in production of intermediate goods and infrastructure was assured mainly by state companies (Lafer, 2002).

During the JK administration, there was a struggle within the state machine between the two competing projects, but rather than one or the other of them becoming dominant, a third project emerged, a 'dependent development' project. This fuelled the engine of the internal market even further, setting aside progressive reforms – urban, agrarian, social security, administrative, and financial – which aimed to pave the way for a less unequal development pattern. This implied an 'open space' for capitalist accumulation to spread from industry to agriculture and services, but without any countervailing forces that could make it less disequalizing for both rural and urban workers. During JK's term of office, civil society was active, and there was a widespread national ideology aiming to promote social inclusion, even though this was not realized, as most government efforts were concentrated on speeding up the growth process.

To make the dependent development project viable politically, a military coup emerged as a 'solution' to the fight between alternative projects, as it allowed for a new pattern of capital accumulation in the country – one that should not be jeopardized by redistributive pressures, as its technocrats argued. The new structure of power grouped together the overarching interests of the new classes (especially international capital and ascendant national capital) and old ones (like the rural oligarchy), with the technocrats as mediators. But this left out of the political space the workers, nationalist bureaucrats, and segments of the urban middle classes, many of whom faced repression or were exiled.

Thus, the military coup of 1964 resulted in the deepening of the dependent development project. By breaking with the triad of nationalism, development and social reforms, it set off other structural reforms that would boost the productive forces of capitalism in Brazil. These reforms distinguished the country's authoritarian regime – the state had a strong hand in economic matters – from the paths followed by most of Brazil's neighbours in the Southern Cone of Latin America, which applied liberal economic reforms. A period of high growth ensued, and lasted until 1980. Growth rates fell after the oil shock of 1973, but remained high during the second half of the 1970s. By then, the military regime had initiated a 'slow, gradual and safe political transition' in the face of a political reaction from trade union leaders, the middle classes, intellectuals, and even segments of the private sector who pledged their commitment to the return of democratic institutions. Nevertheless, in 1980 Brazil was still under military rule.

India's story had some elements in common with Brazil in the early years after independence, but major differences emerged. The struggle for independence consumed the energy of national leaders until the end of the Second World War, but plans for a national development strategy were already being put in place in the 1930s. In 1944, a group of leading Indian industrialists prepared a framework for industrialization and economic development (the 'Bombay Plan') which had considerable influence on economic policy after independence in 1947 (Thakurdas 1945). In some ways, this resembled the national-statist project in Brazil, as it relied on large-scale public sector investment to provide the conditions for private sector growth. This was an important aspect of 'Nehruvian socialism', a nationalist model built around public sector economic leadership and supported by a wide political coalition. But the state played a larger role in India than in Brazil. A Planning Commission was created and a formal five-year planning process was rapidly put in place, its design significantly influenced by the example of the USSR. Nevertheless, there was a partnership with domestic capital, which had benefitted from the transfer of control of businesses with the departure of the British, and from public sector investment, and was highly monopolistic (De and Vakulabharanam, 2013). Industrial and public sector labour was also relatively advantaged. Like in Brazil from 1946 to 1964, economic policy was subordinated to democratic process. However, unlike in Brazil, there was no change in political direction, since the first thirty years after independence saw the Congress party, which had led the independence movement, re-elected in successive general elections and in power at the national level without interruption until 1977.

Table 3.1.1. Political Timeline: 1930 to 1980

Date	Brazil	India	
1930–1950	1930 Revolution – Getúlio Vargas takes office through *coup d'état* 1934 New constitution. The Congress elects Vargas president 1937 Vargas closes Congress and bans political parties; authoritarian regime until 1945 1945 Vargas forced out; new presidential elections 1946 New constitution	1935–37	Provincial autonomy with Congress governments
		1942	'Quit India' movement
		1944–45	Bombay plan for industrialization and development
		1947	Independence
1950–1960	1951 Vargas elected by popular vote with a nationalist programme 1954 Vargas commits suicide under the pressure of the right-wing opposition 1956 Juscelino Kubitschek becomes president, launches Goals Plan.	1950	New constitution adopted; creation of Planning Commission
		1951–56	First Five-Year Plan
		1950s	Indian National Congress in power, led by Jawaharlal Nehru
1960–1970	1961 João Goulart takes office under a parliamentary system. 1963 Presidentialism re-established and political radicalization 1964 Military coup 1968 Increasing repression of leftists and social movements by military regime	1962	War with China
		1964	Death of Nehru
		1965	War with Pakistan
		1965–67	Drought and famine
		1966	Indira Gandhi Prime Minister (until 1977)
1970–1980	1968–73 High rates of growth provide 'legitimacy' for authoritarian government; opposition silenced 1974 President Geisel announces 'slow, gradual and safe' political transition 1979 Amnesty for exiles and spread of demonstrations against military regime	1970–71	War with Pakistan and independence of Bangladesh
		1971	Indira Gandhi re-elected on slogan 'get rid of poverty'
		1975–77	Emergency; Opposition leaders jailed
		1977–79	Janata government

There were also other influential economic currents in India, notably a strong Gandhian tradition, which stressed the simple, local, autonomous community as against Nehru's concern with large-scale industrialization. Traces of this, as well as more business-oriented development models, can be identified throughout the period, but they were secondary forces. There were also important landed interests represented in the Congress party – including both peasant leaders and landlords.

The latter in particular succeeded in delaying and weakening land reform, especially in the populous states of North India (Chibber, 2012).

The 1960s was a period of political crisis, with wars against China and Pakistan and the severe drought and famine of 1965–67. After Nehru's death in 1964, a struggle for control within the Congress party led to the victory of a faction led by his daughter, Indira Gandhi, who engaged in a much more explicitly populist agenda aimed at eradicating poverty. But she never achieved the political dominance of her father, and conflicts with other political forces grew as she asserted her power. Relationships with major economic actors – both business and labour – deteriorated. In the latter half of the 1970s, this led to the suspension of democracy and the imprisonment of her opponents, followed by an election that she lost, an unstable alternative government, and her subsequent return to power. The effect of these conflicts and the instability that they generated was to undermine the longer term state-led development agenda, and to legitimize the demands of a variety of special-interest groups (Kohli, 2012a). There was, therefore, a clear divergence between India and Brazil from the mid-1960s onwards, for the alliance between capital and an authoritarian regime in Brazil led to high rates of growth, while political crisis in India had the opposite effect.

These political developments were closely intertwined with the growth regimes in the two countries, which we consider in more detail below. In both countries, the development paths launched in the 1940s and 1950s proved unmanageable, economically and politically, in the mid-1960s. This led to political changes in both countries. But while the authoritarian regime in Brazil pursued the path of intensive industrial development subsidized by the state, and accompanied by rising inequality, India saw a shift to populist policies aimed at poverty eradication, but which were undermined by decelerating economic growth.

3.1.3 Growth regimes in Brazil and India

As explained in Chapter 2, our analysis is built around regimes of growth and capital accumulation, which reflect the overall relationships between social and economic institutions and political forces. Table 3.1.2 summarizes the features of the key institutions in the two countries up to 1980, under the six major headings identified above: international integration, competition regime, wage labour relations, agrarian relations, monetary and fiscal regime, and the role of the state.

The importance of these different institutions was not the same in the two countries. In Brazil, two institutional forms dominated, although not in a homogeneous or continuous way: the pattern of international integration and the role of the state, built on an increasingly oligopolistic production system.

Wage labour institutions were basically subordinate, adapting to the overall growth regime, and the same was true of fiscal and monetary policies. Agrarian relations changed during this period, not through land reform, but as a result of increasing capital investment, which made labour relations more precarious and heterogeneous, especially after the mid-1960s. The new commercial farms made use of short-term wage contracts and did away with the subsistence plots that were previously cultivated by small peasants, who received in exchange a meagre monetary income.

In the case of India, the state was dominant and international integration was unimportant, while private capital played a subordinate role. As in Brazil, wage labour institutions adapted to the overall growth regime, in that effective structures for protection and representation of labour were mainly restricted to the sectors that were seen as a priority for growth – notably heavy industry. The private sector was oligopolistic, as in Brazil, but more dependent on the state. Agrarian relations evolved rather than being transformed, with limited land reform and the gradual extension of market forces, while the dominant agrarian classes retained influence as a political constituency.

The period up to the mid-1960s

In Brazil, the growth regime up to 1955, which we characterize as 'constrained industrialization' (Table 3.1.2), was initially prompted by the international crisis of 1929, a turning point which moved the driving force of the economy from export markets towards domestic demand. It also inaugurated a new economic role for the state, which in the 1930s and 1940s invested in the industrial sector and in infrastructure, expanded credit, and regulated labour relations to promote the social inclusion of some occupational groups in the urban-industrial sector. The industrial sector, until then driven mainly by the production of primary goods for export, began to play a significant role in the accumulation process.

With strong import restrictions in place, investment responded to the growth of domestic demand, mostly concentrated in the non-durable goods sector, but including production of some industrial inputs, mainly by publicly owned companies. Profit rates were assured by both protection from foreign competition and the labour market structure, with an elastic labour supply and a framework of regulation that discouraged collective bargaining. As a consequence, the accumulation process did not evolve towards greater capital intensity (Cardoso de Mello, 1990).

After 1940, the creation of the minimum wage prevented the cost of labour from rising, as it set an income that was independent of the productivity levels of different industries, thus reducing pressures for wage increases. On the other hand, it also established a floor to labour incomes and fuelled consumer demand, as the growth of employment ensured the expansion of the wage bill (Oliveira, 2003). Short-term credit was supplied mainly by public banks, such as Banco do Brasil, and tax revenues did not increase much as a percentage of GDP, at least until the mid-1960s. Agriculture, even though not yet modernized, was not a source of inflationary pressure, for it was able to deliver the basic goods needed by the increasing urban population by expanding the land frontier and raising productivity in some parts of the country. Agrarian reform, a highly debated issue in the political area, never became public policy.

However, this regime of capital accumulation was short-lived and its mode of regulation unstable, as the time horizon for return on capital was short, social conflicts emerged, and balance-of-payments imbalances increased. The government initially lacked the financial power to expand investment in the dynamic manufacturing sectors, and the same was true of the national private sector. This, however, changed in the 1950s with the creation of Petrobras – the state oil company – and BNDE, which funded important infrastructure projects and basic industries (such as steel). The role of the state – especially the technical expertise within the bureaucracy in the case of BNDE – and nationalistic pressure from civil society, in the case of Petrobras, were strategic in this progress.

This is why a more intensive process of accumulation began in 1956, in the 'heavy industrialization–I' period from 1956 to 1963 (Table 3.1.2), when a triple alliance between the state, the national bourgeoisie, and international capital paved the way for a new growth regime. The key difference with the earlier period lay in the international connection, as the second half of the 1950s was marked by the internalization of the world market. American and European Foreign Direct Investment (FDI) arrived in new Brazilian industries such as automobiles, household appliances, electric power, metalworking, and engineering.

Therefore, in the second half of the 1950s, the national-statist project had already lost influence, presaging the later victory of the dependent development project. Nevertheless, the state continued to play a powerful role in this period, planning investment, mobilizing national and foreign savings, and increasing budget expenditures, albeit without tax reform. However, the structure of aggregate demand did not change, and the increase in productivity was not transferred proportionally to either prices or wages, leading to over-accumulation, due to the high profit rates. Rather than facing scarcity of capital, the growth regime 'drowned' in capital excess (Rangel, 1986), prompting a cyclical crisis (1961–1963) that was accompanied by rising social conflicts, inflation, and balance-of-payments deficits. Even the state bureaucracy, which had underpinned the prior leap forward, became obsolete, as the production structure it had erected had widened its array of interests beyond its capability to control, and its funding sources were depleted. At this point, fiscal deficits and inflation were mounting, and Brazil could not afford to finance its international debt, as the export pattern had not changed. In a polarized political setting, President João Goulart (1961–1964), supported by the labour movement and progressive social forces, was unsuccessful in his attempt to control inflation and renegotiate the external debt. At the same time, unable to establish alliances with the more conservative groups, who were increasingly allied with US interests, he could not bring about the social reforms he advocated.

During this period, up to the mid-1960s, there was an effort at state-driven industrialization in India, like in Brazil, but its character was rather different. After an initial period until 1957, when the Indian economy was relatively open to imports, the country followed an essentially autarkic strategy, with minimum linkage with the international economy. There was virtually no international investment in the Indian economy, transnational firms played little role, and domestic investment was driven largely by import substitution – notably in the production of capital and intermediate goods. Some foreign aid helped to meet financial and food deficits. Up to the mid-1960s, there was no significant growth in exports or imports. The lack of international investment meant that capital accumulation depended essentially on domestic savings, increasingly through the government; by the 1960s, over half of all investment was public. This required the government to expand fiscal capacity; with the acceleration of growth after independence, government revenues as a share of GDP doubled between 1950 and 1970, mainly through indirect taxation (Vaidyanathan, 1982).

With little competition from abroad, national markets were basically oligopolistic in industrial goods, other than those that could be produced locally and on a small scale. A national capitalist class benefitted from the indirect subsidies provided by public sector investment in infrastructure, capital goods, and intermediate inputs. Prices were controlled by the government, but allowed for adequate profits. Some key sectors, such as power, were public sector monopolies, where prices were set low.

A high priority after independence was to transform the agrarian structure but, as noted above, landed interests played a blocking role within the political system. Nevertheless, there was limited land reform, which reduced landlessness in some parts of the country, though semi-feudal production relations persisted in others, and many rural workers remained under forms of bondage until the 1980s. In practice, there was relative neglect of agriculture in the planning process, as it received a less than proportionate share of investment, and output growth was relatively slow (Chaudhuri, 1978).

Part of the overall strategy of industrialization in the period after independence involved the creation of an industrial proletariat, which received fair wages and was protected by trade union organization and labour law. Wages were also largely protected from competitive forces (Chibber, 2012). Until the mid-1960s this group, while small, did grow, along with the numbers of public sector workers. It also took industrial action to defend its interests, to the point where Nehru expressed concern about the impact of labour-management conflict on economic development (International Labour Office, 1958). However, the bulk of workers remained in rural areas, where these protections did not reach.

The state dominated economic activity throughout this period, driving growth through public investment and setting rules for private economic activity. The Planning Commission, created in 1950, played a central role in setting economic strategy and resource allocation, and in particular was responsible for the industrialization strategy in the Second Five-Year Plan, associated with the name of Mahalanobis. The government was clearly a more effective economic actor in the Nehruvian period than later on, perhaps because it incorporated potential opponents into a broad coalition, though this also made it more vulnerable to particular interests.

The mid-1960s to 1980

In Brazil, after the military coup of 1964, and up to 1980, there was an even more flexible labour regime than before – with union repression, legislation that facilitated the turnover of labour, and declining real wages – which resulted in income concentration and an increase in profit rates. Helped by new financial (both private and public) and fiscal instruments (subsidies), the economy grew once again, bringing about higher levels of public investment and a new surge of foreign capital. This is what made possible the 'heavy industrialization-II' period (Table 3.1.2). But unlike the earlier period, increases in aggregate demand came mainly from growth of investment (private and public), consumption by the elites, and the rising level of exports, favoured by a policy of currency mini-devaluations. In this way capital accumulation was maintained with government incentives in a quite favourable international setting, at least until 1973. The result was a profit-led accumulation process that increased functional and personal income inequality.

As a result, after the stabilization plan that was implemented in the period 1964 to 1966, growth in GDP soared between 1968 and 1973, reaching a rate of 13 per cent in the latter year, the last of the so-called 'economic miracle'. Economic growth slowed afterwards, but still remained rapid, now with a substantial contribution coming from the capital and intermediate goods sectors, though the economy was heavily dependent on rapidly increasing external debt.

In the 1970s, investment by the state and transnational companies (TNCs) leapt ahead of demand, reinforcing the oligopolistic industrial structure. The share of manufacturing in GDP reached its highest level in Brazilian history. The leading companies, mostly TNCs, relied on a belt of national suppliers, and this entrenched the durables and capital goods sectors in the production system. This was not a version of 'state capitalism', but a model of private capital expansion – pioneered by TNCs – with strong support from the government (Evans, 1979). The regional elites also benefitted from this model, as they were able to attract capital, through public subsidies, modernizing the more backward regions – the Centre-West, the Northeast, and the North – but with less diversified production structures and much higher social exclusion. In these regions, the minimum wage and the labour legislation were less effective, leading to the growth of a new proletariat, mostly in urban areas and largely dependent on precarious jobs.

In other words, a more intensive process of capital accumulation got under way in Brazil, which allowed the country to change its export profile. In 1980, 42 per cent of the value of exports consisted of manufactured goods (Bresser Pereira, 1998). Capital accumulation also spread from industry into services and agriculture. The gaps between sectors widened, but the most important outcome was the increasing inequality within sectors.

In the agricultural sector, up to the late 1950s, the extensive model predominated. Big landowners could use the cheap labour of their quasi-peasants and expand their production for both the internal market and for exports. Output growth depended on access to land and the elastic supply of workers under non-capitalist relations. After the 1960s, there was a segmentation of the market between exporters, who obtained access to new technologies and subsidized credit, and producers for the internal market. The expansion of capitalist employment relations led to the casualization of the rural labour market, now interacting closely with the unskilled urban labour market. Rural workers became mobile and dispossessed of labour rights. On the other hand, a new peasant class emerged, producing mostly for the internal market, but receiving low incomes due to the presence of commercial intermediaries or the lack of credit and technical expertise. While the internal market for foodstuffs was divided between capitalists and small landowners, their goods were highly differentiated and met distinct demand profiles. Land concentration increased, and peasants with small plots could hardly eke out a living even when included in the market (Velho, 1976; Goodman, 1986), thus reinforcing the ongoing process of rural-to-urban migration.

In India, the mid-1960s was a turning point for different reasons. The autarkic economic strategy proved to be unsustainable, as higher growth required intermediate inputs and capital goods beyond the capacity of the domestic economy. Growth faltered. Then, in the mid-1960s, a deep agricultural crisis and famine struck. Along with the political crises induced by war and the succession to Jawaharlal Nehru, there was strong pressure for change. When Indira Gandhi won the internal battle for political power and the 1971 general election, she did so on the back of a populist programme that aimed to treat poverty directly through employment creation and a variety of social programmes under the slogan *Garibi hatao* (eradicate poverty).

While this can be interpreted as a shift of growth regime, as indicated in Table 3.1.2, it rested largely on the same institutions as before. From the late 1960s, there was some growth of exports to meet foreign exchange needs, but it was limited, and proved insufficient to avoid a deep balance-of-payments crisis at the end of the 1970s. The state remained the key economic actor, including on the demand side, since government expenditure rose much faster than either private consumption or investment, partly because of the new emphasis on programmes aimed at reducing poverty. But while public investment remained high, the state-led model failed to deliver high rates of growth in the 1970s. GDP growth remained stuck at 3 to 4 per cent per year, famously described by the prominent economist Raj Krishna as the 'Hindu rate of growth'. Rising government expenditure in a period of low growth led to fiscal deficits and eventually, to financial crisis (Nagaraj, 2012; De and Vakulabharanam, 2013).

There was little change in the structure of industry in this period – which remained oligopolistic and based on domestic capital – and the share of industry in GDP stagnated. Like in Brazil, it was regionally unbalanced, concentrated in the West and South of the country and near major ports. In the 1970s, there were attempts to promote small-scale industries and to control private monopolies, but these had little effect. Over time and especially after the mid-1960s, improved trade union organization and bargaining increased the wage gap between industrial workers and the rest of the workforce. At the same time, there was a growth of precarious jobs and informality in urban areas, especially in personal and domestic services, as economic growth was far too slow to absorb the growing labour force.

There were larger changes in agrarian relations. From the late 1960s, the technological changes known as the Green Revolution spread, along with irrigation, but these too were regionally concentrated (especially in Northwest India). It was widely argued that the Green Revolution led to increasing inequality, because larger farmers were better placed to take advantage of the new methods – they had access to credit and markets and could invest in new seeds and fertilizers. The number of casual agricultural workers grew in both absolute and relative terms, and casual wages hovered around subsistence levels throughout the period (Jose, 1988).

3.1.4   Dynamics of growth and inequality

From 1940 to 1980, Brazil was one of the world's fastest growing economies. In 1980, it had a highly diversified manufacturing industry when compared to other developing countries, which led to the creation of jobs not only in manufacturing but also in modern services. Nevertheless, its social structure was very unbalanced. There was a large informal sector, and a substantial segment of wage earners who were deprived of basic social goods and labour rights, and received at best a minimum wage that diminished over time in real terms. Inequality had risen substantially, especially in the poorest regions of the country, which had experienced higher economic growth rates in the 1970s than the richer areas. The booming economy may have brought about a fall in absolute poverty (Rocha, 2003), but social exclusion became more widespread, especially with respect to health, education, housing, and labour conditions (Singer, 1977). At the same time, the urban middle classes, with better jobs and levels of education, expanded substantially. Yet a growing and increasingly powerful industrial proletariat was starting to fight for better wages and labour rights.

In India, the thirty years of a state-led growth regime from independence up to 1980 succeeded in expanding India's industrial base. But it created a highly dualistic economy, reproducing neo-Fordist industrial relations for a small fraction of the workforce while leaving the great majority in essentially unregulated, competitive labour markets, subject to various forms of vulnerability and exploitation. Productivity gains in agriculture were modest despite the Green Revolution, and growth was insufficient over the period to raise living standards for the population as a whole. There is some evidence that the income share of the highest income groups declined during this period – unlike in Brazil, where a wealthy elite grew – but the income share of the poorest groups hardly rose and poverty remained high.

If we compare the two countries more directly, we can identify some of the factors that underpinned the patterns and paths of inequality. Both countries were initially quite successful in promoting industrial growth, but there were some major differences.

First, in India the expansion of industry was heavily dependent on the state, and did not generate a substantial process of private accumulation, unlike in Brazil. So, after the mid-1960s, the experience of the two countries diverged – growth faltered in India but accelerated in Brazil.

Secondly, the pattern of distribution was different, in that only a small group of industrial workers benefitted in India, while the mass of workers were engaged in casual or low productivity work in agriculture or services. This segmentation persists even today. In Brazil, especially during the 1970s, the industrial workforce expanded significantly. Even though unable to benefit from productivity gains, they were much better off than the huge sub-proletariat concentrated in urban areas (Singer, 1981). At the same time, the growth regime in Brazil was instrumental in expanding a relatively well-off middle class, while in India the growth of this class was slow.

These different outcomes would shape the subsequent trajectories of both countries. In Brazil, democracy would be restored in the 1980s with the support of the new trade unionism that developed in the late 1970s, along with other social movements. In India, industrial workers, fewer in number, were more concerned with defending their specific interests and could not play the same role as their Brazilian counterparts, even when democracy was under threat in the 1970s.

The dynamism of the Brazilian economy lay in the process of rapid capital accumulation. This yielded high returns, due to complementary private and public investment, the low cost of labour – to which rural-to-urban migration contributed by flooding the urban labour market – and the absence of countervailing redistributive policies or institutions. On one side of the coin, there was mounting inequality; on the other, there was a strengthening power of workers and new social actors brought into being by the modernization process itself. In India, neither were productive forces so dynamic, nor was rural-to-urban migration as important. Economic growth proved insufficient to fight poverty, and while inequality was probably somewhat reduced within both urban and rural areas, the urban-rural gap increased. In contrast, in Brazil inequality rose sharply overall, but more within both urban and rural areas than between them.

Table 3.1.2. Growth Regimes and Modes of Regulation in Brazil (1930–1980) and India (1947–1980)

	Brazil			India	
	Constrained Industrialization (1930–1955)	Heavy Industrialization–I (1956–1963)	Heavy Industrialization–II (1967–1980)	Post-Colonial Industrialization (1947–1967)	State-Driven Populist (1967–1980)
Accumulation regime	Extensive with short-lived horizon for return on capital	Intensive with over-accumulation crisis	Intensive, profit-led and disequalizing	Autarkic state capitalist	Inward-looking state capitalist/populist
Institutional forms					
Type of integration in the international economy	External crisis and constant foreign imbalances due to internal market growth with import dependence	Abundance of FDI from TNCs in the capital and durable goods sectors, with sharp foreign imbalances	Fiscal export incentives, mini-devaluations, foreign debt renegotiation, new foreign capital flows (FDI and commercial bank loans)	Very limited; import substitution in capital goods, slow growth of exports. Capital market closed. Foreign managed firms taken over by nationals on Independence	Remaining focussed on domestic economy, higher growth of exports to cover imports of necessities and capital goods. Capital market remains closed
Competition regime	Oligopoly, little capital-intensive industry, predominance of national private and state companies	Oligopoly, differentiated in dynamic sectors and competitive in traditional sectors	Oligopolistic structure expands to other sectors and more backward regions.	Oligopoly, national private companies indirectly subsidized through public sector investment. Growth of public sector monopolies	Some shift towards curbing private monopoly and promoting small-scale industries. But main features unchanged

Cont.

Cont.

	Brazil			India	
	Constrained Industrialization (1930–1955)	Heavy Industrialization–I (1956–1963)	Heavy Industrialization–II (1967–1980)	Post-Colonial Industrialization (1947–1967)	State-Driven Populist (1967–1980)
Wage labour relations	Competitive, no collective bargaining, and large informal sector	Competitive, increased minimum wage and restricted collective bargaining compensated by labour surplus; wages falling behind productivity gains	Competitive, anti-union, wage depreciation until the mid-1970s, plus more flexible use of workforce (increased turnover rates)	State-imposed social protection and fair wages only for small industrial proletariat and public sector workers. Otherwise competitive with stagnant real wages. Women largely excluded except in agriculture	Protected segment remains small, improved organization and bargaining increases wage gap between industrial workers and the rest. Growth of precarious jobs and informality in urban areas. Growth of rural casual labour
Agrarian relations	Very high land concentration with rural workers under non-wage labour relations. The wage labour code is restricted to urban areas and some occupations	Continued high land concentration, but now with strong pressure for agrarian reform, never implemented. Government approves a rural workers' statute in 1963, with very limited effects	Re-concentration of land as agrarian capitalism incorporates new regions and areas. Labour contracts – of seasonal workers living in urban areas – do not improve labour conditions, on the contrary. Emergence of small and family producers with very low incomes	Highly unequal land structure, limited land reform reduced landlessness but persistence of semi-feudal relations in some areas. Slow growth in agricultural productivity after 1960 leads to crisis and famine	Beginnings of technological change (Green Revolution) in agriculture but regionally concentrated. Stagnant wages and growth of landless agricultural labour

Cont.

Cont.

	Brazil			India	
	Constrained Industrialization (1930–1955)	Heavy Industrialization–I (1956–1963)	Heavy Industrialization–II (1967–1980)	Post-Colonial Industrialization (1947–1967)	State-Driven Populist (1967–1980)
Monetary/fiscal regime	State facing fiscal limits, lack of long-term savings mechanisms, Bank of Brazil financing corporate cash flow and some long-term investments	Fiscal limits overcome by monetary expansion, BNDE – supplied long-term credit, and increasing foreign indebtedness	Fiscal and financial reforms leading to redistribution of tax burden, creation of government bond market and stimulus to stock market. External indebtedness becomes a burden	Fiscal capacity of the state expands with acceleration of growth	Lack of diversification of tax base and slow growth, along with increased government expenditure in populist programmes, lead to fiscal deficits and eventually crisis
Role of the state	Overseeing institutional forms above, handling fiscal and foreign imbalances, yet allowing high profit margins, despite low capital intensity	State loses capacity to arbitrate conflicts within the new economic structure, unable to launch new investment or meet social demands	State increases actions to stimulate the economy, with a stronger fiscal and monetary regime, assuring the rise of the productivity/wage gap	State is dominant, driving growth through public investment and setting rules for private economic activity	Dominant but weakened by successive political crises. Growth of government expenditure despite slower GDP growth

Cont.

Cont.

	Brazil			India	
	Constrained industrialization (1930–1955)	Heavy industrialization – I (1956–1963)	Heavy industrialization – II (1967–1980)	Post-colonial industrialization (1947–1967)	State-driven Populist (1967–1980)
Mode of regulation	Unstable, with the pattern of international integration and the role of the state dominating the other institutional forms	Highly unstable, with stronger international integration and the state still preeminent but less coherent	Authoritarian political regime: alignment with the accumulation regime due to exclusion of progressive social forces, albeit subject to economic and political crises	Dualistic state-led industrialization	Dualistic state-led populist, unstable
Income distribution profile	High income concentration; competitive wage relation and corporatist trade union model favour capital accumulation through compressed labour income.	Stabilization of high levels of income concentration up to 1960, due to the minimum wage real levels, then increasing inequality from 1961 to 1963 as inflation goes up.	Higher profit and investment rates, boosting productivity gains with contained wages leads to increasing income concentration; rising income levels for urban middle classes	Little direct redistribution, except through limited land reform and growth of public sector. Some decline in inequality reflects redistribution from the rich to the middle, little change in poverty, and increasing gap between protected workers and others	Continuation of earlier pattern with some redistribution through populist programmes. Real wages of casual workers stagnate, and wage gap between organized industrial workers and others increases. Urban-rural and regional differentials probably increase

Source: Prepared by the authors. For Brazil drawing on Cardoso de Mello (1990) and Oliveira (2003). For India drawing in part on De and Vakulabharanam (2013).

3.2 Macroeconomic Patterns and Outcomes

This section reviews the main macroeconomic characteristics and outcomes of the growth regimes discussed above. The next two sections do the same for labour markets and institutions, and for social policy.

3.2.1   The growth of GDP

In the early years of the twentieth century, there was little difference between India and Brazil in GDP per capita, according to Maddison's figures (Table 3.2.1). But in India, under colonial rule GDP grew slowly in the following decades, and hardly kept pace with population growth. Indeed, Maddison's estimates give a decline in GDP per capita in 1950 compared with the beginning of the century. In 1945, per capita income was estimated by Heston at Rs. 163 per year, equivalent to about US$ 50 at the exchange rate at the time (Rs. 3.3 to the dollar). Other estimates give around Rs. 190, closer to US$ 60 (in 1946-47 prices). Official figures for national income per capita in 1950-51 give Rs. 264 or US$ 53, at the then exchange rate of Rs. 4.79. So, we can conclude that per capita income was US$ 50 to 60 (at current prices).

Meanwhile, Brazil's GDP per capita, which stagnated in the first half of the nineteenth century (Furtado, 1959), grew at 0.6 per cent per year from 1870 to 1930, according to Maddison's data. It was driven mostly by coffee production and other export crops, which generated demand for expanding industries and services, concentrated in the south-eastern part of the country. The city of São Paulo mushroomed during this period; its population jumped from 31,000 inhabitants in 1872 to 579,000 in 1920. Because of the development of this capitalist enclave, when coffee prices fell during the 1929 crisis, there was an industrial base to nurture the process of capitalist development from within the country, and take advantage of its embryonic internal market. By 1950, GDP per capita had reached US$ 290 at current exchange rates, five times higher than India. Adjusted for purchasing power in Maddison's estimates, the difference was smaller, but Brazil's GDP per capita was nevertheless 2.7 times that of India. Also, it was more than twice its value in constant dollars in 1910, as opposed to the decline experienced in India over the same period.

Brazil's GDP growth accelerated throughout the period from 1930 to 1980, with average annual real growth rates of 5.2 per cent from 1930 to 1955 (the 'constrained industrialization' period; chart 3.1.2); 8 per cent from 1956 to 1962 (heavy industrialization–I); and 9 per cent per annum from 1968 to 1980 (heavy industrialization–II). The period 1963–1967 was one of economic and political crisis, with falling investment rates, and growth of idle capacity and inflation, in which the annual growth of GDP dropped to 3.4 per cent. The years 1968

Table 3.2.1. Annual Per Capita Income, India and Brazil, in US$ at Nominal Exchange Rates, International Dollars and PPP$, various years, 1910–2013

	Brazil			India			Ratio Brazil: India		
	US$ (Nominal Exchange rate)	1990 GK$* (Maddison Data)	Current PPP$ (World Bank)	US$ (Nominal Exchange Rate)	1990 GK$ (Maddison Data)	Current PPP$ (World Bank)	Nominal US$	1990 GK$	PPP$
1910		769			697			1.1	
1930		1048			726			1.4	
1950**	290	1672		53	619		5.5	2.7	
1965		2448			771			3.2	
1980***	1994	5195		236	938		8.4	5.5	
1990	3087	4920	6475	376	1309	1174	8.2	3.8	5.5
2010	10978	6879		1417	3372		7.7	2.0	
2013	11208		15034	1499		5410	7.5		2.8

Source: Maddison database, see Bolt, J. and J. L. van Zanden (2013); World Bank World Development Indicators; National Accounts for India (Reserve Bank of India – RBI database) and Brazil (Ipeadata).

Note: * Geary-Khamis international dollars; **India, 1950-51; *** India, 1980-81.

to 1980 can be broken into two sub-periods. The first is up to 1973, the so-called 'economic miracle', during which average growth reached 10.7 per cent. The second sub-period is from 1974 to 1980, when the Brazilian economy was hit hard by the international oil crisis, but reacted with the Second National Plan of Development, which involved high investment in intermediate and capital goods, led mostly by state companies. Average growth during this period was 7 per cent.

In India, growth accelerated after independence, averaging 3.9 per cent in the 1950s or about 2 per cent per capita (Table 3.2.2). Growth of 4 per cent was sustained until the mid-1960s, but the drought of 1965-66 severely affected agricultural production and subsequently growth declined, averaging 3.4 per cent in the 1970s. These growth rates should be set against population growth of a little over 2 per cent per annum. It was this unspectacular performance which, as we saw above, came to be known as 'the Hindu rate of growth'. This reflected the failure of an intensive process of planning to generate growth rates comparable to those that the East Asian economies were already achieving in the 1960s and 1970s – or for that matter those achieved by Brazil. By 1980, India's GDP per capita had reached US$ 236 in current dollars against US$ 1994 in Brazil, 8.4 times higher. The gap was less after adjusting for price differences, but was still 5.5 times, according to Maddison's estimates (Table 3.2.1).

Table 3.2.2.A. Real Growth Rates of GDP and Major Sectors by Decade, Brazil, 1950–1980 (% Per Year)

	Agriculture	Manufacturing*	Services**	GDP
1950s	4.1	9.3	7.2	7.1
1960s	3.8	6.8	5.7	6.1
1970s	4.3	9.2	8.4	8.7

Source: Ipeadata/Brazilian System of National accounts, IBGE.
Note: *For the industrial sector as a whole, data are available only from 1971. Mining not included.
            **Services include all subsectors.

Table 3.2.2.B. Real Growth Rates of GDP and Major Sectors by Decade, India, 1950–1980 (% Per Year)

	Primary	Secondary	Tertiary	GDP
1950s*	3.1	6.3	4.2	3.9
1960s*	2.4	5.6	4.8	3.7
1970s**	2.0	4.2	4.5	3.4
1950-51 to 1964-65***	2.9	6.7	4.6	4.1
1965-66 to 1980-81***	2.8	4.0	4.3	3.6

Source: Drèze and Sen (2013) and National Accounts.
Note: *1999-2000 prices; ** 2004-05 prices; *** excluding the drought year 1965-66.

3.2.2 Capital accumulation and the pattern of final demand

Brazil's remarkable GDP growth was accompanied by a gradual increase in gross fixed capital formation over the three periods identified in Table 3.1.2, with its share in GDP increasing from an average of 12 per cent in the first period (1930 to 1955) to 21 per cent in the third (1967–80). The peak rate of investment (23 per cent) was reached in the second half of the 1970s. As can be seen in Table 3.2.3, the share of the public sector in gross capital formation fell as the investment rate rose. However, public investment was very dynamic throughout the period. Moreover, if state enterprises are taken into account, its overall share was still close to 40 per cent of gross fixed capital formation throughout the 1970s. For the year 1974, an analysis of around 700 companies showed that state-owned ones accounted for 63 per cent of total capital stock and 39 per cent of profits. Transnational Companies (TNC) came in second place with shares of 20 per cent and 31 per cent, respectively; and private national companies in third place (Suzigan, 1976).

In India too, gross capital formation rose steadily as a proportion of GDP until 1965-66, when it reached 16 per cent; it then declined somewhat, before rising again at the end of the 1970s (Table 3.2.3). In this process, it was the public sector that was the principal driver, with its share in investment rising from a quarter to a half in the first fifteen years, then declining somewhat, before recovering in the late 1970s. In 1980-81, the public sector accounted for just over half of all capital formation. In fact, throughout this period, private capital formation as a percentage of GDP changed very little – it fluctuated between 7 per cent and 10 per cent. And only between a quarter and a third of this was private corporate investment – most was in the household or small-scale sector. The accumulation process was driven essentially by the state. During the whole period, there was virtually no Foreign Direct Investment (FDI). All foreign funds were channelled through the public sector.

It is interesting to note that while capital formation accounted for a somewhat smaller share of GDP in India than Brazil, the difference was not large, and certainly not large enough to account for the considerable difference in growth rates. Public sector investment as a percentage of GDP was actually higher in India than in Brazil. Actually, it was the type of alliance between the public sector and national and international companies that made the difference. Public investment in Brazil paved the way for higher private capital formation than in India, with a substantial contribution by transnational corporations, which were not given access to the Indian market.

Most capital formation was funded out of domestic savings in India. The level of gross domestic savings tracked the level of capital formation fairly closely, since there was essentially no foreign private investment. The opposite happened in Brazil, where FDI jumped in the 1970s (Table 3.2.5), reaching almost 1 per cent of Brazilian GDP.

Table 3.2.3.A. Capital Formation, Brazil, 1950–1980

	Gross fixed capital formation					
Year	Total % of GDP	Public Sector % of GDP	Public Sector Plus State Companies % of GDP	Public Sector as % of Gross Fixed Capital Formation	Public Sector plus State Companies as % of Gross Fixed Capital Formation	FDI (% of GDP)
1950	12.8	4.1	4.4	32.2	34.2	0.3
1955	13.5	2.7	3.3	20.3	24.3	0.7
1960	15.7	4.0	5.6	25.3	35.9	0.8
1965	14.7	4.7	6.8	32.2	46.2	0.7
1970	18.8	4.4	7.3	23.5	38.6	0.9
1975	23.3	3.9	8.4	16.9	36.1	0.9
1980	23.6	2.3	6.6	9.9	28.0	0.8

Source: Ipeadata, IPEA. Brazilian System of National Accounts, IBGE.

Table 3.2.3.B. Capital Formation, India, 1950/51–1980/81

	Gross Capital Formation (% of GDP)	Public Sector Capital Formation (% of GDP)	Public Sector Capital Formation (% of GCF)	FDI
1950-51	10.9	2.8	25.6	*
1955-56	12.6	5.2	41.4	*
1960-61	14.6	7.1	48.8	*
1965-66	16.4	8.6	52.2	*
1970-71	15.3	6.4	41.7	*
1975-76	18.4	9.0	49.0	*
1980-81	18.0	9.1	50.8	*

Source: National Accounts (RBI database).
Note: *Negligible. Capital formation includes change in stocks.

In terms of the overall pattern of final demand (Table 3.2.4), in both countries household consumption was the major component, more so in India, but its share decreased over the period, also more in India, so there was some degree of convergence between the two countries. As noted above, in both countries the share of capital formation increased, and investment was the most dynamic component of final demand in the period up to the mid-1960s, though its growth slowed considerably in India in the 1970s while it accelerated in Brazil. Government consumption expenditure rose slowly in India in the 1950s, but accelerated in the 1960s, especially at the time of the expansion of Indira Gandhi's programme for poverty reduction in the late 1960s and early 1970s. In Brazil, government current expenditure stagnated, and after 1970 declined as a percentage of GDP. This decline occurred not because the role of the state was less important than before, but because after the military coup of 1964 state action was concentrated on fiscal incentives and capital formation, especially through state enterprises, rather than on consumption expenditure. Overall, including capital expenditure, central government expenditures as a percentage of GDP rose in both countries, faster in India than in Brazil, reaching similar orders of magnitude of around 15 per cent in the 1970s (Graphs 3.2.1 and 3.2.2).

The expansion in government expenditure in India was underpinned by a fairly rapid rise in revenues. In 1950-51, government revenue accounted for only some 7 per cent of national income, and the public sector accounted for about 7.5 per cent of total output. By 1970-71, these figures had approximately doubled. But this expansion of the public sector was on a precarious financial base, because direct taxes were quite small, rising from 2.4 per cent of national income in 1950-51 to 3.7 per cent in the mid-1960s, but then falling. This reflected low returns from income taxes, and reliance on stagnant land revenues. Public sector enterprises failed to deliver significant benefits in terms of revenues. These difficulties continued into the 1970s, when the push to increase public sector investment and anti-poverty programmes led to increased deficits and inflationary pressures (Vaidyanathan, 1982).

In the Brazilian case, the gross tax burden as a percentage of GDP increased from 14.4 per cent in 1950 to 24.5 per cent in 1980 (BNDES, 2001), including all levels of government. This increase occurred especially after the tax reform of the mid-1960s, and allowed for the expansion of central government expenditures that is shown in Graph 3.2.2. Compared with the figures for government current expenditure in Table 3.2.4, the difference is because these revenues were channelled mainly to the publicly managed pension system and to investment, so they contributed either to private consumption or to gross capital formation. For instance, pensions represented 20–30 per cent of all government expenditure over the period. However, it is clear that the resources available to the state were distinctly greater in Brazil than in India throughout the period.

Table 3.2.4.A. Share of Components of Final Demand in GDP at Current Prices (%), Brazil, 1950–1980

	Private Consumption	Government Expenditure*	Gross Capital Formation	Net Exports
1950	74.6	11.4	12.3	1.6
1960	72.6	11.5	17.0	−1.1
1970	68.6	11.3	20.5	−0.4
1980	69.1	9.1	24.0	−2.2

Source: Brazilian System of National accounts, IBGE.
Note: *Only government consumption.

Table 3.2.4.B. Share of Components of Final Demand in GDP at Current Prices (%), India, 1950/51–1980/81

	Private Consumption	Current Government Expenditure	Gross Capital Formation*	Exports	Imports
1950-51	84.2	5.4	10.2	6.6	6.4
1960-61	82.2	6.4	13.5	4.1	6.2
1970-71	76.6	8.9	14.5	3.5	3.6
1980-81	75.8	9.7	17.3	5.8	8.7

Source: Government of India, Economic Survey, 2015–16.
Note: *Including change in stocks (hence the difference, for Brazil, with Table 3.2.3). The calculated share for India neglects discrepancies in the National Accounts so as to add to 100, hence the difference with Table 3.2.3.

Graph 3.2.1. Central Government Expenditure as % of GDP, India, 1950/51–1980/81

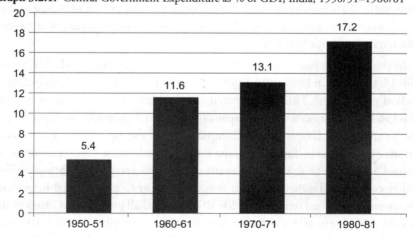

Source: Verma and Arora (2010) and Hall (2010).

Graph 3.2.2. Central Government Expenditure* as % of GDP, Brazil, 1950–1980

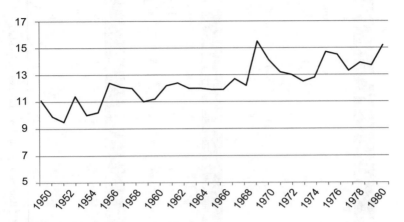

Source: IBGE (2006).

Note: *Includes consumption, capital formation, and transfers.

In Brazil there was a significant change in the role of external trade, which now increased even faster than GDP for both exports and imports in the 1970s. This brought about an opening of the economy, even though the internal market was still the main engine of growth. For instance, imports increased 24 per cent per year and exports 22 per cent in the 1970s. The trade profile changed markedly. On the export side, the share of industrial goods in total exports began to increase in the heavy industrialization–I period and this trend was reinforced dramatically during heavy industrialization–II (Table 3.2.5), while exports of commodities declined in relative terms over the whole period. On the import side, there was also a decline in the share of all imports other than machines and equipment, manufacturing inputs, and fuel.

The external sector played a much more limited role in India. Exports hardly grew up to the mid-1960s, and foreign exchange constraints sharply limited import growth after the exhaustion of the sterling balances in the mid-1950s.[2] Imports consisted mainly of capital goods, intermediate inputs, and cereals. Both exports and imports accelerated after the 1960s, but remained well under 10 per cent of GDP. Unlike in Brazil, the overall pattern of exports did not greatly change. Half of all exports were manufactures throughout the period, but these were heavily concentrated in traditional sectors like textiles, garments,

---

[2] The sterling balances were assets in foreign exchange that corresponded to loans from India to Britain during the Second World War.

Table 3.2.5.A. Selected Economic Indicators, Brazil, 1940–1980

	1940	1947	1950	1955	1960	1963	1967	1970	1980
GDP per capita (R$ of 1999)*	1,072	1,291	1,502	1,796	2,282	2,433	2,554	3,123	5,586
Real minimum wage (R$)*	616	309	258	730	993	588	540	521	596
Inflation (FIPE consumer price index – annual change)****	9.3	23.3	3.7	18.4	32.2	80.5	25.3	17.5	84.8
Foreign debt (US$ million)***	–	625	559	1,395	3,738	3,612	3,440	6,240	64,259
FDI (US$ million)***	–	55	39	79	138	87	115	392	1,910
Export pattern (% distribution)**									
Basic goods	83	80	91	90	86	83	79	75	42
Semi-manufactured goods	14	13	8	8	12	13	9	9	12
Manufactured goods	3	8	1	1	3	4	12	15	45
Import pattern (% distribution)**									
Fuel	16	9	8	22	19	18	12	11	44
Industrial inputs	22	15	15	23	21	25	27	29	20
Machines and equipment	29	40	37	30	37	31	33	39	21
Other	33	36	40	25	23	26	28	20	15

Source: *IBGE (2006); **MDIC. *Projeto Aprendendo a Exportar: 200 Anos de Comércio Exterior Brasileiro;* *** Brazilian Central Bank. Time series; Ipeadata.

Table 3.2.5.B. Selected Economic Indicators, India, 1950/51–1980/81

	1950-51	1960-61	1963-65	1970-71	1976	1980-81
GDP per capita (in 1999–2000 rupees)	6,147	7,270		8,159		8,590
Real unskilled wages (industry)*			7.28		11.85	
Real unskilled wages (agriculture)**				1.52		1.65
Average annual inflation, % (10 years prior to date)		0.4		6.2		8.0
Foreign debt (% of GDP)	0.4	6.6		16.3		19.2
FDI	–	–		–		–
Export pattern (% distribution)						
Food including oils	27.8	33.9		29.4		30.7
Fuel and raw materials	15.5	18.1		17.2		6.6
Manufactures including chemicals and machinery	49.2	44.8		47.9		55.8
Import pattern (% distribution)						
Food	20.1	19.6		14.8		3.0
Fuel and raw materials	27.1	20.0		24.9		55.3
Manufactures including fertilizers and chemicals	23.2	28.5		29.5		22.5
Machinery and capital goods	26.6	29.7		24.7		15.2

Source: Vaidyanathan (1982); Government of India, *Economic Survey*, 2010-11; RBI database; Drèze and Sen (2013).

Note: *Rupees per day. Source: Ministry of Labour and Employment, Government of India, Annual Report, 2002-03, and Indian Labour Journal, September 2006.
**Rupees per day in 1960 prices (Drèze and Sen, 2013).

leather, and jewellery. Imports of food declined, reflecting in part the success of the Green Revolution, but the costs of raw materials rose sharply, and their share in total imports doubled (Table 3.2.5).

Lastly, foreign debt expanded significantly in Brazil after 1967, during heavy industrialization–II (Table 3.2.5). After the oil crisis, the government opted to invest heavily in capital goods, industrial inputs, and new sources of energy – using state companies to borrow money in the international market – notwithstanding the sharp deterioration of the country's terms of exchange. As a consequence, 1980 found Brazil immersed in foreign debt, jeopardizing the capacity to invest of both private and public companies (Baer, 2014). From 16.8 per cent of GDP in 1971 it rose and peaked at 52.8 per cent in 1984. On the other hand, an integrated and diversified industry came to life, which led to large trade surpluses in the 1980s in some dynamic manufacturing sectors – a remarkable contrast with other Latin American economies (Castro and Pires de Souza, 2004).

None of this happened in India; foreign debt did not play a large role except in the context of balance-of-payments crises, especially the one at the end of the 1970s which led to a change of growth regime, and FDI was negligible.

3.2.3   The sectoral composition of output and employment

These macroeconomic trends were built on very different sectoral production structures in the two countries.

Already in 1950, agriculture accounted for less than a quarter of GDP in Brazil, against over a half in India, and the gap widened in the following decades. From 1947 to 1980, the growth of the Brazilian economy (6.4 per cent per year on average) was led by the manufacturing sector, which grew at 8.6 per cent per year over the period. Manufacturing increased its share of GDP from 19.3 per cent in 1947 to 33.7 per cent in 1980 (IBGE/ Ipeadata), though the secondary sector as a whole was still smaller than the very heterogeneous tertiary sector, which represented around half of GDP throughout the period. Whenever manufacturing growth slowed, as in the 1960s, it affected service sector growth, because of the inter-sectoral links between them. Construction – reflecting the pace of urbanization – also evolved in parallel with manufacturing throughout the period, though a little faster. Agriculture's output growth was stable throughout the period, around half the average growth of overall GDP. However, because of its lower growth, the share of agriculture declined precipitously until 1970, and it accounted for only 10 per cent of GDP in 1980 (Table 3.2.6). But agriculture was heterogeneous. Modern agriculture – especially in new commodities like soya and in areas such as the Mid-West – might have achieved growth close to that of the manufacturing sector, while traditional agriculture lost ground.[3]

The accumulation process led by manufacturing industry spread and affected the dynamics of other sectors. In so doing it created a new social structure in a country that was rapidly urbanizing, as capital was increasingly concentrated in large urban centres, followed by the labour force, as people left rural areas for the growing metropolitan areas.

In India, agriculture was the dominant sector throughout. Together with mining it still accounted for almost 40 per cent of output in 1980 (Table 3.2.6). In 1950, the secondary sector as a whole provided only some 14 per cent of GDP, and manufacturing on its own not much more than 10 per cent, but like in Brazil, manufacturing was seen as the engine of growth. A strategy of investment in capital-intensive industry initially generated a high rate of growth of manufacturing, which increased its share steadily in the early years after independence. However, the expansion of manufacturing mainly occurred during the period up to the mid-1960s, when its share in GDP had reached close to 15 per cent. After that date the growth of manufacturing output fell sharply and its share in output stagnated, while that of services, whose growth was less affected, started to rise. By 1980, the share of industry in India's GDP, at 16 per cent, was less than half that of Brazil.

In fact, in India, manufacturing industry was mainly an urban island in a predominantly rural sea. The growth of large-scale, capital-intensive industry was not complemented by the expansion of light manufacturing of consumer goods or by rural industrialization. The outcome was a segmented industrial structure with large enterprises and conglomerates, on the one hand, and cottage industries, on the other, with few linkages between them. As a result the spread effects were much weaker than in Brazil.

---

[3] With the available data, we cannot examine intra-sectoral heterogeneity, especially in terms of productivity. We cannot say that industry as a whole was modern; nor can we say that agriculture as a whole had low productivity, while the services sector also combined high and low productivity segments.

Table 3.2.6.A. Sectoral Composition of GDP, Brazil, 1950–1980 (%)

	Agriculture	Secondary*	Tertiary
1950	24.3	24.1	51.6
1960	17.8	32.2	50.0
1970	11.6	35.8	52.6
1980	10.1	40.9	49.0

Source: Ipeadata/Brazilian System of National Accounts, IBGE.
Note: *Includes manufacturing, mining, construction, and public utilities.

Table 3.2.6.B. Sectoral Composition of GDP, India, 1950/51–1980/81 (%)

	Primary	Secondary	Tertiary
1950-51	53.7	14.4	29.5
1960-61	49.8	17.9	30.1
1970-71	43.8	21.4	32.7
1980-81	38.3	23.0	37.6

Source: National Accounts (RBI database), at constant (2004–05) prices. Primary includes mining.
Note: The total is not exactly 100 in the RBI database.

The import-substitution policy: manufacturing as the engine of growth

Why did industrialization take a different path in India and Brazil? Both governments saw industrialization as the principal method not only to modernize and raise the rate of growth of their economies, but also to break away from dependency on other countries. In Brazil, it was seen as an alternative, a way to change centre-periphery relations with its reliance for growth on the exports of primary products. In India, industrialists, who had actively supported the national freedom movement, considered that freedom from colonialism could only be possible if it were linked to economic independence. In both countries, then, the leitmotiv was import substitution and the construction of a broad national manufacturing capacity. In both countries the public sector played a leading role, dominating in intermediate goods and infrastructure, while consumer goods were mainly left to the private sector. In Brazil, the private sector, both domestic and transnational, also expanded production of capital goods, following a 'tripod model' (Baer, 2014). In India, capital goods remained mainly within the public enterprise sector, the autonomy of the private sector was more limited, and foreign enterprises were excluded.

In Brazil, the National Economic Development Bank (BNDE, later renamed BNDES) was created in 1952 to play a central role in supporting new or expanding national industrial enterprises. At first, most of its loans were directed to enterprises of the public sector, especially to electricity and transport. Then, a core group of firms in traditional (textiles) and modern industries (such as machine tools, auto parts, and steel) began to adapt foreign technology and develop capabilities in engineering, design, product quality, and distribution. These firms were able to raise productivity and become competitive in external markets. But this was not the case for the majority of firms, which specialized in supplying the low end of the market. The outcome was a highly heterogeneous industrial structure in terms of technological development, quality of production, and productivity. Nevertheless, overall industrial efficiency increased. Labour productivity in manufacturing industries grew at a rate of 8.7 per cent from 1945 to 1960, 2.7 per cent in the 1960s, and 6.9 per cent in the 1970s.

By the early 1960s, Brazil had a fairly large and diversified industrial structure. The share in industrial output of traditional industries – such as textiles, food products, and clothing – had dropped while transport equipment, machinery, electric equipment, and appliances and chemical industries expanded. The 1962–1967 period was less dynamic, but the post-1964 reforms and other policies of the military government, together with a booming world economy, created conditions for very rapid growth between 1968 and 1973. As a result, import of capital goods and basic and semi-processed inputs increased sharply (Hudson, 1997; Table 3.2.5). The diversification in industrial production also led to the diversification of exports: the share of manufactured and semi-manufactured goods in exports rose from 15 per cent in 1960 to 57 per cent in 1980 (Table 3.2.5). But the domestic market dominated; the total share of exports in GDP was low, averaging 5.9 per cent over the 1950–1960 period, and increasing to only 6.8 per cent over 1970–1980 and to 10 per cent at the end of the period (Aldrighi and Colistete, 2013).

Despite this success, industrialization in Brazil failed to overcome both underdevelopment and dependency. Furtado (1974) coined the term 'industrial underdevelopment' to describe Brazil's experience, as economic policy rendered the historically embedded structural heterogeneity even more complex. On the one hand there were low productivity activities, not confined to the agricultural sector, aimed at either the internal or export markets. On the other there were more capital-intensive activities, especially in the production of durable goods controlled by TNCs, which initially targeted the internal market by supplying goods to the middle classes, whose numbers grew due to the very nature of the disequalizing growth regime. This deepened the social and regional gaps accumulated during the process of industrialization, and also distorted the productive structure in favour of the expansion of TNCs.

India depended more heavily on the public sector, with a state-directed industrialization model in the 1950s that was inspired by Nehru's and Mahalanobis' conceptions of modernization and planning.[4] The emphasis was on heavy industry, the public sector assumed a leading role, and investment in the private sector was to be carried out according to the requirements of the overall national plan, and not on the basis of private profitability. The Five-Year Plans emphasized technological self-reliance and were inward-oriented. Anything that could be produced in the country, regardless of the cost, should not be imported. High tariff walls protected the manufacturing sector.

The government intervened extensively through a wide variety of measures. Controls were exercised on productive capacities, production, and prices. The most important were industrial licensing, import controls, export subsidies, administered prices, and strict control of investment by multinationals (Singh, 2008, p. 5).

The rate of industrial growth surged during the first decade and a half of Indian planning, but started decelerating in the mid-1960s. This occurred despite the creation of sizeable capacities in a wide range of organized industries through public investment. This slowdown was the result of several contributory factors. The potential of import substitution had reached a plateau, and the sluggish growth in agriculture impinged on the growth of the domestic market. Dependence on imports of basic and intermediate goods increased substantially and led to a foreign exchange bottleneck. By the end of the 1970s, the country was faced with decelerating exports, a worsening balance of payments, and stagnating industrial growth. However, this was a rather different situation from that in Brazil; the latter had relied on foreign debt to complete its industrial park in the 1970s, while manufacturing output and exports were rising, which led to an external debt crisis when growth fell after 1980. In India, the balance-of-payments crisis reflected structural problems in the domestic economy, not exposure to foreign loans, as in the Brazilian case.

Indian manufacturing was, and still is, characterized by a bimodal concentration of productive power. As big business houses had been obtaining a disproportionate share of industrial licences in the 1950s and 1960s, an official

---

[4] The Mahalanobis model (a variant of Leontief's input-output model) was used for the Second Five Year Plan. It emphasized rapid industrialization on the basis of a two-sector model.

committee recommended that they be given licences for setting up industry only in core and heavy investment sectors. Small scale industrial units were protected through the reservation of a large number of items for their exclusive production as well as the provision of fiscal, financial, and legislative incentives. This policy encouraged entrepreneurs to expand horizontally with more small units, rather than vertically with larger middle-sized units (Mazumdar and Sarkar, 2009).

Nevertheless, the growth in output in both manufacturing and services was concentrated in the registered or modern parts of the sectors. The share of the public sector in manufacturing output, 7 per cent in 1960-61, rose to 26 per cent by 1980-81. Overall, the share of registered manufacturing in all manufacturing rose from 47 per cent in 1950 to 56 per cent in 1970 (but then ceased to grow further). Growth in the tertiary sector was high for modern services, such as banking and public administration (over 6 per cent), and low for personal services (2.3 per cent) (Pais, 2014). The productivity (and wage) gap between this formal or organized sector and the unorganized sector of small and household enterprises was extremely large.

The difference in outcomes between the two countries is striking, especially after the mid-1960s, when manufacturing stagnated in India and grew rapidly in Brazil. Up to that point, large-scale manufacturing was the driving force in both countries. But the Indian model, driven by public investment in capital-intensive manufacturing, delivered less growth in both output and productivity than the Brazilian model based on private domestic and foreign capital. In Brazil, the industrial structure developed in a more balanced way than in India, with most production chains internalized, and only the more technology-intensive goods imported. After 1965, manufacturing lost its leading position in India (and never recovered it). In contrast, manufacturing growth – especially durable goods – was the motor of the 'Brazilian miracle'. But in both countries heterogeneity increased, with large differences in productivity and dynamism between different parts of the manufacturing sector. In fact, this heterogeneity played an important role in structuring inequality in the two countries, first of all through its impact on the labour market.

The structure of employment

In neither country was the growth of output of manufacturing industry accompanied by a proportionate increase in employment and labour income in the sector. In Brazil, the structure of employment broadly tracked the pattern of output (Table 3.2.7), but the amplitude of the changes in employment was smaller. Agriculture still provided 30 per cent of employment in 1980 (down from

60 per cent in 1950), much higher than this sector's share of output, implying lower average productivity levels than in the rest of the economy. The secondary sector accounted for 25 per cent of employment in 1980, much lower than its share in output, reflecting the greater capital intensity of the sector. Meanwhile, employment in the tertiary sector grew while its share of output stagnated, so relative productivity declined. To illustrate the dimension of change in the sectoral distribution of employment over the period, agricultural employment increased 30 per cent from 1950 to 1980, against an increase of 466 per cent in the services sector and 531 per cent in the manufacturing sector; the latter accounted for 16.5 per cent of all employment in 1980 compared to 7.5 per cent in 1950.

In India too, the increase in the share of manufacturing (and to a lesser degree, services) in output was not matched by a corresponding increase in employment. In fact, in India this gap between the growth of output and the growth of employment in the secondary sector was much greater than in Brazil. The employment share of the sector did increase, but by less than 3 percentage points in 30 years, less than half the increase in the output share, while employment in the primary sector (essentially agriculture) hardly fell at all until the 1970s. Moreover, the increase in employment in the secondary sector mainly occurred after its period of high output growth had ended (Table 3.2.7).

Table 3.2.7.A. Sectoral Distribution of Employment, Brazil, 1950–1980 (%)

Sector	1950	1960	1970	1980
Agriculture	59.9	54.0	44.3	29.3
Secondary (including mining)	14.2	12.9	17.9	24.9
Tertiary	25.9	33.1	37.8	45.8
Total	100	100	100	100

Source: Demographic Census, IBGE.

Table 3.2.7.B. Sectoral Distribution of Employment, India, 1951–1981 (%)

Sector	1951	1961	1971	1981
Primary	72.4	71.9	72.0	68.8
Secondary (including mining)	10.6	11.7	11.5	13.5
Tertiary	17.0	16.4	16.5	17.7
Total	100	100	100	100

Source: Census of India.

But even more than the overall sectoral pattern of employment, there was a qualitative difference between the two countries in the structuring of the labour market. In Brazil, the share of registered workers in all manufacturing jobs was around two-thirds in 1980, compared with less than 20 per cent in agriculture. We discuss the labour market in more detail in the next section, but broadly speaking Brazil in this period created an industrial proletariat, in the sense of a regular wage labour force centred on the manufacturing sector. But the economy was not driven by rising wages – the share of labour income in manufacturing value added fell from 22 per cent to 15 per cent between 1940 and 1980, showing the secondary role of wages in the growth regime and the widening gap between productivity and labour income. The real minimum wage, after rising up to 1960, fell again in the 1960s and early 1970s, only recovering in the second half of this decade. However, in 1980 it was no higher in real terms than in 1940 (Table 3.2.5). The benefits from growth were concentrated on a better-off upper- and middle-class group, and the gap between this group and wage workers as a whole widened. This configuration was subsequently important in the restructuring of Brazilian institutions in the 1980s.

In India, the growth of employment in regular wage work in manufacturing was much slower. The wage labour market was dominated by the mass of informal, casual workers. Regular workers, many of them in the public sector, were relatively protected, with interests and means to defend those interests, which were in important ways different from those of casual workers. This was much closer to the 'labour aristocracy' model than in Brazil, but the size of the protected work force was small and their real wages low in absolute terms, even if higher than casual workers (Section 3.3).

Another important dimension of inequality was regional. In Brazil, there was a huge regional concentration of the industrialization process. In 1970, the State of São Paulo accounted for 58 per cent of all manufacturing output, and a somewhat lower share of manufacturing employment (Cano, 1998). A regional development strategy was drawn up for the Northeast, after the creation of Sudene[5] in 1959, but it promoted a process of industrialization that benefitted only the large cities and was restricted to some manufacturing sectors. During the 1970s, the growth of manufacturing did start to become less concentrated, with industrial units expanding in states outside the Southeast region, some of them even moving to the Northeast, and manufacturing employment increased

---

[5] The Superintendency for the Development of the Northeast, created under the leadership of the Brazilian economist Celso Furtado, but subsequently used by the military regime in ways that he had not intended.

faster in this decade in the Northeast than in the Southeast. But the share of manufacturing in all employment in the Northeast was still only 8.4 per cent in 1980, against 22 per cent in the Southeast.

The regional pattern of growth varied in India as well. Wide variations already existed in the level of industrial development across states at the time of independence. In the 1950s, policy mechanisms and instruments were devised to mitigate these disparities: establishment of central public sector undertakings in less industrially developed regions, use of 'backwardness' of regions as a criterion in industrial licensing, special packages for development of industrial infrastructure in poorer states, and special fiscal and financial incentives for industrial development in backward areas. But despite the stated objectives the disparities persisted. In 1967, the four most advanced industrialized states accounted for 62 per cent of the licences approved while the four least industrialized received only 16 per cent (Thakur et al., 2012). As long as the central government was in the driving seat, there was an attempt to ensure that the benefits of growth were regionally dispersed, but it is likely that regional disparities started to grow from the mid-1960s onwards. We return to this issue in Section 5.2.

3.2.4   Inequality and poverty

The slow growth of the Indian economy was insufficient to make a substantial dent in poverty. While estimates vary, the balance of the evidence is that the percentage of the population below the poverty line fluctuated, but in the end was not much different in 1980 from the level at the time of independence – around half of the rural population, and rather more than a third of the urban (Drèze and Sen, 2013, Table A.5, based on Datt and Ravallion, 2010). Since the population had grown, this implies that the absolute numbers of poor had risen substantially. Real wages in agriculture fluctuated during this period, but if there was any upward trend it was modest. Insofar as there was an increase in real wages, it mainly concerned industrial workers (Table 3.2.5).

As for inequality, the evidence is mixed. There is some evidence of decline in inequality in the period after independence as measured by National Sample Survey expenditure surveys. The Gini coefficient of inequality of household expenditure, which averaged around 0.34 to 0.35 in the 1950s, declined to 0.31 to 0.32 between 1965 and 1980 (World Income Inequality Database, UNU-WIDER). There is also evidence of decline in the share of top incomes during this period. Using income tax records, Banerjee and Piketty (2005) found that the income share of the top 1 per cent fell sharply from 14 per cent in the early 1950s to less than 5 per cent in 1980. On the other hand, urban-rural differentials may have increased, at least up to the mid-1960s. Since poverty did not decline, and real wages in agriculture failed to rise significantly, we can infer that any improvements in income distribution consisted mainly of redistribution from the rich to an intermediate class of industrial workers, white-collar workers, bureaucrats and perhaps middle peasants. However, the size of the group of regular waged and salaried workers was quite small, as we saw above.

In Brazil, almost the opposite story can be told. The booming economy led to a large fall in poverty in absolute terms, especially in the 1970s. Between 1970 and 1980, the percentage of the population below the poverty line fell by almost a half, to about 35 per cent (Rocha, 2003), due mainly to high growth. At the same time, poverty had become increasingly an urban problem. Whereas more than half of the poor lived in rural areas at the beginning of the decade, in 1980 almost 60 per cent were urban. What is more, the decline in absolute poverty did not necessarily mean better living conditions, as slums were widespread, especially in metropolitan areas, and the quality of elementary schooling and access to health services had deteriorated in the meantime.

This poverty decline is related to the dynamics of the labour market. Minimum wages were set by the government during military rule. Falling in real terms from 1964 to the early 1970s, the minimum wage moved upwards in the mid-1970s, but over the decade as a whole the level remained stable. However, more workers started to earn wages above the minimum level, especially in cities in which the industrial workforce was concentrated.

Alongside the decline in absolute poverty, inequality increased, especially within urban and rural areas, but also within regions, with the poorest regions, like the Northeast, showing the highest Gini coefficient of income inequality. From the 1960s on, when the first systematic empirical studies on income inequality in Brazil were carried out, this is well documented through the Demographic Censuses. Over the period from 1960 to 1980, the poorest 50 per cent of households, who in 1960 received 18.6 per cent of all income, lost 5 percentage points. Conversely, the higher strata increased their share considerably. In 1980, the richest 10 per cent received half of all income, a gain of 9 percentage points since 1960; while the richest 5 per cent received nearly 40 per cent of total income. Unfortunately, most of these data refer only to labour income as measured in the Demographic Censuses. But at the same time, income from capital rose much faster than labour income. From 1940 to 1980, while total GDP per capita grew over 400 per cent, the purchasing power of the minimum wage decreased. Average wages performed better, but still grew much more slowly than productivity. The share of profits in GDP thus moved upwards in the 1970s – from 50 per cent to 58 per cent (IBGE, 2006). The greater pace of capital accumulation also led to increasing inequality in labour incomes, due to the diversification of the production structure, and the widening of the wage scale, in a context of a constrained minimum wage and authoritarian control over union activities.

The picture in India can be summarized as an effort at industrialization that petered out in the 1960s, and sluggish growth of the economy as a whole. There was some redistribution of income, but not enough, or not sufficiently directed to the poorest groups, to substantially reduce poverty, and the growth of both the industrial workforce and the middle class was slow. One consequence was to limit the increase in internal demand for consumption goods, which constrained industrial growth. This weak performance was compounded, in the second half of the 1970s, by political and economic crises. In 1980, India's prospects looked poor.

Brazil had a very different experience. A successful push for industrialization had generated high rates of growth and rising incomes, but also widening inequality as the benefits of growth were concentrated on upper income groups. A large, increasingly affluent group provided the bulk of domestic demand. Although weakened by the oil shocks of the 1970s, and a contested military regime, the economic foundations for continued high growth appeared to have been laid.

The 1980s were to belie these expectations for both countries.

3.3 Labour Market Structure and Labour Institutions

Labour markets developed in different ways in the two countries in the decades before 1980. This was partly because of economic structures – sectoral patterns, production systems and productivity – and partly as a result of the underlying labour institutions and their dynamics. These two aspects of the labour market are of course interdependent. Labour institutions – patterns of organization, job access, law, and regulation – are embedded in the very functioning of the labour markets. At the same time, labour market structures condition the emergence and role of different institutions. This interaction of labour markets and labour institutions configures the growth regime and is a major determinant of the overall pattern of inequality. In both countries, the growth of the labour market was fuelled by workers who were subjected to new forms of work control and social stratification – as they were recruited from different and mainly non-capitalist labour relations, in a complex process that redistributed opportunities and incomes.

This section explores these issues. It starts by presenting the basic shape of the labour markets in the two countries, before discussing the main labour institutions, their role in different segments of the labour market, and how these institutions evolved during the period.

3.3.1   Labour market structures

The different production structures in India and Brazil gave rise to different patterns of employment. In India, in the period before 1980, not only did agriculture account for the bulk of employment, its share showed no sign of decline until the 1970s (Section 3.2, Table 3.2.7). The population was largely rural. Urbanization grew only slowly from 17 per cent in 1951 to 23 per cent in 1981. In 1951, 72 per cent of all workers were in agriculture, some 52 per cent as cultivators and 20 per cent as agricultural wage labourers (16 per cent of male workers and 35 per cent of female workers) (Krishnamurty, 1983). Agrarian systems varied greatly from one part of India to another, with peasant (ryotwari) and zamindari systems being the most widespread. The zamindari system, involving the extraction of rent by intermediaries, often took a 'semi-feudal' form (Bhadhuri, 1973; Prasad, 1987), involving relations of labour bondage, indebtedness and tenancy.

Semi-feudal relations persisted until the 1980s or 1990s in some areas, but declined throughout the period after independence, and rural labour markets developed with a growth of casual wage work among the large numbers of landless rural households. By the end of the 1970s, 27 per cent of male rural workers and 40 per cent of female rural workers were engaged in casual wage labour (Table 3.3.1). The decline of bonded labour meant that workers were increasingly able to move between jobs and wage rates were, at least in part, determined by the forces of supply and demand. However, agricultural growth was slow, and a large labour surplus persisted. Real agricultural wages, which had been broadly stagnant in the decades before independence (Heston, 1982) showed little sign of growth thereafter (Jose, 1974; Roy, 2007). The data in Table 3.2.5 suggest that there might have been some slight increase in the 1970s but, overall, the classic Lewis model of unlimited supplies of labour at a constant real wage seems like a fairly good approximation.

There was more change in urban areas. As we saw in the last section, the growth in industrial employment was slow in the decades after independence, especially in large-scale manufacturing, despite its relatively high output growth. As a result, by the 1960s there was in urban areas only a small section of protected workers, consisting mainly of government employees and an increasingly unionized industrial workforce. Industrial employment did expand after 1970, but growth was concentrated in unregistered manufacturing (and construction) – where there was a higher proportion of informal and unprotected workers – and also in lower-level occupational categories such as sales workers and labourers. At the end of the 1970s, over half of employment in manufacturing outside the household sector was in unregistered enterprises (Deshpande and Deshpande, 1985, cited in Harriss, 1989).

There was, therefore, a growing segmentation of the urban labour market. Almost half of urban male workers were reported to be in regular wage work of one sort or another by the end of the 1970s (Table 3.3.1), but much of this work was clearly unprotected (by law or trade unions). There was also a growing class of casual daily workers in urban areas in unregistered manufacturing, construction and other sectors.

Several urban labour market studies from the 1970s, summarized by Harriss (1989), document this segmentation. There were differences not only in the degree and extent of protection enjoyed by workers in different labour market segments but also in their wages. For instance, wages for casual workers in Bombay were nearly 40 per cent lower than for workers in small enterprises and 65 per cent lower than for workers in factories. In Calcutta, the daily wage rate for casual work in 1977-78 was almost 40 per cent lower than for regular work (Bardhan, 1989). There was very little mobility of workers from one labour market segment to other. Factory workers came from better-off families, while casual labourers came from low-status households, and migration to the city did not modify the status hierarchy of the village. Such patterns were also found in other large cities such as Madras, Coimbatore, and Ahmedabad.

Information on wage trends for this period is patchy. Data reported in the last section (Table 3.2.5) suggest that there was a rise in real urban wages between the mid-1960s and the mid-1970s. Data from Indian Labour Yearbooks reported by Harriss (1989) also suggest that there may have been some increase of 10–20 per cent in real wages in manufacturing in the 1970s; however, not all workers gained. Detailed studies suggest that the gap between skilled and factory workers on the one hand, and casual labourers on the other, was rising. Harriss (1989) concludes that the real wages received by protected workers were rising in the 1970s while those received by casual workers stagnated or declined.

Table 3.3.1. Distribution of Usually Employed Population by Principal Work Status (%), India, 1977-78

	Regular Wage Workers	Casual Labourers	Self-Employed
Rural male	10.8	27.0	62.2
Rural female	3.7	40.0	56.3
Urban male	47.2	18.9	39.9
Urban female	30.8	27.0	42.2

Source: Government of India, National Sample Survey Organization (1997), based on NSS survey 1977-78.

The labour market structure in Brazil evolved in quite a different way, due to the dynamism of the economy, driven by the industrial sector, and the system of labour regulation. The latter was progressively extended to workers in the industrial and services sectors, even though it reached only some segments and occupations. One characteristic that Brazil had in common with India was a structural excess supply of labour to urban areas. But, unlike in India, there was a rapid growth of the non-agricultural workforce, especially after the 1960s, when it overtook the agricultural workforce, which remained stable even in absolute terms (Cacciamali, 1988). The non-agricultural workforce expanded sixfold, soaring from 5 million workers in 1940 to 30 million in 1980. Of the 28 million new workers over this period, 90 per cent were concentrated in urban areas, mostly in non-agricultural activities.

This was possible because Brazil's high growth levels translated into significant job creation in urban areas. The conjunction of population growth and regional migration (mainly rural-to-urban) led to a steady movement of agricultural workers to cities. This reflected not only the availability of jobs in urban areas but also, in many cases, the loss of access to land. Many of the migrants became precarious wage labourers in the urban labour market. Informal employment, calculated by adding the self-employed to unpaid family workers, accounted for 20 per cent of workers in urban Brazil in 1976, while unregistered wage workers accounted for another 27 per cent (Table 3.3.2). Although registered wage work was the most dynamic in this period, only 56.5 per cent of occupied workers were in formal employment in 1976 in the metropolitan region of São Paulo, which was at the forefront of the country's capitalist development process. Limited as it was, this is a distinctive feature compared to the Indian case, for it led to the creation of a substantial industrial proletariat.

In rural Brazil, where labour relations were also deeply changed, there was an increase in the share of wage employment, which reached 35 per cent in 1976. Yet two-thirds of wage workers were unregistered and so outside the purview of labour laws. This was the case, for instance, of workers who accepted to trade part of their monetary income for own production on a piece of land belonging to the landlord. 65 per cent of rural workers were categorized as 'self-employed' or 'unpaid', producing for their own subsistence and also for the market. However, their low pay excluded them from the consumption standards of urban workers. In 1976, Singer (1981) considers that 84 per cent of agricultural workers could be classified as members of the 'sub-proletariat', grouping together non-wage workers and wage workers earning below the minimum wage.

Trends in wage levels in Brazil were greatly influenced by the official minimum wage (Cacciamali et al., 2015). In setting minimum wage levels for the 14 different regions of the country in 1940, the Brazilian government chose values between the average and the lowest market wages. This would ensure that the supply of new workers flooding the market were paid around the minimum wage, and made it more difficult for skilled workers in capital-intensive industries to increase wage differentials compared with the wage floor (Oliveira, 2003), as collective bargaining was rare at the time. It also hindered the process of segmentation of the labour market, at least at the beginning of the industrialization process.

Table 3.3.2. Distribution of Occupied Workers by Labour Market Status, Brazil, Urban and Rural Areas and the São Paulo Metropolitan Region, 1976

	Registered Wage-earners	Unregistered Wage-earners	Non-wage Workers	Total
Rural Brazil	1,633,525	3,207,947	8,866,712	13,708,184
	11.9%	23.4%	64.7%	100.0%
Urban Brazil	12,465,900	6,505,447	4,874,972	23,846,319
	52.3%	27.3%	20.4%	100.0%
Brazil	14,098,815	10,358,852	13,742,010	38,199,677
	36.9%	27.1%	36.0%	100.0%
São Paulo Metropolitan Region	2,507,485	1,049,579	881,450	4,438,514
	56.5%	23.6%	19.9%	100.0%

Source: Computed on the basis of microdata from IBGE/PNAD, 1976.

After falling in the 1940s, both average and minimum wages rose in the 1950s, in part because of union strength, but also due to government policy, even though the increase in wages was not commensurate with the rise in productivity (Table 3.2.5). However, after the mid-1960s, the minimum wage was reduced in real terms, reflecting the wage policy launched by the military regime and the repression of trade unions. Afterwards, and especially during the 'economic miracle' (1968–1973), minimum wages and average wages followed divergent trends. More capital-intensive sectors pushed wages up, though usually less than productivity (Souza, 1999). That is, the wage scale widened.

However, minimum wages were still important for unskilled workers in more traditional industries. In 1973, 37 per cent of manufacturing industry workers in the city of São Paulo had wages less than 50 per cent above the minimum, though this was lower than in 1965 (66 per cent). This ratio varied considerably across regions and sectors. Even more important, as unions started to rebuild their strength in the late 1970s, wage floors negotiated in the most unionized sectors always took the value of the minimum wage as a reference (Sabóia, 1985). Also, while wage inequality was increasing for manufacturing workers, this was even more so for white-collar workers (Hoffman, 1975).

Although the minimum wage in 1980 was much the same in real terms as in 1940, the Lewis model does not seem to apply, especially from 1970 onwards, as real wages rose for many groups of workers, and the minimum wage itself reflected political factors. So the wage rate within the capitalist sector was not set by the subsistence wage outside the formal sector. This is a significant difference with India. Nevertheless, some elements were common to both countries – including the increasingly heterogeneous wage labour relations and the growth of an informal economy. Thus, in both countries, the outcome was a segmented labour market, but the pattern of segmentation was different, for the Brazilian labour market was not dominated by casual and unprotected wage work to the same extent as the Indian. Moreover, the urban labour market in Brazil was dominant, and within it there was not only a sharp increase in the share of formal employment but also a trend towards increasing inequality. In contrast, the share of formal employment in India remained small, rural employment continued to dominate, and there was an expansion of unprotected casual labour in both rural and urban areas.

It should be said, however, that informality – in a context of very low unemployment rates – was also seen as the main problem in the Brazilian labour market (Dedecca, 2005). Despite the fast increase in wage labour, the reproduction of the labour force was not fully integrated into the circuit of productive capital. This can be seen in the importance of non-wage workers, but also in the fact that many wage workers were employed in activities that did not comply with labour laws, and that this was regarded as legitimate not only by employers but also by the workers themselves (Marques-Pereira, 1998).

3.3.2   Labour institutions

Many labour institutions play a role in shaping labour market outcomes – some of them defined by the state, others emerging from the actors of the labour market themselves. These include the framework of labour law and regulation – codes, acts, basic rights, labour contracts, wage regulation – and the institutions involved in worker organization, collective bargaining, and recruitment. How these institutions work, and especially the enforcement (or lack of enforcement) of rules and regulations determined by the state, is related both with the functioning of the labour market itself and with the nature of the political forces that predominate at different times.

The first Vargas administration in Brazil (1930–45) created a labour code that defined the individual labour contract, collective bargaining, trade union structure, overall conditions for exercising an occupation, and the role of Labour Courts. The system of labour regulation in Brazil was limited to urban registered workers and did not include agricultural workers or public employees, as the latter were forbidden to create their own unions. Effective collective bargaining in Brazil became a goal for workers in some specific periods, such as in 1946 with the return of democracy, and from then up to the early 1960s. This ended with the military coup in 1964, when the government started dictating wage levels.

The individual labour contract had to be registered in a booklet (*Carteira de Trabalho e da Previdência Social*) issued by the Ministry of Labour, where the employer entered the employee's personal data, his/her occupation, working hours, and the wage. Should the employer fail to enter the worker's contract data in the *Carteira de Trabalho* or to comply with the labour code, the employee could petition the Labour Court claiming registration and pecuniary compensation. As used in this section, and in other sections, the term 'registered employment' refers to employment with a *Carteira de Trabalho*.

The labour contract included clauses that had already been recognized in international labour law by the 1930s, notably in the international labour standards of the ILO, the recognition of basic social rights by the League of Nations and the German experience with the Weimar Constitution, along with some elements created by the Vargas governments. Some protections worth highlighting were the minimum wage and wage floors by occupation; regulation of working hours, overtime, vacations, weekly rest, and respective pay; safety and health at the workplace; dismissal compensation and stability after ten years' work for the same company; and protection of women and under-age children.[6]

Collective bargaining agreements and conventions[7] were legally binding, and had to be complied with by all workers and employers party to the negotiation, represented by their respective unions/associations, even if they were not individually or voluntarily associated with the agreement. The law ruled void any agreement contrary to government economic policy. As the unions were state-controlled, collective bargaining was limited in practice, except during periods when the organization of workers was stronger, as between 1946 and 1964 and in the late 1970s. The main idea of the corporatist system was that the labour price should be kept 'out of the market' (Vianna, 1978).

On the other hand, if the parties to a collective bargaining process failed to reach an agreement, the demands of the workers' union as well as the employers' justification for not accepting them would be referred to the Labour Justice system for settlement, and a court would rule and create jurisprudence. This institution was made up of, in rising hierarchical scale, Reconciliation Boards (*Juntas de Conciliação*), Regional Labour Courts, and the Supreme Federal Labour Court. Representation in these bodies was tripartite – one judge, one employer, and one employee representative – but most of the latter were lawyers, bureaucrats, and former union leaders, many of them co-opted by the state.

There was no right to spontaneous strike, only the right to *legal strike*, i.e., authorized by the Labour Justice system. Non-compliance with the law or with any institutional decision was punishable with fines, job suspension, dismissal, deportation from the country in the case of a foreign worker, loss of the right to run for election to representative bodies for each professional category, and even trade union suppression and arrest of labour leaders.

In Brazil, minimum wage-setting, collective bargaining, the role of Labour Courts, and state policies for professional training and social assistance (the so-called 'S System') were applied only to registered wage-earners. For an important

---

[6] Titles I to IV of the Brazilian Labour Law [Consolidation of Labour Laws (CLT–from Portuguese *Consolidações das Leis Trabalhistas*)], which has 510 articles.

[7] A collective bargaining agreement is struck between one trade union and one employers' association, whereas a convention is signed by more than one employers' association. Conventions take precedence over agreements.

segment of the labour market, this meant that wages, training, and access to rights were left to the market or to relations that assumed rather clientelistic forms.

India also put in place rules governing basic conditions at work, minimum wages, working hours, overtime, safety and health at work, dismissal and stability, etc., through the Factories Act (1948), Minimum Wages Act (1948), the Industrial Disputes Act (1947), the Contract Labour Act (1970) and other laws. Both the Centre and States could legislate on labour matters, which gave rise to regional variations. India did not ratify (and has not ratified) the basic ILO Conventions No. 87 (Freedom of Association and Protection of the Right to Organize) and No. 98 (Right to Organize and Collective Bargaining), on the grounds that there are legal provisions for forming collective associations and compulsory arbitration in the country's own labour code. Brazil, on the other hand, ratified Convention No. 98 (in 1952), but not Convention No. 87, because of the specificity of its trade union system. But, in the Indian labour code, much less attention was paid to collective bargaining, which was generally left to the discretion of private players; the government intervened only if negotiations failed and caused industrial unrest.

The Constitution of India laid strong emphasis on basic rights of equality and freedom and focussed on the need to eradicate poverty and all forms of discrimination. The dignity of human labour and need to protect and safeguard the interests of labour is enshrined in the Constitution in Chapter III (Articles 16, 19, 23, and 24) and Chapter IV (Articles 39, 41, 42, 43, and 54). The Directive Principles of State Policy, in Article 39 (Part IV) of the Constitution, direct the state to secure to all its citizens the right to adequate means of livelihood, and equal pay for equal work for both men and women; however, this section is not justiciable by law.

There is a clear contrast between the two countries in terms of the legal framework for the labour market. Brazil's corporatist system established many rights, and procedures to guarantee these rights, but at the same time limited the autonomy of the actors and enshrined substantial control in the state. The Indian system provided greater freedom for the actors of the labour market, and also declared many rights, but provided fewer means for their realization. The judicial system rapidly became clogged and both trade unions and employers' organizations were in practice heavily dependent on state patronage. In both countries, a substantial fraction of employment was effectively excluded from legal protection. But this fraction was much larger in India, partly because of exemptions – notably for smaller enterprises and some sectors – and partly for lack of implementation capacity.

Wages were seen as an important area for state regulation in both countries. We have discussed the implementation of minimum wages in Brazil above. This was a key labour policy with considerable influence on wages in both registered and unregistered employment (Cacciamali et al., 2015). At times, it served as a floor for wages, but at times it also acted as a ceiling.

Legislation for minimum wages was also enacted very early in India (1948). The Minimum Wages Act of 1948 applied in principle to the majority of wage workers, including those excluded under other Acts. It allowed the Central and State governments to fix minimum rates of wages for different employments listed in the Schedules of the Act; these minimum wages further categorized workers in each industry on the basis of skill. Certain criteria were established by the tripartite Indian Labour Conference in 1957 for setting minimum wages. In practice, however, the minimum varied enormously across states and between different occupational groups, and the system became bewilderingly complex. Enforcement was weak outside organized industry and virtually non-existent in rural areas. The minimum wage was generally higher than the effectively unregulated casual wage, but was in practice only applied in regular, organized employment, which paid higher wages anyway. Therefore, the minimum wage was of much less significance in India than in Brazil.

Wage policy in India was not confined to the minimum. A Committee on Fair Wages, which reported in 1949, attempted to establish a principle for wage-setting within a range between the minimum determined by needs and the maximum set by ability to pay. In fact, a wide range of institutions and policies developed around wage-setting, for different categories of workers. For the public sector, starting in 1947 the government periodically appointed Pay Commissions to lay down the principles of wage fixation for Central Government employees, and these then tended to be used as a reference point for other public sector employees. There was some collective bargaining over wages at the enterprise level in the private sector, but this mechanism extended only to a section of the organized sector and excluded large portions of the workforce. There were also Wage Boards established for certain industries and occupations, though these were mostly rather ineffective (Subramanian, 1977). Despite this institutional complexity, however, the wages of most workers were effectively set in the market.

Among other labour institutions, the mechanisms for job access have always been highly segmented in India into formal and informal; rural and urban; skilled and unskilled; and casual and regular. Not all workers have equal access to the labour market. Information about the availability of jobs is shared very unevenly and the process for accessing particular jobs has often been a privilege of only a few. Hiring for jobs across all sectors has been influenced by factors like caste, community, language, regional affiliation, family background, social networks, and of course educational level. These factors operate in different ways in public and private sectors; in agriculture, industry, and services; in the formal and informal economy; and in urban and rural areas.

Historically, the recruitment of the industrial labour force depended on intermediaries – jobbers – who controlled the flow of labour and acted as agents of industrial firms. After independence, the role of the jobber declined, but recruitment remained narrowly based around networks of patronage and influence. Despite the creation of formal institutions such as Employment Exchanges in the public sector in the 1950s and 1960s, informal mechanisms of recruitment like the system of personalized referrals remained more popular among employers, because the formal methods were either inadequate or costly. In a system of referrals, the worker or the contact who introduces or recommends the new recruit assumes the responsibility for ensuring the quality and attributes of the worker; the advantage for employers is that this reduces the risk of indolence, misbehaviour, and protests (Papola, 1992). The net result, however, was to concentrate access to industrial jobs within a relatively small fraction of the population.

In Brazil, too, the process of recruitment was mostly informal – the Public Employment Service was created only in the late 1970s, and performed poorly. So, job access depended on the personal networks of unskilled workers, who flooded into the rapidly expanding urban areas. These consisted mainly of migrants from rural areas, especially from the Northeast, occupying jobs in civil construction and in services, where they tended to work as self-employed or unregistered wage workers. Workers with educational credentials that were scarce at the time – like middle school and college – or vocational training qualifications could obtain access to a relatively good, more stable position in the labour market and earn a wage that was higher than the minimum wage.

The labour institutions in the two countries thus had many elements in common, notably in terms of the goals of protection of workers and their wages through the labour codes, and informal systems of access to jobs which tended to perpetuate existing hierarchies. But Brazil's corporatist system reached a much larger fraction of the workforce, simply because of the much larger size of the formal economy. It also was an important element of labour control, especially under authoritarian regimes, and much more so than in India. On the other hand, the labour code functioned as a promise for new entrants in the labour market, even if it failed for many. It raised expectations and defined in the minds of all workers what a 'good job' should be like (Cardoso, 2010). This created a common identity for the working class – even if shattered by the dynamics of the labour market – that would reappear in the different guise of social citizenship later on during the formulation of the 1988 Constitution. In contrast, India's working class was fragmented. India's labour institutions were more a reflection, outside a small formal sector, of traditional patterns of access and differentiation, notably by caste and gender, and of personalized and clientelistic relationships between employers and workers in informal production.

On the whole, labour laws were not designed to reduce inequality. Indeed, it can be argued that they may have contributed to worsening inequality, to a different extent in each country, as their implementation proved limited and incomplete. A regular wage worker was entitled to a guaranteed wage as well as benefits in matters of sickness, disability, and other forms of social protection in both countries. But for the remainder of the economically active population engaged in informal work – such as casual daily workers, self-employed workers, domestic workers or non-registered wage workers – these conditions were not met. The laws proved to be more effective in some regions than others, and further deepened regional inequality in both countries. So the legal system was inherently disequalizing, as it granted advantages to some while failing to reach others.

3.3.3 Labour relations and the role of trade unions

Perhaps even more than the legislative framework, the difference between Brazil and India in the role and importance of trade unions is striking today, and these differences have their roots in the period before 1980.

Trade unions in India have a long history. They were preceded by workers' welfare associations in the cotton, jute, textile, and railway industries. These included the Bombay Millhands Association (started in 1890) and the Amalgamated Society of Railway Servants (1907), among others (Morris, 1965). An increase in the numbers of wage-earners gave rise to class consciousness among workers and slowly, workers in the Ahmedabad mills organized themselves to demand better wages and welfare services. Such agitations eventually led, in 1920, to the formation of the All India Trade Union Congress (AITUC) – the first trade union federation in India.

The labour movement in India was closely linked to the struggle for independence and was instrumental in carrying out grassroots mobilization, with key national leaders being active members of these unions. In 1947, the Indian National Trade Union Congress (INTUC) was formed by the Indian National Congress to serve as an alternative to the AITUC, and one which would act as a dependable ally for Congress policies. This marked the first step towards state control of the labour movement (Bhowmik, 2013). It was believed that the state would be the leading employer in the years following independence, and that unions would have to play a much less antagonistic role in order to maintain industrial peace during the period of national reconstruction. This gave rise to a situation in which the labour movement became heavily dependent on the state for protective legislation and its implementation and for solving industrial disputes.

In the period immediately after independence, the Indian government's industrialization policy resulted in the development of industrial clusters in different locations, such as the cotton textile industry in Bombay and Ahmedabad, and the jute industry in Calcutta. This led to the rapid growth of trade unions. The central government at that time, as an employer and as regulator of the public sector, played a major role in determining wages and working conditions. Due to strong political linkages and a centralized structure of trade unions, collective bargaining was also greatly politicized (Bhattacherjee, 1989; Ahn, 2010). Then, in the period from 1967 to 1979, industrial stagnation limited the expansion of the trade union movement. And during the Emergency from 1975 to 1977, the right to strike was suspended and union activities were restricted (Ahn, 2010). Thus, the trade union movement as a whole was weakened at the same time as it became increasingly divided through the diverse political affiliations of different federations.

Overall, it can be argued that in the years following independence the Indian state projected itself as the protector of workers, through its various policies and interventions (especially by the Labour Department). But it aimed at the same time to make workers and trade unions increasingly dependent on government support. To perpetuate this dependence, the government selectively passed laws that granted workers protection yet simultaneously worked towards reducing the role of unions. For example, the Industrial Disputes Act (1947) ostensibly protected workers by curbing the employer's right to terminate employment and to shut down establishments. However, in practice, it prevented unions from going on strike in case of an unsettled dispute, and thereby greatly diminished their bargaining power. Further, as noted above, labour laws enacted in this period often applied only to certain sectors of the economy – typically, to those legally interpreted as an 'industry' (Sankaran, 2007) – and left out a large share of casual, contract, and self-employed workers. The existence of multiple categories within the workforce, with differing rights and entitlements, weakened the bargaining capacity of unions.

In Brazil, the first decades of the twentieth century saw strong political activities of workers in the most important urban centres. They fought for better wages and labour conditions through their local trade unions or mass movements, but these were not recognized either by employers or by the state. Workers became institutionally recognized as social actors only in the 1930s and 1940s. During this period, the state machinery in Brazil was completely reconfigured to put in place the preconditions for a capitalist economy. The Vargas administration (1930–45) considered the worker as a privileged target who was to be protected and tutored by social policy. To access social rights and obtain recognition as a citizen, the worker had to be registered in an occupation established by law. This concept of 'regulated' citizenship was based on occupational stratification rather than membership of a community or adherence to a set of political values (Santos, 1979). This administration co-opted the workers' autonomous movement; attracted the workforce to the economy's dynamic centre; and incorporated and subordinated wage-earners in some sectors, especially those linked to the industrialization process run and promoted directly by the state.

The union/association structure was set and regulated by the Ministry of Labour. A single union/association for a given territorial base – the smallest was the municipality – had to be registered with and get approval from the Ministry to be able to operate.[8] The Ministry set the number of categories of trade unions and trade associations symmetrically, the former (employees) on the basis of occupational categories and the latter (employers) on the basis of economic sectors. Public civil servants were not allowed to establish unions.

A minimum of five trade unions in the same occupational category or in the same economic activity was required to establish a state-level federation. At least three federations were required for the establishment of a nationwide confederation. Finance was provided by one day's wages of every worker – collected by the company itself and deducted from the wage bill – and by a percentage ranging from 0.002 per cent to 0.8 per cent of the amount of capital recorded by each company in its register (the *Junta Comercial*). The guiding notion was that trade unions should symbolize the spirit of harmony between workers and employers. The duties of the representatives of capital and labour, convened in reconciliation and arbitration boards, were to solve conflicts, answer consultations on professional matters, and eventually extend rights and

---

[8] Title V of CLT.

procedures to the whole of the working class. This tutelage-based corporatist structure was maintained over time, although it did not prevent unions from organizing horizontally during the democratic period (1946–1964), when they tried to challenge some of its elements.

During the military government (1964–85), the corporatist system remained unchallenged at first, and was even reinforced. The government's repressive policies directly impacted labour institutions and relations. A new policy was introduced, which made this institutional framework more flexible. Especially after 1966, when a fund (FGTS[9]) was created to provide a redundancy payment, it became easier to lay off workers,[10] and this led to a rise in turnover rates. The unions went through a phase of exacerbated tutelage. This was highly contested during the rise of the 'new unionism' in the late 1970s, which paved the way for the emergence of independent unions, which sought to enhance collective bargaining and develop a bottom-up strategy to defend the workers' right of association.

The system of labour relations weakened the bargaining power of the working class, either through trade union laws or by granting rights only to certain occupational sectors. Thus, it led to a fragmentation of interests among the workers themselves – both between registered and unregistered wage workers and between wage workers as a whole and those not subject to capitalist labour relations.

Summing up, we can see that in both countries the state attempted to co-opt and control the trade union movement, through different means, and to different degrees. It can be argued that the labour relations system was less strategic for the growth regime in India than in Brazil, as it remained confined in India to the public sector and the rather small urban modern private sector. Nevertheless, it contributed to growing inequality between different groups of workers – notably between regular industrial workers and casual labour, and between urban and rural areas, for there was little effective organization of agricultural labour, except in the plantation sector.

In the case of Brazil, where the capitalist sector created many new jobs, the labour institutions – especially the corporatist union structure – played a strategic role in ensuring that productivity gains in industry were not shared

---

[9] Fundo de Garantia do Tempo de Serviço (Severance Pay Fund).

[10] Before 1966, if a formal wage worker were fired, he or she would receive an amount equivalent to one month's wages for every year worked at the same company. After ten years, the workers obtained stability in their jobs. After 1966, the government did away with job stability, and instead 8 per cent of the worker's wages were deposited in a bank account that could be accessed after dismissal.

with workers. In rural areas, the modernization of the agricultural sector brought new labour relations, but these proved to be even more precarious than before, as workers lost their small plots of land and were unable to claim their rights – unlike their urban counterparts. The wage gaps between different groups of workers within the labour market widened. Overall, the way in which the labour institutions developed in Brazil in the 1960s and 1970s was an important cause of the increasingly unequal pattern of income distribution, reinforced by the authoritarian regime and its anti-labour stance.

The consequences of these diverse structures and institutions for inequality cannot be summed up in any simple way. Both labour markets were unequal, but in different ways. In both the state played an important role, to assure capital accumulation and growth, promote industrial peace, and protect at least some workers. The state also responded to different interests at different points in time, and at some times played an equalizing and at others a disequalizing role. But it can be said that the reach and impact of the state was greater in Brazil, since the share of the labour market that it influenced directly was greater. Over most of the period, however, the interest in rapid industrialization took precedence over workers' rights and incomes, and labour market institutions were moulded to serve perceived national goals. The persistence of a low-wage labour market in both countries, but particularly in India, reflected the limits of state intervention and the abundant labour supply, which India's growth was far too slow to absorb productively. The institutions of the labour market reflected this excess, which mainly emerged as underemployment in casual employment or low-productivity self-employment, rather than unemployment, since only a fraction of workers had the resources needed to engage in an extended job search.

3.4 The State, Social Policies and Inequality

In both Brazil and India, a wide variety of social policies were implemented in the decades before 1980. Many of these were aimed directly at reducing poverty or inequality or at providing a degree of economic security. So alongside the role of the state in the overall growth regime, which, as discussed above, often underpinned an unequal pattern of growth, a range of policy instruments was introduced with a view – or so it was expressed by policy-makers – to redistributing resources or changing the pattern of opportunities.

Social policy is not a well-defined or clearly bound concept. In conventional usage, it covers several different fields of state action.

- First, there is social protection, in the sense of policies that protect or insure against contingencies, extending from unemployment to ill health, and from maternity to old age.

- Second, some social policy redistributes resources directly (food security and nutrition programmes, cash transfers of various sorts, employment creation through public works programmes).

- Third, a variety of policies aim to overcome particular disadvantages. They include, in addition to direct redistribution, job reservations and development policies aimed at specific groups, such as small and marginal farmers.

- Fourth, there is policy that delivers a 'social' service. Education and health are the most prominent examples, along with care and related activities.

All of these elements were present in both countries as social policy was expanded in the mid-twentieth century, but the balance between them was completely different. In Brazil, social policy was organized around social insurance of the type that had been developing in Europe. The 1934 Constitution, and later on the Labour Code, provided for workers' social protection and pension benefits, health insurance, and measures related to elementary and secondary education. These were not universal, however, because the social rights and social security of different categories of workers were connected with their occupational status and wages, and mainly benefited registered urban workers. Access to health services, for instance, was linked to occupational status. Moreover, large sections of the population were not covered by the social protection system, and did not have access to education, especially from secondary level onwards. Much less attention was given to redistributive measures and to policies towards vulnerable and deprived populations.

In India, social policy in the colonial period was limited in scope. After independence in 1947, a new set of priorities was reflected in the Constitution. In particular, the 'Directive Principles of State Policy' spelled out the state's obligations to promote welfare, security, livelihood, and social justice, and to reduce inequality. The Constitution also included special provisions for deprived castes and tribes, minorities, women, and children. These gave rise to policies such as job reservations for Scheduled Castes and Tribes and targeted rural development programmes. But universal social security was seen as infeasible for a poor agrarian economy; instead, specific policies aimed to improve the levels of living of the poor, through subsidized food grains and public works programmes. Meanwhile, investment in education and health took second place to the drive for industrialization.

3.4.1 Social protection and redistribution

In Brazil, the constitutional provisions that established social protection for workers, publicly managed pensions, and other benefits at first covered only some employees in the urban formal sector, but coverage was gradually extended. Pensions were introduced in the 1920s for railroad workers (under the Workmen's Compensation Law 1919 and the Eloy Chaves Law of 1923). From the 1920s until the 1980s, significant and incremental steps were taken towards making social security more comprehensive and wider in scope. In the 1930s, the federal government put in place a pension system in which retirement and pension institutes were organized for broad professional categories, each with its own rules of contribution and benefits. This fragmentation remained until the military regime in the 1960s, when the National Social Security Institute (INPS, from the Portuguese *Instituto Nacional de Previdência Social*) was established and standardized benefits and contribution rates. Moreover, the government became responsible for expenses related to pension system administration. At the end of the 1960s and in the early 1970s, pension coverage was extended to occupational categories beyond formal urban workers, such as the self-employed and domestic and farm workers. However, their inclusion in the pension system was incomplete, and based on different rules for benefits and requirements.[11]

Therefore, the public social security system became the dominant means for social protection in Brazil during this period. It was characterized by compulsory regulation of social rights, which were bound to legal labour relations and varied with workers' economic activity and their contribution to the Social Security Institutes. The wage labour relationship determined the type of contract and access to the social security system. Thus, a regularly hired worker with a formal contract was entitled to sickness, disability, and old age insurance,[12] as well as access to health services and vocational training, and often to housing programmes and leisure and cultural services. But this system left out about half of the economically active population. A large fraction of rural workers, the self-employed, unregistered wage earners and domestic workers in urban areas were not covered. In reality, social citizenship was recognized only for some (Müller, 1986).

However, as we saw in the last section, this set of labour and social rights formed part of the expectations of most of the new workforce migrating to

---

[11] For a more detailed discussion of the development of social policy in Brazil, see Fagnini (2005) and Medici *et al.* (1993), among others.

[12] Unemployment insurance was introduced only in 1986.

urban areas, and represented symbolically to workers the foundations of a 'good life' and better social status (Cardoso, 2010). But because these rights were not universalized, they came to be regarded mostly as privileges, which made it easier for employers to 'negotiate' 'some' rights with their unregistered workers, as if they were not entitled to them.

Moreover, in terms of civil and political rights, it is important to stress that the illiterate did not have the vote in Brazil until 1985, and that civil rights were constrained by the passive role of the judiciary, especially for the most vulnerable groups – blacks, women, and the illiterate.

The incomplete coverage of the formal system was to a limited degree compensated by public action in the field of social assistance. The first such action was the creation in 1938 of the National Council of Social Service (CNSS, from the Portuguese *Conselho Nacional de Serviço Social*), which was to regulate the foundations of social service in the country. However, social services were actually provided through private institutions, especially the Catholic and other churches, while public participation was basically limited to supporting those institutions. Thus, before the 1988 Constitution, social assistance was not developed as public policy. One of the few government initiatives was the For-life Monthly Income (RMV, from the Portuguese *Renda Mensal Vitalícia*), a social security benefit created in 1974 to meet the needs of the destitute elderly over 70 years of age, destitute disabled or work-incapacitated people, and other non-contributors to the National Social Security System.

In India, too, there was some development of conventional social security for the formal labour market. The first major programme was launched in 1952. It was known as the Employees' State Insurance (ESI) Act and provided medical benefits, cash benefits in compensation for employment injury, death, sickness, and maternity benefits. Legislation for old age benefits was also initiated in 1952; some such benefit was already being extended to coal mineworkers. Old age benefits were to be administered by the central government, which could delegate implementation to States. An Employee's Provident Fund (EPF) Scheme was also introduced.

By the end of the 1960s, these schemes had significant coverage – 3.7 million persons in the ESI and 5.3 million in the EPF (Government of India, 1969) – but this compared with a total labour force of 227 million in 1971 (Mitra, 1978). In reality, these protections were essentially confined to the organized sector, both public and private. Not only was this a small fraction of the workforce but, as we saw above, its share hardly grew in the decades after independence. In the segmented labour market, access to social protection remained confined to the relatively advantaged but restricted group of regular workers.

Instead, social policy focused on targeted interventions to reduce poverty and deal with extreme vulnerability. During the period of the first three Five-Year Plans, i.e., from 1951 to 1966, it was understood that industrialization and growth would 'solve' other issues in the longer term. The social measures initiated at that time, such as the Ration System (in 1950) (which provided highly subsidized/free food rations) and some public works programmes to create employment, aimed mainly to reduce poverty in rural areas.

Public works as a means of income support in times of famine or economic crisis have a long history in India, going back at least to Ashoka,[13] and (unlike in Brazil) this was seen as a significant instrument of social policy in the period up to 1980. For instance, in the Third Five-Year Plan (1961–66), it formed part of a major attack on unemployment (Rodgers, 1972). An influential publication in 1970 advocated making employment in public works the core of any action to reduce poverty (Dandekar and Rath, 1970). Such schemes faced many difficulties in implementation, and the impact on unemployment was small, but they were again a central part of the 'garibi hatao' (eradicate poverty) campaign launched in 1971. In 1978, the State of Maharashtra introduced an employment guarantee programme in rural areas based on the provision of work in public works, which would be the forerunner of the much larger employment guarantee scheme introduced in the 2000s.

But public works were clearly not enough on their own. A concern with unemployment and underemployment grew in the 1960s. There were efforts to promote labour-intensive technologies in small-scale manufacturing (Papola, 2013), and in 1978 the government launched the Integrated Rural Development Programme (IRDP) to expand self-employment. The 1970s also saw the launch of the Minimum Needs Programme and Indira Gandhi's Twenty Point Programme, which aimed to improve education, health, housing, and nutrition among lower-income groups in both urban and rural areas on the basis of a series of specific plan allocations and projects. However, these programmes did not create employment on any substantial scale and fell far short of providing general social protection.

The role of social sector development was more significant in reducing poverty in some of the States with the lowest poverty ratios. At various dates,

---

[13] An Ashokan rock edict in present-day Gujarat, dating to the third century BCE, spelled out the details of how public works should be implemented to create employment at times of famine.

Kerala, Tamil Nadu, and Karnataka achieved rapid poverty reduction through state intervention, especially in the social sector. In Kerala, the efforts of the rulers of the princely States of Travancore and Cochin in the field of education prior to independence, and of the Communist Party of India (CPI) government elected in 1957, played an important part in achieving lower poverty levels (United Nations, 1975). Ration shops functioned more efficiently than in other parts of India (covering almost one-third of cereal requirements by the early 1970s) and a school meals programme reached a substantial fraction of children.

The other important aspect of Indian social policy was targeting disadvantage. The colonial regime initiated some positive discrimination for 'depressed classes' in the early 1900s, and influential leaders such as B. R. Ambedkar supported and expanded this after independence. A proportion of jobs in the public sector were reserved for Scheduled Castes and Scheduled Tribes, and a wider system of job reservation for backward castes was implemented in some States. Such reservation policies played a different role in different parts of the country. In Tamil Nadu, for instance, the early mobilisation of Other Backward Classes (OBCs) (who constitute the majority of the population) and reservations for them in government services and education were important instruments for countering the inegalitarian social structure. But the issue of affirmative action became extremely politicized. In response to this agitation, at the end of the 1970s, a Commission was established, which recommended an expansion of the system of reservations to a larger number of castes (Government of India, 1980). However, because of the political volatility of the issue, it was implemented only much later, and remains controversial today. Evaluation of the impact of reservation policies is ambiguous, and even when discriminated groups gain access to employment they remain concentrated in low-level positions. However, this has also to do with other disadvantages of these groups, such as lower levels of education. These issues are discussed further in Chapters 4 and 5.

3.4.2   Education, health, and other social services

In India, expenditure on social services, including education and health, was included in the Five-Year Plans, but as a share of all expenditure it declined after the First Plan (when it was about 24 per cent of total plan expenditure) stabilizing between 17 and 18 per cent thereafter (Table 3.4.1). The percentage of plan outlay devoted to education, health, and other welfare measures fell over time (the last of these included rehabilitation), compensated by an increase in family planning, sanitation, and housing. Meanwhile, central government expenditure as a percentage of GDP increased continually until the 1980s (Section 3.2.2 above, Graph 3.2.1).

Table 3.4.1. Plan Allocations to Social Policy (% Distribution), India, 1951–1979

	First Plan 1951–56	Second Plan 1955–61	Third Plan 1961–66	Fourth Plan 1969–74	Fifth Plan 1974–79
All social services	24.0	18.3	17.4	18.9	17.3
Education	7.6	5.8	6.9	4.9	4.3
Health	3.3	3.0	2.6	2.1	1.9
Family planning	0.0	0.1	0.3	1.8	1.2
Water and sanitation	1.7	1.8	1.2	2.9	2.8
Housing and urban development	-	-	1.5	1.7	2.9
Other welfare	9.8	5.8	4.1	4.7	4.1

Source: Government of India, Central Statistical Office (1983), pp. 148–9; Government of India, Ministry of Finance (1987), pp. S-31 and S-32.

After independence, education policy in India was greatly influenced by Nehru's approach, which gave priority to building 'centres of excellence' in higher education rather than universalizing primary education (Kohli, 2012b). It can certainly be said that primary education did not get the emphasis it deserved, but the number of primary schools and students did nevertheless increase substantially during the early post-independence period. Education, and especially literacy, started to receive greater priority in the 1960s, and policy steps were initiated towards universalizing primary education, though by 1980 this was far from achieved, especially for girls. There were considerable regional disparities, with school enrolment much higher in South India than in the North. The 1960s and 1970s saw the growth of private sector participation in education, especially higher education; and by 1980, almost one-third of colleges in India were private-aided. This privatization of higher education occurred much before economic liberalization.

This early failure to spread basic education clearly had adverse consequences on inequality, which persisted for decades and indeed, persist today (Drèze and Sen, 2013; Section 5.4). Even in 1981, only 55 per cent of boys and 38 per cent of girls aged 6 to 11 were enrolled in school. Adult literacy was just 41 per cent (55 per cent for men and 25 per cent for women), and the literacy of 7 to 14 years old at that time (who were therefore 42 to 49 years old in 2016) was not much higher at 51 per cent.[14]

---

[14] Census data for 1981 reported in the *National Human Development Report 2001* (Government of India, 2002), Tables 4.12 and 4.7.

In Brazil, public social expenditure (education, health, and social security) rose after the 1930s, especially up to 1962. In the 1930s, it represented around 15 per cent of total government expenditure for all administrative levels (central government, States, and municipalities), and reached 26 per cent in 1948 – that is, after the 1946 Constitution – before climbing to 30 per cent in the early 1960s. At this date, social expenditure amounted to 6.5 per cent of GDP (Pires, 1995). During the military regime, expansion of social policies was more quantitative than qualitative, as the aim was to offer the rapidly increasing workforce basic services but not to universalize social sector protection. However, data for 1972 show that 8.8 per cent of GDP was being spent on social policies (Oliveira, 1999). This probably has to do with the increasing share of social security (but for registered workers only) and new areas such as subsidized loans for housing, benefiting especially middle-income groups. However, the expansion of public expenditure on education and health did little to reduce inequality – quite the contrary, actually, if the poor quality of these systems is compared to the growing private services provided for those who could pay.

In Brazil, the 1934 Constitution ruled that everyone was entitled to education, ensuring mandatory and public, free-of-charge, primary education. Subsequently, education in Brazil was governed by two important laws, one addressing higher education and the other primary and secondary education: Law to specify Guidelines and Bases for National Education, 1960 (LDB, from the Portuguese *Lei de Diretrizes e Bases da Educação Nacional, 1960*).

However, the level of education in Brazil advanced slowly in this period. In 1988, approximately 20 per cent of the population aged 15 and over was illiterate, and in rural areas 37 per cent. The average level of schooling was 5.1 years of study, much below the 8 years established by the LDB, while only 5 per cent of those aged 18 to 24 were enrolled in higher education. Besides the problem of the age-grade gap, the education system in Brazil suffered from a shortage of schools and a high percentage of unqualified teachers. And like in India, there was a growth in the supply of private educational establishments aimed at the middle and upper classes.

In neither country, then, could it be said that education was playing an equalizing role; on the contrary, it tended to reinforce existing disparities.

There was also considerable inequality in access to health services in the two countries, though the reasons were different. In India, during the first two decades after independence, health planning concentrated on managing epidemics, and operated through campaigns such as those against malaria, smallpox, tuberculosis, and other diseases. Social aspects of health were largely ignored. Healthcare resources were skewed in their distribution across rural and urban areas, with urban areas receiving more than 75 per cent of resources in the first decade after independence. Even basic facilities were hard to come by and were unevenly distributed. In fact, the Fifth Five-Year Plan acknowledged that urban health facilities had been built at the cost of rural health facilities. Resources and manpower constrained the expansion of healthcare throughout the period – despite innovations such as introduction of Auxiliary Nurses and Midwifes (ANMs) and community health workers.

Plan expenditure on health fell from 3.3 per cent of plan allocations in the First Five-Year Plan (1951–56) to 1.9 per cent during the Fifth (1974–79). Over the same period, expenditure on family planning increased from 0.1 per cent to 1.3 per cent. India was the first country to adopt a government family planning programme in 1951. Initially, it was run through voluntary organizations, but by the Third Plan it had its own department and by the Fifth Plan, it had the highest outlay among the health sub-sectors. Nevertheless, because of attempts in the 1970s to introduce forced sterilization, the programme lost public support.

In Brazil, access to health services depended, like access to social security, on occupational status. The pension institutes of each professional category were responsible for the healthcare of the workers they insured, under the Ministry of Social Security. Wealthier individuals used private health services. The poorest and those outside the formal labour market could access free healthcare services from the Ministry of Health and philanthropic organizations such as Santas Casas and public hospitals. The expansion of healthcare also benefitted from the greater coverage of social security. In 1971, the Fund for Social Assistance and Social Security of Rural Workers (FUNRURAL, from the Portuguese *Fundo de Assistência Social e Previdência do Trabalhador Rural*), established the right to access health and social services for rural workers and their dependents. In 1974, healthcare coverage was extended to any person in a situation of urgency or emergency, regardless of social security contributions. However, these rights were seldom enforced.

To sum up, in the period from independence up to 1980, India first gave priority to growth as the means to achieve social goals. Broadly, it could be said that social policy went through three phases in the period between independence and 1980. The first phase largely ignored social policy. Little attention was paid to social insurance, which reached only a small fraction of workers, so the great majority of workers had little social protection. Some redistributive measures were initiated in the early period after independence, but their scope was limited. The expansion of the public health system was also slow. Some efforts were made to develop social infrastructure through local programmes, notably through rural community development. But all of these programmes were sharply constrained by resources. This was followed by a phase (during the 1960s) when the need for social policy was more widely recognized but little action was taken. Then, after the economic crisis and famine of the mid-1960s, Indira Gandhi's government introduced a variety of redistributive anti-poverty programmes. But implementation was patchy, and there was not much impact in the end – the proportion of the population below the poverty line at the end of the 1970s had hardly declined in comparison with the 1950s (Section 3.2.4).

Brazil's approach to social policy was entirely different. Starting in the 1930s, Brazil introduced social insurance along the same lines as European countries, including in particular pensions and health insurance, but also disability, housing, and other benefits. These were contributory systems linked to formal employment, largely organized by occupational category. While initially this only reached a small fraction of workers, the process of industrialization created an expanding working class, so that by the end of the 1970s a larger fraction of the population was covered. Nevertheless, this social security system covered mainly workers in registered employment and hardly reached the self-employed or rural areas. So, there was an unequal pattern of social protection, which mirrored the inequality within the labour market. Redistributive policies were less important, and were largely managed by private (often religious) organizations, though some state policies were developed. Healthcare gradually spread beyond occupational health insurance to reach the population as a whole, so that emergency services were available for all, but in 1980 coverage was still very incomplete.

Thus, in Brazil, there was social protection for a substantial fraction of workers, but access to social policies was highly segmented and selective. There was also inequality within the group of protected workers. This was because social security contributions – mainly wage-based – reproduced the inequalities generated in the different segments of the labour market. Lastly, it should be mentioned that the urban/rural divide – already tremendous, due to the gap in working conditions and employment relations – was widened further by social policies.

The narrow scope of social policies in both countries in this period had to do not only with the political coalitions that shaped public policies but also with the rationale of the growth regimes. In India, the slow pace of growth did not allow for universal social policies; in Brazil, wider social protection would have been competing with the profit-led strategy of economic growth, in which government expenditure paved the way for private sector expansion.

Nevertheless, it is clear that the scope and impact of social policy in 1980 was much greater in Brazil than in India. This was partly because of the much larger formal labour market, through which social protection was mainly delivered, and partly because the Brazilian state had greater resources. But this was not enough to offset the mounting levels of income inequality in an increasingly urbanized society characterized by a highly concentrated ownership of assets in both urban and rural areas.

4

India and Brazil from 1980 until 2014

Chapter 4 pursues the approach adopted in Chapter 3 for the period from 1980 to 2014. In the first section, a broad overview of the period is provided for both countries. It connects the political context (the political timeline in Table 4.1.1) with economic policies in the light of the changing growth regimes. The following sections of the chapter successively consider the macro-economics of accumulation and growth (4.2); labour institutions and labour markets (4.3); and the role of the state (4.4), relating them all with the outcomes in terms of inequality.

4.1 Political Context, Economic Policies, and Growth Regime

By the end of 1970s, with the global economy in deep crisis and the exhaustion of the Fordist growth regimes in developed countries, both Brazil and India faced turbulent times. In the 1980s, the rise in international interest rates led to a sharp contraction of world trade and a debt crisis in some countries of the periphery, mostly in Latin America and Africa. Growth rates fell around the world, and economic institutions were restructured to serve the interests of the increasingly globalized private sector, especially TNCs and major financial groups, providing the foundations for the subsequent phase of deregulated globalization.

Given the histories of the two countries up to that point, it would seem that Brazil's economy was better placed to face the turbulence. After all, despite weaknesses in the late 1970s, thirty years of high growth in Brazil had laid the foundations of a powerful industrial economy. Meanwhile, India had faced both economic and political crisis with a model that was delivering declining rates of growth and stagnant living standards. But the result was the opposite: India embarked on a period of increasing growth, while Brazil found itself mired in the 'lost decade'.

In fact, Brazil's 'success' was related to its deep integration into the capitalist world economy of the 1960s and 1970s. This can be characterized as subordinated integration, as the country opened its internal market to TNCs and became deeply indebted to commercial banks by taking loans with floating interest rates. In the new context, Brazil's industrial sector was hard hit and the public sector severely affected by the sharp increase in foreign debt. In India, the external crisis was much less intense, largely because the country's ties to the global economy were weaker. This permitted India – or its policy makers – to ultimately, though not immediately, embark on the opening of its economy as a part of the effort to stimulate the internal market.

Economic liberalization was to dominate the policy agenda in the following decades in Brazil and India as in much of the world. But that was not obvious in 1980, and change occurred progressively. In both countries, the decade of the 1980s marked a transition towards a new growth regime, but whereas in India this was a transitional period with limited reforms, in Brazil the previous growth regime foundered in a decade of economic turmoil. The economic stabilization of the 1990s made it possible to implement liberal reforms, but these did not lead to the resumption of stable economic growth in the context of a highly unstable global economy. A new growth regime seemed to emerge after 2000 – which combined the economic policies launched in 1999 (fiscal surpluses, a floating exchange rate, and interest rates adjusted to inflation) with redistribution and labour market regulation – but this proved to be short-lived, as we will show in this chapter. Meanwhile, in India there was progressive implementation of liberalizing economic reforms by different governments after 1991, which has been sustained up to the present. Table 4.1.2 summarizes the key features of the growth regimes from 1980 onwards. The remainder of this section provides an overview of how these regimes played out in each country, and their consequences for growth and distribution.

4.1.1 Political context and the State

In both countries, the political environment changed in the 1980s, but the change was more gradual in India than Brazil. The new Congress government, restored to power in 1980, did not immediately abandon the populist policies of the 1970s. In fact, it introduced new social policy initiatives and reinforced others. But it was much more open to coordination with business interests than before, providing some tax breaks and subsidies, and embarking on some limited deregulation of the domestic market (Kohli, 2012b; Nagaraj, 2012). After Indira Gandhi's assassination in 1984, Rajiv Gandhi pursued the same line, with a focus on innovation and technological upgrading. At the same time, the leading role of the state was not questioned, public investment remained high, and the economy remained insulated from the global market. Government policy during this period became much less hostile to the private sector than before, in a way that has been characterized as pro-business rather than pro-market (Rodrik and Subramanian, 2004).

Larger changes occurred in the 1990s. The Congress government was voted out of office in 1989, but returned to power in 1991 in the wake of a financial and balance-of-payments crisis. This government had a wider agenda of liberal economic reform, triggered by an IMF loan, but also reflecting criticism of earlier strategy within the government (Ahluwalia, 2002; 2016). The reform, put into effect by Finance Minister (and from 2004 to 2014 Prime Minister) Manmohan Singh, for the first time included a measure of both internal and external deregulation. Throughout the 1990s, there was no clear parliamentary majority, and there was a succession of governments of different political hues, but reform policies were carried forward by all, albeit quite cautiously. While business had benefited from protection earlier, there was now a substantial business lobby in favour of across-the-board deregulation. This reform laid the foundations for a shift in the process of capital accumulation, as private business, essentially domestic but eventually including multinational companies, started to increase investment rates as the economy accelerated (De and Vakulabharanam, 2013).

In 1999, a coalition government came to power led by the Hindu nationalist party, the Bharatiya Janata Party (BJP). But it lost the next election in 2004, partly because its slogan of 'Shining India' failed to recognize the adverse social fall-out of a model that concentrated the benefits of higher growth on a fraction of the population, especially the urban upper middle class. The Congress-led government that came to power in 2004 continued the gradual extension of liberalizing reforms. But it also implemented a variety of social policies to compensate for the failure of the economic model to create enough employment or distribute incomes to the population as a whole. These included debt forgiveness for farmers, the MGNREGA to create employment for the rural poor, strengthening of the Public Distribution System (PDS) to provide subsidized food, the right to education, and other policies. Not all of these policies were new, but they took on new significance within the new growth regime. The employment guarantee scheme, MGNREGA, was particularly significant, successfully raising rural employment and income levels in much of the country. The government also raised the reference minimum wage in 2004, though subsequently it was allowed to stagnate in real terms. During this period, living standards were generally

Table 4.1.1. Political Timeline since 1980

Date	Brazil	India
1980–1990	1980 Creation of Workers' Party 1982 Party of the Brazilian Democratic Movement (PMDB from Portuguese *Partido do Movimento Democrático Brasileiro*), the opposition party to the military rule, wins elections in most states 1984–85 Tancredo Neves becomes president, but dies, and is replaced by José Sarney 1986 Members of the constitutional assembly elected 1988 New constitution approved	1980 Indira Gandhi returns to power 1984 Indira Gandhi assassinated, succeeded by her son Rajiv Gandhi 1989 Congress loses election
1990–2000	1990 Fernando Collor wins first direct presidential election since 1960 1992 Impeachment of Collor 1994 Launch of the Real Plan 1995 Fernando Henrique Cardoso president until 2002 1999 Devaluation of Real followed by economic crisis	1990–1999 Succession of unstable minority governments 1991 Rajiv Gandhi assassinated 1991 Economic reforms launched 1999 BJP comes to power in coalition government
2000–2010	2003 Lula assumes the presidency for the following 8 years 2005 Corruption scandal involving parties of the governing alliance	2004 Congress defeats BJP and returns to power 2009 Congress-led government re-elected on platform of high growth and social policy
2010–Present	2010 Lula's former chief of staff Dilma Rousseff elected president 2014 Dilma narrowly re-elected after close political battle 2015–16 Brazil faces economic recession, aggravated by political crisis 2016 August Rousseff is impeached in what has been described as an institutional *coup d'état*	2010–14 Corruption scandals weaken Congress-led government 2014 BJP wins election and forms government 2014 Abolition of Planning Commission

rising and poverty diminishing. But the government was ultimately voted out of power in 2014 in the wake of corruption scandals and falling growth rates.

Throughout this period of liberalization, the government was attempting to play a much more limited role than before – of regulator and promoter, rather than planner. By 2010, public investment was down from a half of all investment to a quarter. At the same time, the state was seen as an ally by business interests, some of which aimed to take advantage of mineral resources, commercial farming options, and industrial production without regard for social or environmental considerations. There were considerable tensions between policy, business, bureaucratic, and judicial systems in the implementation of the process of reform (Kohli, 2012a).

There was an even sharper divide between the 1980s and the previous decade in Brazil. In the years after 1980, Brazil's political institutions were reconfigured in the midst of a stagnant economy with steeply rising inflation levels. The military regime was discredited on both economic and political grounds. Finally, it imploded, without violence, in the face of an alliance of social actors whose goal was to restore a democratic order and, eventually, to bring about a new development strategy, though its contours were quite vague at the time. New social forces emerged, in particular a reconstructed trade union movement and new political parties. During this period, the state was greatly weakened, and subordinate to the new international setting and the need for economic stabilization. In the early 1980s, the central government assumed responsibility for private external debt, thus jeopardizing domestic public spending. At times, it appeared to have completely lost control as inflation accelerated.

A new constitution was promulgated in 1988, incorporating a wide range of democratic rights and social principles. However, its main advances could not be implemented in the context of economic instability due to increasing inflation levels, which reached over 80 per cent per month in 1989. The old growth regime was exhausted, but the political preconditions for a new one were not yet in place. When the indirectly elected presidential candidate Tancredo Neves died before taking office, José Sarney, his vice-president, became president. Sarney was an important representative of the ruling party during the dictatorship, while the party he subsequently moved to, the PMDB, was increasingly dominated by the traditional elites, displacing progressive forces.

Monetary stability returned in the 1990s. The key was the Real Plan which, in 1994, finally brought inflation under control. Its principal architect, Fernando Henrique Cardoso, then Finance Minister, came to power as President in 1995 and embarked on a series of structural reforms, guided by the pursuit of productivity gains through the reorientation and reduction of the state's role in the economy and by the liberalization of international trade and finance (Franco, 1999).[1] Thus, the government recovered some economic policy capacity, but played a less active role, privatized public enterprises (in the mining, steel, telecommunications and energy sectors, among others) and remained dependent on the ups and downs of international markets. This was also a period of tension with the labour movement as a result of some efforts to flexibilize labour markets. In the end, the liberalization strategy proved to be unsustainable in a context of a series of financial crises that struck the global economy in the second half of the 1990s. The Brazilian economy suffered severely – unlike the Indian economy, which was still relatively protected from international financial flows, because it had not yet opened its capital market.

This was one of the reasons why India and Brazil diverged in the 2000s. In Brazil, there was in effect an attempt to change the growth regime. In India, there was greater investment in social policy by the new government after 2004, but essentially as a complement to an unchanged central strategy of liberal reforms. In Brazil, on the other hand, there was a qualitative change. The Cardoso government of 1994–2002 had in fact introduced a number of important social policy instruments (Comunidade Solidária, Bolsa Escola) as a complement to the process of liberalization, which could be compared with the policies of the later Congress government in India. But there was a more substantial shift with the arrival in power of the Workers' Party (PT for Portuguese *Partido dos Trabalhadores*) led by President Lula da Silva. The new government widened the scope of both economic and social policies. Government investment, consumption, and social transfers were gradually increased. Central government social expenditure grew faster than GDP, following a pro-cyclical pattern (Guerra et al., 2015). At the same time, there was a sharp increase in the purchasing power of the minimum wage, and a wider social protection net, which increased the real incomes of workers and reduced social and economic inequality.

However, the reformist stance of the Lula government, and of his successor Dilma Rousseff after 2010, was weakened by the need for a majority in Congress, where political power was shared with centre-right politicians and leading members of the Brazilian business class. Despite its left-wing credentials, the PT government, from the outset, used orthodox financial tools to calm the markets and engaged with the private sector.

---

[1] It is striking that in both countries the finance minister who managed the process of liberalization in its early stages subsequently became president (Brazil) or prime minister (India). This parallel between the two countries might be considered as a coincidence, but it does underline the centrality of liberalization in national politics.

Both India and Brazil were hit by the global recession that started in 2008, and deepened after 2011. There were also major corruption scandals in both countries, which undermined the credibility of the ruling parties. This ultimately led to the fall of the government in both countries, but in entirely different ways. The Congress government in India was decimated in the 2014 election, and the BJP returned to power with a parliamentary majority. In Brazil, the PT government just survived a close-run presidential election in 2014, but was incapable of taking advantage of its victory in the face of deep economic recession, finally losing power in 2016 as a result of the impeachment of President Dilma Rousseff. We return to these developments in the final chapter.

4.1.2 Economic liberalization

In both countries the essential differences between the periods before and after the early 1990s lie in the roles of the state and of private business in a liberalized economy, on the one hand, and the type of international economic integration, on the other (Table 4.1.2). Both countries were increasingly influenced by global economic forces after 1990. But increasing openness also made the domestic economy more vulnerable to instability in the global economy, especially in Brazil, with the consequence that the growth regime was less coherent and sustainable.

In India, in 1980, the state was the prime economic actor, the Planning Commission determined resource allocation and defined development strategy, and the public sector accounted for half of all investment. The move from a largely state-controlled regime to an increasingly market-based regime started in the 1980s, with a freeing-up of some administrative controls on investment and production in domestic markets. But the Indian economy remained protected by many restrictions on foreign trade and capital flows. While both exports and imports grew in this period, their share in GDP did not rise, and private foreign capital inflows were negligible, except in technology-sharing agreements with domestic firms. However, higher growth led to growing demands for imports, which ultimately led to a balance-of-payments crisis at the end of the 1980s, one of the factors that sparked economic reforms in 1991.

The reforms widened domestic deregulation and extended it to the external market. Deregulation was neither comprehensive nor immediate (licensing remained in many industries and it was more than a decade before consumer goods were opened to imports; Ahluwalia, 2016). The state remained an important economic actor, but a much wider range of opportunities was opened up for private investment and production with less administrative oversight. This triggered a shift in corporate behaviour, an increase in private investment, and an accelerating growth rate of GDP (Rodrik and Subramanian, 2004). Nevertheless, the economy remained heterogeneous, with production of goods and services concentrated on the one hand in small firms and businesses operating in a competitive market, and on the other in an oligopolistic structure controlled by a relatively narrow group of business families and conglomerates (Mazumdar and Sarkar, 2009). In some sectors (telecommunications, automobiles) multinationals started to play an important role. The manufacturing sector as a whole failed to take off, but construction and modern services boomed (Section 4.2 below).

Deregulation of the external sector was a central component of reform. Tariff protection remained, and was sometimes high (still averaging 30 per cent in 2000); but import licensing was reduced, foreign exchange controls were relaxed, and the Indian economy rapidly integrated into global markets for goods and services. The latter was of particular importance because the manufacturing sector was weak and uncompetitive. On the other hand, liberalization of capital markets was much slower (Rodrik and Subramanian, 2004), and while multinationals became increasingly active in India, they were mainly interested in accessing the growing domestic market. Foreign direct investment rose, but was only 5 per cent of all investment twenty years after the reform started.

One result of this slow opening up of capital markets was that India was relatively little affected by the Asian Financial Crisis of 1997–1998, which severely affected the economies of East and Southeast Asia first, and subsequently Latin America, especially Brazil and Argentina (Stallings, 1998). But exports and imports continued to grow rapidly.

In 1980, Brazil was already open to the global economy through FDI in manufacturing industry, access to external loans, and low tariffs for goods not produced in the internal market. This was one reason for the depth and duration of its economic difficulties in the 1980s. Not only did Brazilian exports shrink – though recovering after 1984 – but there was also a crisis of solvency of the huge foreign debt. Attempts to curb foreign imbalances by currency devaluation worsened the overall picture through their inflationary impact, and the heterodox stabilization plans intended to control inflation had only short-term results. Trade surpluses throughout the decade were assured by recession (fall of imports) and higher exports of manufacturing goods, the latter reflecting diversion to external markets of production for which domestic demand was stagnant (Castro and Pires de Souza, 2004). The outcome was a decade of low growth, an informalization of economic activity and an expansion of precarious employment relationships (Table 4.1.2, first column).

In the 1990s, efforts at liberalization focused on the pattern of international integration, with the opening up of trade and the end of restrictions for FDI in some sectors, most notably in services. As a consequence, the economy was severely hit by increasing competitive pressure from abroad. Economic stabilization was achieved through a combination of high interest rates and an overvalued exchange rate. Together with the absence of consistent industrial and technological policies, this was unfavourable for Brazilian corporate capital, which reacted by reducing product lines, importing capital goods, and outsourcing many activities (Castro, 1999). Investment rates were volatile despite the large inflow of FDI, attracted by economic liberalization and state-sponsored privatization under the aegis of the BNDES. Mostly, FDI aimed not at new investment but rather at the acquisition of existing public and private assets. The oligopolistic structures that dominated industry before 1980 were maintained and even reinforced; for instance, these expanded to the service sector. Open unemployment and informal employment rose considerably throughout the 1990s, affecting social groups that had been protected from these phenomena in the earlier industrialization period.

So, during this period, external constraints, interacting with economic policies at home, were a major factor in the failure of the attempt to put a new growth regime in place in the 1990s. Stopping inflation required an overvaluation of the currency, which led to a loss of competitiveness on global markets, trade deficits, and vulnerability to short-term capital flows, attracted by high interest rates, as high yields were offered on public bonds to finance Brazil's debt. In this context, Brazil became easy prey for capital flight during speculative attacks after the 1994 Mexican crisis, the 1997–1998 Asian crisis, and the 1998 Russian crisis, eventually leading to the forced devaluation in 1999.

Brazil was now inherently dependent on short-term capital to close the current account deficit. Rising interest rates at home discouraged investment aimed at expanding new capacity. In terms of economic performance, GDP growth during the Cardoso period was meagre – 2.3 per cent per year on average. Moreover, there was a large fall in the share of the industrial sector in GDP and a deterioration of labour market conditions. In contrast, India's liberalization of the capital account was more cautious, its GDP growth was fuelled by domestic private investment, and it faced no external crisis after the beginning of the 1990s until the global financial crisis of 2008.

These contrasting situations in the 1990s took India and Brazil in quite different directions after 2000. The Indian economy responded positively to liberalization. As deregulation was gradually extended, private investment rates increased, and growth accelerated from decade to decade after 1980. In the first decade of the twenty-first century, the annual growth rate reached almost 10 per cent for several years before the recent slowdown in the wake of the global financial crisis. This growth has been unevenly distributed across economic sectors, and there has been a substantial shift of the share of value-added from wages to profits, but real wages and incomes have been rising across the economy as a whole, and absolute poverty has dropped steadily (Section 4.2). Nevertheless, there is little doubt that an elite group has benefited disproportionately from the new economic model, and the concentration of the accumulation of capital in a relatively small group of families and businesses is likely to accentuate this further.

By the time the global financial crisis started in 2008, steps towards external deregulation had gone further than at the end of the 1990s, and the Indian economy was more vulnerable to international instability. Growth rates fell, in large part the result of lack of growth in export markets and of the continuing weakness of India's manufacturing sector. But the economy returned to growth rates of 7 per cent or more relatively quickly after the crisis.

In Brazil, after the Asian Financial Crisis, and after nearly a quarter of a century of stop-and-go, the economy resumed growth in 2004. But, unlike in India, the growth path was built on a new institutional framework, which attempted to overcome some of the failures of the 1990s. We present this as an attempt to launch a new growth regime in the third column of Table 4.1.2. In part, this reflected a new international environment, and in particular a cycle of economic expansion in the United States, together with the changing role of China in the international division of labour. It should also be acknowledged that devaluations in 1999 and 2002 were important as they increased the competitiveness of Brazilian exports and stimulated an import substitution process in some sectors of manufacturing industry. Tight monetary and fiscal policies were also maintained, in the context of growing internal demand, which encouraged the inflow of all types of foreign capital – both productive, long-term investment and short-term movements. But these conservative economic policies were accompanied by major changes in the orientation of the state, social policy, and labour market regulation, aiming to change the pattern of growth and the distribution of its benefits.

The commodity boom helped to significantly improve Brazil's foreign accounts, foreign debts decreased, exports rose (benefiting from higher commodity prices, but there was also an increase of manufacturing exports), and international reserves were boosted. The result was a recovery of growth accompanied by a decline in inequality, aided by other economic policies such as the expansion of credit, especially by public banks, and to a lesser extent, public investment in infrastructure and state-owned enterprises (Barbosa, 2013).

Nevertheless, this growth regime was unbalanced. It combined redistribution to workers with the maintenance of high interest rates, absence of tax reform, and low levels of public investment. There was also a pattern of international integration that limited the capacity of the country to benefit from the dynamism of the internal market, because currency revaluation after 2005 hampered the movement up the production chain to higher value activities, especially in manufacturing. When a less favourable international setting emerged after 2008, current account deficits grew once again, while growth of GDP and investment began to slow in 2011–2013 and the economy went into deep recession after 2014. In sum, changes were not made to the mode of regulation that could unleash a new growth regime or bring more coherence to the incomplete one in place, and the share of investment in GDP was still below 20 per cent. While Brazil does not now face the same classic balance-of-payments problem of the past, the challenge lies in how to raise growth and productivity levels in the new international context, without undermining the social advances made in the past decade.

There is, therefore, a sharp contrast between the two countries. Throughout the period, the success or failure of Brazil's growth regime has been heavily dependent on the nature and degree of its integration into the global economy. The success in reducing inequality in the last decade has been facilitated by a favourable international environment, and also by its interaction with a dynamic internal market, encouraged by state policies. However, in the wake of the 2008 crisis, and in a much less favourable international environment, the growth regime proved fragile. Although social policies were maintained, at least up to the fall of the PT government, they now were being implemented within a stagnant economy, which led to unsustainable fiscal deficits.

In India, on the other hand, the international economy has not been nearly so central to economic and social performance. Nevertheless, as the Indian economy modernizes and increasingly opens its markets for goods and capital, international factors play an increasing role. But the challenge is different from that in Brazil. It is not that a change of growth regime is needed because of the loss of effectiveness of a set of economic policies – the scenario is rather one in which the economic model still delivers growth, but at the same time growing inequality, with implications for its sustainability in the long term.

4.1.3   Labour and the agrarian structure

Two other sets of institutions identified in Table 4.1.2 have played a role in these changes in the growth regime – labour and agrarian relations. Agrarian relations, although still important, were becoming less central in both countries, but labour institutions were more significant – especially in Brazil, where labour institutions and regulation were key for the attempt to unleash a new growth regime in the 2000s.

In neither country did the deregulation of investment and trade extend to the labour market. But in India, throughout the period since 1980, labour legislation was slackly applied, and the extent of casual, contract, and other forms of unstable and precarious wage labour was enormous and growing (Section 4.3 below). It was widely commented that the rapid growth of the Indian economy was 'jobless', in the sense that the employment elasticity of growth was low; and, in particular, there was little creation of regular, protected jobs in the formal economy (Papola and Sahu, 2012). The share of such jobs stagnated until at least 2005, and while it started to rise slowly thereafter, it was still less than 7 per cent of all employment in 2011-12. Employment in the public sector, which was the reference point up to the 1980s, declined after the economic reforms, which shifted resources towards the private sector. The informal economy continued to account for the bulk of employment (so growth was not really jobless – the issue was the type of jobs), and the great majority of informal workers had little security or protection.

Market forces increased in rural areas, where casual labour also grew, as did circular migration to urban areas, but self-employment in small-scale agriculture continued to dominate. Labour market opportunities differed greatly between men and women, and between different social groups, as the labour market was highly fragmented. Trade unions remained weak and almost invisible in the private service sector, which dominated the economy. Although there were regular calls for greater flexibility in the Indian labour market, in particular because of legal restrictions on dismissals, in practice this did not hinder the liberal growth regime.

In Brazil, the situation was somewhat different even in the 1980s and 1990s. The 1980s was a period of informalization of labour relations, though it was also an important period for the reconstitution of the trade union movement. Then, in the low-growth 1990s, a rise in productivity reflected the laying-off of workers and growth in outsourcing and informalization rather than an expansion of productive capacity (Kupfer, 2012). Open unemployment and informal employment rose in this period, and real living standards declined from 1999 to 2003. Nevertheless, there were important innovations, notably the introduction of a system of unemployment insurance in 1986 and a reinforcement of training institutions in the 1990s, even though disconnected from other labour policies.

The role of labour institutions changed substantially under the PT government. The wage relation no longer played a subordinate role; instead, it now contributed positively to macroeconomic performance, as rising real wages added to the growth of aggregate demand, driven by a steadily increasing real minimum wage and social transfers. A central feature of this period was a reformalization of wage labour, so the minimum wage was also applied to an increasing share of workers. Brazil was one of the few countries to show substantial growth in formal employment in this period. In the 1980s and 1990s, there had been growth of both unemployment and precarious forms of work, and this was true of India as well. But after the turn of the century, the paths diverged, as the informal economy continued to grow in India while Brazil started to reverse that trend.

With respect to agrarian institutions, the situations of Brazil and India could hardly be compared. In India, older forms of bondage and feudal structures tended to disappear, and in many parts of the country agricultural production was dominated by middle and rich peasants, who also came to political power in some states. The agrarian system changed slowly, becoming increasingly integrated into national markets for commodities and labour. Green Revolution technology spread rapidly in the 1980s, and continued to spread thereafter, but public investment in irrigation and power fell away in the 1990s, and so did agricultural growth (Bhalla and Singh, 2012). In some regions, capital entered rural areas through either the production of commercial crops or the supply of seeds and other agricultural inputs, but severe problems of farmer indebtedness ensued. Agricultural growth recovered after 2005, but the share of agriculture in GDP declined, and rural development was relatively neglected.

In Brazil, implementation of agrarian reforms was slow. An increasing share of rural labour had access to social protection, a process that started in the 1990s. But peasant agriculture was relatively unimportant in terms of GDP compared with the expansion of agribusiness. This made rural areas appendages of urban areas, and fuelled the development of the growth regime as a whole. Investment in modern agriculture became an engine of growth, as it increasingly used inputs from manufacturing and services. However, because of its low share in GDP, it could not by itself drive the growth in demand.

On the other hand, small producers were better placed in the internal market, benefiting from wider access to credit and growing demand in urban areas. Since the bulk of agricultural labour worked in family farms, this was an important source of poverty reduction, together with the expansion of social security to rural areas, the Bolsa Familia programme (Section 4.4), and better access to credit. In addition, rural consumption patterns changed and aligned with those in urban areas, thus reducing the urban-rural divide. This occurred without any substantial change in the concentration of wealth in Brazilian agriculture, as land was still highly unevenly distributed – indeed, increasingly so.

4.1.4   *The overall pattern of growth and distribution*

The overall pattern of inequality reflects these histories and growth regimes in two ways: in the power and class relations that mould the different institutions underpinning the growth regime; and in the economic consequences – especially market opportunities and outcomes – that derive from its overall structure.

The broad picture is the following. Liberalization and high growth in India drove inequality upwards after the 1980s, due to the pattern of private investment, the less interventionist state, and a rather flexible labour market with excess labour supply and high levels of informality and migration. The mechanisms lay partly in the competition regime and the pattern of international integration (Table 4.1.2), both tending to concentrate incomes and shift factor shares from wages to profits; partly in the persistent informality of wage labour relations; and partly in the limited role of the state. Nevertheless, the rise in inequality up to 2004-05 seems to have since been halted or at least slowed after that date by the redistributive programmes implemented by the Congress-led government, at least up to the change of government in 2014.

It is also true that absolute poverty has been declining. But absolute poverty is not a sufficient yardstick in a rapidly growing economy, and relative poverty has certainly increased, as social expectations rise faster than the means to satisfy them. And the growing inequality that has accompanied high growth has generated many new conflicts of interest and aspirations.

There are also indications of an increasing diversity of experiences across India. Rural areas have clearly gained less than urban areas; and, since the majority of the population still lives in rural areas, this is an important divide. It also seems that growth is regionally concentrated, so that regional inequality is growing. This may be moderated by growing migration, but the tendency for growth to be concentrated in certain major urban centres risks leaving backwaters across the country with a stagnant economic base. Finally, the process of market-driven growth seems unlikely to overcome some of the key embedded inequalities, between castes and communities, between genders, between those with assets and those with none, and between the more and less educated. Differentials in wages and employment opportunities between these social categories remain large. We examine these issues further in later sections of this book.

In Brazil, the growth of inequality to exceptionally high levels peaked in the late 1980s, when high inflation levels disproportionately affected the poor, who have few assets. By the same token, the stabilization of inflation at low levels in the 1990s helped to reduce inequality, but this was at least partly offset by growing unemployment and informalization. Nevertheless, as noted above, some innovative social policies were introduced in the Cardoso period, which aimed at overcoming social exclusion and evening out opportunities in the educational system. Inequality started to decline after the mid-1990s. But it was the PT government that came to power in 2003 that started to address the extremes of inequality. The main factors were the rising real minimum wages along with the recovery of the labour market and large-scale cash transfers to families. State policies and labour market institutions therefore played an important role in offsetting the disequalizing tendencies of liberalized markets.

The outcome was a substantial fall in the standard measures of inequality, starting in the latter part of the 1990s and accelerating after 2003 (Section 4.2). This fall in inequality and a parallel fall in poverty, in a democratic political setting, is a substantial achievement. But progress was halted in 2014 and, partially, reversed in the period of severe recession (2015–2016). As in India, some of the inequalities – among social groups and regions – are deeply entrenched. For instance, white-to-black and male-to-female income differentials fell up to 2013, mostly by virtue of the increase in the minimum wage, but they remain substantial, and larger than the relative educational attainment of these groups could explain. Furthermore, poverty and inequality have fallen less in the poorest regions – like the Northeast – than in the richest ones, as the former lack the dynamic labour markets of the latter.

Despite differences between the two countries in the overall role of the state, there were some parallels in the efforts of the government in both countries to put in place social programmes to counter the disequalizing effect of liberalization (Section 4.4). But in Brazil the effort and impact were significantly greater. This is a key difference between the two countries: Brazilian labour market and social policies delivered significantly better outcomes in terms of social protection and redistribution than in India, despite lower GDP growth levels and investment rates. And while some of this difference reflected the differences in economic and social structures and productivity levels, it is also clear that the Brazilian government after 2003 had a broader social vision and a stronger base of support in the trade union movement and civil society, which was strategic for the configuration of the growth regime as a whole.[2] Meanwhile, high growth in India certainly spills over to rising living standards for a majority of the population; but there must also be doubts about the sustainability of a model of high growth without greater redistribution.

---

[2] This is no longer the case after the change of government in 2016; Chapter 7.

Table 4.1.2. Growth Regimes and Modes of Regulation in Brazil and India since 1980

	Brazil			India	
	Economic Crisis (1981–1989)	Economic Liberalization (1990–1999)	Internal Recovery with Redistribution (2000–2014)	Transitional (1980–1991)	Liberalizing (1991–)
Growth regime	Crisis of the previous growth regime	Liberalized growth regime, subjected to currency crisis, and downplaying the role of the internal market	Internal market growth benefiting from the international context and the increasing role of the state	Inward-looking partial liberalization	Increasingly open liberal regime with limited redistribution
Institutional forms					
Pattern of international integration	Negative effects of external debt crisis are worsened by a new hike in oil prices and fall of commodity prices; capital flight during the whole period	With the exchange rate pegged to the dollar after the Real Plan, current account deficits increase fast. New inflow of FDI in a variety of sectors, helped by privatizations. External debt again escalates	Increase of trade surplus (partly because of the boom of commodity prices), expansion of greenfield FDI, and reduction of foreign debt.	Very limited international integration; share of imports and exports in GDP low and stagnant. Negligible FDI but some technology partnerships	External liberalization of trade, with rapid rise in both exports and imports; gradual opening up to FDI with increasing presence of multinational companies (and Indian multinationals operating abroad).

Cont.

Cont.

	Brazil			India	
	Economic Crisis (1981–1989)	Economic Liberalization (1990–1999)	Internal Recovery with Redistribution (2000–2014)	Transitional (1980–1991)	Liberalizing (1991–)
Competition regime	Oligopoly, protected from international competition due to the devaluation of the currency and the stagnant internal market	Oligopoly expanded to the services sector, now with the entry of global TNCs. Creation of new regulatory agencies reinforces oligopolistic structure and accepts high profit margins in telecommunications, energy etc.	Oligopolistic structure is rearranged with new strategies from the leading companies – TNCs and national – to get better position in the more dynamic internal market; internationalization of some national business groups	Some domestic deregulation of prices and investment led to greater competition, along with widening of state-business coordination. Continued political support to agrarian interests	Increased competition from abroad and within some domestic sectors, though much large-scale industry and modern services still oligopolistic and controlled by a few business families
Wage labour relations	Unaltered from pre-1980, the more organized unions are able to peg wages to inflation; other segments of the workforce lose purchasing power	Attempts to reduce labour costs and reform Brazilian Labour Code. Expansion of unregulated segments of workforce, non-registered workers, and the informal sector	Expansion of formal jobs with a substantial increase of the minimum wage in a context of recovery of trade union pressure leading to collective bargaining	Deterioration in industrial relations and weakening of trade union influence. Little growth of regular, protected work, and little change in labour institutions. Growth of large-scale casual labour market in both urban and rural areas, but rising wages.	Little increase in protected/formal work despite economic growth. Informal, competitive employment relations dominate – but wages grow as demand for casual labour increases. Women disadvantaged in outsourced production. Growth of casual labour in rural areas and increase in migration.

Cont.

Cont.

	Brazil			India	
	Economic Crisis (1981–1989)	Economic Liberalization (1990–1999)	Internal Recovery with Redistribution (2000–2014)	Transitional (1980–1991)	Liberalizing (1991–)
Agrarian relations	Unaltered, with the expansion of agricultural frontier to the West and north and the creation of landless rural workers' movement (MST)	Agrarian reform gets under way, but without complementary policies, cannot prevent further land concentration. Rural pensions to workers implemented, which contributes to reduction of poverty in rural areas	Agrarian reform continues at a slow pace, now with a set of complementary policies (credit, market and technical support), but still constrained by the huge expansion of agribusiness	Spread of technologies to middle peasants who increasingly dominate agrarian system rather than former landlords. Increase in agricultural productivity and rising wages	Rural areas relatively neglected, but some larger scale capitalist investment in commercial crops. Increased integration in wider labour and commodity markets
Monetary/ fiscal regime	Tough monetary policy contributes to further worsening of fiscal capacity of the state, which bails out the debt contracted by the private sector.	Inflation stabilization is managed through exchange rate-peg, as fiscal deficits increase. High interest rates lead to mushrooming of the internal public debt	Low inflation, helped by currency revaluation. GDP growth permits higher public spending; credit expansion by public banks. This equation is eroded after 2010.	Fiscal capacity of the state expands with acceleration of growth, but expenditure rises faster leading to growing deficits	Reduced reliance on external tariffs, government finance stable as share of GDP, government debt first increases then declines with high economic growth

Cont.

Cont.

Cont.

	Brazil			India	
	Economic Crisis (1981–1989)	Economic Liberalization (1990–1999)	Internal Recovery with Redistribution (2000–2014)	Transitional (1980–1991)	Liberalizing (1991–)
Role of the state	Totally subordinate to the new international setting, losing its autonomy over economic and social policies	Active, albeit subordinate, as the economic policy depends on the ups and downs of foreign capital movements	State action is stronger in both economic and social policies. More active role of BNDES (Brazilian development bank) and public investment since 2006. Social policies have a wider scope though not universal	Public sector investment remains high but greater accommodation with and support for business interests. Increased expenditure on social programmes.	Liberal economic reforms implemented by both Congress- and BJP-led governments. Reduced state intervention but Complementary social policies introduced after 2004. Greater regional diversity. Growth of corruption.
Mode of regulation	Shattered, as capital accumulation horizon is shortened and TNCs move away from the country	Higher competitive pressure brought about by liberalization raises criticisms from social movements and, later on, also from industrial groups	Wide coalition of interests including different capital groups, workers, and social movements, without substantial structural reforms	State-business coordination in market protected by tariffs and administrative regulation	Market coordination with state support to business and some social transfers

Cont.

	Brazil			India	
	Economic Crisis (1981–1989)	Economic Liberalization (1990–1999)	Internal Recovery with Redistribution (2000–2014)	Transitional (1980–1991)	Liberalizing (1991–)
Income distribution profile	The highest income inequality levels in Brazilian history due to the uncontrolled inflation, unemployment, and informalization	Inequality falls somewhat after the stabilization of inflation but then stays at still high levels. Profits increase faster than wages but do not lead to productive investment	Fall of labour income inequality due to new labour market conditions (job growth, formalization and rising minimum wages) and social policies (Bolsa Família, and social security programmes).	Little direct redistribution by the state and little change in inequality overall. Some decline in poverty mainly because of rising casual wages.	Upper income groups gain from economic reform and increase in profit share, although real wages rise and poverty falls, especially after 2005. Rising inequality despite redistributive programmes such as rural employment guarantee. Benefits of growth concentrated in urban areas and some regions

Source: Prepared by the authors. For India, also drawing on De and Vakulabharanam (2013).

4.2 Macroeconomic Patterns and Outcomes

4.2.1 The growth of GDP

Until 1980, there were some common elements in the growth paths of India and Brazil. Between 1950 and 1980, both countries followed a state-promoted capital-intensive, protective, import substitution-based growth regime that delivered higher rates of growth than in the past. The process of industrialization went much further in Brazil, and generated a much higher growth rate of GDP than in India; and the contrast between socialist, democratic India and the right-wing military dictatorship in Brazil after 1964 was extreme. But there were at least some similarities in the way the development path was conceived.

Table 4.2.1.A. Real Growth Rates of GDP and Major Sectors by Decade, Brazil, 1980s to 2014 (% Per Year; 2010 Prices)

	Agriculture	Secondary	Tertiary	GDP
1980s	2.4	0.2	2.7	1.6
1990s	3.7	2.2	2.2	2.5
2000s	4.0	2.8	3.7	3.6
2011–2014	2.3	0.1	0.7	1.6

Source: National Accounts System, Reference 2000, IBGE (Ipeadata).

Table 4.2.1.B. Real Growth Rates of GDP and Major Sectors by Decade, India, 1980s to 2014-15 (% Per Year; 2004-05 Prices)

	Primary	Secondary	Tertiary	GDP
1980s	3.5	5.5	6.6	5.2
1990s	3.3	6.2	7.5	5.9
2000s	3.2	8.5	8.9	7.6
2010–11 to 2014–15	2.7	5.8	7.9	6.3

Source: Drèze and Sen (2013); National Accounts (RBI database and Economic Survey, 2015-16).

Note: 1. Indian data refer to the financial year April to March. Data for the 1980s cover growth from 1980-81 (April to March) to 1990-91, etc.

2. In India, a substantial change in methodology was applied by the Central Statistical Office after 2012-13, using 2011-12 basic prices. The figures in the bottom row of the table use the new methodology, except for 2010-11 when only the old series is available. In the period for which both estimates are available, the new method gives a higher rate of growth of GDP (by 0.8 per cent in 2012-13 and 1.6 per cent in 2013-14).

3. In Brazil, the secondary sector includes mining, civil construction, and public utilities. In India, the classification is similar, except that mining is included in the primary sector.

As we saw in the last section, in the decade of the 1980s the trajectories of the two countries diverged in a spectacular fashion. In India, growth started to accelerate, finally leaving the 'Hindu rate of growth' behind (Table 4.2.1). Growth increased in all sectors, but unlike in the early years after independence, the leading sector was not industry but services, which would be the fastest growing segment of the Indian economy for the next thirty years. Agriculture also grew faster than before, thanks to the spread of the Green Revolution.

In Brazil, on the other hand, the 1980s was a decade of crisis and low growth. The rising foreign debt had to be serviced in a period of high international interest rates. Devaluation fuelled inflation, which peaked at 1,637 per cent per year in 1989. In contrast, inflation in India was quite stable and usually in single digits. The stabilization plans for the Brazilian economy, while not successful in controlling inflation, negatively affected economic growth, with GDP growing at an annual average of 1.6 per cent in the 1980s – which meant effectively no growth in GDP per capita against 6 per cent in the 1970s. The economy underwent its first economic recession after the industrialization process from 1981 to 1983, leading to high rates of open unemployment. Due to the weakening of the internal market, the manufacturing sector was the hardest hit – its annual growth was less than 1 per cent during the decade, with positive growth only because of exports, compared to 9.2 per cent in the 1970s.

The process of liberalization in the 1990s also had opposite effects in the two countries. In India, growth continued to accelerate in the 1990s, after the economic reforms that started in 1991-92, averaging almost 6 per cent in the decade as a whole. While reforms gradually opened up the economy to foreign trade, capital accounts were initially tightly controlled. Foreign direct investment rose, but remained very small, while foreign debt declined as a percentage of GDP and did not play an important role in the overall macroeconomic outcomes (Table 4.2.2). The deficit on international trade grew, but was largely compensated by a growth in invisibles (including private remittances and exports of services), and the remaining deficit was financed with little difficulty.

In Brazil, in contrast, the economy grew at a real annual rate of just 2.5 per cent in the 1990s, and in a very unstable fashion; one might say that it started to have a 'Hindu rate of growth'. The Real Plan and accompanying stabilization reforms successfully controlled inflation in 1994, but at the cost of an overvalued currency and high interest rates. Opening up to the international economy in that situation led, unsurprisingly, to a rising current account deficit (from US$ 6 million in 1993 to US$ 33 billion in 1998) and a growth of FDI, attracted by the economic liberalization and privatizations of state-owned enterprises (from US$ 1.3 billion in 1993 to US$ 29 billion in 1998). Unlike in India, Brazil's foreign debt nearly doubled, growing by almost US$ 120 billion from 1994 to 1999. While economic liberalization helped finance the foreign deficit, it also brought extreme vulnerability to foreign capital flows and speculative movements, and a series of international financial crisis in the latter half of the 1990s drove the growth of the economy down to 2 per cent from 2001 to 2003.

Only in 2004 did Brazil resume higher growth, averaging about 4.8 per cent a year until 2008. During the Lula period as a whole (2003–2010), the average growth was 4.0 per cent. In the 2000s, a new international cycle of economic expansion and increasing demand for commodities helped improve Brazil's foreign accounts. Gross external debt as a share of GDP, which reached more than 40 per cent in 1999 – the year of currency devaluation – dropped to 12 per cent in 2010.

India did even better in terms of growth, and exceptionally high growth rates of 9 or 10 per cent were recorded in some years after 2000. For the first decade of the twenty-first century, average growth was 7.6 per cent per year, by far the highest in the country's history, and very close to the 'Brazilian miracle' rates of growth before 1980. Foreign debt fell and inflation remained stable.

The global financial crisis that started in 2008 looked at first as though it would have only a temporary effect on growth in both countries. A fall in growth in 2009, larger in Brazil than in India, was followed by recovery in 2010. The crisis did not immediately have major effects on Brazilian exports, as the quick recovery of China and other emerging economies helped sustain export demand. Neither employment nor real average income was much affected. The same was broadly true of India, which rapidly returned to high growth.

But, as the crisis continued, GDP growth dropped substantially in both countries. In India, there was a period of lower growth (2011–2013) as recession persisted in the global economy. Thereafter, growth started to recover – but how much is difficult to judge, because of statistical changes which have produced some non-comparable numbers. Official estimates indicate that the growth rate rose from a minimum of 5.3 per cent in 2012-13 (compared with 2011-12) to 7.6 per cent in 2015-16, despite stagnant exports and private investment. Brazil was less fortunate. During 2011–2014, GDP grew at a rate of 1.6 per cent – the same level as the 1980s – driven like in India by household and government expenditures. But unlike in India, this situation led, in 2014, to a near-stagnant economy – the growth rate was 0.1 per cent – which combined increasing current account deficits, due to the overvalued currency, which displaced local production by imports, with rising inflation levels. After 2014, the Brazilian economy went into a deep recession.

Table 4.2.2.A. Macroeconomic Indicators, Brazil, 1980–2013

	1980	1992	2001	2010	2013
GDP per capita (in 2013 R$)	17,950	16,890	18,760	23,870	24,527
Consumer price index (% change per year)*	99.3	1,119	7.7	5.9	6.4
Current account (US$ billion)**	−12.7	6.1	−23.2	−47.3	−91.0
Current account (% of GDP)	−5.3	1.6	−4.2	−2.2	−4.2
FDI, % of GDP**	0.8	0.5	4.1	2.3	4.0
Gross foreign debt (US$ billion)***	64	136	210	257	353
Gross foreign debt, % of GDP***	27.0	35.1	37.9	12.0	14.6
Real effective exchange rate index (1994=100)**		103	117	74	101
Real interest rate (% p.a.) ****	−20.8	34.1	9.5	3.2	4.7

Source: *National Consumer Price Index (IPCA), IBGE (Ipeadata).

Note: **Brazil Central Bank.

***Author's calculations based on the gross foreign debt and balance of payments series, Central Bank of Brazil time series.

****Authors' calculations based on the benchmark interest rate (SELIC) and the FIPE Consumer Price Index; series from Ipeadata.

Table 4.2.2.B. Macroeconomic Indicators, India, 1980/81–2014/15

	1980-81	1990-91	2000-01	2010-11	2014-15
Per capita net national income (in 2004–05 rupees)	11,711	15,996	22,491	39,270	47,384
Consumer Price Index (CPI) for industrial workers, average annual increase, previous 10 years (per cent)	8.0	8.1	8.7	6.5	8.2*
Current account (US$ billion)	–2.8	–9.7	–2.7	–48.1	–26.8
Current account, % of GDP	–1.5	–3.0	–0.6	–2.8	–1.3
FDI, % of GDP	0	0.3	1.1	1.9	2.0
Foreign debt, % of GDP	19.2	28.7	22.5	19.6	25.9
Real effective exchange rate (6-country index; 1993–94 = 100)	**	**	103	126	122
Real interest rate*** (%)	–4.3	4.3	5.4	–4.5	1.6

Source: National Accounts (RBI database); Economic Survey, 2012-13, 2015-16.

Note: *Previous four years.

**Not available from RBI. However, the rupee depreciated against the SDR by an average of 9 per cent per year over this twenty-year period, much higher than the inflation differential with India's main trading partners, which implies a substantial fall in the real exchange rate.

***This is estimated as the call/notice money rate, as reported by the Reserve Bank of India, minus the inflation rate over the previous year measured by the rise in the consumer price index for industrial workers.

4.2.2   Capital accumulation and the pattern of final demand

The shift of economic strategy in the 1980s and the economic reforms of the
1990s transformed the pattern of capital accumulation in India. In the 1980s,
the overall rate of capital formation rose significantly (Table 4.2.3). In the first half
of the 1980s, this was driven by the public sector, which accounted for more than
half of all investment. But in the late 1980s, the rate of private capital formation
started to rise. The effect on the overall rate of capital accumulation was limited
because after 1985 public sector investment declined as a share of all capital
formation. This process accelerated after the 1991-92 economic reforms. By the
mid-2000s, public investment was down to a quarter of the total, but private
investment had risen from 9 per cent of GDP in 1980 to 14 per cent in 1990,
16 per cent in 2000, and 26 per cent in 2010 (though, after peaking in 2011, the
share declined up to 2014-15). This sustained the high rate of output growth,
though clearly a disproportionate share of investment went into construction and
real estate, and relatively little into manufacturing. In this process, investment
from abroad played little role. Foreign direct investment rose from nothing in
1980 to 3.5 per cent before the crisis and then fell to around 2 per cent of
GDP in 2010–15 (Table 4.2.2), but still accounted for less than a tenth of all
capital formation. This can also be seen in the figures for gross domestic saving
(Table 4.2.3), which tracked gross domestic capital formation fairly closely.
Most saving was in the household sector, but private corporate saving rose
steadily as a share of all savings, from 11 per cent in 1990 to 16 per cent in
2000, 23 per cent in 2010 and 38 per cent in 2014-15. Meanwhile, the share of
the public sector shrank from parity around 1990 to only one-tenth as large as
private corporate savings in 2014.

In Brazil, gross fixed capital formation, which had grown at an average rate
of more than 10 per cent in the 1970s, fell as a share of GDP in the 1980s,
to less than 20 per cent of GDP after 1990 (Table 4.2.3). In the 1990s, the
regime of liberalization with low and unstable economic growth led to a fall
in investment (from 21 per cent of GDP to 17 per cent), the opposite of the
pattern in India. Most of this decline concerned investment in public enterprises.
With the recovery of growth in the 2000s, investment also recovered, especially
after 2005, when there was an increase of public investment as a share of GDP,
due to the Growth Acceleration Programme launched during the second Lula
term. But it still remained low when compared to the historical record, and only
half the figure in India, where the state was nevertheless losing ground in overall
capital formation. Even so, the state played an important role in the capital
accumulation process in Brazil, with a gradual decrease in interest rates and

measures to expand credit. But the investment rate – 19.5 per cent in 2010 – remained far below India's peak of 36.5 per cent of GDP, and fell slightly after 2010.[3]

Table 4.2.3.A. Capital Formation, Brazil, 1980–2013

	Gross Fixed Capital Formation* (% of GDP)	Public Sector Capital Formation Excluding Public Enterprises (% of GFCF***)	Public Sector Capital Formation Including Public Enterprises (% of GFCF)
1980	23.6	9.9	28.0
1985	18.0	13.6	28.5
1990	20.7	18.1	25.2
1995	18.3	12.3	19.6
2000	16.8	10.7	14.3
2005	15.9	11.0	-
2010	19.5	14.2**	-
2013	18.2	-	-

Source: National Accounts System, Reference 2000, IBGE (Ipeadata).
Note: *Does not consider change of stocks.
**Data for 2009.
***Gross fixed capital formation.

Table 4.2.3.B. Capital Formation, India, 1980/81–2014/15

	Gross Capital Formation (% of GDP)	Public Sector Capital Formation (% of GDCF *)	Gross Domestic Saving (% of GDP)
1980-81	19.2	50.8	17.8
1985-86	20.6	50.8	18.4
1990-91	26.0	42.5	22.9
1995-96	25.3	32.9	23.6
2000-01	24.3	30.4	23.7
2005-06	34.7	24.0	33.4
2010-11	36.5	24.4	33.7
2014-15	34.2	22.7	33.0

Source: National Accounts (RBI database); Economic Survey, 2015-16. Public sector capital formation includes public enterprises.
Note: *Gross domestic capital formation.

---

[3] However, more recent data with 2010 as the reference year show a minor increase in the investment rate from 20.5 per cent in 2010 to 21 per cent in 2013, then falling abruptly from 2014 to 2016.

Foreign direct investment in Brazil had boomed at the end of the 1990s and continued to increase in absolute terms, but in 2010 it fell as a share of GDP to 2.3 per cent, lower than at the end of the 1990s, but now more closely related to the expansion of productive capacity (Table 4.2.2).

The rise in the pace of capital accumulation in India shows up clearly in the pattern of final demand (Table 4.2.4). In the 1980s, the pattern of growth of final demand was not greatly different from the 1970s, so the trends of the 1970s continued. The share of government expenditure and of investment continued to rise, while that of private consumption continued to fall, and there was little change in the share of exports and imports. De and Vakulabharanam (2013) characterize this period as led by government expenditure, but it does not seem significantly different from the 1970s in that respect. The real change occurred with the economic reforms in the early 1990s. The share of both private and public consumption expenditure declined in the period from 1990 to 2010; and the share of capital formation, exports, and imports shot up, especially after 2000. By 2010, high economic growth was clearly driven by growing investment and exports as a result of the process of liberalization – though, as we have seen, the sectoral pattern of this growth was quite unbalanced, and neither of these components provided the same impetus to GDP growth after 2010 (and especially after 2012).

Further, and closely connected with the reduced importance of the state in both investment and consumption, both tax and other public revenues failed to rise as a proportion of GDP after the end of the 1980s. For the following twenty-five years, overall government revenues, divided approximately equally between state and central government receipts, fluctuated around an average of about 20 per cent of GDP. After reaching about 22 per cent in the late 1980s, government revenues fell to a minimum of 16.5 per cent in 1998-99, before recovering to some degree, mainly after 2004. This pattern was largely due to variation in tax revenues – other revenues, which reached about a quarter of all receipts in the 1980s, showed a systematic tendency to decline after the 1990s. However, the proportion of direct taxes (including income taxes) did rise during this period, from less than 20 per cent in the 1980s to over 40 per cent in the most recent decade.

In Brazil, in the 1980s, it was mostly government expenditure and the growth of net exports that ensured that the economy did not stay in open recession throughout the whole period. In the 1990s, private consumption – following the fall of inflation – took the lead, whereas investment, government consumption, and the external sector did not provide much fuel to the engine of growth. The most striking figures are for the 2000s, as they differ from the assumptions of much analysis of the Brazilian economy. The share of private consumption in GDP fell at least up to 2008. Meanwhile, investment, government expenditure, and net exports were responsible for the acceleration of economic growth after 2004. Nevertheless, the increase in wages and household credit played a fundamental role in that they encouraged investment and led to an increase in government revenues, especially since private consumption still accounted for 60 per cent of total demand. Interestingly, the latter once again became the main driver of demand when the economy lost momentum, that is, after 2011, when investment fell and the gap between imports and exports widened. In 2014, when economic growth was just 0.1 per cent, it was once again private and government consumption that offset a fall of 4.4 per cent in total investment.

From 2000 onwards, that is, both during the economic upturn but also after 2011 when GDP growth was much slower, government expenditures did rise in Brazil. This rise was helped by an increase in the tax ratio – after growing in the 1990s to 33 per cent of GDP it continued to increase, reaching 35 per cent in 2013. However, unlike in the 1970s, most of the expenditure was directed to government consumption or to pensions and social transfers, as public investment remained low compared with the past. Also, despite the relative tax decentralization promoted by the 1988 Constitution, since the mid-1990s there has been a centralization of tax revenues. In terms of the tax composition, 22 per cent is made up of direct taxes, a figure that would be close to 30 per cent if pension contributions are considered, still lower than in India despite the higher Brazilian GDP per capita.

Table 4.2.4.A. Share of Components of Final Demand in GDP (%), Brazil, 1980–2013

	Private Consumption	Government Expenditure	Gross Fixed Capital Formation	Exports	Imports
1980	69.1	9.1	23.6	9.0	11.2
1990	59.3	19.3	20.7	8.2	7.0
2000	64.4	19.2	16.8	10.0	11.7
2010	59.6	21.2	19.5	10.9	11.9
2013	62.4	22.0	18.2	12.6	15.0

Source: National Accounts System, Reference 2000, IBGE (Ipeadata).

Growth and Inequality

Table 4.2.4.B. Share of Components of Final Demand in GDP (%), India, 1980/81–2014/15

	Private Consumption	Government Consumption Expenditure	Gross Capital Formation*	Exports	Imports
1980-81	78.9	10.1	18.0	6.0	9.1
1990-91	68.0	11.9	24.9	6.9	8.3
2000-01	64.6	12.6	23.4	12.8	13.7
2010-11	56.0	11.4	34.4	22.0	26.3
2014-15	57.6	10.9	32.6	22.9	25.9

Source: RBI database, Economic Survey 2015-16.
Note: *Including stocks but excluding valuables (hence the difference with Table 4.2.3). In current prices.

Overall, the difference in trend between the two countries is striking. In 1980, the level of capital formation was higher as a share of GDP in Brazil than in India, but it fell before stabilizing after 2000. Meanwhile, capital formation rose substantially in India, to almost double the percentage in Brazil. In contrast, government consumption rose in Brazil, while in India it declined after peaking around 2000, so that by 2014 it was only half of the level of Brazil. The external sector showed a similar trend in both countries, with exports and imports rising – a logical consequence of external liberalization – but much more strongly in India. Meanwhile, the share of private consumption declined substantially in India – the counterpart to the growth in capital accumulation – while it fluctuated in Brazil with no clear trend. So, Brazil directed more resources towards current government expenditure, while India directed more resources towards investment and away from private consumption. This is a key difference in the growth regime, with consequences for both growth and inequality. The pattern of investment in India, concentrated in the corporate sector, in construction and in real estate, was an important factor in the rise of inequality after 1990.

4.2.3   The sectoral composition of output and employment

As Table 4.2.1 shows, the sectoral pattern of growth was also quite different in the two countries. The main exception was agriculture (or in the case of India the primary sector), where growth averaged 3 to 4 per cent in both countries – though the nature of this growth was different, reflecting the increased production of commodities (soybean, coffee, and many others) in Brazil and cereals and other basic foodstuffs in India. However, both secondary and tertiary sectors grew much faster in India than Brazil.

The increase in growth rates in India produced a very substantial change in the sectoral balance of the Indian economy (Table 4.2.5). The primary sector declined steadily, accounting for only one-fifth of output by 2014. The share of the secondary sector as a whole increased somewhat, but this was largely due to growth in construction and public utilities – the share of manufacturing in GDP mainly hovered between 14 per cent and 16 per cent.[4] All the action was in the tertiary sector which, as a whole, gained 15 percentage points between 1980 and 2010. Within this, the share of finance, real estate, and business services increased from 11 per cent to 16 per cent. There were also large gains for trade and transport, but the share of social and personal services (which includes government) hardly increased. The growth of the secondary sector accelerated after 2000, but much of this was again due to high growth of construction activity, rather than manufacturing. Agriculture could not maintain the growth of the 1980s; agricultural output continued to expand at a historically respectable pace, but did not accelerate in the same way as the rest of the economy.

Table 4.2.5. Sectoral Composition of GDP, 1980–2014 (%)

	Brazil			India		
	Primary**	Secondary	Tertiary	Primary	Secondary	Tertiary
1980*	10.9	44.1	45.0	35.4	24.3	39.9
1990	8.1	38.7	53.2	29.0	26.5	44.2
2000	5.6	27.7	66.7	23.0	26.0	50.5
2010	5.3	28.1	66.6	18.2	27.2	54.6
2014***	5.7	25.0	69.3	20.0	27.4	52.6

Source: National Accounts (IBGE and RBI database); Economic Survey, 2015-16.
Note: *1980-81, 1990-91, etc. for India. Current prices.
**Primary refers to agriculture in Brazil; mining is included in secondary, as are construction and public utilities.
*** Because of the change of statistical methodology, data for India for 2014-15 are not strictly comparable with 2010-11.

The same trend of a rapidly increasing share of the tertiary sector is found in Brazil, reaching close to 67 per cent in 2000 and then stabilizing. This partly corresponded, as in India, to a fall in the share of the primary sector, but this is somewhat misleading because a great deal of the value-added from agri-business is considered to be part of the industrial and tertiary sectors. Agriculture did

---

[4] Planning Commission data tables, December 2014 (http://planningcommission.gov.in/data/datatable/index.php?data = datatab). An increase was reported after 2011 but appears to be an artefact of the change in methodology (Nagaraj, 2015, *inter alia*).

grow in the late 1990s and the 2000s, but not fast enough to increase its share of total output.

However, the main difference with India concerns the share of the secondary sector, which fell considerably. This was mainly the result of the shrinking of the manufacturing base, especially in the 1980s and 1990s; the manufacturing share of GDP declined rapidly from 35 per cent in 1985 to 27 per cent in 1994. From 1995 to 2009, this share fluctuated around 18 per cent, then falling to reach just 13 per cent in 2013 (IBGE-Ipeadata).[5] In recent years, there has been a great deal of concern in Brazil about what has been labelled 'deindustrialization' (Nassif, 2008; Bonnelli and Pessoa, 2010). Some authors even argue that Brazil has faced a 'Dutch disease' due to the rising prices of commodities, which led to an overvalued currency (Bresser-Pereira and Marconi, 2010). However, during the upswing of the economic cycle there was an absolute increase in manufacturing employment, value-added, and exports, though this was reversed during the slowdown in growth from 2011 to 2014, after the financial crisis, when imports from the US, Europe, and China flooded into Brazil.

On the other hand, in the 2000s, the share of the secondary sector as a whole slightly increased, thanks to investment in construction and public utilities. During the expansionary phase of the economic cycle, inter-sectoral relations between services, manufacturing, construction, and agriculture strengthened the internal market, with a positive impact on labour market outcomes.

These changes in output structure were reflected in an attenuated form in the pattern of employment in both countries (Table 4.2.6). In India, the share of agricultural employment declined, but a great deal more slowly than its share of output, as it still accounted for nearly half of all employment in 2011-12. The relative productivity of the agricultural sector fell from 56 per cent of the all-India average to 34 per cent. The share of employment in the secondary sector rose much faster than its share of output, but this mainly reflected the creation of casual employment in the construction sector. Employment in manufacturing rose more or less in proportion to output. It was in the tertiary sector that employment growth fell behind output growth. After the 1991 reforms, public sector employment fell, which explains the lack of growth of employment in social and personal services. Employment in trade and transport expanded rapidly, but finance and business services created relatively few jobs despite their rapid expansion.

---

[5] There was a break in the series after 1994.

Table 4.2.6.A. Share of Employment by Industrial Sector (%), Brazil, 1980–2012

Sector	1980	1992	2001	2004	2008	2012
Agriculture	30.4	26.5	19.7	19.3	16.4	13.3
Manufacturing industry	16.4	14.6	13.6	14.9	15.3	14.1
Construction	7.6	6.4	6.7	6.5	7.6	8.9
Trade	10.8	12.2	14.3	17.5	17.6	18
Services	30.4	35.5	40.8	36.6	38.2	40.2
Public administration	4.4	4.8	4.9	5.1	5	5.6
Total	100	100	100	100	100	100

Source: 1980 Demographic Census/IBGE and PNAD/IBGE for the following years.
Note: Data from 1980 and the other years are not fully comparable.

Table 4.2.6.B. Share of Employment by Industrial Sector (%), India, 1981–2011/12

Sector	1981	1983	1993-94	2004-05	2011-12
Agriculture & related	68.8	68.6	64.0	56.3	48.9
Total Secondary Sector	13.5	13.8	15.0	18.8	24.4
Mining	0.6	0.6	0.7	0.6	0.5
Manufacturing	11.3	10.6	10.6	12.3	12.8
Electricity	0.4	0.3	0.4	0.3	0.4
Construction	1.6	2.3	3.2	5.7	10.6
Total Tertiary Sector	17.7	17.6	21.1	24.9	26.7
Trade and Hotels	5.5	6.3	7.6	10.9	11.5
Transport	2.7	2.5	2.9	4.1	4.4
Finance and Business	0.2	0.7	1.0	1.7	2.6
Social and Personal	7.4	8.1	9.6	8.2	8.2
Total	100	100	100	100	100

Source: Institute for Human Development, 2014; based on various rounds of NSS data on
   employment and unemployment, except 1981 from Nagaraj (2012), and from Census data,
   not fully comparable.

In industry, after 1991, internal and external deregulation spurred a move towards increasing capital intensity. By 2007-08, India had moved away from labour-intensive, low-technology industries towards scale-based, capital-intensive, medium-technology industries. Medium-technology segments accounted for about 75 per cent of manufacturing in terms of value-added, while low-technology industries had declined to 22 per cent, and high-technology segments remained low and stable around 3 per cent (Aggarwal and Kumar, 2012). This was one reason why the growth of manufacturing employment was slow, although low-technology manufacturing continued to account for over 50 per cent of the sector's employment. After 2000, manufacturing employment showed more volatility. It grew rapidly between 1999-2000 and 2004-05, led largely by export-oriented industries such as garments, textiles, leather, and diamond cutting. However, after 2008, due to the worldwide economic slowdown, these same industries suffered sharp employment declines (Thomas, 2012).

In Brazil, the distribution of employment evolved in a markedly different way. The share of agriculture in employment fell less sharply than its product share, as in India, reaching 13.3 per cent in 2012, with 12.2 million workers, almost two-thirds of them on small landholdings with more often than not low productivity levels. On the other hand, the modern agricultural sector became even more capital-intensive. Most of the fall in employment was concentrated in the 1990s, and it occurred in both relative and absolute terms.

In the manufacturing sector, there was a decrease in employment in the 1990s, whereas an increase in its growth between 2001 and 2008 meant the creation of 3.6 million jobs. In the 2000s, the employment-output elasticity proved to be quite high, above 1. But the sector as a whole failed to increase its share in all employment, fluctuating between 13 and 15 per cent. Nevertheless, in absolute terms the size of the industrial proletariat grew, now including more skilled workers. Moreover, manufactures based on science, engineering, and knowledge, which accounted for 28 per cent of the total value-added of the manufacturing sector in 1970, rose to 46 per cent in 2008. This gain was offset by the dramatic loss in importance of labour-intensive industries – their share dropped from 32 per cent in 1970 to 17 per cent in 2008. The natural resource-based industries roughly maintained their participation, over 30 per cent (Nassif et al., 2013).

The private services sector, which increased its employment share rapidly between 1980 and 2000, lost some ground in the following years, recovering its share only after 2009 with the slowing of the economy, which mostly affected tradeables. It is important to notice the increasing share of trade, construction, and public services in overall employment since 2001. Moreover, the growth in the share of public sector employment is in sharp contrast to the decline in India.

In both Brazil and India, the evolution of manufacturing has become a source of concern, as its capacity to absorb the shift of labour out of agriculture has proved to be limited. With the share of manufacturing losing ground, in the case of Brazil, or stagnating, in the case of India, the development of services was crucial to absorb surplus labour. In both countries, the growth of services has been largely driven by domestic final demand. It is directly affected by the rise in household incomes and changes in the distribution of incomes. For India, Nayyar (2012) estimated that the share of services in private final consumption expenditure was 17 per cent in 1981, 21 per cent in 1991, 27 per cent in 2000, and 44 per cent in 2009. Arbache (2012) estimated the share of services in Brazilian household expenditure at 62 per cent. The disparity in per capita income, the relative size of the middle class (larger in Brazil), and their respective expenditure patterns explain the difference between the two countries.

Though a much smaller contributor to the demand for services than household expenditure, the growth of service exports accelerated after 2000. In India, the average annual growth rate exceeded 24 per cent during the first decade of the century. Software and business services represented 74 per cent of total service exports in 2010. In Brazil, the annual growth rate was lower but still substantial at 14 per cent. Historically, Brazil has run a deficit in its trade in services. But a recent shift towards sectors with higher growth in international trade, such as business services, points to a potential for increasing the country's exports more than its imports in the medium to long term (Oliveira, 2013).

In Brazil, since 1995, jobs created in the service sector have been concentrated in public administration and commerce. These sub-sectors are less technology-intensive and less complementary to productivity growth in other sectors. In addition, the service segments that are expanding fastest employ relatively few highly qualified workers. Productivity increase over 1995–2006 mainly reflected intra-sector gains rather than a shift to jobs of higher quality (Vargas da Cruz et al., 2008).

In India, the services sector has become the mainstay of the growth process. It is the largest and fastest-growing sector. But the increase in employment has not been commensurate with the increase in the contribution of the sector to total GDP, and there are marked and widening differentials in earnings across sub-sectors. Education is an important entry barrier to remunerative and high-quality employment, but the supply of highly skilled workers has not kept pace with demand, causing wages to increase faster for higher-skill services. The change in skills composition, rising wage inequality within the sector, and the regional concentration of modern services has contributed to India's overall increase in inequality.

4.2.4   Inequality and poverty

It is not easy to trace the connections between these macroeconomic patterns and the overall levels and trends of inequality and poverty. The latter reflect changing productivity differentials across sectors and regions, patterns of employment and wages, the shares of different groups in value-added, and the accumulation and distribution of wealth, but the relationships are complex and often indirect. For instance and as noted above, the high rate of capital accumulation in India is certainly one of the factors in the growth in inequality, but the precise mechanisms are not easy to evaluate. The growth of corporate savings probably reflects high returns to investment and the accumulation of wealth in that sector. In the household sector, relatively high savings rates among middle and upper classes would also tend to reinforce inequality. Real estate booms have certainly generated a highly unequal pattern of capital gains.

A classic mechanism by which economic growth may lead to growing inequality is if there is a substantial shift of employment towards higher productivity sectors. This is the foundation of Kuznets' inverted U-shape curve. But, in India, as we have seen, while the share of employment has declined in agriculture, the corresponding increase has been concentrated in construction, trade, and hotels and restaurants. These are generally low-productivity sectors with a high proportion of low-paid, casual work. The occupational shift towards higher skilled, protected employment has been quite limited, especially since the share of public sector employment started to decline after the economic reforms. Nor have there been large changes in the relative productivity of different sectors. Primary sector (agricultural) labour productivity was only 26 per cent of that in industry in 1983; in 2011-12, it had actually risen to 32 per cent, largely because of the expansion of construction, which is included within industry. Compared with the service sector, in the same period, agricultural labour productivity had fallen from 21 per cent to 17 per cent. Considering that GDP had been multiplied by a factor of 5.7 in this period, these are not large changes. So the contribution of these inter-sectoral shifts to growing inequality has probably been modest.

In Brazil, in 1980, after the industrialization process, agriculture had a productivity of 15 per cent of the national average, whereas productivity in industry was 28 per cent higher and in services 42 per cent higher. Productivity was 8.3 times higher in industry than in agriculture. We should also not forget that these average levels abstract from the sometimes even more important differences within each sector.

In the following decades, there were interesting changes. In the 1980s, productivity fell for every sector except agriculture, which experienced a small increase, so sectoral differentials declined. In the 1990s, agricultural performance improved, industry showed a very small increase, but service sector productivity went down substantially, as this was the sector where most of the informal and low-productivity activities developed. In the 2000s, there was another shift in productivity differences between sectors. Agricultural productivity continued to rise, by 4 per cent per year, but still only reached one-third of overall average productivity in 2009. Productivity in services rose by 0.5 per cent a year, but industry recorded an annual fall of 0.8 per cent. At the end of the period, the industry to agriculture productivity ratio had fallen to 3.7.

There was, therefore, a degree of convergence across sectors. This could be considered a 'negative' trend, insofar as it reflected a relative decrease of productivity in industry, especially manufacturing, and only a slow increase in the service sector (de Negri and Cavalcante, 2014). However, the poor productivity performance in the industrial sector also reflected the high pace of employment generation compared to output growth. In any case, this convergence certainly played some role in reducing wage differentials and also inequality.

Another important macroeconomic dimension of inequality is the functional distribution of income. In India, there has been a very substantial reduction in the wage share in organized industry, and perhaps also in organized service sectors (for which data are not available). In the National Accounts, the overall profit share rose from 8 per cent in 1980-81 to 22 per cent in 2007-08 (the latest year available), at the expense of both wages and 'mixed' income (which includes self-employment). The trend can be seen more clearly in organized industry, where wages and salaries accounted for over 50 per cent of value-added in the 1980s, but this declined to 40 per cent in the 1990s and has varied between 25 and 35 per cent since the mid-2000s (Graph 4.2.1). Inversely, the profit share leaped from 20 per cent in the 1980s to between 50 and 60 per cent in the 2000s. There has therefore been a substantial shift of income from labour to capital, which is surely an important element of the growth in inequality. However, the most recent data suggest that there is a slow reversal of this trend as real wages rise.

Graph 4.2.1. Factor Shares in the Organized Manufacturing Sector, India, 1981/82–2013/14

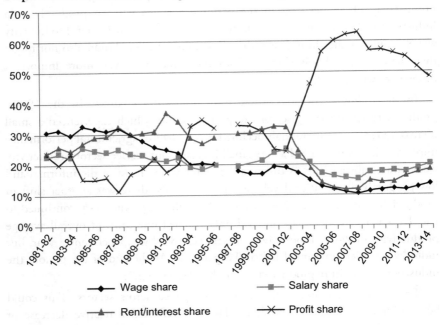

Source: Government of India, Annual Survey of Industry.

Graph 4.2.2. Factor Shares in GDP, Brazil, 1990–2009

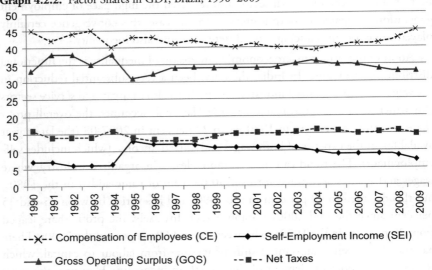

Source: System of National Accounts/IBGE.

In Brazil, at the beginning of the period from 1990 to 2009, and again at the end, labour income (compensation of employees) was around 44 per cent of GDP, compared with capital income (gross operating surplus) of 33 per cent. These percentages moved in opposite directions during the period, with the capital share rising up to 2004, and the labour share recovering afterwards (Graph 4.2.2). However, these data should be used with caution, as they do not account for differences between sectors. They also do not allow for a breakdown of different sources of income from capital (rents, profits, and interest). Self-employment income was more or less stable over the period, at around 10 per cent. In 1995, it jumped to 14 per cent due to the fall of inflation, which led to an increase in the prices of non-tradeable goods. This also happened in the 2000s, but this time it was more than compensated by slower growth in jobs for the self-employed, so there was a small decrease in the self-employment income share.

Another way to look at the overall pattern of distribution is in the trend of labour incomes in relation to overall output or income per capita (we look at the distribution within labour incomes in the next section). In India, real wages grew at much the same rate as Net National Income (NNI) per capita during the 1980s, and also in the early years after the economic reforms. But from 1999 onwards, while wages continued to rise, they rose more slowly than NNI (Graph 4.2.3). This is exactly what would be expected in the light of the shift in the functional distribution of income from wages to profits, which also accelerated after the turn of the century. Rural wages rose a little faster than urban, and no doubt faster than output per capita in rural areas, since the growth of agriculture

Graph 4.2.3. Pattern of Change in Real Net National Income Per Capita and Average Real Wages in Urban and Rural Areas, India, 1983–2011/12 (Index, 1983 = 100)

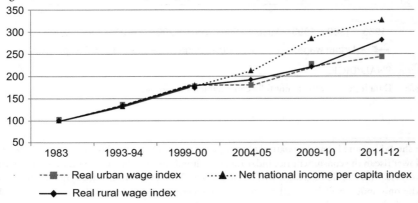

Source: NSS, unit level data, and National Accounts.

was relatively slow.[6] There was a decline in the rural-urban per capita expenditure ratio throughout this period (Table 4.2.7). So, if rural wages rose faster than urban wages, it implies that non-wage incomes in rural areas (essentially farmer incomes) rose more slowly than non-wage incomes in urban areas. Since capital income is concentrated in urban areas, this seems quite plausible.

In Brazil, after a recovery in both GDP per capita and wages between 1983 and 1989, wages suffered a major fall during the 1989–1993 period of recession (Graph 4.2.4). After the Real Plan (1994) and up to 1998, wages and output broadly moved in the same direction. Following the currency devaluation in 1999, GDP per capita rose very slowly, while labour income fell steeply up to 2003, opening a huge gap between the trends in GDP per capita and in labour income. After 2003, average real wages increased faster than GDP, a trend that was maintained even after the global crisis, and which corresponds to the shift in functional distribution of income towards wages discussed above. In this regard, Brazil is almost the mirror image of India.

Graph 4.2.4. Pattern of Change in Real GDP Per Capita and Real Average Labour Income (Urban and Rural), Brazil, 1983–2011 (Index, 1983 = 100)

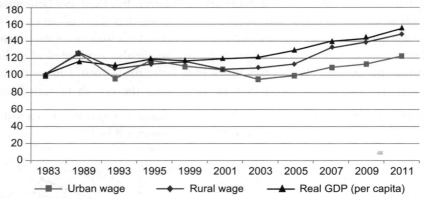

Source: PNAD/IBGE.

Note: Data for the 1980s are not fully comparable to the following years.

---

[6] It should be noted that the relatively better performance of real rural wages is in part due to a slower rise in the consumer price index for agricultural workers than in the index for industrial workers. This should be treated with some caution. Moreover, the CPI for agricultural labour (the only index available for the complete time period) is not necessarily an accurate guide for rural non-agricultural workers, while the CPI for industrial workers may not be a good reference for the urban middle class. We use these indices in the absence of better alternatives.

Graph 4.2.4 shows that like in India, rural wages rose faster than urban in Brazil, especially in the recent period (2003–2011). The ratio of urban wages to rural wages fell from 2.3 in 1983 to 1.9 in 2011.

The overall changes in inequality of household income and expenditure in the two countries can be seen in Table 4.2.7 and Graphs 4.2.5 to 4.2.7. The tables and graphs are based on income in the case of Brazil, and household expenditure per capita in the case of India. Only expenditure data are available in India in a long time series, while the same is true for income in Brazil. We therefore cannot directly compare the absolute figures for the two countries. In general, it is observed that the distribution of income is less equal than that of expenditure, because richer households save more, expenditure is more stable than income over time, and the expenditure of richer households is more prone to underestimation.[7] However, we can expect trends in inequality of income and of expenditure to be broadly similar; so we consider that it is reasonable to compare the trends in the Indian and Brazilian data.[8] In addition, while the table reports household income per capita for Brazil, in the graph we show individual labour income, because household income per capita is not available from the Census data before 1980. However, comparing the table with the graph we can see that the order of magnitude and the trend for the two measures are similar after 1983.

In India, it can be seen that up to the 1990s, the overall Gini coefficient of household expenditure per capita was fairly stable, all the way back to the 1960s (Graph 4.2.5). But after the turn of the century the Gini coefficient rose, especially in urban areas (Table 4.2.7). There was also a decline in the ratio of rural incomes to urban incomes, which contributed to the increase in inequality. However, the overall level of inequality did not rise much further after 2005.

Other evidence also suggests that the process of growth was disequalizing in this period. An analysis of income tax data shows that the income share of the top 1 per cent, which had been declining before 1980, rose from 5 per cent of all income at this date to 9–10 per cent by 2000, and further to 12 per cent in 2012 (Piketty and Saez, 2012; India, Economic Survey 2015-16, Box 7.1). The main

---

[7] A direct comparison of income inequality with expenditure inequality is possible for 2004-05 in India, using the National Council of Applied Economic Research (NCAER) Human Development Survey. The income Gini coefficient was 0.54 against a Gini of 0.40 for expenditure (estimated using data from that survey, so slightly different from Table 4.2.7); Rodgers and Soundararajan (2016). A similar exercise for Brazil in 2008-09 gave a smaller difference, an income Gini of 0.57 against an expenditure Gini of 0.53.

[8] In the next section we look at wage inequality, which is more directly comparable between the two countries.

underlying factor is probably an increasing concentration of wealth, as has been documented by Anand and Thampi (2016). They show that the Gini coefficient of household wealth inequality (all assets) rose from 0.65 in 1991 and 0.66 in 2002 to a remarkably high figure of 0.74 in 2012.

Table 4.2.7.A. Inequality of Per Capita Household Income, Brazil, 1983–2011

	1983	1993	1999	2005	2009	2011
Gini coefficient of household income per capita						
Rural	0.521	0.572	0.539	0.497	0.475	0.482
Urban	0.574	0.588	0.579	0.557	0.531	0.520
Total	0.597	0.602	0.593	0.565	0.536	0.527
Rural-urban ratio of average per capita income						
	0.43	0.48	0.45	0.49	0.53	0.52

Source: PNAD/IBGE.

Table 4.2.7.B. Inequality of Per Capita Household Expenditure, India, 1983–2011/12

	1983	1993-94	1999-2000	2004-05	2009-10	2011-12
Gini coefficient of household expenditure per capita						
Rural	0.304	0.286	0.258	0.305	0.300	0.311
Urban	0.339	0.344	0.341	0.376	0.393	0.390
Total	0.326	0.326	0.325	0.363	0.370	0.375
Rural-urban ratio of mean per capita expenditure						
	0.68	0.61	0.57	0.52	0.52	0.54

Source: National Sample Survey. For the years 1983, 1993-94, 2004-05, and 2011-12, computed from unit-level data. For 1999-2000, the figures were taken from the National Human Development Report 2001 (Government of India, 2002). For 2009-10 from Motiram and Vakulabharanam (2011). Rural-urban ratios from unit-level data, Ahluwalia (2011), and Government of India (2002).

Note: The measures refer to inequality of household expenditure per capita, weighted by household size (i.e. an estimate of inequality among individuals, but not allowing for intra-household inequality).

In Brazil, inequality peaked in the early 1990s due to the extraordinarily high level of inflation, then started to fall after the introduction of the Real Plan in 1994 (Table 4.2.7 and Graph 4.2.5). The decline accelerated after 2003. This reduction was larger for urban areas and for states with higher GDP per capita levels, as they have more structured and broader-based labour markets, the main factor behind the fall in inequality. Here, also, the case of Brazil is opposite to the Indian, as the ratio of rural to urban incomes rose in the long term while it fell in India. So urban-rural inequality increased in India but declined in Brazil.

Another way of presenting the same data, which gives a different perspective on the overall distribution, is in terms of the percentage of all income received or expenditure made by households grouped by their income or expenditure ranking. Graph 4.2.6 shows that in India, the share of all expenditure by the top 10 per cent of households rose from 29 per cent in 1983 to 33 per cent in 2010, while that of the bottom 50 per cent fell from 27 per cent to 24 per cent in the same period, confirming the widening of the gaps. In Brazil, in contrast, the top 10 per cent lost income share, from around 48 per cent – from 1980 and for most of the 1990s – to around 43 per cent in the 2000s, that is, the opposite of India (Graph 4.2.7). The bottom 50 per cent increased their share from 12 per cent to 14 per cent, while the intermediate group of 40 per cent of households also gained about three percentage points. In India, once again in contrast to Brazil, the intermediate and bottom groups both lost share in total expenditure per capita, especially the latter, while the top group gained 4 percentage points. So, India redistributed from the bottom half and the middle of the distribution to the top; Brazil mainly redistributed from the top to the middle and the bottom.

Graph 4.2.5. Gini Coefficients of Labour Income (Brazil) and Household Expenditure Per Capita (India), 1960 to 2011

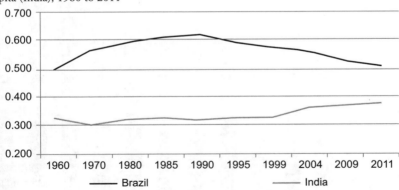

Source: Brazil: 1985 onwards, computed on the basis of PNAD/FIBGE data. Earlier years, Census data (1960, 1970, 1980). India: Mainly NSS. For 1983 onwards, Table 4.2.7B. For earlier years, UN-Wider World Income Inequality database (WIID) V3.3 (http://www.wider.unu.edu/research/Database/en_GB/database/).

Note: Indian data refer to household expenditure per capita. Brazilian data refer to individual labour income. See discussion of comparability in the text. The years in the horizontal axis refer to Brazil. For 1980 to 1995, the Indian data relate to approximately two years earlier than the date indicated in the graph, and for 1999 onwards, these are the NSS surveys overlapping with the year following that indicated.

Graph 4.2.6. Distribution of Total Per Capita Expenditure by Population Share, India, 1983–2011/12

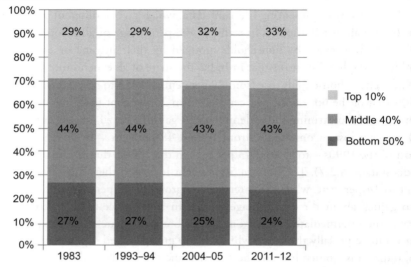

Source: Prepared on the basis of NSS unit level data for each year.

Graph 4.2.7. Distribution of Total Per Capita Income by Population Share (%), Brazil, 1979–2011

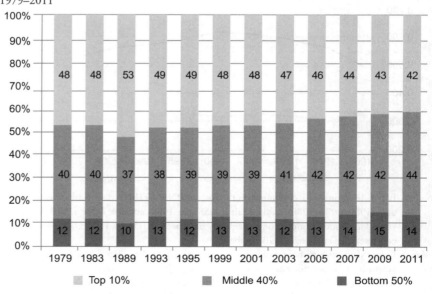

Source: Prepared on the Basis of PNAD/IBGE micro-data.

For the case of Brazil, if we add income from wealth – now available through personal income tax data – to labour income measured from survey data, inequality among adults is not only much higher than reported above, but also remained almost unchanged from 2006 to 2012. Between 2009 and 2012, the bottom 50 per cent received around 12 per cent of all income (against 14 per cent of income from household data), while the top 10 per cent received 62 per cent (against about 42 per cent from household data) (Medeiros et al., 2014). However these numbers cannot be directly compared with India, because the source and method of calculation are different.

The incidence of poverty gives yet another perspective. In India, while inequality rose, overall poverty rates came down (Table 4.2.8). After allowing for changes in the methodology used to calculate poverty, it can be inferred that absolute poverty declined by some two-thirds over the 30 years starting around 1980. The rise in inequality, therefore, was much more than offset by the positive impact of growth on incomes among the poor. On the other hand, with growing inequality, relative poverty increased. The absolute poverty lines that are used to calculate the proportion of the population that is poor are increasingly questioned in India; they are completely out of line with the expectations of people in an increasingly well-off society, who no longer aim only at bare subsistence.

Poverty fell even more than inequality in Brazil.[9] Around 28.5 million people escaped from absolute poverty, reducing the share of poor households from 35 per cent in 2001 to 16 per cent in 2011 (Table 4.2.8). If compared to 1990, when the proportion below the poverty line was almost 45 per cent, this means a reduction of almost two-thirds in the poverty rate in two decades.

In the most recent period, the fall in poverty was sharper in rural than in metropolitan areas, thanks to cash transfer policies such as Bolsa Familia, rural pensions, and the Continuous Cash Benefit Programme (BPC – from Portuguese *Benefício de Prestação Continuada*), the latter providing a payment equal to the minimum wage to the elderly and disabled people in areas where the labour market is almost absent (Section 4.4). Poverty in metropolitan areas also declined, but at a much lower rate, so that in 2011, there was not much difference between metropolitan and rural areas in terms of the proportion of poor people, whereas in India rural poverty has always been higher (double the urban rate in 2011-12). As a consequence, today around 85 per cent of the poor in Brazil live in urban

---

[9] For the Brazilian case, the poverty line was based on the methodology devised by Sônia Rocha (1997), who calculated different minimum consumption standards for different areas of Brazil.

areas – totally different from India. Understanding these very different social contexts is important for devising strategies to promote inclusive growth.

Table 4.2.8.A. Percentage of the Population below the Poverty Line, Brazil, 1980–2011*

Area	Poverty (%)							
	1980**	1990	1993	1995	2001	2003	2007	2011
Metropolitan areas	27.2	41.4	45.1	31.2	37.4	39.8	28.9	17.8
Non-Metropolitan Urban areas	32.7	40.0	40.4	31.2	31.7	32.1	22.4	13.8
Rural areas	45.6	56.8	51.6	41.5	42.1	39.7	27.2	18.5
Total Brazil	35.3	44.2	44.1	33.2	35.1	35.6	25.1	15.6

Source: Computed on the basis of PNAD/IBGE micro-data.
Note: * Poverty line set in accordance with methodology proposed by Rocha (1997).
        **For 1980, Demographic Census data. Rocha (2003).

Table 4.2.8.B. Percentage of the Population below the Poverty Line, India, 1973/74–2011/12

	Rural		Urban		Total	
	A	B	A	B	A	B
1973-74	56.4		49.0		54.9	
1983-84	45.7		40.8		44.5	
1993-94	37.3	50.1	32.3	31.8	36.0	45.3
2004-05	28.3	41.8	25.7	25.7	27.5	37.2
2011-12		25.7		13.7		21.9

Source: Government of India, Planning Commission (2013), and earlier Planning Commission documents.
Note: A: Lakdawala Committee method.
        B: Tendulkar Committee method (introduced in 2011-12; also calculated for some earlier years to permit comparison).

Summing up these patterns, the contrasts between the two countries are striking. Since the 1980s, in both countries poverty rates have fallen by around two-thirds. But in Brazil, this was achieved despite relatively low and unstable rates of growth by virtue of a shift of both primary incomes and government social expenditures towards lower income groups, resulting in a sharp decline in overall measures of inequality. In India, it was achieved largely through trickle-down from high growth, but accompanied by growing inequality. As a result, it can be said that in Brazil both relative and absolute poverty declined, while in India the decline in absolute poverty was accompanied by an increase in relative poverty. It is also interesting to note a parallel change in both countries after 2003, for the trend towards declining inequality was strengthened in Brazil, and that towards increasing inequality weakened in India. But this may have been a temporary phase. In both countries, in the wake of the global financial crisis, there have been economic and political changes that could well reverse these trends.

Of course, these broader patterns give only part of the story. In the next section, we look at wage inequality in more detail, and in Section 5, we examine some of the underlying factors, looking more closely at the divides between social groups.

4.3 Labour Market Structure and Labour Institutions

After 1980, labour markets in both countries were affected by the shifts in the national growth regimes and in the global economy, but the pattern of change was different in the two countries. In India, labour institutions did not change much initially, and until the 1990s, the overall structure of the labour market evolved only slowly. However, as growth accelerated, some segments of the labour market tightened, wages rose, labour institutions were questioned, and new inequalities developed. In Brazil, in contrast, the deep economic crisis and the process of re-democratization in the 1980s put different and opposing pressures on the labour market and its main institutions. On the one hand, democracy and the new Constitution brought a new set of labour institutions and rights. On the other, economic crisis and liberalization fostered informalization and flexibilization. This opposition prevailed in the 1990s, and was partially overcome with a move towards stronger labour institutions in the 2000s, which emerged in a different political and economic framework.

4.3.1 Structural changes in the labour market

As we saw in the last section, the increase in economic growth in India after 1980 generated changes in the structure of output and employment. The importance of the primary sector declined, and the share of services increased. At the same time, and for the first time, real wages started to grow. However, these macro-level changes did not modify the basic structure of the labour market, which as a result of the pattern of growth up to that point was segmented in two principal ways

(Section 3.3). The first was a dualism in the production system. A substantial share of employment (but much less of output) was, and remains so today, in the large, informal, low-income economy known in India as the unorganized sector. It includes small, private enterprises employing less than ten workers and the self-employed working in both agricultural and non-agricultural activities. The great majority of workers in this sector are excluded from labour regulations covering conditions of work, social security or dismissal, and even when they are technically included – under the minimum wage legislation, for example – enforcement is weak (National Commission for Enterprises in the Unorganised Sector-NCEUS, 2009). Unionization rates are low. Most agricultural production, with the exception of plantations, is usually considered part of the unorganized sector, though its institutional structure is different from the urban informal economy. Of course, the 'unorganized' sector is in reality highly organized, but through social and informal mechanisms (Harriss-White, 2003). This is in sharp contrast to the 'organized' sector, which is subject to labour legislation, and in principle provides regular jobs, standardized wages and salaries, social security benefits, and often unionization and collective bargaining.

The second dimension of segmentation concerns the nature of the employment relationship. Over half of all employment in India is self-employment, essentially in the unorganized sector. This is a heterogeneous category, including a substantial segment of marginal, survival activities, many low-productivity household enterprises, but also some high-income professionals and employers. Wage employment too is heterogeneous. A large proportion of wage work is casual and paid on a daily basis. The organized sector generates some regular jobs, protected by contract and social security, but even within the organized sector there are many casual or temporary jobs, such as cleaning, security, and other services, while a great deal of work is outsourced to the unorganized sector. Sectors like construction, trade, and personal services have predominantly relied on casual wage labour and self-employed workers and continue to do so (Papola, 2013).

In the period prior to 1980, there had been some increase in employment in the organized sector, although it was still small as a proportion of all employment. But after 1980, the share of organized employment declined (José, 1994). Over the subsequent twenty years, industrial employment and, especially, service sector employment grew, but mainly in the unorganized sector. At the end of the 1990s, 90 per cent of employment was still in the unorganized sector (Graph 4.3.1 and Table 4.3.1). Then, after the turn of the century, the share of employment in the organized sector started to rise, though it still accounted for only one-sixth of employment by 2011-12.

Graph 4.3.1. Distribution of Workers by Employment Status, India, 1983–2011/12 (%)

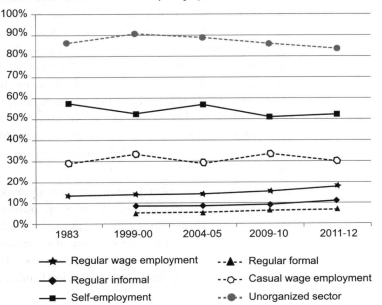

Source: Computed from unit-level data of the corresponding National Sample Survey (NSS) rounds; IHD (2014).

Note: UPSS measure of employment (Usual Principal and Subsidiary Status).

Table 4.3.1. Distribution of Workers by Employment Status*, India, 1983–2011/12 (%)

Share (%) in total Employment of:	1983	1999–2000	2004-05	2009-10	2011-12
Regular wage employment	13.5	14	14.3	15.6	17.9
Regular formal	**	5.4	5.6	6.4	6.8
Regular informal	**	8.6	8.6	9.2	11.0
Casual wage employment	29	33.3	28.9	33.5	29.9
Self-employment	57.5	52.6	56.9	51.0	52.2
Unorganized sector	86.4	90.7	88.9	86.0	83.6

Source: National Sample Survey, various rounds. Prepared by Ajit Ghose for the 2014 India Labour and Employment Report (Institute for Human Development, 2014). Slightly revised estimates are reported in Ghose (2016).

Note: *Employment status refers to Usual Principal and Subsidiary Status (UPSS).
**A breakdown of regular employment into formal and informal in 1983, comparable with later years, is not available because of changes in the information available from the NSS.

Meanwhile, casual wage employment continues to dominate the labour market. Its share in all employment has fluctuated, but with no long-term trend (Graph 4.3.1). At the same time, despite a fall in the share of agricultural employment, where of course many workers are self-employed on their own farms, the overall share of self-employment declined by only 5 percentage points between 1983 and 2011-12. There has been very little increase in the share of regular wage employment since 1983, and even less increase in regular, formal wage employment since 1999-2000. The percentage of informal workers in organized sector wage employment increased from 41 per cent in 1999-2000 to 58 per cent in 2011-12, when less than 7 per cent of all employment was regular, formal work,[10] and much of this was in the public sector.

It is widely believed that economic liberalization has had an important influence on this trend, visible in measures like downsizing, outsourcing, privatization of public services, increases in 'precarious' employment in old and new occupations (e.g., call centre work) and the reappearance of sweatshops. All these have resulted in the expansion of informal employment, where workers do not have security of tenure or protection against contingent risks (Sundar, 2011; Srivastava, 2015).

These structural inequalities in the labour market are clearly a major aspect of inequality overall, because they imply patterns of inclusion and exclusion, different lifetime employment experiences, and differences in wages and incomes.

Female participation in the Indian labour market is low. Female employment accounts for less than one-third of all employment, and grew less than male employment over the past three decades. The marginalization of women in the labour market can be seen in their exclusion from regular, well-paying jobs and in restrictions on their mobility. At the same time, a large percentage of women, particularly in rural India, are involved in part-time economic activities that are poorly measured by national surveys. This results in under-reporting of the economic participation of women (IHD, 2014). Working women are more likely than men to be in self-employment (mainly as unpaid family workers), and less likely to be in regular wage work. We return to these issues in Section 5.1.

In the Brazilian labour market, while similar segmentations are present, their balance is quite different. In particular, the size of the organized labour market in Brazil is much larger than in India. This was already the case at the end of the

---

[10] These figures were estimated for the 2014 India Labour and Employment Report (Institute for Human Development-IHD, 2014). Updated estimates for some of these figures can be found in Ghose (2016), but the revisions are small and do not change the overall pattern.

1970s, as we saw in Section 3.3. In 1976, according to the National Household Survey (PNAD/IBGE), 64 per cent of the occupied population (combining rural and urban areas) was in wage work, 37 per cent registered and 27 per cent unregistered. Registered wage work in Brazil can be compared with regular, formal wage work in India, where it accounted for only 5.4 per cent of all employment in 1999-2000, and probably less in the 1980s. Although an 'unorganized' – informal – sector existed in Brazil, in the sense of self-employment and unpaid work, it was much smaller than in India. In 1976, it accounted for 36 per cent of the workforce in Brazil, but a lower share of around 20 per cent in urban areas, as against 65 per cent in rural areas.

However, in Brazil, labour market trends in the 1980s were deeply negative. Unemployment rose, real wages dropped – more for unregistered than for registered wage-earners – and there was an increase in the share in employment of both unregistered wage workers and the self-employed. Even so, there was no significant change in the basic structure of the labour market, shaped during the years of fast growth. Even in 1993, just after the period of economic crisis, the degree of formalization of the Brazilian labour market remained much higher than the Indian (Table 4.3.2 and Graph 4.3.2). But there was an erosion of real labour income, which not only worsened the living standards of workers but also contributed to the deterioration of macroeconomic conditions.

Table 4.3.2. Distribution of Workers by Employment Status as a Percentage of Total Occupied Population, Brazil, 1993–2012

	1993	1995	1999	2003	2005	2009	2012
Private registered wage-earners	30.1	30.8	29.7	31.9	33.6	37.4	41.8
Public employees	6.4	7.3	7.1	7.1	6.8	7.6	7.8
Non-registered wage-earners	17.8	16.9	18.1	18.7	18.6	17.1	15.7
Self-employed	22.5	24.5	24.9	23.7	22.7	21.4	21.3
Domestic workers	7.2	7.7	7.9	8.1	8.1	8.2	7.1
Unpaid and subsistence economy	16.0	12.9	12.3	10.6	10.1	8.2	6.3
Total	100.0	100.0	100.0	100.0	100.0	100.0	100.0

Source: Computed from PNAD/IBGE micro-data.

This situation changed in the 1990s and the 2000s, when there were two markedly different trends (Graph 4.3.2). Up to the turn of the century, there was no increase in the number of registered wage employees in the private sector (and a small increase in the number of public employees), while self-employment and unregistered wage employment rose. In 1999, the share of these two groups, taken together, exceeded the share of private registered wage workers by 33 per cent. But from 2000 onwards, the picture was very different. Formal work was boosted, while self-employment and unregistered work grew much more slowly. The latter even recorded a decrease in absolute numbers after 2008. As a consequence the share of private registered wage earners reached 13 per cent higher than the combined share of unregistered wage workers and the self-employed.

In Table 4.3.2, the categories for employment status in Brazil are presented in a way that allows for a comparison with India. After having stabilized at around 37 per cent of all jobs in the 1990s (employers excluded), public and private formal employment jumped to close to 50 per cent in 2012. This figure can be compared with the 6.8 per cent of regular formal wage workers in India at that date. At the end of the period, unregistered wage work, the nearest available equivalent of casual labour in India,[11] had fallen to 15.7 per cent (against 30 per cent in India). However, the self-employed, together with domestic workers and the subsistence economy – more important in rural areas – still represented almost 35 per cent of the total occupied workforce in Brazil. So, while the overall picture shows a more structured labour market than in India with a large share of formal workers, at the same time unregistered wage work, self-employment, domestic work, and family-based activities still accounted for half of all workers.

Nevertheless, the reformalization of the Brazilian labour market after 2000 stands in remarkable contrast to the persistent informality of the Indian. Even if we consider only urban areas in India – which is perhaps a better comparison with highly urbanized Brazil – formal, regular, wage work accounted for only 17.5 per cent of employment in India in 2011-12. This is not much more than one third of the share of registered wage workers in Brazil. Moreover, this proportion has hardly changed in India, while it has risen substantially in Brazil.

---

[11] In reality, casual work in India is not equivalent to unregistered work in Brazil, because there is little casual daily employment in Brazil, and no equivalent system of worker registration in India. However, these employment statuses identify the key segmentations in the labour market of the two countries, and can therefore be considered to play a structurally similar role.

Graph 4.3.2. Trend in Number of Workers by Employment Status, Brazil, 1992–2011

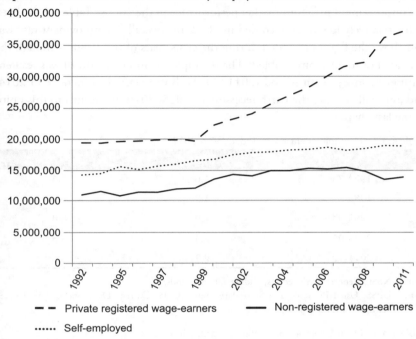

— — Private registered wage-earners   —— Non-registered wage-earners

······ Self-employed

Source: Based on PNAD/IBGE micro-data.

In Brazil, the other important labour market outcome is open unemployment. Because of the nature of the Brazilian labour market – with a larger share of formal, waged work than in India – open unemployment plays a different role in labour market adjustment. In India, unemployment is essentially structural, and does not change much over time. Table 4.3.3 shows that in India 'usual status' unemployment (over the past year) has been quite stable at around 2 per cent, while 'daily' status unemployment, which reflects mainly the inability of casual labourers to find work every day, has fluctuated in a range of less than 3 percentage points over forty years. Variations in economic activity are absorbed largely in self-employment and the sharing of casual work rather than in open unemployment.

In Brazil, on the other hand, open unemployment responds to conjunctural forces and is an important labour market indicator. Unequal exposure to unemployment is a significant aspect of labour market inequality in Brazil. This is especially true for urban areas, more than for rural areas, where the labour market is less developed. The unemployment rate increased fast in the 1990s, reached almost 10 per cent, and fell thereafter to 6.2 per cent in 2012, due to the improvement in labour market performance in the 2000s (Table 4.3.4). Even at the relatively low levels recorded in 2012, the overall unemployment rate was still above the figures recorded during the crisis years of the 1980s – though the data are not totally comparable.[12] The unemployment rate in Brazil was resilient during the low-growth period (2011–2013). But it started to increase in 2014, and especially during the harsh recession of 2015–2016. We return to this point in the last chapter.

Table 4.3.3. Unemployment Rates, India, 1972–2012

Year	UPSS	CDS
1972-73	1.6	8.4
1983	1.9	8.3
1993-94	1.9	6.0
2004-05	2.3	8.3
2011-12	2.2	5.6

Source: NSSO, reports on the corresponding survey rounds.
Note: UPSS: Usual Principal and Secondary Status: CDS: Current Daily Status. For detailed definitions, IHD (2014), box 2.1.

Table 4.3.4. Open Unemployment Rates, Brazil, 1983–2012

Year	Total	Rural	Urban
1983*	4.9	1.1	6.4
1989*	3.0	1.0	3.7
1993	6.2	1.5	7.7
1995	6.1	1.6	7.5
1999	9.6	3.0	11.6
2003	9.7	2.5	11.2
2005	9.3	2.8	10.8
2009	8.3	3.2	9.3
2012	6.2	2.9	6.8

Source: PNAD/IBGE.
Note: *Due to methodological differences, figures from the 1980s are not strictly comparable with later years.

---

[12] In addition to statistical changes, the introduction of unemployment insurance in the 1990s, absent in India, has helped some workers survive periods of unemployment without driving them into informal work.

In India, the main exception to the argument that open unemployment is of secondary importance concerns young people, especially those with higher educational qualifications.[13] The rise in education level has increased the job aspirations of youths, but the higher education system has on the whole failed to provide the skills and qualifications demanded by modern industry and services. There is, thus, a mismatch between the expectations of young people and the availability of jobs. In fact, the Indian economy faces a paradoxical situation where, on the one hand, young people (aged 15 to 29 years) are searching for higher-paying decent employment while, on the other hand, industry is suffering from a shortage of skilled labour. So, in the past two decades, despite high growth, there has been a persistently high unemployment rate among young people (Table 4.3.5). A significant proportion of young people also fall back on self-employment or low-paying contractual employment while they search for better jobs.

Table 4.3.5. Youth Unemployment Rate (15 to 29 Years), India, 1999–2012 (%)

	1999-2000	2004-05	2009-10	2011-12
Rural male	5.1	5.2	5.5	6.1
Rural female	3.7	7.0	6.5	7.8
Urban male	11.5	10.0	7.9	8.9
Urban female	16.6	19.9	17.2	15.6

Source: Government of India, National Sample Survey Office (2014).

There is a similar pattern in Brazil. Even though the open unemployment rate for youth fell over the period 1999–2012 (Table 4.3.6) in urban areas, it is much higher for this age group than for the workforce as a whole, especially for women, for whom it was still 16 per cent in 2012. In rural areas, where unemployment is usually very low (Table 4.3.4), it rose during this period for both men and women of this age group. Moreover, it is more than twice as high for young women as for young men in these areas. Since the young are on average better educated than the rest of population, the problem is usually seen as one of higher aspirations among these groups than can be met by the jobs available. So, in Brazil, like in India, there seems to be a mismatch between supply of and demand for educated workers.

---

[13] There is also an unemployment problem among the poorest groups, especially those with disabilities or other disadvantages that impede access to the labour market. We do not analyse that issue here, but unemployment rates are widely found to be high among the poorest groups in urban areas. Rodgers (1989), Table 1.2, gives data for several countries.

Table 4.3.6. Youth Unemployment Rate, Brazil, 1999–2012 (%)

	1999	2005	2012
Rural male	4.1	3.9	4.4
Rural female	8.2	8.5	9.7
Urban male	15.1	14.5	9.7
Urban female	22.5	22.7	15.8

Source: PNAD/IBGE.

4.3.2 *Wage and income differentials*

As noted in Section 4.2, there has been a substantial rise in real wages in India since the 1980s. Graph 4.3.3 shows the broad trend in regular and casual wages compared with Net National Income (NNI) per capita. Real wages grew for both labour market categories through most of the period since 1983, though they grew less than NNI per capita after 2000. Regular workers did better than casual workers until 1999-2000, but then did less well, especially between 2009-10 and 2011-12, when growth in casual wages accelerated.[14] In contrast, in Brazil (Graph 4.3.4), real wages have not changed greatly since 1983, although they have fluctuated over time, and have been rising since 2003 from the low levels reached in the early 2000s. Like in India, wage growth was lower than GDP per capita growth up to the end of the 1990s, but the gap shrank somewhat between 2003 and 2011. The incomes of unregistered wage workers and the self-employed even rose faster than GDP per capita. Wages of registered workers stayed fairly constant in real terms over the period as a whole, while those of unregistered workers fell sharply in the 1980s and then gradually recovered, reaching their 1983 level again only in 2011.[15]

---

[14] We used the consumer price index for agricultural labourers to deflate casual wages, and the consumer price index for industrial workers for regular workers. This is an imperfect approximation, but there are no price series specifically for these groups. The price index for industrial workers has generally risen faster than that for agricultural labour, which may bias the real wages of regular workers downwards. If we replace the consumer price indices by the GDP deflator to calculate real wages for both groups, regular wages do better than casual throughout the period (though still lower than NNI per capita).

[15] In India, we rely on the quinquennial NSS surveys for wage data. Regular wage data are available on a more frequent basis only for a few occupations (mainly in agriculture). Therefore, there are fewer data points for India than for Brazil, where annual (actually, monthly) data are available.

Graph 4.3.3. Real Net National Income Per Capita and Average Real Wages for Regular and Casual Workers, India, 1983–2011/12 (Index, 1983 = 100)

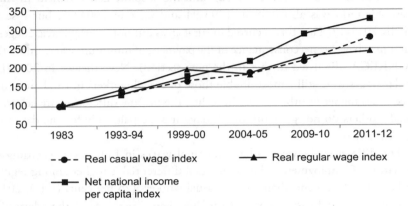

Source: Computed from NSS unit-level data and National Accounts.

Graph 4.3.4. Real GDP Per Capita and Real Labour Income (Registered and Unregistered Wage-earners and Self-employed), Brazil, 1983–2011 (Index, 1983 = 100)

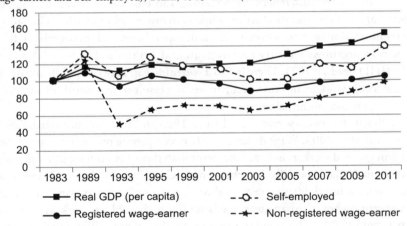

Source: Computed from PNAD/IBGE micro-data.
Note: Data for the 1980s are not fully comparable with the following years.

This is a very large difference between the two countries, but part of it reflects the economic and political crisis in Brazil in the 1980s, to which there was no Indian counterpart. Graphs 4.3.5 and 4.3.6 confine our analysis to the more recent period and trace changes in real wages in detail since 1993 for casual/unregistered and regular/registered workers in rural and urban areas. It can be seen (Graph 4.3.5) that the rise in wages in India was substantial for all groups (with the exception of the period between 1999-2000 and 2004-05).

However, the ratio of casual to regular wages changed little in urban areas (0.38 in both 1993-94 and 2011-12), and the absolute gap widened. In rural areas, this ratio was also 0.38 in 1993-94 and 0.37 in 2004-05, but rose to 0.46 by 2011-12. That this occurred in rural areas but not in urban areas suggests that it may have been a consequence of the payment of minimum wages under the MGNREGA (discussed further in the next section). Nevertheless, in 2011-12, regular wages were still almost double those of casual workers in rural areas and three times higher in urban areas. In reality, the income differences are larger, as casual workers do not get work on all days and are paid only for the days that they actually work.

The differences between urban and rural wages in India vary according to the nature of employment. The urban-rural differential is higher among regular workers, at 49 per cent, than among casual workers (25 per cent) (IHD, 2014, Table 4.1). A rural casual worker earns less than 7 per cent of the salary of a public sector employee. There is also a persistent wage differential between male and female workers, though it is narrowing (Section 5.1). Another significant trend is that wage differences are widening substantially between managerial/ supervisory workers and production workers in organized industries. The ratio of the remuneration of 'non-workers' (clerical, supervisory, and managerial staff) to workers in organized industry rose from around 1.5 in the 1980s to 3.5 around 2010 (IHD, ibid., p.107). There is also a widening gap between public sector and private sector workers in some occupations as a result of the awards of successive public sector pay commissions.

In Brazil, the twenty-year period from 1993 to 2012 saw sustained rises in wages only after 2003. Wage differentials between private registered wage-earners and unregistered workers in Brazil are lower than those between regular and casual workers in India, especially in urban areas (Graph 4.3.6). In 2012, registered wages were around 90 per cent higher than unregistered in rural areas and 45 per cent higher in urban areas; the latter figure showed a remarkable fall from 78 per cent in 2003. This trend towards a reduction of wage differentials in urban areas is partly explained by the fact that some unregistered workers obtained registered jobs during the period. Meanwhile, the remaining unregistered wage-earners have been performing tasks similar to their registered counterparts. This has led to a less intense segmentation of the labour market, or at least one that manifests itself in other ways, such as the overall level of wages and the minimum schooling required for each type of job. In addition, the rising minimum wage has been an important factor in pushing up the wage floor. Rural differentials have not narrowed, but there has been a larger rise in the real wage in rural areas, so the gap with urban areas has been reduced.

Graph 4.3.5. Real Wages of Regular and Casual Workers in Rural and Urban Areas, India, 1993/94–2011/12 (in 1993-94 Rupees Per Day)

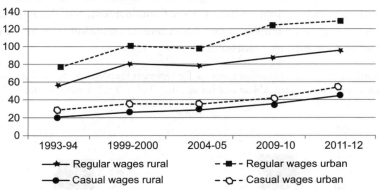

Regular wages rural ── Regular wages urban ── Casual wages rural ── Casual wages urban

Source: NSS Reports of the survey years concerned.

Graph 4.3.6. Real Wages of Registered and Unregistered Wage-earners in Rural and Urban Areas, Brazil, 1993–2012 (in 2012 Reais Per Month)

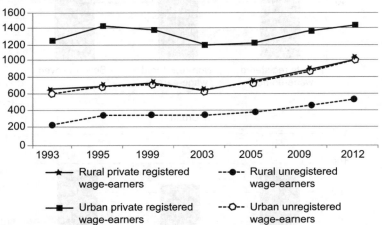

Rural private registered wage-earners   Rural unregistered wage-earners

Urban private registered wage-earners   Urban unregistered wage-earners

Source: PNAD/IBGE.

In Brazil, we can also compare incomes in self-employed and wage-employed households (this refers to the employment status of the household head) (Graph 4.3.7). This gives the following picture in 2012: in both urban and rural areas, there is virtually no difference in income between private registered wage-earners and the self-employed. For the country as a whole, the income gap between individual registered wage workers (including those in the public sector) and the self-employed fell from 32 per cent in 2003 to 13 per cent in 2011. These are average figures, and so do not take into account the higher inequality of per capita income among self-employed households, but the downward trend is significant. It probably reflects a growth of demand for wage labour, which not only reduces the supply of labour to self-employment, but also implies that those who remain self-employed face better market conditions due to the rising incomes of wage-earning households.

Graph 4.3.7. Per Capita Household Income for Different Employment Status Categories of the Household Head, Brazil, Urban and Rural, 2012 (Index, 2012 Average = 100)

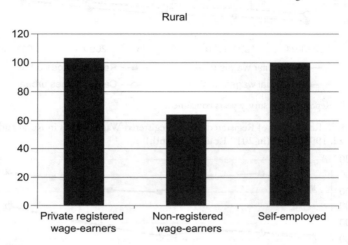

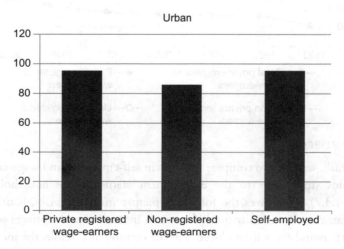

Source: PNAD/IBGE.

Note: The average (=100) includes two categories not presented here, employers and public employees, both with higher than average incomes.

It is more difficult to get information on the relative incomes of wage and self-employed workers in India, but a proxy is provided by per capita consumption at the household level. In 2011-12, in both urban and rural areas, consumption levels were higher in self-employed households than in casual wage households but lower than in households headed by regular wage workers (Graph 4.3.8). The ratios seem to be fairly stable over time. Relative to wage-earners, then, on average, the self-employed are worse off in India than in Brazil. This no doubt reflects the importance in India of low-productivity, supply-driven self-employment as an alternative to casual wage work and the excess labour supply in parts of the labour market.

Graph 4.3.8. Per Capita Household Expenditure for Different Employment Status Categories of the Household Head, India, Urban and Rural, 2011-12 (Current Rupees Per Month)

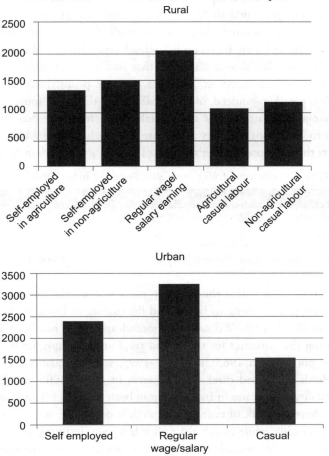

Source: Computed from NSS unit-level data.

These patterns of segmentation and the corresponding differences in employment status are therefore important sources of wage inequality, and they interact with other factors influencing labour market inequality such as gender, caste, race, and region (we discuss these in Chapter 5). It is therefore interesting to explore what proportion of overall wage inequality can be attributed to these structural characteristics of the labour market.

Table 4.3.7 shows the overall Gini coefficients of wage inequality in India and Brazil for the period 1983 to 2011-12. There are two striking results here. First, wage inequality has been of the same order of magnitude in the two countries over the past thirty years, the Gini coefficient averaging a little under 0.5 in both countries. This contrasts sharply with the picture based on household income and expenditure presented in Section 4.2 (Graph 4.2.5), which showed that inequality in India was much lower than in Brazil. But, as we commented there, the estimates for India are based on household expenditure and those for Brazil based on income. We should also note that income from self-employment is excluded from the estimates in Table 4.3.7, as are profit, interest, and rental income. It is possible – indeed, likely – that adding these two sources of income would change the pattern, but the available data from the National Sample Survey in India do not allow us to explore this further. In any case, this result contradicts the widespread belief that Brazil is more unequal than India.

Table 4.3.7. Gini Coefficients of Wage Inequality, Brazil and India, 1983–2012

	1983	1993–1995	2004–2005	2011–2012
Brazil	0.56	0.52	0.46	0.41
India	0.47	0.46	0.51	0.47

Source: India: Computed from NSS unit-level data. Brazil: Computed from PNAD/IBGE unit-level data.

The second result is that the trends in the two countries are quite different, with wage inequality falling in Brazil, and fluctuating in India, with an upward tendency until 2004-05. We can see more clearly what has been happening by separating the estimates for urban and rural areas (Graph 4.3.9). First, it is striking to note that in 1983 and 1993–1995, wage inequality was greater in Brazil in both urban and rural areas, whereas in 2004–2005 and 2011–2012 wage inequality was greater in India, again in both areas. In urban areas of India, which is where the bulk of economic growth is occurring, wage inequality has been rising steadily, while in urban Brazil it has been declining steadily. In rural areas, there is less difference between the two countries, with a downward trend in both countries, more pronounced and consistent in Brazil than in India.

Graph 4.3.9. Trends in Wage Inequality (Gini Coefficient) in Rural and Urban Areas, India and Brazil, 1983–2012

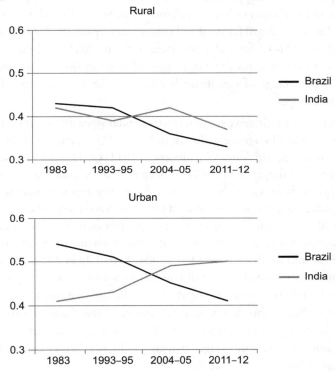

Source: India: Computed from NSS unit-level data. Brazil: Computed from PNAD/IBGE unit-level data.

Note: '1993–95' refers to the 1993-94 National Sample Survey and 1995 PNAD data. 2004–2005 refers to the 2004-05 National Sample Survey and 2005 PNAD data. 2011–12 refers to the 2011-12 National Sample Survey and 2011 PNAD data.

In India, the increase in wage inequality in 2004-05, followed by a decline in 2011-12, was essentially a rural phenomenon. It is possible that this pattern in part reflects a surge of low-productivity employment in a period of rural distress (Himanshu, 2011), due to poor harvests before 2004-05, followed by a series of good agricultural years. And we have already noted the likely impact of higher wages paid in employment under the MGNREGA after 2004-05. In any case, the difference in pattern between rural and urban areas is striking.

How much of this overall pattern and trend of wage inequality can be explained by the segmentation of the labour markets in the two countries? A first indication can be provided by decomposing the Theil index of wage inequality.

Decomposition is a standard technique for establishing, in accounting terms, what proportion of inequality is due to variation within groups, and what proportion to the difference between them.[16] Graphs 4.3.10 and 4.3.11 give the results for India and Brazil for rural and urban areas separately. We have estimates from 1983 to 2011-12 for India and from 1995 to 2011 for Brazil. For each year, the first column gives the Theil index of wage inequality and the second column the percentage of this inequality that can be attributed to differences between the groups.

Taking rural areas first, we see that casual-regular wage differences account for about one-third of all wage inequality in India in 1993-94 and 2004-05, up from 19 per cent in 1983, and falling to a quarter in 2011-12. This is a very substantial part of inequality (larger than the other factors that we examine in Section 5), especially when we consider that measured inequality also reflects measurement errors, regional patterns, interpersonal differences, and many other factors. The decline in 2011-12 probably reflects a tightening labour market for casual labour, which is certainly a major factor in the decline in inequality overall (the Theil index in rural areas declines from 0.37 in 2004-05 to 0.28 in 2011-12). In Brazil, the contribution to inequality of differences in wages between registered and unregistered workers is smaller, but it too declines in the most recent period. In the case of Brazil, this may reflect the impact of the rising minimum wage, which affects unregistered workers as well as registered, although less in rural areas. In contrast, minimum wages (which we discuss further below) have less influence in India.

In urban areas, the differences in wages between casual and regular workers and between registered and unregistered workers account for a much smaller fraction of wage inequality than in rural areas, no doubt because there is much more inequality within regular work in urban areas. A downward trend in the contribution to the Theil index is also visible in both countries, so much so that registered-unregistered differences account for only 3.4 per cent of wage inequality in 2011-12 in Brazil (against 12 per cent in India). This is partly because the wage gap between registered and unregistered workers has been declining, as we saw above. But, in addition, the formalization of the labour market in Brazil implies that the numbers of unregistered workers have been declining, which

---

[16] This method and its application are discussed in more detail elsewhere; see Cacciamali et al. (2015) and Rodgers and Soundararajan (2016). The Theil index is a more convenient measure for this purpose than the Gini coefficient because it is easier to decompose. The pattern of inequality given by the two measures is broadly similar in the case of the wage distribution.

reduces the measured contribution of registered-unregistered wage differentials to overall inequality. So, by 2011, this aspect of labour market segmentation was not a major influence on wage inequality in Brazil. On the other hand, the casual-regular wage gap remains an important source of inequality in India.

Graph 4.3.10. Decomposition of Wage Inequality by Employment Status (Regular and Casual Work), India, 1983–2011/12

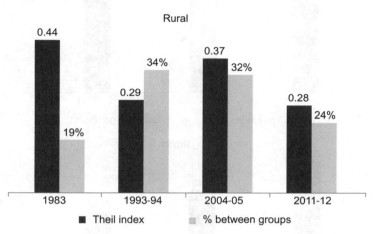

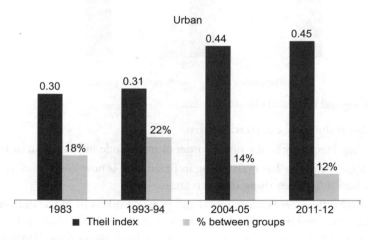

Source: Computed from NSS unit-level data.

Note: For each year the first column gives the total value of the Theil index of wage inequality; the second column the percentage of the Theil index that can be attributed to difference between the groups.

Graph 4.3.11. Decomposition of Theil Index of Wages by Employment Status (Registered/Unregistered Work), Brazil, 1995–2011

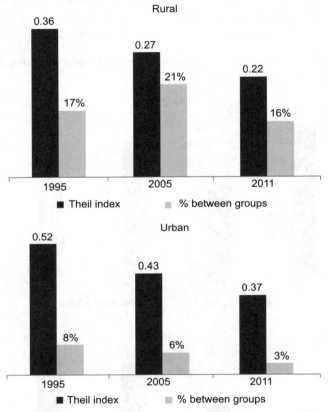

Source: Computed from PNAD/IBGE micro-data.

From this analysis, we can conclude that

- Wage inequality is of a similar order of magnitude in Brazil and in India;
- Wage inequality has been falling in Brazil, and is now lower than in India, where it has been rising in urban areas;
- Wage differences between casual and regular workers in India, and between registered and unregistered workers in Brazil, contribute substantially to this inequality, but this contribution has been falling, especially in Brazil; and
- The fall in wage differences between registered and unregistered workers is an important part of the overall decline in wage inequality in Brazil, and the similar fall in casual-regular wage differences in India has no doubt been an important reason why wage inequality has not risen further there.

4.3.3 Changes in labour institutions

The labour market outcomes discussed above reflect both the pattern of economic growth and the underlying labour institutions, including labour market regulation and the role of trade unions. This section considers some of these institutional factors, how they have been changing, and their consequences. We start by comparing the overall institutional framework of the labour market in the two countries, and then look in more detail at the minimum wage, one particular policy area that directly affects labour market inequality.

The broad institutional framework

As we saw in Sections 3.1 and 3.3, both India and Brazil had built a framework for labour market regulation before 1980 that aimed to establish key rights and protections within a wider labour code. This code was confined largely to the formal economy, and so did not cover the workforce as a whole in either country. But since the formal economy was much larger in Brazil, the coverage there was greater than in India. Brazil's model of industrial relations had a corporatist foundation, and provided instruments for labour control that were used especially by the military regime in the 1960s and 1970s. India's model was more liberal in inspiration, but there was a substantial gap between ambition and realization.

The political movement that brought dictatorship to an end in Brazil also endeavoured to change labour institutions. The 1988 Constitution modified the concept of citizenship and consolidated, broadened, and universalized social rights. In particular, it brought together a number of rights that were scattered over the Labour Code and ascribed them the status of fundamental rights.

In India, although the Emergency in the 1970s had suppressed some labour rights, there was little lasting effect. The labour code in the 1980s was extensive and complex, though effectively it applied only to a restricted group of workers. The code continued to rest on a foundation conceived in the 1940s and 1950s (as discussed in Section 3.3), with relatively minor changes, and with some regional variations, since labour was a subject on which both the centre and states could legislate.

In the 1990s, as part of the liberalization agenda, the governments in both India and Brazil aimed to reduce labour costs and create new labour contract modalities in order to increase the flexibility of the workforce. In both countries, the business community frequently argued that low growth rates and insufficient labour demand could only be overcome if labour regulation were made more flexible, which implied restricting labour rights and reducing constraints on labour use. And in this decade, in both countries, the governments adopted an approach that weakened the impact of labour regulations – without a marked change in the institutions themselves, and mostly bypassing them – for instance by neglecting enforcement and allowing employers to set their own rules on some aspects of labour relations, which ultimately impacted the hiring, firing, employment conditions, and pay of workers.

But after the 1990s, the paths in the two countries diverged. In India, labour market flexibility continued to be seen as part of the process of economic liberalization, and some steps were taken to promote it. In Brazil, on the other hand, after 2000 there was a reformalization of the labour market and a strengthening of labour market institutions. This was an important factor in the different trends in overall inequality in the two countries.

In India, much of the debate about labour market regulation centred on Chapter V-B of the Industrial Disputes Act (1947), which states that in factories with 100 or more workers, the firm has to seek the state's permission before retrenching a worker. But this Act had not prevented layoffs in the Indian manufacturing sector when required. As noted by Papola (1992), a large number of workers were laid off in the 1980s from two industries – cotton textiles and food products – which earlier accounted for one-third of the total employment in the organized sector. In the 1990s, new practices such as voluntary retirement schemes (VRS) made it easier to fire workers, and between 1997-98 and 2003-04 some 730,000 employees were reported to have lost their jobs (Sood et al., 2014). In addition, a spread of subcontracting arrangements bypassed the regulations that applied to formal wage employment, so that employers could differentiate between a core group of permanent workers and a larger contract labour workforce (Srivastava, 2015). Despite being theoretically restricted by a 1970 Act, the proportion of employment under such arrangements in organized manufacturing rose from 10 per cent in 1995-96 to 25 per cent in 2009-10, according to data from the Annual Survey of Industries (Sood et al., 2014).

Nevertheless, it was – and still is – widely argued that the failure of the Indian economy to create more formal jobs can be traced to restrictions on layoffs, and that rigidities in Indian labour regulations have made it difficult for Indian industries to operate in a globally competitive environment. As a result, successive Indian governments have adopted measures to facilitate greater flexibility in the labour market with a view to promoting domestic investment and attracting global capital. Initially, this was mainly through changes in legislation at the state level, alongside court judgments that favoured employers (Srivastava,

2015). Among central government actions, the UPA governments (2004–14) created an increasing number of special economic zones where strikes and trade union activities were restricted (ILO, 2012). The present BJP government has proposed a series of reforms to existing labour laws that would increase the overtime limit for workers, raise the enterprise size threshold for the application of various regulations, including the requirement of government approval in case of dismissals, and make trade union registration more difficult. Some of this is a welcome simplification of the mind-bogglingly complex structure of regulation, but it also aims to promote more flexible employment relationships in the interests of growth (Lerche, 2015; Gopalan, 2016). Combined with underfunded labour inspection (Srivastava, 2015) and deliberately weak enforcement in some states, it is clear that labour market regulation is being eroded. Significant exceptions, however, include action against child labour and bonded labour; in these cases, international pressure for fair trade clearly played a role.

In Brazil, some measures were introduced to promote labour market flexibility in the 1990s, and like in India enforcement of the Labour Code was weakened. The main idea was that the 'negotiated' should prevail over the 'legislated', bringing less 'rigidity' to the labour market. But flexible labour rules – such as increased temporary labour, fixed-term labour contracts, and part-time contracts – had little impact on the market, and not only because of union resistance (Cacciamali and Brito, 2002). Increasingly, it became apparent that low levels of employment growth and high unemployment levels in that period were due not to labour rigidity – which is why the new rules were seldom used – but to low and uneven economic growth, which negatively affected labour demand. Also, the growth in unregistered wage work seemed to fit better with enterprise goals of reducing labour costs.

In contrast, regulation on working hours and wages through the so-called 'hour banks' and 'profit-sharing schemes' had considerable impact, with more workers subject to these normative innovations (Krein, 2007). These mechanisms continued even during the period of formalization of wage labour relations in the 2000s.

It should be borne in mind that while formally the Indian system of labour regulation is almost as extensive as the Brazilian, the latter is much more deeply embedded in society. The system of a signed labour card (Section 3.3) highlights the rights of workers and employers, Labour Courts are widely respected, and trade unions are much stronger (below). In particular, the formation of a PT-led government in 2003 relied heavily on trade union support – especially from CUT (United Workers Confederation, from Portuguese *Central Única dos Trabalhadores*),[17] the main trade union centre in Brazil, which was created right after the PT and has strong links with it – and part of its policy agenda reflected trade union demands and was supported by local trade unions. The new government reinforced labour inspection, actively promoted labour registration and steadily raised the minimum wage (discussed further below); hence the rapid growth in formal employment (Graph 4.3.1), which contrasts with the situation in India. Most importantly, despite their political and ideological differences, in 2007 the six recognized trade union centres launched a 'Worker's Agenda for Development with Inequality Reduction' (DIEESE, 2012).

This does not mean that labour market flexibility was completely off the agenda in Brazil in the past decade, on the contrary. There have recently been some efforts to revise labour legislation to make it easier to hire labour services without a contract, for instance, or for retail workers to work on Saturdays and Sundays. And a new law makes it easier for firms to outsource not only support services but also core production activities.

Thus, while the trend towards formalization in the 2000s offered a counter-argument against the rigidity thesis formulated in the 1990s, the same argument returned in the midst of the recession of 2015–2016.

However, it is clear that strong labour institutions played an important role in the reduction in inequality in Brazil. Among these labour institutions, trade unions were central.

Brazilian trade unions played a prominent role in defending workers' rights in the face of military dictatorship and liberalization, and during the period of high unemployment in the latter part of the 1990s. And since the main political opposition during that period drew much of its strength from the workers' movement, unions also had political influence. In fact, the formalization of employment relations also increased union membership, even if unionization rates fell, as we describe below. During the period of improving labour market performance in the 2000s, collective bargaining was increasingly generalized in the formal sector, and most of the unions obtained a wage increase above inflation rates, although this process was very uneven. It is often argued that unions mainly represent the interests of formal workers but, unlike in India, these constitute a majority of wage workers in Brazil. Moreover, although most of the members of the main trade unions came from sectors that paid three to

---

[17] In 2014, according to data from the Ministry of Labour, unions affiliated to CUT accounted for 34.3 per cent of all unionized workers, followed by Força Sindical (FS) and União Geral dos Trabalhadores (UGT), with 12.6 and 12 per cent, respectively.

five times the minimum wage, they nevertheless pressed for the minimum wage to increase at the same rate as the nominal GDP.

However, it is striking that the unionization rate fell in Brazil in the 2000s. In 2011, it was a little above 20 per cent of wage-earners, having fallen both for manufacturing – from 30.2 per cent in 2001 to 28.6 per cent in 2011 – and in the rest of the economy, where it declined from 25 per cent to 20 per cent over the same period. According to Campos (2014), microeconomic, demographic, and political factors may explain this unexpected trend in a buoyant labour market. Companies outsourced much more and moved production to less unionized regions of the country; a new segment of workers was made up of youth with less experience of unionization, usually concentrated in low-skilled parts of the services sector; and trade union centres were more concerned with the public policy agenda than with the need to spread unionization to these new segments of the workforce. Furthermore, it should be stressed that in the 1990s, contrary to what would have been expected, the unionization rate rose despite the disorganization of the labour market. This was related mainly to new entrants, like public employees, who were not allowed to form a union before the 1988 Constitution, and rural workers, whose unionization levels were very low. As a result, the unionization rates were already relatively high at the beginning of the 2000s, and a further rise would have called for a more active union policy aimed at expanding its membership.

There remain issues of freedom of association and representation, which are a legacy of the military period. A union reform aimed at increasing union representativeness was attempted in the first term of President Lula but was not completed. The only change was the legal recognition of national union centres, which now also receive part of the funds collected through the union tax (to which there is no counterpart in India). The present system creates a divide even among formal workers, as some unions are stronger than others, since the level of unionization varies with formalization rates in each sector, and also by region, because of the lack of centralized bargaining.

The present union system allows just one union to represent each category of worker in every municipality, and assures the payment of a mandatory union fee by law, alongside its structure in federations and confederations. It should be noted that reforming this system was one of the main goals since the creation of PT and CUT in their pursuit of more autonomous unions engaged in national collective bargaining in different sectors. The fact that this was not achieved during Lula's terms of office points to the benefits of the present system for the national union centres, and also reflects the very broad political coalition which did not see this as strategic. For instance, business representatives – well represented in government – wanted to trade reform of the union system against change in the labour law, allowing for negotiation on some of the items of the Labour Code through collective bargaining. This led to a stalemate, and no change in either the union system or the Labour Code while the PT was in government.

In India, the trade union movement remains politically fragmented, and this is a source of weakness. Major strikes in the early 1980s were unsuccessful, and unions are today largely concentrated in the public sector, with some presence in larger manufacturing and mining companies, and in some specific occupations. It is true that there are regions – Kerala, for example – and sectors – including public utilities – where unions are strong. And while the number of industrial conflicts appears to have declined in recent years, their scale has increased (Sundar, 2015). But available figures, which are quite unreliable, suggest that only some 5 per cent of the non-agricultural workforce is unionized, and that the numbers have been declining in the post-reform period (IHD, 2014). One factor is an overall decline in public sector employment, which has reduced the influence and collective bargaining potential of the unions. Even within the public sector, unions have been unable to prevent the increasing contractualization of employment. This, too, reduces the influence of unions, since casual, temporary, and contract workers largely remain unorganized (Srivastava, 2001). Another adverse influence on unionization has been the growth of the service sector, where unions are resisted. Unions have particular difficulty entering modern services such as the IT sector and private finance and business services.

On the whole, the traditional, politically affiliated unions failed to capitalize on the gains from accelerated output growth, and one consequence was the emergence of 'independent unions', with no political affiliation, which focused on negotiating higher wages and other benefits for their members (Bhowmik, 2012; Ahn, 2010). This was associated with a shift in the pattern of collective bargaining from centralized negotiation aimed at regularizing employment to productivity-linked decentralized and cooperative wage bargaining in both the public and the private sectors. In the private sector, decentralized bargaining permitted employers to pay different wages across different plants depending on the strength of the union and on the productivity of the plant (Bhattacharjee, 1999).This also allowed unions to make gains where they were strong, although it implied less solidarity between workers in different firms and greater wage inequality overall.[18] Indian firms have also in recent years tried to create and recognize unions of their own from company loyalists among workers, even if they constitute a minority of the workforce, to create alternatives to non-cooperating unions that refuse to accept flexibility in collective bargaining. In the public sector, long-term agreements were reached in which higher wages for workers were combined with increased labour flexibility and higher output per worker (Venkataratnam, 2003). Unions agreed to such terms to safeguard their existence in an environment of intensified product market competition.

Trade unions in India remain capable of large-scale coordinated actions, notably the mobilization of millions of workers in national strikes, for instance in September 2016. This strike was a vehicle for protest against labour reforms and for promoting many specific demands, including higher minimum wages, rights for contract workers, and restrictions on FDI and on privatization. But the political impact of these mobilizations appears to be limited.

All of this basically concerns the organized sector, which as we have seen accounts for only a small fraction of employment in India. Yet, the most important challenge is the large number of the working poor engaged in low-productivity activities in small and household enterprises and farms in the unorganized sector, both wage workers and self-employed. The low earnings of these workers are compounded by precarious working conditions and terms of employment. This sector tends to be defined negatively as the sector where many legal regulations and labour laws are not applicable, and not much attention is paid to how the 'unorganized' are actually organized. In 2004, the government established the National Commission for Enterprises in the Unorganised Sector, which made many recommendations for improvements in working conditions and incomes (NCEUS, 2009). However, few of its recommendations have been put into practice. One exception was the Unorganized Workers' Social Security Act, 2008, which recognized those concerned as workers and aimed to provide them with social security benefits. But the Act did not specify the social security rights to which the workers are entitled, and progress in implementation has been slow (Sankaran, 2012; Kannan, 2014).

In India, traditional trade unions have, on the whole, not been very successful in expanding their activities into the unorganized sector. This is at least in part

---

[18] Actually, the rise of independent unions is similar to what happened in Brazil in the late 1970s, under military rule, leading to the so-called 'new unionism', with the marked difference that the Brazilian unions favoured sectoral collective bargaining at that time as well as the creation of national union centres.

because the interests of regular, formal workers often do not coincide with those of casual, unorganized workers. Nevertheless, in recent years, there have been successful union activities in some parts of the unorganized sector such as brick kilns, dockyards, bidi workers, and street vendors. In some areas, there has also been large-scale organization of agricultural labourers. SEWA (the Self-Employed Women's Association), which organizes women workers engaged in informal employment, such as in domestic work, construction, or home-based industry, has become a significant actor. It has helped women workers increase their bargaining capabilities, develop skills, and improve their access to finance. Popular movements in favour of the right to work and the implementation of the employment guarantee scheme (MGNREGA) have also contributed to increasing awareness among informal workers. But these efforts are far from comprehensive, often local, and their power is limited in the face of market forces.

Overall, in India, it is hard to judge how large a role these institutional patterns and changes have played in the trends of inequality. The failure of formal employment to grow eroded the strength of trade unions by reducing the space for collective bargaining. The most striking change was in fact a rise in real wages, in both rural and urban areas, and in both regular and casual employment. But this cannot readily be attributed to trade union activity, since it was as large, if not larger in non-unionized sectors as in unionized. Likewise, the role of labour legislation was not very visible, especially since the legislation itself did not change much, and the main issue was the effectiveness of enforcement. But there is a presumption that the weakening of labour institutions and the strengthening of market forces permitted greater variation in wages to emerge; an obvious case in point is the lower wages paid to contract workers.

In Brazil, in contrast, it is clear that the institutional changes played an important part in reversing the rise in inequality from the mid-1990s onwards, in which union activities, minimum wage legislation, and labour market formalization all played an important role. However, as shown above, the trade union role was mainly one of support to inclusive public policies; in fact differences in union power in different sectors of the labour market, in the absence of a union reform, may have reinforced wage inequality. If this was not the case, it was largely because of the impact of the minimum wage. The passing of the law that permits greater outsourcing will be a turning point, hampering the access to labour rights for large segments of the labour force and no doubt leading to a more unequal labour market.

Minimum wages

Among labour market institutions with an impact on inequality, minimum wages are sufficiently important to merit separate attention. By setting a floor to wages, they truncate the overall distribution, and so protect the incomes of groups that are particularly vulnerable to exploitation or discrimination.[19]

As noted in Section 3.3, the role played by minimum wages is quite distinct in Brazil and India, due to differences in the nature, coverage, structure, and implementation of the system. In Brazil, the minimum wage is an important policy instrument around which other labour market policies are built. It also acts as a benchmark for other payments such as social security benefits and pensions. In India, on the other hand, minimum wages have a more limited effect despite – or because of – a complicated structure that varies by state and occupation.

In Brazil, the national minimum wage was well established by 1980, even though this did not prevent many unregistered workers from receiving a wage below this floor in certain occupations and regions. It was reinforced by the 1988 Federal Constitution, which specifies a 'nationally unified minimum wage,'[20] established by law, capable of satisfying [workers'] basic living needs and those of their families.' In theory it has 100 per cent coverage; however, enforcement is clearly less than perfect in informal wage work. Nevertheless, the share of workers receiving less than the minimum wage fell from 24 per cent in 1989 to 16 per cent in 2013 (but 35 per cent in the case of unregistered workers) despite a substantial rise in the level of the minimum.

In India, the legal framework is provided by the Minimum Wages Act of 1948. This law is applicable to both organized and unorganized sectors so long as the industry concerned is included in the Schedules of the Act. The Act gives both the central and state governments the right to fix minimum rates of wages for different employments listed in the Act. Since 1996, there is a national floor

---

[19] This section draws on M.-C. Cacciamali et al., *Minimum Wage Policy in Brazil and India and its Impact on Labour Market Inequality*, New Delhi, IHD Working Paper, 2015, which also reviews some of the empirical literature.

[20] When the minimum wage was created in Brazil in 1940, it had 14 different regional values. In 1963, this jumped to 38, leading to fragmentation. During the military rule, and especially after 1974, the number of regional minimum wages was reduced, and the differences between them went down. At the beginning of the 1980s, there were only three regional minimum wages, and the system was finally unified in 1984.

wage which should, in principle, serve as the lowest limit for state minimum wages, but it is non-statutory and so is not legally enforceable. Otherwise, there is a complex system of multiple minimum wages which vary between occupations and across states, with little overall coherence. These minimum wages are, on the whole, poorly enforced. Legally, they cover around two-thirds of workers, and so extend deep into informal employment. However, in practice, labour inspection and enforcement cannot reach much of the informal labour market. Just under 40 per cent of casual workers and 20 per cent of regular workers received less than the minimum wage in 2011-12, according to NSS data – a figure that had however declined from 48 per cent in 2004-05 in the case of casual workers.

The significance of a minimum wage for inequality depends on the level at which it is set. The long-term trend in the minimum wage in Brazil is given in Graph 4.3.12. It can be seen that that the real level fell after the 1970s, with a decline in real terms of some 40 per cent between the late 1970s and the mid-1990s. Since then, there has been a steady rise in its value, especially after 2004, although it has not yet recovered the level of the 1950s. Minimum wages have been rising faster than average wages – the ratio of the minimum wage to average wages rose from 0.30 in 1999 to 0.46 in 2013. Along with an increased formalization of employment, this has clearly led to some compression of the wage scale.

Graph 4.3.12. Trend in the National Minimum Wage, Brazil, 1940–2014 (in 2014 Reais)

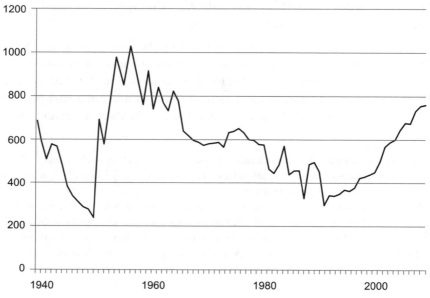

Source: Ipeadata.

In India, the real national floor wage was approximately constant from 1996 to 2004, at about Rs. 47 per day in 2001 prices. After an increase in 2004, it again remained approximately constant at about Rs. 59 per day in 2001 prices, with occasional adjustments for inflation. An increase in 2015 brought the real value to Rs. 60 in 2001 prices (Rs. 160 in current prices). This constant real floor wage after 2004 contrasts with the large increase in average real wages. So, the ratio of the minimum to the average wage has declined.[21] State-level minimum wages for unskilled occupations, on the other hand, have tended to be fairly close to the observed casual wage in rural areas, and to be about half the casual wage in urban areas. They are, therefore, high enough to have a significant impact on wage inequality if they are enforced.

What is the overall impact of the minimum wage on inequality in the two countries? Estimates by Belser and Rani (2011) for 2004-05 suggest that in India the full implementation of the national floor wage would have reduced the Gini coefficient of wage inequality from 0.50 to 0.41. This assumes that there would be no negative impact on employment, but a substantial impact on inequality remains even after a reduction in employment is allowed for. Similar calculations for 2011-12 give a smaller impact on inequality, because average wages had in the meantime risen faster than the national floor wage.

In the case of Brazil, a similar calculation for 2012 gives only a small decrease in the Gini coefficient for wage inequality, from 0.40 to 0.37. But this is largely because most workers already receive at least the minimum. In fact, in the past twenty years, the minimum wage has clearly acted as an instrument for labour market convergence. The steady rise of the minimum wage led to a reduction of wage disparities between men and women, whites and blacks, rich and poor regions, and also highly and less skilled workers, as the latter tend to earn a wage close to the minimum while the former receive higher wages that are not indexed in the same way.

In India, the minimum wage cannot play this role because of the multiple rates of minimum wages that differ across different groups of workers, and across regions and different industries. The absence of any definite criterion for fixing wages and poor levels of enforcement and inspection have rendered minimum wages much less effective as an instrument for promoting equality in the labour market than in Brazil.

---

[21] A central government proposal to raise the floor substantially has been floated, but not implemented yet. In 2016, a large increase in one minimum wage (for central government unskilled non-agricultural workers) was announced in an effort to head off the strike mentioned above. Whether a broader change of policy will ensue remains to be seen.

One should bear in mind that the large increase of minimum wages in Brazil since the turn of the century was brought about in a context of growing output and high levels of job creation. In part, this reflected the effect on aggregate demand of this minimum wage rise and of collective bargaining for workers getting above the minimum wage. In other words, a rising minimum wage was part of a virtuous circle in which rising wages led to a growth of consumer demand and of production, which in turn made it possible to raise the minimum further. However, with the crisis of the growth regime in Brazil – which became clear from 2011–2013, and especially afterwards – the virtuous circle has been broken. It seems unlikely that the minimum wage can continue to play this role of reducing inequality, though it may help to prevent it from increasing again.

The minimum wage was therefore at the core of the equalizing growth regime in Brazil during the 2000s, but has played only a secondary role in India. A substantial rise in the national minimum wage in India, if enforced, could alter the very nature of the growth regime. But, perhaps for that reason, it would have to overcome considerable political opposition.

Other labour market institutions and policies with a bearing on inequality

The minimum wage is not the only labour market intervention that has a direct impact on inequality. We consider some relevant labour market policies when discussing social policy in the next section, notably employment creation programmes and anti-discrimination policy. Another important area concerns institutions for the development of skills and job placement.

As noted in Section 3.3, the system of employment exchanges in India did not replace informal networks and mechanisms before 1980, and this remains true today. In practice, insofar the official system contributes to labour market information and job search, it is confined to a relatively small fraction of the labour market. The Brazilian Public Employment Service (SINE, from the Portuguese *Serviço Nacional de Emprego*) plays a more substantial role, because of the larger formal labour market, and because of its role in the management of unemployment insurance. There is a literature on the functioning of these institutions, but little evidence on the consequences for labour market inequality. In fact, with the creation of the Workers' Support Fund (FAT, from the Portuguese *Fundo de Amparo ao Trabalhador*), the 1988 Constitution ensured a sizeable and stable source of income to provide financing for an unemployment insurance system, while surplus funds were channelled to the Public Employment Service and training policies. This was an important step towards the functional regulation of the labour market, even though lack of integration and coherence between its major components has always been a bottleneck, especially for unskilled workers, who are subject to high turnover rates.

There has been more research and policy effort devoted to skill development and training. The ways skills are imparted and acquired, the ways qualifications are interpreted and rewarded, and the pathways they provide into employment, are labour institutions with a direct bearing on labour market inequality (Barbosa et al., 2015).

In many industrialized countries, the divide between Vocational Education and Training (VET), on the one hand, and an academic education (above a certain level of schooling), on the other, corresponds to a divide in the labour market and a class division in society. Vocational education can play the role of a second-class track for those who fail to reach academic standards (often related to the origins of the children concerned). In India and Brazil, on the other hand, even the formal VET system reaches only a small fraction of the population concerned, so there is a threefold division between those with academic education, those with a VET qualification of some sort – a group within which there is a variety of situations as well, in terms of the type and quality of the training provided – and those with neither. The last is the largest group in both countries, though to a much greater extent in India. Of course, most of those without formal qualifications acquire skills of some sort, but they do so in informal ways, usually on the job.

In recent years, in both Brazil and India, VET has moved up the political agenda. It is seen as a key mechanism in facilitating entry in the labour market, including for social groups that would otherwise be excluded. It is, thus, seen as a social mobility tool, one that is all the more effective when the economy generates better jobs with increasing productivity levels. But while it is a facilitator of opportunities, training creates institutional and individual differences and incentives that may exacerbate inequality in the labour market and in society in general, especially if employment creation is inadequate (Sadgopal, 2016).

In both India and Brazil, the formal VET system reaches only a small fraction of the population concerned and, especially in India, the bulk of the labour force acquires skills informally. In practice, because of the educational qualifications required to enter the vocational training systems, there is a stratification of the work force. Formal training is associated with higher wages, so these unequal training systems are likely to reinforce labour market inequality. The proportion without VET is higher among Scheduled Castes, Scheduled Tribes, and backward classes in India; similarly, in Brazil, there is more access to VET among whites than non-whites. In India, VET is lower among rural residents than urban, and twice as many men as women have vocational skills (both formal and informal).

There are policy efforts to overcome these shortfalls in both countries. In Brazil a large, federally funded programme known as the National Programme of Access to Technical Education and Employment (PRONATEC from Portuguese *Programa Nacional de Acesso ao Ensino Técnico e Emprego*) aims at the productive inclusion of targeted social groups, such as youth, unemployed workers, and the poorest and more vulnerable segments of the population. In India, while there is no large programme of this type, the Ajeevika Skill Development Programme, launched in 2011, caters to the training needs of rural youth. Recent figures suggest that around 30 per cent of beneficiaries have been SCs, 15.4 per cent STs, and about 8.9 per cent minorities (Government of India, Ministry of Rural Development (MoRD), 2015). This suggests that the programme is reaching a much higher percentage of backward groups than their proportion in the population.

Despite these efforts, it is clear that the present vocational training policies in both countries tend to reinforce labour market inequality. This is not only a question of the training institutions themselves. Training as a policy also has to be accompanied by industrial and development policies that create employment opportunities to apply the skills; and this is particularly important for poorer and vulnerable groups whose access to decent jobs is limited.

4.3.4 Summing up

Overall, India and Brazil have some labour market issues in common, and many differences. In the recent period of higher growth in both countries, Brazil has been much more successful than India in converting growth into formal jobs. Many labour institutions in India protect the interests of insiders rather than the work force as a whole and, except in the small formal part of the economy, the representation of workers is weak and the quality of their jobs poor. Both countries face similar challenges in terms of the need to strengthen collective bargaining and to extend it to a larger proportion of workers. While there has been some decline in union power in recent years in India, trade unions in Brazil have been able to consolidate their strength, but mainly in the public sphere, since unionization rates fell in the private sector, despite improved labour market performance. Nevertheless, large sections of the workforce remain unorganized in both countries. This is a greater challenge for India than for Brazil, since the Indian labour market remains dominated by informal work.

Labour institutions to protect workers were somewhat weakened in both countries during the process of economic reform and liberalization in the 1990s. The labour market performed poorly in both countries in this period, with little creation of formal employment in India despite increased growth, and a rise in open unemployment in Brazil. In the 2000s, in Brazil labour institutions were strengthened in a more favourable political and economic environment, whereas in India the acceleration of economic growth coincided with some erosion of labour protection without substantial institutional change, and eventually some improvement in employment performance.

These findings need to be set in the context of the growth regimes in both countries. In Brazil, the 1990s saw a fall in wages and low economic growth. When economic growth resumed, it was built on rising wages and greater emphasis on labour rights – especially for workers receiving around the minimum wage – and this brought about a fall in inequality of labour income. This, in turn, fed into the dynamism of the internal market. In India, on the other hand, economic growth depended on sectors that were mostly capital-intensive or relied on highly skilled labour (IT services, for example). While there was some spillover into demand for casual labour in construction and some services, the primary factors driving growth lay elsewhere. This macroeconomic dynamic – compounded by the availability of a large reservoir of low-cost unskilled labour in rural areas – created the conditions for widening inequality. So in both countries, the strength or weakness of labour institutions has played an important role in determining how the pattern of economic growth impacts on inequality.

4.4 The State, Social Policies and Inequality

4.4.1 The context

In both Brazil and India, there was a change in the role of the state in the decades after 1980. But the historical circumstances were different, and so were the consequences for social policy. In Brazil, the military regime was weakened and collapsed in the face of increasingly assertive social movements. A return to democracy was consolidated in the 1988 Constitution, which restored social rights and entitlements that had been suppressed under the dictatorship, and went much further, establishing new rights and provisions for social policies. However initially, in the context of hyperinflation and economic instability, social policy took a back seat. In the wake of the defeat of inflation by the Real Plan, Fernando Henrique Cardoso came to power in 1995 with an agenda that combined economic liberalization with new social policy programmes, including some cash transfer policies aimed at the poor population. But his period of government was hamstrung by an overhang of rising public debt and high interest rates, which led to low rates of economic growth. Moreover, social policy was seen as mainly as subordinate to economic policies, with the exception of education.

India's transition was more gradual, but no less profound. The reduced economic role of the state, starting in the 1980s and accelerating in the 1990s, was not accompanied by any reduction in social policy spending. Indeed, there was an increase in the share of GDP devoted to education in the 1980s (Vijay Shankar and Shah, 2012). But neither was there any substantial investment in social policy to offset the disequalizing effect of market forces. After the introduction of economic reforms in the early 1990s, a succession of governments was more concerned to promote an acceleration of growth than to introduce new social programmes or to broaden the scope of social security. Social policy continued to mainly take the form of 'ad hoc responses to particular demands emanating from groups that (at least temporarily) have acquired some degree of political voice' (Ghosh, 2002).

In 2002 in Brazil and 2004 in India, a political reaction led to the election of governments with greater social commitment. This was especially so in Brazil, where the Workers' Party, brought to power with the support of trade unions and social movements, put in place a series of policies to redistribute resources to the poor, while maintaining relatively conventional macroeconomic policies. In India, the political coalition that came to power in 2004 introduced a number of social policies. These included a 20-per-cent increase in the real national floor minimum wage and, above all, the MGNREGA (which we discuss below), but without directly confronting the private interests that had developed under liberalization.

4.4.2 Public sector expenditure on social policy

In India, the basic character of social policy did not change after 1980, and its share of GDP remained broadly constant. The percentage of Plan expenditure devoted to social services (health, education, welfare, housing, water and programmes for particular groups) hovered between 14 per cent and 16 per cent in the three five year plans between 1975 and 1990. At the beginning of the 1990s, the social sector as a whole accounted for 7.5 per cent of GDP (Graph 4.4.1), of which four-tenths was for education (Graph 4.4.2). And, apart from some increase in pension payments, it remained at much the same level until 2007-08. During this period, total government expenditure first fell as a percentage of GDP, then increased, and then stagnated; social expenditure first rose as a proportion of government expenditure, and then stabilized. There was no long-term trend in either, and the share of GDP devoted to the social sector was not substantially different before and after the economic reform (Joshi, 2006). After 2007, both total government expenditure and the proportion devoted to the social sector rose, with social sector expenditure reaching a little over 10 per cent of GDP after 2009 (Graph 4.4.1). This reflected, in particular, some growth in education, social security and welfare policies, food subsidies, and both urban and rural development (Graph 4.4.2). Since this was a period of rapid growth of GDP, the absolute levels of expenditure rose quite substantially after 2006-07.

To define the social sector, we rely on the categories in the official Ministry of Finance public finance statistics (Government of India, Ministry of Finance, 2015). For the purposes of our estimates, we include in the social sector

- Most of the 'Social and community services' under the heading 'Developmental expenditure' in the public finance accounts (excluding broadcasting, scientific research, and some others);
- 'Rural development' expenditures ('urban development' is already included under social and community services);
- 'Food subsidy' (included in the accounts under 'non-developmental expenditure');
- Two components of 'Social security and welfare', one under 'Non-Developmental expenditure' and the other under 'Social and community services';
- 'Pension and other retirement benefits' under 'Non-Developmental expenditure'.

Public sector pensions and the like are not usually treated as part of the social sector in the Indian literature, but in Brazil all pensions are included with social security expenditures, so we include them in India too to make the data more comparable. Graph 4.4.2 groups these expenditures in five categories, defined in the footnote to the graph.

Direct comparisons between India and Brazil are still delicate, because the concept and accounting of social spending is different in each. For instance, urban and rural development expenditures that are classed as 'social' in India (and include employment creation through public works) may not be treated the same way in Brazil. Nevertheless, the numbers give some indication of the relative size and trend of social sector expenditures in the two countries.

In Brazil, the renewal of political institutions after the fall of the military regime was also reflected in social policy. As we noted above, the 1988 Constitution enlarged the concept of citizenship, consolidating, broadening, and universalizing social rights. To deliver on these rights, public funds for education, health, and social insurance were put in place. The result was a steady rise in the share of

GDP devoted to social policy, rising from a low point of 15 per cent in 1992 to 25 per cent or more over 2009–2014 (Graph 4.4.3). There was a substantial increase in both the 1990s and the 2000s. Within this there was a significant growth of social security spending – from 9 per cent of GDP to 14 per cent of GDP. A universal health programme was put in place, accounting alone for some 5 per cent of GDP by the end of the period.

These social expenditures are incurred at all the levels of the Brazilian federation, not only the central government. This is important, as the 1988 Constitution establishes some minimum rates – 25 per cent for spending on education, for instance, for states and municipalities, whereas the rate for the central government is 18 per cent of net fiscal revenues. This allowed for the expansion not only of the educational services but also of public employment in education, and substantially increased the number of teachers in absolute terms and as a percentage of all employment. In India, too, a great deal of social policy is financed and implemented at state level, with a mix of often overlapping state and central programmes. Because of regional variation in priorities and in implementation, the thrust and effectiveness of social policy is quite different in different parts of the country (Shariff et al., 2002).

Graph 4.4.1. Total Government Expenditure and Social Sector Expenditure as a Percentage of GDP; and Social Sector Expenditure as a Percentage of Total Expenditure, India, 1990/91–2013/14

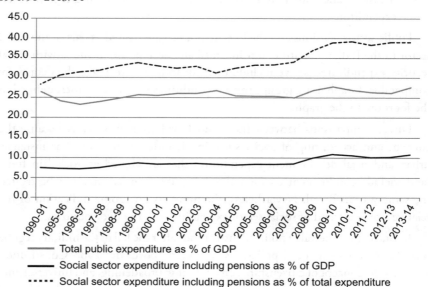

Source: Computed from Indian Public Finance Statistics, Annual Reports, Ministry of Finance, Government of India (http://finmin.nic.in/reports/ipfstat.asp).

Graph 4.4.2. Expenditure on the Social Sector as a Percentage of Gross Domestic Product, India, 1990/91–2013/14

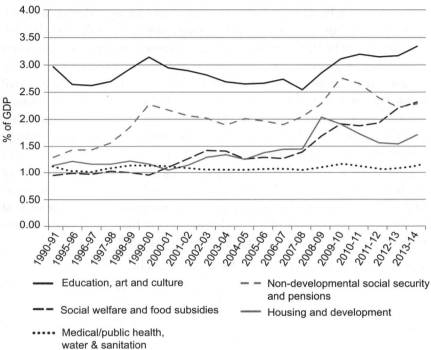

Source: Computed from Indian Public Finance Statistics, Annual Reports, Ministry of Finance, Government of India (http://finmin.nic.in/reports/ipfstat.asp). This extends with more recent data a graph presented in Palriwala and Neetha N. (2011).

Note: The category 'social welfare and food subsidies' includes 'family welfare', 'labour and employment', developmental expenditure on 'social security and welfare (P)' and 'food subsidy'. The category 'housing and development' includes 'housing', 'urban development', and 'rural development' (the last of these includes MGNREGA expenditure). The category 'non-developmental social security and pensions' includes 'pension and other retirement benefits' and non-developmental 'social security and welfare (NP)'.

In this period, then, the clear difference between India and Brazil was in the scale of social policy – the share of GDP devoted to social policy in Brazil averaged around two and a half times that in India. In addition, since 1988, social policy was to a greater degree built on universalistic principles in Brazil. In India, a small minority had access to social insurance in formal work, but the majority depended on a variety of targeted public programmes, mostly aimed at households below the officially defined poverty line (or in the case of affirmative action, defined caste groups). Moves towards universalization in the 2000s were partial, and not accompanied by a commensurate increase in resource commitments. In contrast, while Brazil moved towards a universal coverage principle in 1988, it committed resources on a large scale, though only in the following decades. Of course, the tax burden from this has generated resistance – and some important redistributive programmes like Bolsa Familia and certain benefits for the elderly are means-tested (below) – but the higher levels of output per capita in Brazil provided greater scope for redistribution than in India. So, once the government was fully committed to social policy, its redistributive policies had a significant impact on inequality. In India, in contrast, social policy was less well funded and redistribution aimed mainly to alleviate poverty.

These differences in the scale and shape of state social policies are of course in part the result of different political trajectories and coalitions in the two countries. But they also reflect different structures of the labour market, the higher levels of poverty and the importance of the rural population in India, and more generally the smaller resource base for state action in India than in Brazil.

Graph 4.4.3. Public Social Spending as a Percentage of GDP, Brazil, 1991–2014

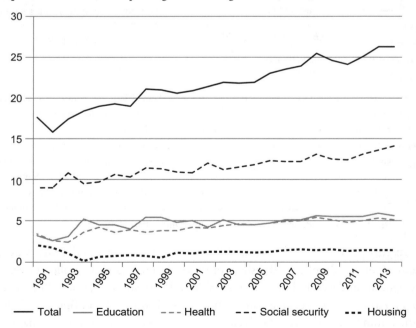

Source: Computed from the Economic Commission for Latin America and the Caribbean Social Expenditure Database.

4.4.3 Social security and social transfers

One of the most striking differences between India and Brazil concerns the reach and design of social security. Public expenditure on social security and social welfare, although rising, accounted for less than 5 per cent of GDP in India in 2013-14 (Graph 4.4.2; sum of the social welfare and social security figures) against 14 per cent in Brazil (Graph 4.4.3). The size of the gap is striking, especially since the Indian figure includes food subsidies and all social and family welfare policies as well as pensions. Before 1980, Brazil had laid a foundation of conventional social security (pensions, health insurance, accident insurance, social assistance) for registered workers. During the 1980s, there was some loss of formal employment, but the 1988 Constitution reinforced the entitlements to social security, and introduced new mechanisms to deliver it. In particular, an important change in the wake of the 1988 Constitution was the establishment of the Workers' Support Fund (FAT). This Fund was (and still is) financed directly by taxes on the revenues of private enterprises and public institutions, which ensured a sizeable and stable source of income to fund unemployment insurance and other labour market policies.

Another breakthrough of the 1988 Constitution relates to the recognition of social assistance as a non-contributory public policy within the Social Security System, laying the foundation for the creation of large-scale cash transfer programmes. This was consolidated in the Single Social Assistance System (SUAS, from the Portuguese *Sistema Único da Assistência Social*) in 2005, which regulates funding and sets the rules for fund allocation and programme implementation. Among the federal social assistance programmes that were created the most important are the Continuous Cash Benefit Programme (BPC, from the Portuguese *Benefício de Prestação Continuada*), the Programme for the Eradication of Child Labour (PETI, from the Portuguese *Programa de Erradicação do Trabalho Infantil*), and the Family Allowance Programme (PBF, from the Portuguese *Programa Bolsa Família*). We discuss the last of these further below.

Despite this formal progress, during the 1990s the share of registered workers with access to the full range of social security stagnated, and the proportion of unregistered workers and the self-employed rose. Some innovative programmes were introduced in parallel with the regular social security system, notably Comunidade Solidária, an attempt to mobilize local actors and communities around a variety of actions to fight poverty, and Bolsa Escola, a programme of cash transfers to households dependent on the school enrolment of children. However, the persistence of high poverty rates throughout the period up to 2002 (Section 4.2) suggests that these programmes had limited impact.

During the 1990s, there was a debate about the form that social policy in Brazil should take. According to one influential line of thought (Barros, Henrique and Mendonça, 2001), Brazil is not a poor country, but an unequal country with a large poor population, and in this situation redistributive policies would be more effective to reduce both income inequality and poverty. The implication was that the design of social policies in Brazil should be reformed, especially with a view to targeting the poor.

This does not detract from the importance of universal policies, which have better redistributive impacts when well designed (Lavinas and Garson, 2004). According to this alternative line of thought, targeting the poor makes sense only if there is an expansion of universal social policies. Otherwise, absolute poverty may fall, and even inequality in terms of income, but without leading to greater social mobility.

This debate is especially important, because social policies in Brazil were historically relegated to a secondary position, subordinated and limited to general guidelines determined by economic policies. Actually, this began to change with the first mandate of Lula, who favoured a model built on the joint design and implementation of social and economic policies. In this view, social policies (including the increase in the purchasing power of the minimum wage) would stimulate the internal market by increasing demand for household consumption. In turn, the acceleration in economic growth with social redistribution would provide a better life for the great mass of the people, raise the supply of wage goods, and create jobs that did not demand high skill levels. The complementarity is such that Kerstenetzky (2012) called them 'economically oriented social policies' and 'socially oriented economic policies'.

After 2002, two other factors came into play. The first was an increasing formalization of the labour market (Section 4.3), which raised the proportion of the workforce with access to regular social security. And, alongside this, a number of complementary programmes were put in place, reflecting the above discussion of targeting in social programmes. Of these, by far the most important was Bolsa Familia (PBF), which grouped together the several cash transfer initiatives of the previous government, enlarged the population covered and increased the value of the benefits.

Launched in 2003, the PBF is a conditional cash transfer programme for poor families that is contingent on medical and nutritional check-ups of children, school enrolment and attendance of children and teenagers aged 7–17 years, and participation in food education programmes. To be eligible for the PBF, the household has to be registered under the *Cad Unico*, a single register that identifies households below an income threshold, and which is used for all federal government social programmes. The cash is transferred, preferably, to the female head of the household, and can be withdrawn using a debit card. The amount transferred to each household varies with the poverty situation and the number of family members.

From about 6.6 million households in 2003, the PBF met its target of 11 million households in 2006. In 2014, it was covering about 14 million households. Expenditure on the PBF amounted to 0.5 per cent of Brazil's GDP in 2014 (Table 4.4.1) and about 2.5 per cent of total government expenditure. The size of the transfers was very different across regions; in the Northeast, they covered almost 50 per cent of the population of some small cities and rural areas, and the cash transfers amounted to more than 50 per cent of the budgets of their municipalities.

Table 4.4.1. Amount Effectively Transferred as Benefits under the Bolsa Familia Programme (Total and % of GDP)

Year	2003	2004	2005	2006	2007	2008	2009	2010	2011	2012	2013	2014
Amount (billion Reais)	0.57	3.79	5.69	8.23	9.95	10.85	13.20	13.68	17.36	21.15	24.89	27.18
% of GDP	0.03	0.19	0.26	0.31	0.33	0.34	0.37	0.37	0.40	0.45	0.48	0.49

Source: Ipeadata (partly from Santos, 2010).

The PBF has led to a reduction in extreme poverty, better health and educational outcomes, as well as a reduction in income inequality between households and regions. In a decade of PBF implementation, extreme poverty was reduced from 9.7 per cent to 4.3 per cent. The PBF was responsible for a 12–18 per cent decrease in the poverty headcount index, and a 24–31 per cent decrease in the squared poverty gap index in 2009 (Higgins, 2012). Soares (2012) also finds that the PBF's effectiveness in reducing inequality has been quite high, especially given the modest amounts transferred. PBF accounts for around 16–21 per cent of the total fall in inequality in Brazil since 2001. However, the bulk of the fall in inequality is explained not by the PBF but by labour income, which increased due to the new jobs created in the formal sector and the increase in the minimum wage over the period (Barbosa et al., 2015). The percentage contribution of each source of revenue to the reduction of inequality varies considerably across regions and even within them, once we separate urban and rural areas.

In India, the reach of regular social security is limited by the small proportion of workers in formal jobs – only about 7 per cent of all workers in 2011-12 (as we saw in Section 4.3), hardly higher than in the 1980s. Efforts to strengthen social security have, therefore, consisted mainly of a series of efforts to transfer resources to the poor, or to extend different aspects of social protection to the unorganized sector or to informal workers (Kannan, 2015). There are two quite different strands here, which reflect the conventional distinction between, on the one hand, social insurance – covering contingencies such as health, old age, accident, etc. – and on the other social assistance, consisting mainly of transfers, which aim to compensate for low incomes.

In India, since before 1980 there has been a mosaic of specific programmes at the national or state level that have provided social assistance, mainly to those below the poverty line. These include ex gratia payments to widows or to the disabled, and a large subsidy programme for housing for the poor (Indira Awas Yojana, now renamed Pradhan Mantri Gramin Awaas Yojana). Other non-contributory schemes include the National Social Assistance Programmes for Pensions (old age, disability, and widow) for poor households introduced in 1995. Some states have successfully implemented a range of such programmes (notably Kerala and Tamil Nadu; Kannan, 2015). Pensions for disadvantaged groups are quite well established, reasonably well implemented, and reach a substantial population (26 million individuals) (Chopra and Pudussery, 2014) – though the amounts paid (by both state and central governments) are quite small. The Midday Meals Programme for school children has made an important contribution to improving child nutrition and encouraging school attendance. The impetus for many of these schemes derives from local campaigns and awareness, sometimes with judicial support, which forces them onto the political agenda (Drèze, 2004).

The most important such programme is the public distribution system or PDS, which provides subsidized food grains to those below the poverty line. Other commodities are available to a varying degree in different parts of the country, but food grains are the most important item. In various forms, this programme has been active since the 1950s. In parts of India where it works well, it has made a substantial contribution to meeting the basic food needs of a large section of the poor population, providing a ration of food grains at 10–20 per cent of market prices. The main problem with the PDS has been its implementation, with substantial possibilities for leakage and corruption, and coverage of the target population which is low in some states. It also implies a large-scale process of public procurement and distribution of food grains, which is not easy to manage. Nevertheless, the PDS has certainly played an important role in reducing the extent of hunger in India.

Like many such programmes, the PDS is targeted at the poor population. Prior to 1997, there was in principle universal access to a ration of subsidized food grains, but in practice only a fraction of the population benefited, because of weak implementation. The 1997 reform aimed to increase the subsidy and concentrate it on the poor. The problem, however, resides in the identification of beneficiaries. Surveys have been conducted from time to time to identify the 'Below Poverty Line' (BPL) population, but the results are much contested, for the criteria to define who is poor and who is not are arbitrary and widely misapplied (Drèze and Sen, 2013), and measurement is subject to many biases. Under the National Food Security Act, 2013, the method of identifying beneficiaries was improved using the results of the Socio-Economic and Caste Census, 2011, and the share of the population covered increased; but it is often argued that universal programmes would be more efficient. However, a universal approach meets considerable political resistance.

Despite its problems, there is strong evidence that the PDS has had a substantial impact. Himanshu and Sen (2013) estimate that food transfers (PDS and Midday Meals Programme) have lifted a significant proportion of households above the poverty line, from 1.3 per cent of the population in 1993-94 to 4.8 per cent in 2011-12. It therefore has certainly helped to contain the rise in inequality. Based on a survey in nine states, Khera (2011) finds that the PDS has made a considerable contribution to food security, with some variation across the country, while in states where it works well a large majority of beneficiaries prefer access to food grains in kind rather than cash transfers.

The other aspect of social security, concerned with protection against contingencies for unorganized sector workers, has mainly been dealt with on an ad hoc occupational or local basis, with the creation of welfare funds and limited schemes to provide accident or health insurance. The National Commission on Enterprises in the Unorganized Sector (NCEUS; Section 4.3) made a number of recommendations on how to extend social protection on an essentially non-contributory basis (NCEUS, 2008). Policy follow-up was at best partial, but it did lead to the passing of the Unorganized Workers Social Security Act, 2008, which provides the beginnings of a universal minimum pension scheme for those below the poverty line, and basic health insurance for unorganized sector households. While authors of this idea have been critical of its limited implementation (Kannan, 2015), there is evidence of increasing coverage (to 42 per cent of the BPL population in 2012).

These social policy initiatives in India are less comprehensive than in Brazil. But this is partly because there is a tradition in India, almost absent in Brazil, of large-scale public works programmes as a means of transferring incomes to the poor through employment creation. As noted in Section 3.4 above, such efforts have a long history, and they continued to be part of the standard set of policy instruments after the 1980s, at both national and state levels, in particular as a response to drought, famine, or seasonal unemployment. A particularly important manifestation was the Maharashtra Employment Guarantee Scheme, which started at the end of the 1970s (Acharya, 1990). The successful implementation of the concept of an employment guarantee in Maharashtra provided the model for the Mahatma Gandhi National Rural Employment Guarantee Act, 2005 (MGNREGA), a central element of social policy in the past decade.

The MGNREGA guarantees a minimum of 100 days of unskilled, waged employment (or in the absence of available employment, an unemployment allowance) to each rural household in a year. The employment provided is in local public works projects, based on bottom-up village development planning. The programme is self-targeting and provides beneficiaries a stipulated daily wage set for each state.

The MGNREGA was more comprehensive than its predecessors, and also more effective due to its legally binding nature. In particular, it establishes a right to employment. Since 2008-09, it has been providing over two billion person-days of employment per year (Table 4.4.2). By 2010-11, it was reaching almost 40 per cent of rural households (Pankaj, 2012, p. 19). Expenditure on MGNREGA as a percentage of GDP peaked at around 0.6 per cent in 2009-10, though it fell to around 0.3 per cent in 2014-15, as the programme declined somewhat and GDP rose (Chari 2014; Jagannath 2014; India, Ministry of Rural Development, 2016).

Extensive evaluation of the MGNREGA suggests that employment guarantee remains an aspiration rather than a reality in many parts of the country (Dutta et al., 2012), and the programme is subject to a variety of criticisms (Shah, 2015). Nevertheless, it has provided a safety net for the rural poor, led to reduction in poverty and hunger, and created physical infrastructure in rural areas. Women have benefited as much as men (Table 4.4.2), and there has been a closing of gender wage gaps (Mehtabul, 2012). It has had multiplier effects on aspects such as rural-urban migration, and the daily payment under MGNREGA has also served as a de facto minimum wage in many areas (Ghosh, 2014).

The proportion of Scheduled Castes and Tribes participating in the MGNREGA has also been substantially higher than their proportion of the general population, though their participation rates have been declining more recently (Table 4.4.2).

Table 4.4.2. Progress and Performance of MGNREGA, 2006/07–2013/14

	2006-07	2007-08	2008-09	2009-10	2010-11	2011-12	2012-13	2013-14
Percentage of women beneficiaries	40	43	45	49	48	48	51	53
Percentage of Scheduled Caste (SC) beneficiaries	25	27	29	30	31	22	22	23
Percentage of Scheduled Tribe (ST) beneficiaries	36	29	25	22	21	18	18	17
Total employment provided (million person days)	905.5	1,435.9	2,163	2,835.9	2,571.5	2,187.6	2,304.8	2,202.2

Source: Ministry of Rural Development, Government of India, in Papola and Sahu (2012); updated with information from Ministry of Rural Development website.

The MGNREGA has clearly helped in increasing employment and reducing poverty. Even though its link with inequality is difficult to establish, it can be said that it has helped to prevent further deepening of inequalities, and its impact on rural wages has probably been an important factor in the decline of wage inequality in rural areas after 2004-05. Nevertheless, the resources allocated to the programme have been declining and it appears to be given lower priority by the BJP government elected in 2014.

4.4.4   Labour market policy

As noted above, employment programmes have played a significant role in social policy in India, but very little in Brazil. However, for other labour market policies the reverse is true – they have been seen, to a much greater extent in Brazil than in India, as important aspects of social policy with a bearing on inequality.

This statement needs a little qualification. Employment protection legislation in India, for example, clearly has a social policy objective. And social security policy cannot be divorced from the analysis of the labour market. But – with the important exception of job reservations, which we discuss below – labour market policy has been a less significant instrument in efforts to reduce inequality or poverty in India. Likewise, with respect to employment policy in Brazil, while there have been employment programmes such as PROGER (Generation of Employment and Income Programme from the Portuguese *Programa Geração de Emprego e Renda*), which supports micro and small enterprises, these are rather peripheral to the main thrust of social policy.

However, other types of intervention in the labour market have played a central role in social policy in Brazil. This is particularly so for minimum wages and, to a lesser extent, training (both of which were discussed in Section 4.3). Minimum wage policy alone is estimated to account for 35 per cent of the fall in inequality of household income between 1995 and 2014 (Foguel, 2016).

There is one other labour market policy that should be discussed in this context because of its importance in India: job reservations for disadvantaged groups. Affirmative action for disadvantaged social groups has been a constant theme in India since colonial times, and increasing proportions of public sector jobs, and positions in public educational institutions, are reserved for both deprived and intermediate caste groups. Initially foreseen in the Constitution of India for SCs and STs (as discussed in Section 3.4) reservations were extended in 1992 to many OBCs, consisting of a large number of middle or poor castes, on the basis of the Mandal Commission Report (Government of India, 1980).

In some states, reservations or preferences were also extended to Muslims, many of whom were economically disadvantaged and included in the OBC category, as was recommended by another committee (the Sachar Committee) in 2006. Public sector job reservations for SCs were initially set at 15 per cent, and for STs at 7.5 per cent, with an additional 27 per cent reserved for OBCs, though there is some variation across states and types of employment. The Supreme Court of India has capped reservations at a maximum of 50 per cent, though this has been exceeded in some states.

This policy is of course intended to compensate for the disadvantage of particular groups, and it has certainly had some impact, as the share of SCs and STs in public sector employment has risen over time. But it is confined to the public sector, which has a small and shrinking share of all employment. Occasional suggestions that the policy should be extended to the private sector are fiercely resisted. But, at the same time, this policy clearly contributes to the fragmentation of the labour market, as each group attempts to claim its share of jobs. It is in some sense an extreme case of the targeting of social policies, and its effectiveness in reducing inequality has to be questioned, since SCs and STs are still relatively disadvantaged, even in the public sector, more than 60 years after the policy was introduced. Implementation of the policy becomes complex as efforts are made to prevent the benefits being captured by a 'creamy layer' of better-off groups among the disadvantaged castes, and it arguably reinforces caste identities and conflicts rather than gradually eliminating them.

Unlike caste in India, state action to tackle racial inequality in Brazil has not relied on job reservations, rather focusing on improving access to quality education for non-whites (below), and – together with unions – encouraging equality practices in companies (Cacciamali et al., 2009). In addition, the Brazilian government criminalizes discrimination practices. In 2010, the federal government created the Secretariat for Policies to Promote Racial Equality (SEPPIR in Portuguese: *Secretaria para a Promoção da Igualdade Racial*), which enacted the Racial Equality Statute (in Portuguese *Estatuto da Igualdade Racial*, Law No. 12, 288, of July 20, 2010). In 2013, the Secretariat established the National System for the Promotion of Racial Equality (in Portuguese *Sistema Nacional para a Promoção da Igualdade Racial* (SINAPIR) regulated by Decree No. 8136/2013). This system organizes and coordinates institutional spaces to implement policies and services to overcome racial inequalities in general, especially those faced by traditional African descendants' communities. We return to these issues in Section 5.3.

4.4.5   Education and health

Education

Education policy of course plays a central role in determining the distribution of life chances and labour market inequality. Section 5.4 explores the educational patterns and outcomes in the two countries, and their connections with the labour market, and we only briefly discuss some basic features of education policy here.

In India, educational performance has been weak in international comparison (Drèze and Sen, 2013). A slow expansion of education in the decades after independence (Section 3.4) was followed by a renewed effort in the 1980s, notably through the New Education Policy under the Rajiv Gandhi government in 1986, which paid special attention to women, SCs and STs, and to school infrastructure. Public spending on education as a proportion of GDP rose during this decade. Nevertheless, after 1990 it remained stuck at 2.5–3 per cent of GDP until 2007-08, not much more than half of that in Brazil, despite several major initiatives. Although there was progress towards universal primary schooling, and despite the investments made in education, imbalances between regions, genders, and rural and urban areas remained stark. In 2013, Drèze and Sen wrote that 'school education in India is in a terrible state' (ibid., p. 139).

A watershed in the Indian education landscape was the Right to Education Act, which was introduced in 2009. The Act makes it a right for all children in the 6–14 age group to receive free and compulsory education, and it also mandates private schools to reserve 25 per cent of their places for the 'weaker' sections. However, the Act does not address the quality of education, which remains a major problem. Panchayati Raj Institutions (local self-governance institutions) are also engaged in literacy efforts and adult education, but their effectiveness is questionable. Nevertheless, expenditure on education as a proportion of GDP has been rising after the passage of the Act (Graph 4.4.2). Schemes targeting both secondary and higher education were launched in the early 2010s, and the present government is developing a new education policy, though progress has been slow.

There has been an increasing emphasis on privatization, and the state seems to be withdrawing from some aspects of the provisioning for education, especially at the higher levels. This is of concern, because the privatization of education thus far has been mainly extractive, with little added value to quality. Moreover, the ability of households to invest in private education is a direct reflection of their economic status; so the expansion of the private system, especially at the post-secondary level, is an important factor perpetuating inequality across generations. As schooling at the lower levels has universalized, the key inequalities have moved up the education system, first to secondary and then to tertiary levels. Further privatization and increase in costs of education are likely to make the education system even more exclusionary.

In Brazil, education is guaranteed as a citizen's right and as a state duty. The federal government's current educational policy was systematized by the Education Development Plan (PDE from the Portuguese *Plano de Desenvolvimento da Educação*) in 2007, an effort to fight poor performance in basic education and broaden access to non-obligatory schooling levels. In secondary education, a nationwide examination was established in 1998, the ENEM (from the Portuguese *Exame Nacional do Ensino Médio*). It was reformulated in 2009, and it is used nowadays for admission to public federal universities and private universities. The expansion of the higher education system started to be reinforced in 1994 with significant participation of the private sector. In the 2000s, several public education institutions were created, mostly focused on technical and technological education, and in regions where the supply was insufficient, especially in the Northeast and North. But, as Graph 4.4.3 shows, there has been only a very slow increase in the share of GDP devoted to public expenditure on education.

The guidelines, goals, and strategies for educational policy until 2024 were laid out in 2014 in the National Education Plan (PNE, from the Portuguese *Plano Nacional de Educação*). Among the various elements of the Plan, a major focus is the discussion and development of the Common National Base Curriculum, which is the standardization of the academic curriculum in each segment of basic education into four areas: languages, mathematics, natural sciences, and humanities. However, it has proved difficult to reach a consensus on the content of the proposed curriculum.

The importance of the private sector for expanding higher education has obvious consequences for inequality, since access depends on ability to pay. As a result, a number of government programmes have been created to offset disadvantage. The University for All Programme (ProUni, from the Portuguese *Programa Universidade para Todos*), started in 2004, provides full or partial scholarships in private higher education institutions for students coming from poor households. The Federal Universities Restructuring and Expansion Plans Support Programme (Reuni, from the Portuguese *Programa de Apoio a Planos de Reestruturação e Expansão das Universidades Federais*), created in 2007, was successful in dramatically increasing access to and keeping students in higher education. And the Student Financing Fund (Fies, from the Portuguese *Fundo de Financiamento Estudantil*), which started in 2010, provides loans to finance students in fee-paying higher education.

One notable achievement of the Brazilian educational system has been that the average educational attainment of women is higher than that of men, and the gap is widening.

Both Brazil and India also attempt to compensate for economic disadvantage by reserving places in educational institutions, especially at the higher education level. In India, since 1982, reservations in public educational institutions have paralleled those in public sector jobs, and a variety of scholarships and other programmes are targeted at disadvantaged groups. However, as in the labour market, the overall impact is weakened by the growth of private education, where reservations do not apply. It was in recognition of that problem that the Right to Education Act imposed quotas for weaker sections on private educational institutions (as noted above). However, it is not clear how effectively this is enforced. In Brazil too, and unlike in the labour market, there are affirmative action policies in public educational institutions, most of which adhere to a quota system for disadvantaged social groups, such as blacks, indigenous groups, and public school students, or implement screening and place-filling procedures. However, as discussed in Section 5.4, while gaps between blacks and whites in educational achievement are narrowing at lower and middle educational levels, the change is less significant at the tertiary level, suggesting that the impact of these policies is still limited, even though not negligible.

Health

In Brazil, before the 1980s, access to adequate health services was to a large degree associated with formal employment. The 1988 Constitution cut this tie, recognized the right to health (like that to education) as inherent in citizenship and a state duty, and made it obligatory for the state to provide for the health needs of every individual. This broader access to and coverage of health services was made possible with the creation of the Single System of Health (SUS, from Portuguese *Sistema Único de Saúde*), a public network of health-related actions and services, based on universal and equal access and decentralized management. Nonetheless, the health system faces funding and management problems. As shown in Graph 4.4.3, public health spending as a percentage of GDP grew consistently, but slowly, from 3.4 per cent of GDP in 1991 to 5.1 per cent in 2014. But service providers are poorly paid, and there is limited availability of skilled professionals for the public health system. Despite these problems, the system is nationwide and integrated, and provides services for all medical specializations. The creation of the Pact for Health (*Pacto pela Saúde*) in 2006 and of the More Health Plan (*Plano Mais Saúde*) in 2007 was an attempt to meet the challenge of universal health care, which still remains. There are also partnerships established with public or private non-profit organizations through the Brazilian Popular Pharmacy Programme (*Farmácia Popular do Brasil*) in 2004, which provides free medication for chronic diseases and other essential medicines at low cost.

India has made much less progress. Before the 1980s, health policy had relied on the five year plans. As a consequence of the Alma Ata Declaration on primary health, a National Health Policy was drawn up in 1983. It was a break from the past, as it put emphasis on quality and efficiency, rather than targets, and also invited a much larger role from the private sector. However, with respect to implementation, it could not live up to its progressive tone. But the next decade did see substantial investment in health infrastructure in rural areas, even though problems of quality and lack of manpower remained. Privatization of health care took place at a rapid pace during this period, and various subsidies and soft loans were given to private players. A number of new paradigms – such as specialization, health for the underprivileged, monitoring, and state-specific strategies – became part of health policy discourse, but quality and efficiency did not improve (Duggal, 2001).

There has been an acknowledged shift in perspective towards more active social health policy since the 2000s. The National Rural Health Mission was launched in 2005, and in 2013 was expanded to include both rural and urban areas – it also commits to more than doubling health expenditure to reach 2–3 per cent of GDP (Srivastava, 2013). But (and as can be seen from Graph 4.4.2), since 1990 the actual share has been more or less constant at a little over 1 per cent, far below the level in Brazil. Another major development was the introduction in 2008 of the cashless health insurance policy extended to BPL households and unorganized sector workers. This programme, the Rashtriya Swasth Bima Yojana, is based on government payments to private health insurance companies. By the end of 2013, more than 35 million households had been enrolled in the scheme.

The rapid growth of the private health sector has in part substituted for shortfalls in the public system, but brings with it a variety of dangers (Drèze and Sen, 2013). In particular, it reinforces inequality in access to health services, and in their quality. In reality, there is world-class healthcare available for those who are able to pay, but this is only true for a fraction of the population. Meanwhile, among the reasons for excessive indebtedness among the poor, large private health expenditures are distressingly common.

4.4.6 Summing up

We can see that there are fundamental differences in approach to social policy between Brazil and India, differences which in part derive from the power and orientation of the state, but which are also embedded in the ways public policy is conceived. These condition the success and failure of policies in particular domains, and directly affect the capacity of the state to influence inequality.

- First, the share of GDP devoted to social policy is much greater in Brazil.
- Second, in Brazil the core of social policy is provided by conventional social security, while in India it is built around need-based programmes.
- Third, social policy in India is to a large extent aimed at poverty reduction, rather than inequality, whereas in Brazil, reducing inequality is also seen as a valid goal in its own right.
- Fourth, in India programmes tend to be more targeted and particularistic, while in Brazil they tend to be based on a principle of universal access (though it is true that universalistic, rights-based principles have gained ground in India, while the PBF and some other programmes in Brazil select beneficiaries on the basis of an income criterion).
- Fifth, India has a tradition of employment creation in public works as a means of transferring resources to the poor, which is almost absent in Brazil. In Brazil, on the other hand, labour market policy, even though concentrated on passive policies (unemployment insurance) and the minimum wage, has tried to establish active programmes aimed at the poor population (such as the training programme PRONATEC, discussed in Section 4.3), much more than in India.

These differences in framework and philosophy make it rather risky to make direct comparisons between the effectiveness of particular policies in the two countries, because a policy instrument that works in one setting may well fail in another. That is, clusters of policies need to be seen together. There is, for instance, a tendency for Bolsa Familia in Brazil to be compared with MGNREGA in India as a means for transferring resources to the poor and reducing inequality. But Bolsa Familia works in a context where there is a wider social security system, with particular family structures and educational opportunities, trade union organizations, and legal protections in the labour market. The MGNREGA operates in a rural context with seasonal unemployment where other social security instruments are lacking and legal protections are weak, but there is a public distribution system providing food subsidies, housing programmes, and other local policies. Moreover, cash transfers, wage policies, education policies, employment policies, and effective labour market regulation do not reach the same populations, so multiple measures of inequality are needed to capture and compare their impacts.

Clearly, it is the set of policies as a whole that needs to be compared, even if they are not designed as a coherent whole. The reality is that efforts to reduce inequality are only likely to be successful where a package of complementary policies is put in place.

The effectiveness of implementation also has to be part of the comparison. In India, social programmes have long been plagued by high levels of corruption and leakage, though there is evidence of improvement in recent years (for instance Khera (2011) and the comments above on the PDS). There is currently a move towards the use of a new system, which involves a unique personal number for all individuals along with biometric information in a central database (Aadhaar), to authenticate the identity of those who are entitled to benefits under some social programmes. Payments would then be made directly to Aadhaar-linked bank accounts (Economic Survey, 2015–16, Volume 1, Chapter 3). This system is expected to reduce leakages and reduce costs but in rural India, especially in some of the less developed parts of the country, a system that relies on new technologies, connectivity, and personal bank accounts risks excluding many from their entitlements (Drèze, 2016b). In Brazil, the social policy system already involves identification of beneficiaries through individual identity numbers (CPF from Portuguese *Cadastro de Pessoas Físicas*) and household registration (the CadUnico register, which also contains information such as income levels used to establish entitlement), and payments through bank cards. The technology is less ambitious than that proposed in India, the reach of the banking system greater, and the population more urban. As a result, the system functions quite effectively, with relatively low levels of exclusion and fraud.

In India, for much of the period since independence it could be said that – formal sector social security apart – most social policy could hardly be distinguished from other policies aimed at poverty alleviation and development. Certainly food subsidies and public works programmes could be seen in that way. Policies for health and education were far from universal. This started to change in the 1980s, and some states made real progress. However, it is in the 2000s that social policies started to be expanded to the point where they began to have a significant impact across the country. The 2000s also saw the transformation of some social policy goals into enforceable rights – such as the right to education, 100 days of employment under the MGNREGA, and the National Food Security Act – reflecting many years of campaigning and advocacy by pressure groups. There was also a visible increase in the resources devoted to social policy after 2007. While the social policies in themselves have not reversed the trend towards greater inequality, they have certainly provided a brake.

In Brazil, the foundation of declining inequality in the first decade of this century was rising minimum wages, the large-scale creation of formal employment, expansion of universal social policies (education and health), social benefits linked to the minimum wage (BPC and rural pensions), cash transfers through Bolsa Familia, and a variety of local policies, including microcredit schemes, creation of cooperatives, training, and other areas. The promulgation of the 1988 Federal Constitution was a social policy milestone in Brazil. The definition of social security and the recognition of social rights and respective state duties led to substantive broadening of access to public services. These actions have increased the numbers of the socially insured, especially in rural areas; secured a universal right to health; and widened access to education to the population as a whole, particularly secondary and higher education for the low-medium strata of the population. Moreover, cash transfer programmes helped to reduce poverty and income inequality, especially from the 2000s on. However, most social policy areas suffer from a chronic problem concerning the lack of societal participation in their management, while funding for the system's expansion requires the establishment of a new political pact between local, state, and federal levels of government to define their budgetary contributions. These crucial challenges must be tackled if there is to be a more consistent reduction of the country's inequalities, for which a tax reform – changing the regressive nature of the system – seems to be a precondition.

One can see some elements of convergence between India and Brazil. In particular, the move towards a rights-based approach is common to both. Nevertheless, large differences in scope, priority, and effectiveness remain. Cash transfers are regarded as effective mechanisms in Brazil, but are contested in India, where they are seen as a way to marketize processes that are not well managed by the market. Moreover, in both countries, existing policies have created lobbies and interest groups that are resistant to change. Universal programmes are less widespread in India, where group identities are stronger. Nevertheless, in both countries it is clear that social policy has played an essential role in dealing with unacceptable inequalities.

5

Key Divides and Cleavages
Ruptures, Continuities, or Adaptation?

The historical and structural forces that we have discussed in the preceding chapters mould the trajectories of economies and societies, but they act along with other factors, divides, and cleavages present in each society that have their own influence on the pattern of inequality. These different forces are not independent of the growth regime, but they reflect distinct and persistent social relationships that merit separate analysis. In this section, we look at four factors. The first is gender, and the inequalities with which it is associated. The second is regional inequality. The third relates to identity in the form of race, caste, community, or tribe. And the fourth is education. As we see below, these four dimensions of inequality cannot be treated in the same way. Gender inequality is by its nature pervasive, and the same is true of race and tribe and in India, caste, but in ways which take different forms at different times and in different places. Regional inequality may be intrinsic to the growth regime, which more often than not takes advantage of regional disparities; at the same time, it is intertwined with gender, racial, and educational inequalities, which vary across the territory. And education is about raising capabilities as much as about identity, but it also plays a role in the creation or perpetuation of labour market inequality.

This chapter looks at each of these factors, separated for the sake of clarity, in the context of the long term historical analysis presented in preceding chapters. It explores the contribution of each factor to labour market inequality, comparing the patterns and trends in the two countries since the 1980s. A final section brings these elements together in an exploratory multivariate analysis.

5.1 Gender Inequality and the Labour Market Insertion of Women[1]

Section 4.3 reviewed overall labour market structures and outcomes, but labour market patterns are sharply differentiated by sex. Gender equality in the labour market depends on the nature of women's inclusion, on how women reconcile their productive and reproductive roles, and on the kind of employment they have access to. This is conditioned by economic, social, and cultural factors. This section looks into the differences and similarities in women's employment in Brazil and India. But, first, we briefly review the evolution of four factors that impinge on female labour force participation: fertility rate, place of residence, educational status, and care regime.

5.1.1 Four factors impinging on female labour force participation

Fertility

In 1950, Brazil and India had a similar total fertility rate (TFR)[2] – around six children per woman. Fertility has declined in both countries since the 1960s, but faster in Brazil than in India. By 2010-11, the TFR was 1.8 in Brazil and 2.4 in India (Graph 5.1.1).

In India, where a family planning policy has been in place since the 1950s, there was initially little change in fertility. In the 1970s, drastic steps – such as compulsory sterilization – were taken to curb fertility, which resulted in popular resistance and a setback to the programme. However, by the end of the 1980s, a notable fertility decline was observed in all parts of the country and in all sections of the population, though to varying degrees (Kulkarni, 2011). But the preference for sons translated into a relative neglect of the girl child and, more recently, into sex-selective abortions,[3] made possible by technological progress, all of which led to a sex ratio that was unfavourable to women.[4] The decline in the sex ratio was particularly sharp in richer Indian states such as Punjab, Haryana, Gujarat, and Maharashtra (Sen, 2001).

---

[1] This section was prepared by Janine Rodgers.

[2] Total fertility rate measures the average number of children that would be born per woman in a population if all women lived to the end of their childbearing years.

[3] Though sex-selective abortions are illegal, ways of bypassing the law have been developed.

[4] The female-male ratio of the population under age 6 fell from 94.5 girls per 100 boys in 1991 to 92.7 girls per 100 boys in 2001 (Sen, 2001).

Graph 5.1.1. Total Fertility Rate, Brazil and India, 1950–2011

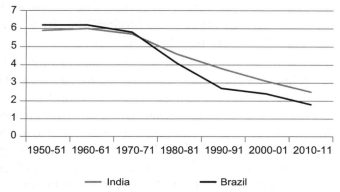

Source: World Population Prospects, United Nations Population Division.

In Brazil, demographic changes occurred despite the absence of an official family planning policy. Abortion was illegal, and the Catholic Church was opposed to birth control, but Brazilian women embraced family planning any way they could. The rapid decline in fertility was achieved primarily through abortion[5] and female sterilization. The decrease in fertility has been pervasive, and has extended through all social strata, racial groups, and regions, though fertility remains higher in the Northeast (Martine, 1996; Goldani, 2001).

In the two countries, there is an inverse relation between fertility and both income and education (Berquó and Cavenaghi, 2005 and 2014; Drèze and Murthi, 2001; Kaur, 2000).

Urbanization[6]

The place of residence is important, as economic activities and access to services differ in rural and urban environments. At the time of the 2001 Census, the majority of Indian women (71 per cent) aged 15 to 64 lived in rural areas, while the overwhelming majority of Brazilian women (84 per cent) lived in urban areas.[7]

Brazil experienced an early and fast urban transition. The redistribution of population within the country followed two directions: a rural-urban stream – the most important – and a frontier expansion towards the interior. A characteristic

---

[5] Estimates of abortion for Brazil in 1996 vary between 800,000 and 1.1 million (Goldani, 2001).

[6] The definition of 'urban' varies between India and Brazil, but the urbanization gap is so wide that the broad trends still hold true.

[7] Percentages have been calculated based on data from the United Nations Statistics Division (http://data.un.org, accessed on 12 July 2014).

of rural-urban migration was the higher rate of female out-migration from rural areas, especially among younger age groups. This process resulted in a 'masculinization' of rural areas (Martine and McGranahan, 2010). In 2000, the urban sex ratio was 1062 women per 1000 men.

In contrast, urbanization in India has been slow and its growth exclusionary. The urban space has become increasingly unaffordable for rural people because of land prices, lack of access to basic services, and regular slum clearances (Kundu, 2012). Migration for work is strongly gendered, but in contrast to Brazil more men than women migrate to towns. Women and children tend to stay behind in their village of origin, while men seek to diversify their activities to supplement or improve household income. This has resulted in a 'feminization' of agriculture. In 2001, the sex ratio in urban areas was 900 women per 1000 men.

Educational attainment

In 1980, men were better educated than women in both countries. But literacy rates were much higher in Brazil than in India – 76 per cent for adult men and 73 per cent for adult women in Brazil, against 55 per cent for adult men and 25 per cent for adult women in India. In Brazil, the gender literacy gap was reversed in the 1980s and, nowadays, women are more educated than men. In India, though the adult female literacy rate doubled between 1980 and 2007, the gender gap remains substantial (25 percentage points) (World Bank, World Development Indicators).

Differences in education are reflected in the distribution of the labour forces by educational attainment (Graph 5.1.2).

In 2010-11, 60 per cent of female workers in India either had no education or had not completed primary education; in Brazil, this proportion did not exceed 7 per cent. Conversely, the share of the female labour force with either secondary or tertiary education was 61 per cent in Brazil and 27 per cent in India. In India, the relationship between female labour force participation and education interacts with factors such as class and caste, and tends to follow a U-shaped curve (Chatterjee et al., 2013; Klasen and Pieters, 2012). In Brazil, it interacts with race and follows an ascending trend (Bruschini, 2007; Barbosa, 2014).

In 2010, in Brazil, the average number of years of schooling was higher among female workers (8.8 years) than among male workers (7.7 years).[8] It is interesting that the educational profile of the Indian female labour force in 2010 was fairly similar to that of the Brazilian female labour force in 1995.

---

[8] IBGE: *Síntese de Indicadores Sociais 2010*, Graph 9.6, p. 254.

Graph 5.1.2. Labour Force Distribution by Educational Attainment, Brazil and India 1994–2011 (%)

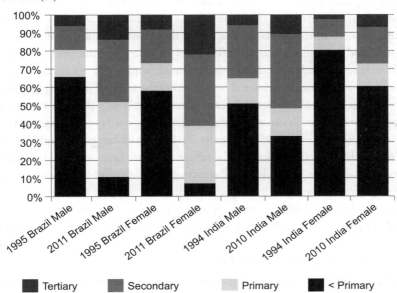

Source: ILO-KILM, 8th Edition, Table 3.

Care regime

Women perform the bulk of reproductive and care tasks. This is crucial to their role in the economy, as it impacts their ability to seek paid work. How problems of care are addressed in a society has important implications for the achievement of gender equality. Care can be provided by the family, the state, the market, and social networks (the 'care diamond'; see Razavi, 2007).

In Brazil, there has been substantial investment in day-care facilities, and this has had a direct impact on women's employment. Crèches and pre-school institutions have enabled mothers to work, lengthen their working time, and aspire to better terms of employment (Sorj and Fontes, 2009). Since the late 1970s there has been a significant expansion of public crèches and pre-school nurseries. However, their number remained insufficient, and by 2005 almost half of the available places were provided by private institutions. The impact of day-care facilities has permeated all social classes, with poorer families benefiting more, as higher income strata also had the option of alternative care strategies such as paid domestic help. However nowadays an increasing number of middle-class families show a preference for paid crèches.

In India, the ideology of 'gendered familialism' in public discourse and policy, which emphasizes care as a familial and female responsibility, is central to the dynamics of care practices. The care regime is essentially an 'ad hoc summation of informal, stratified practices' shaped by the economic and social inequalities of work and livelihoods and by deficiencies in state economic and social policy (Palriwala and Neetha N., 2011). Institutional support to reconcile work and family responsibilities is weak and mostly takes the form of poorly-implemented government policies. Childcare entered government policy through a concern to improve nutrition levels and lower infant and child mortality rates (Integrated Child Development Scheme-ICDS), and enhance 'human resources' through education (Early Childhood Education-ECE) rather than to help women to reconcile work and family responsibilities. Those programmes suffer from poor coverage, bad implementation, and inadequate funding. So support for care takes place mainly within the family context. It is provided by members of the extended family or paid help, but the market provision of care is growing in urban areas.

5.1.2 Labour force participation

The labour force participation of women remains well below that of men in both countries (Graph 5.1.3). Men's long-term trends in participation have been similar in the two countries – above 80 per cent of the adult population and slowly decreasing – but those of women have been different. Women's participation has increased in Brazil while it has stagnated and even decreased, recently, in India. In 1980, the gender gap in participation in both countries was substantial and of similar magnitude: 53 percentage points in Brazil and 54 percentage points in India. Thirty years later, the gap had been cut by half in Brazil but remained wide in India. In 2010, the female labour force participation rate in India (29 per cent) was half that in Brazil (59 per cent).

Brazil has thus experienced a substantial increase in female labour force participation since the mid-1970s. The increase has affected all age groups and the peak of participation is in the 30–39 age group (Barbosa, 2014). In recent decades, important changes occurred in the family structure. There has been an increase in the number of female-headed households and in the number of families with two breadwinners. This has been reflected in the profile of the female labour force: the proportion of older women and married women with children has increased (Bruschini, 2007).

In India, female labour force participation has historically been low in international terms, but the current low level remains a puzzle. Why has it remained so low despite rapid economic growth, rising education levels, and decreasing fertility? Several explanations have been put forward: undercounting of women's activities; social norms and legal entitlements that deny or restrict women's access to resources such as land, credit, skill training, and education; an education effect; and an income effect. But a major reason has been the lack of employment opportunities for women (Neetha N., 2009; Chandrashekar and Ghosh, 2011; Sankaran and Madhav, 2011; Hirway, 2012; Kannan and Raveendran, 2012; Chatterjee et al., 2015;).

Graph 5.1.3. Labour Force Participation Rate, Females and Males Aged 15+, Brazil and India, 1980-81 to 2010 (%)

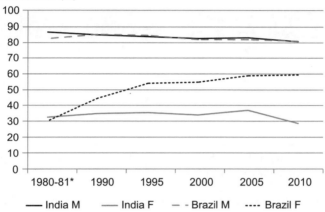

Source: ILO-KILM, 8th edition, Table 1a, ILO estimates.
Note: *1980-81 figures are taken from Table 1b based on national estimates.

In India, since 1990 the secular trend of female participation has been downwards in all age groups, more so among the young, as girls stay longer in education. The peak of participation is in the 35–44 age group, later than in Brazil. In rural areas, social norms impose some restrictions on the mobility of young women, and women join the labour force in their post-reproductive years (Rustagi, 2010). Before the 1990s, workforce participation was relatively stable, but in the post-liberalization period, the amplitude of fluctuations around the long-term trend has increased.[9] A peculiar feature of female employment has been the counter-cyclical responsiveness of women's work participation to economic fluctuations. This is true for a majority of workers who might be classified as 'reserve' labour, that is, women, children, and the elderly (Himanshu, 2011).

---

[9] In rural India, fluctuations are of a much bigger magnitude than in urban areas, as employment is seasonal and women tend to enter the labour force at times of economic hardship ('distress employment') and exit it when the situation improves.

Rural-urban differences in women's labour force participation rates are significant (Table 5.1.1). Participation has been higher in rural areas than in urban areas, but this pattern was reversed in Brazil in 2011. In India, labour force participation of women in urban areas has always been substantially lower and more stable than in rural areas. In recent years, female labour force participation has been declining in rural areas, but has remained stable in urban areas. However, in urban Brazil, the female labour force participation rate is more than three times that in urban India.

Table 5.1.1. Female Labour Force Participation (15+) by Location, Brazil and India (%)

	1993–95	1999–2001	2004–05	2011–12
Brazil rural	64	60	64	53
Brazil urban	51	53	57	55
India rural	33	30	33	25
India urban	16	15	18	16

Source: For Brazil, computed on the basis of IBGE/PNAD data. For India, NSS Employment and Unemployment Reports, various rounds.

In Brazil the highest rate of female labour force participation is found among the so-called 'developing middle class',[10] or the segment of the working class that has been able to increase and diversify its consumption thanks to the rise in real income. In contrast, in India, the peak of female participation is found among the poorest segments of the population (ILO-KILM, 8th edition). This shows that the relation of women to the labour market is different in the two countries. For a majority of women in Brazil, paid work is an empowerment strategy, while for low-income women in India an economic activity is a poverty alleviation strategy. Nevertheless, there is a small group in India, especially women with some education, for whom work is empowerment.

Unemployment

In both countries, unemployment figures disaggregated by sex show that women are more affected by unemployment than men (Graph 5.1.4). But the gender gap is much wider in Brazil, where unemployment plays a different and more important role in labour market adjustment (Section 4.3).

---

[10] 'Developing middle class' = between 4 and 13 US dollars per capita per day, PPP (Source: ILO-KILM 8th Edition, Table 18b).

In India, the unemployment gender gap started to increase after 2000. On the one hand, there is an aspiration-reality mismatch among the better educated for lack of acceptable jobs outside agriculture. Young women and men, who are encouraged to pursue secondary education, aspire to a regular white-collar job. But new jobs are created mostly in the informal sector. This is a problem that the state needs to address to reap the benefits of the demographic dividend. On the other hand, manufacturing employment declined during the second half of the 2000s, and women workers, in particular in export-oriented industries such as textiles and garments, constituted the majority of workers who lost their jobs (Thomas, 2012).

In Brazil, although women have always had higher unemployment rates than men, the gender gap started to widen in the 1990s, which shows that the opening process of the Brazilian economy has affected men and women in different ways (Menezes-Filho and Scorzafave, 2009). The evolution of unemployment by level of education shows that all groups experienced a rise in unemployment, but the group with 8–11 years of schooling was the most affected.

Graph 5.1.4. Unemployment Rate by Sex (%)

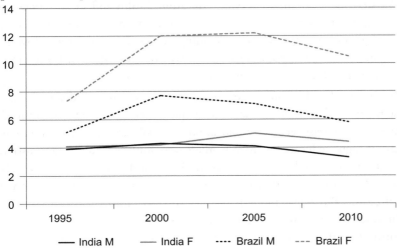

Source: ILO-KILM, 8th Edition, Table 9a. KILM adjusts unemployment estimates to an international standard, hence the difference with totals in Tables 4.3.3 and 4.3.4.

5.1.3 Sectoral structure of employment

Agriculture is the major employer of both male and female workers in India, while the services sector is the prime employer in Brazil. In both countries, women workers display a greater sectoral concentration than men (Graph 5.1.5). In India, the concentration in agriculture is gradually diminishing but more rapidly among male workers. In contrast, in Brazil the concentration in services has increased for both sexes, slightly more among women.

Agriculture in India and domestic service in Brazil have played a similar role in labour market adjustment: they have been the default employment, where women crowded in the absence of more remunerative and desirable work. But this has somewhat changed in Brazil during the 2000s.

Structural changes in the labour market have been slower in India than in Brazil. This is true not only for aggregate employment but also for changes in the industrial affiliation of workers and their employment status. In 2009-10, 88 per cent of women workers and 80 per cent of men workers in Brazil were engaged in a non-agricultural activity; in India, the respective numbers were just 35 and 55 per cent.

In Brazil, women have been able to penetrate traditional male occupations to a certain extent, though traditional female occupations have maintained their gender composition over the past thirty years (Madalozzo, 2010). Almost half of women workers (46 per cent) are concentrated in sectors that conform to gender stereotypes: domestic service, education, health and social services, and other community services, while only 9 per cent of male workers are found in those activities. In India, the corresponding figures were 9 per cent of women's employment and 5 per cent of men's (ILO-KILM, Table 4c). The low figures are due to the predominance of employment in agriculture.

In India, the distribution of female workers across industries changes substantially with education. Access to white-collar service jobs is confined to women with at least secondary education. In 1987, the majority (almost two-thirds) of highly educated women workers were found in public administration and education, though this share had declined to 45 per cent by 2009. New avenues for women's employment have opened up since liberalization and globalization. But while modern services (finance, insurance, real estate, and business services) have increased their share of GDP and opened new employment opportunities, they accounted for only 1.1 per cent of female employment in 2009-10. 'Consequently, highly-educated women are increasingly working in typically less skilled industries such as textiles, wholesale and retail trade, or do not enter the labour market at all. For low-skilled women, employment has shifted from agriculture into textiles, construction, and domestic services' (Klasen and Pieters, 2013, p. 10).

Graph 5.1.5. Distribution of Male and Female Employment by Aggregate Sector, Brazil (1995–2009) and India (1994–2010(%)

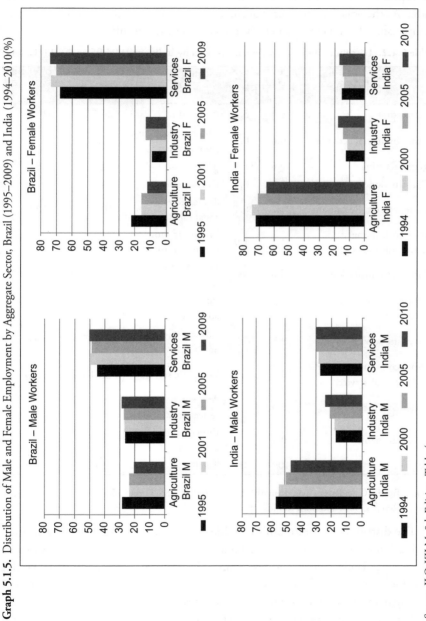

Source: ILO-KILM, 8th Edition, Table 4a.

Since occupational profiles are very different in rural and urban areas, and the vast majority of Brazilian women workers live in urban areas, it is more appropriate to focus the analysis on a comparison of urban Brazil with urban India. As the agrarian structures of the two countries are very dissimilar, a direct comparison of rural employment in the two countries is difficult.

Table 5.1.2. Distribution of Urban Female Workers by Industry, 1993/95 and 2011/12 (%)

	Brazil			India	
	1995	2011		1993-94	2011-12
Agriculture	6.3	3.1	Agriculture	24.7	10.9
Other industrial activities	0.6	0.3	Mining, Electricity, gas and water	0.9	1.3
Manufacturing	10.0	11.7	Manufacturing	24.1	28.7
Construction	0.5	0.6	Construction	4.1	4.0
Trade, Hotels, Restaurants	21.2	26.1	Trade, hotels, restaurants	10.0	12.8
Transport, storage, communications	1.1	1.9	Transport, storage, communications	1.3	2.7
Public administration	4.8	5.7	Finance, insurance, real estate	1.9	4.5
Education, health, and social work	19.8	18.2	Public administration		2.6
Domestic service	19.7	16.5	Education, health, and social work		18.0
Other community, social, and personal services	10.1	6.3	Domestic service	33.1	8.3
Other activities	6.0	9.4	Arts, entertainment, recreational		0.3
Non-classifiable	0.0	0.1	Other service activities		5.9
Total	100	100	Total	100	100

Source: Brazil: Calculations based on IBGE data; India: NSS Employment and Unemployment Reports, 50th and 68th rounds.

The distribution of economic activities among the urban female labour force in Brazil and India is presented in Table 5.1.2. In 2011, the top three sectors in Brazil were 'Trade, hotels, and restaurants', 'Education, health, and social work', and 'Domestic service'; together they accounted for 60 per cent of all urban employment of women. 'Trade, hotels, and restaurants' now employs more than a quarter of urban women workers. This branch registered the biggest increase in female employment between 1995 and 2011. 'Domestic service', which until the beginning of the 2000s was the primary employment opportunity for urban women, has lost some ground, but still represents more than 15 per cent of the urban female labour force. On the other hand, 'Manufacturing' accounts for only 12 per cent. The textile industry – a major employer of women – lost 27 per cent of its jobs between 1990 and 1998 (Menezes-Filho and Scorzafave, 2009).

In India the three main sectors of activity for urban women were 'Manufacturing', 'Education, health, and social work', and 'Trade, hotels, and restaurants'. Together they employed 60 per cent of the urban female labour force in 2011-12. The two noticeable differences between Brazil and India lay in 'Manufacturing' and 'Trade, hotels, and restaurants'. The incidence of 'Manufacturing' is almost two-and-a-half times higher in India than in Brazil. Now it accounts for 29 per cent of urban female employment. The Indian performance is due to the garment industry, and in particular to outsourcing of activities to homeworkers, which enables them to reconcile domestic responsibilities with paid work. On the other hand, the incidence of 'Trade, hotels, and restaurants' in India is less than half that of Brazil. Social norms tend to restrict the interaction of women in the public sphere. In urban India, 'Domestic service' is the fastest growing employment for women since 2000.

5.1.4   Work and employment status

As we saw in Section 4.3, there are some striking differences between Brazil and India in the work status of the labour force. The majority of Indian workers (52 per cent in 2011-12) are self-employed, which results from both the dominance of small-holding agriculture as well as a deficit of decent jobs outside agriculture. In Brazil, the majority of workers (70 per cent) are employees (wage workers, registered or unregistered). Since 1995, the proportion of employees increased in both countries, more so in Brazil, especially among women workers.

Self-employment covers three distinct segments of workers: employers, own account workers, and unpaid family workers, with different opportunities for economic empowerment.[11] The share of employers is small; it hovers around 1 per cent of the female labour force in India and around 2.5 per cent in Brazil. The share of own account workers in India was more than three times higher

---

[11] In the WIEGO (Women in Informal Employment: Globalizing and Organizing) pyramid of segmentation in the informal economy, based on average earnings and poverty risk, employers are at the top of the pyramid of segmentation, unpaid family workers are at the bottom, and own account workers are in an intermediate position. In the literature, a distinction has also been made between 'autonomous' self-employed, 'subordinate' self-employed, and 'subsistence' self-employed (Biles, 2009).

than in Brazil, and that of unpaid family workers more than five times higher. The gender gap within the latter segment was substantial in India (34 per cent of women and 11 per cent of men) but much lower in Brazil (6 per cent of women and 3 per cent of men). Unpaid family workers are more numerous in rural areas where women work on family farms, and own account workers in urban areas where home-based work is outsourced from manufacturing enterprises.

Though there are significant differences in income and education and training among the self-employed, a large proportion undertake own account work as a survival strategy if they fail to get wage employment. In the absence of ownership of productive assets and access to capital, they undertake poorly paid activities in the informal economy as a last resort. Women working as own account workers or unpaid family workers are more vulnerable to inadequate earnings, low productivity, lack of social security, and lack of voice. The proportion of female vulnerable workers in India was more than three times higher than in Brazil (ILO-KILM, 8th edition).

But the picture is somewhat different when breaking down data by location. The contrast is sharp between rural and urban areas.

Graph 5.1.6 presents a breakdown of the labour force by sex and location in 1995 (1993-94 for India) and 2011–2012 for the categories of self-employed and employees. The category of employee is broken down into registered and unregistered workers in Brazil, and regular and casual workers in India (Section 4.3).

In rural areas, self-employment is the dominant employment status for men and women in both countries, but its incidence has been decreasing except for Indian women. Among Indian men, it has been replaced primarily by an increase in casual wage labour, while in Brazil it has been mainly compensated by an increase in the incidence of registered workers, especially among men, with the spread of the agribusiness sector.

In urban areas, the change in status has been more pronounced among women than among men. In Brazil, the dominant status is that of registered worker; between 1995 and 2011, this category increased by 17 per cent among men and 37 per cent among women. In India, the incidence of regular work remained stable among male workers but increased by 53 per cent among the female labour force.

As seen in previous chapters, the degree of formality differs substantially between the two countries. India is characterized by a dualistic labour market with a small minority of organized sector regular workers and a majority of low paid casual workers. Over 90 per cent of working women are crowded in the unorganized/informal economy (Verick, 2013). In recent years, most new jobs created in the organized sector have been informal. In manufacturing, women find employment increasingly as temporary or contract workers (Thomas, 2012). In Brazil, the gender gap in access to formal employment is much smaller than in India. The proportion of women in informal employment outside agriculture decreased from 49 per cent in 1990 to 40 per cent in 2011 (Agénor and Canuto, 2013). Informality varies between occupations; for example, 70 per cent of domestic workers are unregistered wage-earners (IBGE-PNAD 2012).[12]

Graph 5.1.6. Employment Status by Sex and Location, Brazil and India, 1994–2012 (%)

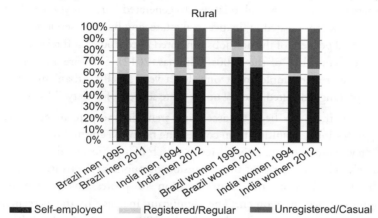

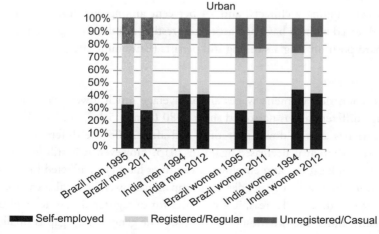

Source: Brazil: Calculations based on IBGE/PNAD data; India: NSS Employment and Unemployment Reports, 50th and 68th rounds.

---

[12] On 2 April 2013, Brazil introduced a constitutional amendment guaranteeing equal rights for domestic workers.

In both countries, women are over-represented in precarious and informal jobs. In manufacturing, women workers tend to concentrate in the garment and textile industries. Flexibilization in this sector has led to an increase in home-based work paid on a piece-rate basis, which means poorly paid and long workdays (Mitra, 2006; Tilly et al., 2013).

On the other hand, highly educated women have been able to access better quality employment in both countries. But in India women accounted for only a small share of the relatively high quality jobs generated in recent years: only 20 per cent of the new jobs created in finance, real estate, and business services during the 2000s, and 10 per cent of the new jobs generated in computer and related activities during the second half of the 2000s (Thomas, 2012). Software and IT-enabled services have created employment only for a very specific urban, metropolitan, English-speaking, educated, mostly upper-caste section of society (Mitra, 2006).

In Brazil, there has been an ascending trend in the percentage of women among professionals resulting from converging factors: a cultural transformation, which drew women to the universities in search of a professional career, instead of a merely domestic activity; the expansion of public and private universities; and the rationalization and transformation of professions, which opened new opportunities for women. The significant increase in the percentage of professional women was consolidated in the 1990s and 2000s. In 2004, there were over 40 per cent of women among lawyers and medical doctors, over 50 per cent among architects, and 14 per cent among engineers. But though some educated women have had access to prestigious jobs, management careers, and board positions, a glass ceiling still persists (Bruschini, 2007).

5.1.5 Wages

In both countries, women's wages are on average much lower than men's, but the wage differential has narrowed since 1980 (Graph 5.1.7). In Brazil, the rate of decline has slowed down over time and after 2008 the differential started to increase, though it decreased again in 2015. However, it is still less than in India. Not all locations and employment statuses have been affected in the same proportion. In Brazil, the gender wage gap is narrower in rural areas than in urban areas and, in both areas, it is narrower for unregistered than for registered workers. In India, the situation is the reverse. The gender wage gap is smaller in urban areas and for regular workers.

In Brazil, only a small portion of the wage differentials in the formal labour force (11–19 per cent) can be attributed to differences in education or experience between men and women. For the most part, the wage gap appears to reflect discriminatory practices and social norms. It also exhibits a non-linear pattern, increasing at higher levels of education. Among those with 12 or more years of schooling, women earned just 58 per cent of men's salaries in 2008 (Agénor and Canuto, 2013; Madalozzo and Martins, 2007; van Klaveren et al., 2009). The decline of the aggregate gender wage gap has been driven to a significant degree by changes in individual characteristics, led by increasing female education, but the unexplained variation, potentially indicative of direct wage discrimination, has remained positive and significant (Salardi, 2012). Cacciamali and Rosalino (2008) have shown that the discriminatory component of the wage gap increased in the 2000s and was larger for white than for non-white women workers.

Graph 5.1.7. Female/Male Wage Ratio, Brazil and India, 1983–2012

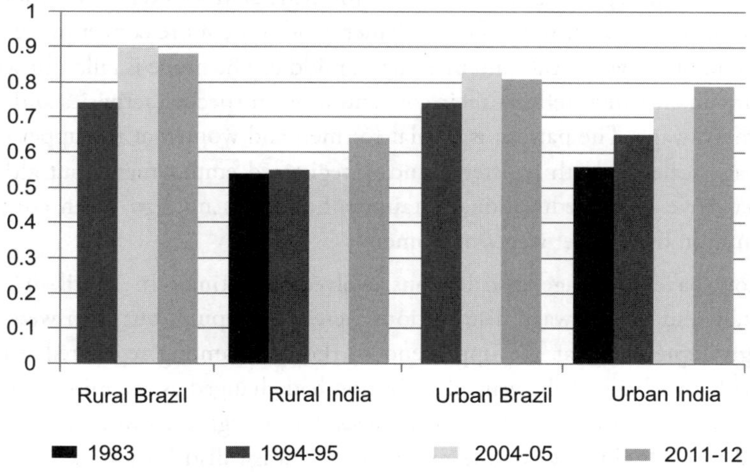

| | 1983 | 1994-95 | 2004-05 | 2011-12 |

Source: Brazil: IBGE/PNAD data; India: NSS data.

In India, across different categories and locations, women earn 20–50 per cent less wages than men. For rural casual, urban regular, and urban casual work, the gap has narrowed to a greater or smaller degree, with the maximum improvement in urban regular employment (IHD, 2014: 105). But male-female differentials in regular wages in rural areas have widened: the average female wage was 72 per cent of the male wage in 1983 and 63 per cent in 2011-12. This could be explained by the entry of women in poorly paid new occupations in education and health (Ghosh, 2009). The wage disparity varies with the sector of activity. On average, the gender wage gap is lower in regular urban manufacturing (75 per cent) and economic services (79 per cent). The widest disparity was found in casual social, community, and personal services (51 per cent). The gap declined with the increasing level of education for regular work in both rural and urban areas, except for graduate and higher education in urban areas. In the casual labour market, however, education seems to put women at a relative disadvantage (IHD, 2014: 105).

Wage distribution

Graph 5.1.8 presents histograms of the distribution of wages across gender and work type in urban areas for 2011 in Brazil and 2011-12 in India. The distribution of male wages is in dark grey and that of women in light grey. To facilitate the presentation, log wages are used and standardized to a mean of zero.

In Brazil, the male and female wage distributions overlap all along the distributions for both registered and unregistered workers. Wage dispersion is wider for unregistered workers than for registered workers, for whom the minimum wage constitutes a floor. Women tend to be more concentrated at the lower end of the wage scale and men in the middle. The mode is taller for women than for men, which reflects their concentration in specific activities and at the minimum wage. The pattern is similar for men and women at the upper end of the wage scale for both registered and unregistered employment, but although women have higher educational attainment, there is no sign of an education premium in the market wages of women.

How have the wage distributions evolved over time? In Brazil, in 1995, the male and female wage distributions were overlapping, but men were more strongly represented at the upper end of the scale among registered workers. By 2011, the shape of the wage distribution had changed as the minimum wage acted as a floor for registered workers' wages. For unregistered workers, the mode moved to the right towards the middle of the wage distribution, reflecting the increase in educational level and the influence of the minimum wage even in the informal economy. This was the case for both men and women.

In India, the wage distributions of men and women only partially overlap. The male wage distributions for both regular and casual workers are distinctly to the right of the female wage distribution. This means that men predominate at the top and middle levels of the wage scale, and women predominate at the bottom, but women's distributions are bimodal, with a clustering at both lower and higher wages. In 1994, wage disparities between men and women workers were sharper. In 2012, they persisted but the distributions of men's and women's wages are less differentiated.

Neither in Brazil nor in India is the gender pay gap homogeneous along the wage distribution, so further information can be provided by decomposing

Graph 5.1.8. Histograms of Standardized Nominal Log Wages across Gender and Work Type in Urban Areas, Brazil and India, 2011–2012

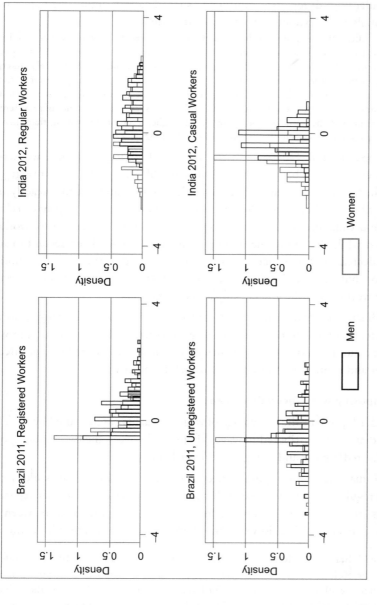

Source: Computed from IBGE/PNAD unit level data for Brazil and NSS unit level data for India.

Note: Light grey – women. Dark grey – men.

wage differentials at different quantiles along the distribution. Salardi (2012) carried out such an exercise for Brazil for the 1987–2006 period, which shows that gender wage differentials exhibit a U-shaped pattern, indicating higher wage differentials at the extremes of the pay distribution.

> These differentials are primarily the result of wage structure effects, which remain positive despite having declined considerably over time, particularly at the bottom end of the pay distribution. The wage structure effect is greater at higher quantiles in the formal market, while in the non-formal sectors the effect of coefficients is considerably greater at the bottom end of the distribution. This suggests the existence of a sticky floor phenomenon for women working in non-formal sectors, while also revealing the existence of persistent glass ceilings in the formal sector where, despite higher levels of endowment than men, women continue to receive lower wages[13] (Salardi, 2012, p. 279).

Deshpande et al. (2015) apply the same methodology to regular workers in India over the period between 1999-2000 and 2009-10, and find that wage gaps are higher at the lower end of the wage distribution and decline steadily over the distribution. They find also that while the average wage gap has declined over the decade, the gap at the first decile (the bottom 10 per cent of workers) increased while the gap in the middle of the distribution (from second to sixth decile) decreased. No change was observed at the top of the wage distribution. They conclude that this implies the existence of sticky floor effects among regular women workers and the absence of glass ceiling effects.

In Brazil, the glass ceiling effect – adverse to women, and strong in formal employment – tends to compress the wage dispersion when the minimum wage increases and, therefore, to reduce inequality. In India, the sticky floor effect is stronger and contributes to increasing overall inequality.

Decomposing wage inequality by sex

Graph 5.1.9 presents the percentage of wage inequality (as measured by the Theil index) that can be attributed to wage differences between the two gender groups for registered/regular and unregistered/casual employment.

In India, the between-group effect is stronger among casual workers than among regular workers, whereas in Brazil it is the reverse. For regular/registered workers, the contribution to wage inequality due to differences between the groups of male and female workers is fairly similar in magnitude in the two

---

[13] In Salardi's Brazilian study, the sticky floor is defined by comparing the 10th percentile pay gap to the 50th percentile pay gap and the glass ceiling by comparing the 90th percentile pay gap to the 50th percentile pay gap. For India, Deshpande et al. (2015) use the definition formulated by Arulampalam et al. (2007): a sticky floor exists if the 10th percentile pay gap is higher than the 25th percentile pay gap by 2 percentage points.

Graph 5.1.9. Decomposition of Theil Index of Wages by Sex and across Employment Status, Brazil and India, 1983–2011/2012, between Group Share (%)*

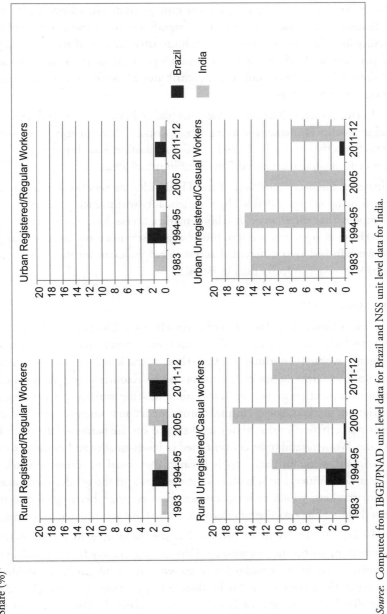

Source: Computed from IBGE/PNAD unit level data for Brazil and NSS unit level data for India.

Note: *Percentage of the overall Theil wage inequality index that reflects wage differences between men and women. See the discussion of decomposition in Section 4.3.

countries. Over time, it varied between 0.9 per cent and 3 per cent. There is an upward trend in rural India while the trend has been more erratic in urban India and in rural and urban Brazil.

The picture is drastically different for unregistered/casual workers. In India, sex differences continue to account for a significant proportion of overall wage inequality for this category of workers in both urban and rural areas, with a peak at 17 per cent in 2005 in rural areas and 15 per cent in 1994 in urban areas. Since then it has declined, but it still contributes 11 per cent in rural areas and 8 per cent in urban areas.

In Brazil, the contribution of wage inequality between men and women to overall inequality is smaller for unregistered workers than for registered workers and much less than in India. In 2011, the contribution was almost negligible, at 0.1 per cent in rural areas and 0.7 per cent in urban areas.

However, the decomposition of the Theil index shows that the dynamics of wage inequality is largely defined by the inequality within each group of workers. This implies that differences in labour market access have strong explanatory power. The primary factor is not so much wage discrimination in work (except in casual work in India) as differential access to employment for men and women, and this is stronger in India than in Brazil.

5.1.6   Conclusion

Gender inequalities in the labour market remain high. Though Brazil has evolved faster than India in terms of fertility transition, urbanization, and educational attainment, women continue to face similar challenges in both countries. Constraints in terms of social norms, access to resources, and discriminatory regulations or practices prevent growth from translating into better gender equality in both labour markets. Socio-cultural norms impact on women's choice of studies, on their participation in the labour market, and on the nature of the work they undertake. Women tend to be concentrated in lower-quality and more precarious forms of paid work. In part, this is because they need to reconcile work and family responsibilities, but it is also the consequence of the gender segmentation of labour markets, which restricts women from entering better paid and more protected work. The neo-liberal reforms seem to have accentuated this tendency.

In India, the development process has not been able to create sufficient employment opportunities for women. Diversification away from agriculture has been limited, and highly educated women who are unable to find suitable jobs do not enter the labour force. Sticky floor effects, strong in India, can be seen in wage discrimination against female casual workers. In Brazil, though some women have had access to better quality employment and prestigious careers, the higher average educational level of the female labour force has not been reflected in relative market wages. Glass ceiling effects, stronger in Brazil, show up in the low return to education.

Gender remains the primary axis of marginalization and segmentation in employment, but it also interacts with other factors of inequality such as caste/race, religion, and regional differences. The market operates within those existing structural inequalities and tends to reinforce them through a cumulative effect.

5.2 Regional Inequality

5.2.1 Introduction

Regional inequality is a major component of overall inequality in the labour market, especially in countries as large and diverse as Brazil and India, which include at one extreme 'backward' areas lacking in both resources and infrastructure and, at the other, modern city complexes with global lifestyles. These differences have historical origins, of course. In India, the backwardness of the state of Bihar, for instance, has much to do with its status as an agricultural backwater during colonial times. Regions with large tribal populations – such as the present-day states of Chhattisgarh and Jharkhand, and several Northeastern states – were left outside the mainstream of development, with the notable exception of mining, which had little local spillover. Economic growth around Delhi and Bombay reflected their status as, respectively, capital and major port. In Brazil, the Northeast, dominated by a conservative rural oligarchy, fell into a relative decline after the middle of the nineteenth century. In the meantime, the dynamic centre of the economy shifted to the former agricultural backwater of the state of São Paulo in the Southeast, thanks to the growth of coffee exports, which paved the way for a substantial expansion of the industrial base. In Brazil after 1930, growth was driven by a rapid increase of industrial output. It was at first concentrated in a small number of major metropolitan centres in the southeastern and southern regions and then, especially after the 1970s, spread to the rest of the country in a more selective and concentrated fashion. Despite the recent industrialization of the Northeast and North, disparities are still striking.

The comparison between Brazil and India is not straightforward because India has a larger population and is more heterogeneous than Brazil. Regional analysis in Brazil has converged on the identification of five large regions of the country with different economic and geophysical characteristics and histories (Map 5.2.1).

Among these regions, the Southeast is the industrial powerhouse of the country, and accounts today for 55 per cent of the country's GDP. However, its large metropolitan areas, especially São Paulo, Rio de Janeiro, and Belo Horizonte – like Recife and Salvador, the main metropolitan areas of the Northeast – are home to much informal labour and housing, not to mention urban violence, which is widespread, especially on the outskirts of the major cities.

Map 5.2.1. Brazil, Regions

Source: IBGE.

The Northeast, the country's poorest region, lagged behind during most of the industrialization process in Brazil. More recently, the region has become an important industrial site – with steel, petrochemical, and automobile factories – and some high-productivity agricultural activities have been boosted, for instance with the expansion of soya production. But a poor subsistence agricultural economy persists, and the metropolitan areas of the Northeast are the most unequal of the country, with much informal work and few backward and forward linkages within the region.

In the large but sparsely populated Northern region, which mainly consists of the less developed Amazon basin, some capital-intensive activities in agriculture, mining, and even manufacturing coexist with a subsistence economy with loose linkages to the market or, at the opposite extreme, strong links that take the form of exploitation.

Thanks to the expansion of a capital-intensive agricultural sector, the Mid-West, the agrarian frontier of the country, has had economic growth rates above the national average since the 1970s, but high levels of productivity growth have not reduced inequality; quite the contrary.

The more temperate South has the best welfare indicators in terms of poverty and employment. Here, a substantial manufacturing industry is linked to a large agribusiness sector. At the same time, small farmers in the South tend to be more productive than in other parts of the country.

The main economic and social indicators of each region are related to their position within the overall growth regime, spearheaded by the Southeast, by virtue of its power of capital accumulation (Castro, 1971). The other regions adapt – in part through state intervention and regional planning projects enacted by the central government, usually subject to political influences – in a rather ad hoc way to the dynamism of the economic core of the country. This has not changed substantially with the changes of growth regime in the 1990s and the 2000s, as even though other regions grew faster, the Southeast has some extent benefited from their growth.

There is no comparable, consensual regional breakdown for India. The history of South India is quite different from the North, but both are heterogeneous. The East tends to be poorer and less developed than the West, but the former includes the relatively more developed area around Kolkata, while the latter includes less developed areas in Gujarat, Rajasthan, and Madhya Pradesh. Much regional analysis is undertaken at the level of individual states, but these vary enormously in size and economic specificity. To facilitate comparison with Brazil, five regions were identified, consisting of groups of states, on the basis of similarity in terms of output and expenditure per capita, poverty, and urbanization. These regions are the Northeast, including West Bengal, Assam, and nearby hill areas; a group of poor states in the centre of the country; the Northwest, covering a rather heterogeneous group of states from Kashmir to Rajasthan, including Delhi; the South and West, a relatively more industrialized region extending from Gujarat to Tamil Nadu; and the state of Kerala, which is so different from the others that it is better to keep it apart (Map 5.2.2). In reality, there are more than five distinct regions in India, but limiting the number to five permitted a more direct comparison with Brazil. The annex to this section explains the rationale for this regional breakdown and lists the states in each region.

The Northwest includes high-productivity agricultural areas such as Punjab and Haryana, where there has been investment in irrigation and rapid spread of new technologies, which has raised rural incomes. It also includes the administrative capital, Delhi. Industrial output has grown in some parts of the region, but the tertiary sector dominates. Overall, this is an advanced region with a relatively successful social and economic model.

The Centre region, including the large states of Uttar Pradesh and Bihar, has generally suffered from poor governance and the presence of exploitative agrarian structures until recent times. Low investment in public infrastructure has discouraged private investment, and low literacy and large gender inequalities persist. Many parts of this region have suffered from high levels of violence and endemic corruption, and population densities are high. The result has been persistent backwardness and poverty.

The South and West (referred to as 'South/West' below) includes important industrial areas in Gujarat, Maharashtra, and Tamil Nadu, the manufacturing heartland of India, as well as cities such as Bangalore and Hyderabad, which have become the home of new, high-technology service activities. There is a high level of urbanization. This is the region where private capital accumulation has been greatest.

The Northeast is a geographical region more than a homogenous economic one, since it extends from Kolkata to remote hill areas. Kolkata has not shared in the industrial growth of western and southern India, and the hill areas have remained on the margins of the national economy.

Finally, Kerala is quite different, with a distinctive form of social organization, large-scale migration to the Gulf, and consequent high income levels and wages. It also has close to universal literacy. Kerala's social and political conditions are different from other parts of India, and this also drives the economic indicators, making the state a special case.

Map 5.2.2. India, Regions

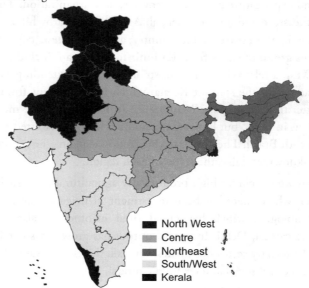

Source: Prepared by the authors.

5.2.2   The pattern of regional inequality

The importance of these regional differences can be seen by comparing some key indicators across regions in both countries (Tables 5.2.1 to 5.2.4).

In Brazil, the regional differences are large (Table 5.2.2). Output per capita in the Northeast is only 48 per cent of the national average while in the Southeast, which accounts for almost half of Brazil's population, it is over 30 per cent higher. The clear distinction is between the North and Northeast on the one hand, and the rest of Brazil on the other. Incomes are lower in the former and a larger percentage of the population is rural, while manufacturing industry is concentrated in the Southeast, which accounts for 60 per cent of the country's manufacturing output. Some decentralization has occurred since the 1970s, and in the 2000s important manufacturing groups – both Brazilian and foreign-based – have established plants in the Northeast, but the share of manufacturing in regional GDP is still only 12 per cent against 20 per cent in the Southeast and South (Table 5.2.1).

Rates of urbanization are now high in all regions, but a quarter of the population still lives in rural areas in the North and Northeast. The main difference between regions in rural areas is the high incidence of poverty in the Northeast and the North, where many workers still make their living from small plots and subsistence economies, poorly linked to the market. The poverty rate in the rural Northeast was 27.2 per cent in 2011 compared to 7.4 per cent in the rural Southeast. Actually, the Northeast is the only region in which per capita household income in rural areas is less than half of that in urban areas. At the other extreme, this rural-urban income ratio reaches 63 per cent in the South.

However, we should bear in mind that poverty is more concentrated in urban areas throughout Brazil, and inequality is higher in metropolitan areas. So the regional problem is not confined to a single region, but shows up everywhere. Dynamism and 'backwardness' seem to interact in different places within the integrated internal market (Bacelar, 2006).

Table 5.2.1. Regional Production Structure, Brazil, 2011 (%)

	Agriculture	Mining	Manufacturing	Construction	Services	Total
Northeast	7.7	1.3	12.1	6.9	72.0	100.0
North	10.9	4.4	14.5	7.7	62.6	100.0
Mid-West	11.4	0.4	7.9	5.1	75.1	100.0
Southeast	2.9	2.6	19.1	5.0	70.4	100.0
South	9.0	0.2	21.7	5.0	64.0	100.0
Brazil	5.8	1.9	17.2	5.4	69.6	100.0

Source: Regional Accounts of Brazil/IBGE/Ipeadata.

Table 5.2.2. Regional Inequality Indicators, Brazil, 2011

	% Share of National Population (Demo-Graphic Census, 2010)	Per Capita Household Income (R$)		Poverty (% of Households)	Per Capita GDP (R$ 2010 Prices)	Urban (%)	Wage (R$)		Private Registered Wage-earners (% of all Workers)		Adult Literacy (%)		Gini Coefficient of Household Per Capita Income
		Rural	Urban				Registered	Unregistered	Farm	Non-Farm	Male	Female	
Northeast	27.8	347	716	22.0	9,703	73.7	1179	822	4.7	32.4	79.5	83.0	0.538
North	8.3	465	796	17.7	12,984	74.7	1022	602	4.5	29.5	87.9	89.2	0.536
Midwest	7.4	685	1234	12.2	26,017	90.8	1374	1133	29.2	40.6	93.0	93.2	0.535
Southeast	42.1	645	1193	11.2	26,503	93.4	1336	959	25.3	49.6	95.2	94.5	0.504
South	14.4	767	1204	4.5	22,794	85.1	1523	1063	10.0	50.8	95.1	94.2	0.471
Brazil	100	505	1064	13.5	20,133	85.0	1379	878	11.3	43.9	90.4	90.9	0.527

Source: PNAD and Regional Accounts of Brazil (IBGE) and Ipeadata.

Table 5.2.3. Regional Inequality Indicators, India, around 2011

	% Share of National Population*	Monthly Per Capita Expenditure 2011-12 (Rs.)		Poverty % of Households 2011-12	Per capita Net State Domestic Product 2010-11 at 2004-05 Prices (Rs.)	Urbanization 2011(%)	Male Casual Wage 2011-12 (Rs./day)	Regular Workers % 2011-12	Literacy % 2011 Male	Literacy % 2011 Female
		Rural	Urban							
Northwest	13.9	1879	2772	10.5	51246	37.5	200	26.2	85.1	68.1
Centre	39.5	965	1780	34.1	21327	20.9	124	9.7	79.2	59.0
Northeast	11.4	1213	2251	24.2	30221	25.0	137	16.4	82.1	71.5
South/West	32.4	1481	2680	15.1	49406	41.7	161	23.4	84.5	69.6
Kerala	2.8	2355	3044	7.1	49873	47.7	350	22.5	96.0	92.0
India	100.0	1287	2477	21.9	35993	31.2	155	17.9	82.1	65.5

Source: First, sixth, ninth and tenth columns, Census of India (2011); second, third and fourth columns, Government of India, Planning Commission (2013); fifth column, Government of India, Ministry of Statistics and Plan Implementation database; seventh and eighth columns, Institute for Human Development (2014).

Regions: Northwest: Delhi, Haryana, Himachal, Jammu/Kashmir, Punjab, Uttarakhand, Rajasthan;
Centre: Bihar, Chhattisgarh, Jharkhand, Madhya Pradesh, Odisha, Uttar Pradesh;
Northeast: West Bengal, Assam, smaller States of the Northeast;
South/West: Gujarat, Maharashtra, Andhra Pradesh, Karnataka, Tamil Nadu.

Note: *Excludes some small States and Union Territories.

In terms of regional production structure, the Southeast is the region with the largest share of production in every sector. But if we look at the sectoral distribution of output within regions (Table 5.2.2), some features deserve mentioning. The Mid-West has the highest share of both agriculture and services, while the other sectors are below the Brazilian average. The Northeast is more balanced, with a substantial contribution from agriculture and manufacturing, and an above-average share of services, but still with a higher percentage of low-productivity activities, especially in the informal economy. The North has a relatively high share of output in agriculture, mining, and construction. Its substantial manufacturing base depends to a great extent on the free zone of Manaus, an industrial enclave. The South and Southeast are very similar; the main difference lies in that agriculture is less important in the latter, which has also a strong service economy, and provides the rest of the country with high productivity inputs. However, even with only 2.9 per cent of the region's production coming from agriculture, this still represents 27 per cent of this sector's total output in Brazil, larger than that of any other single region.

In India, the poorest region, the Centre, has per capita output, expenditure, and wage levels that are 20–40 per cent below the all-India average (Table 5.2.3); poverty rates are high, urbanization and literacy are low, and regular workers are few. The Northeast is also relatively poor, but much closer to the all-India average. The other three areas have similar levels of output per capita – about 40 per cent higher than the all-India average – but different profiles otherwise. The South/West region is more urbanized, and has a high share of manufacturing (Table 5.2.4), but wages and poverty indicators are not much better than the all-India average. The Northwest, which includes Delhi, has the highest share of regular workers and relatively high wages. Kerala is a case apart, partly because of the inflow of remittances from migrants to the Gulf. It has by far the highest wages, lowest poverty, and highest literacy.

Rural-urban differences are at least as important as the wider regional pattern. Rural household expenditure per capita is hardly more than half of that in urban areas, and this difference is found within all regions, though somewhat less in the Northwest and Kerala, which have higher levels of urbanization. Wages for regular workers are about 50 per cent higher in urban than in rural areas (not shown in the table); for casual workers, the difference is less, about 25 per cent, and unlike for regular workers this difference has been declining over time.

Table 5.2.4 shows how these differences are closely inter-related with regional differences in the production structure. The poor central region is much more heavily dependent on agriculture than the average, but the three higher-income regions have different production bases. The South/West has the highest share of manufacturing, while the Northwest includes both the productive agricultural areas of Punjab and Haryana and the capital, Delhi, where both public and private services dominate. Kerala's high income is sourced largely from services and construction in addition to remittances from abroad.

Table 5.2.4. Regional Production Structure, India, 2012–2014 (% of NSDP)

	Agriculture	Mining	Manufacturing	Construction	Services	Total
Northwest	19.9	1.3	11.1	8.8	58.9	100
Centre	27.8	2.7	8.2	10.5	50.8	100
Northeast	23.2	1.9	8.3	7.2	59.5	100
South/West	15.2	1.0	16.2	8.5	59.2	100
Kerala	14.1	0.6	7.7	17.2	60.4	100
India	19.7	1.5	12.3	9.2	57.3	100

Source: RBI database. Compiled from state-wise data for the most recent year, 2012-13 or 2013-14.

If we compare the pattern of regional inequality in the two countries, it can be seen that in both there are two regions that are poorer and three that are richer. In Brazil, output per capita is lower in the North and the Northeast, and poverty is higher; the same is true of the central and northeastern regions in India. In fact, in both countries the gaps between these two poorer regions and the others are large, and the same pattern is found for household expenditure or income per capita and urbanization. So it is clear that there is one major regional divide in both countries, and that there are other, generally smaller differences within each of the two parts of the country. It is also the case that the ranking of the two poorer regions is quite consistent across these socio-economic indicators. In India, indicators for the central region are systematically below those for the Northeast; in Brazil, the Northeast is worse than the North. So, we can say that in both countries there is one particularly deprived region, the Northeast in Brazil and the Centre in India, and one relatively deprived region, the North in Brazil and the Northeast in India. On the other hand, differences among the relatively better-off regions are less consistent.

However, the patterns of poverty in the poorest regions of each country are different, for in India poverty is still mainly rural, while in Brazil it is mainly urban. This is related to the nature of each country's growth regime, for industrialization in Brazil prompted high rates of migration which shifted poverty from rural to urban areas.

These regional patterns also carry over to labour market inequality. Graphs 5.2.1 and 5.2.2 present the regional patterns in the two countries with respect to two labour market indicators – the share of formal employment (regular work in India and private registered work in Brazil), and casual wages in India and wages of unregistered workers in Brazil – comparing the levels of each region with the national average. The regions are presented in ascending order of output per capita from left to right in the graphs for both countries. For both indicators, it can be seen that like for output per capita and poverty, the northern and northeastern regions are at the bottom in Brazil and the central region and the Northeast in India.

Graph 5.2.1. Percentage of Regular/Registered Work by Region, 2011–2012

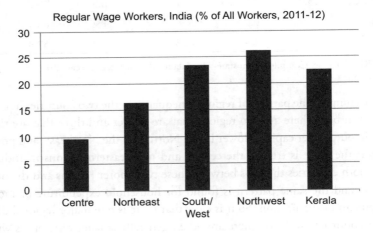

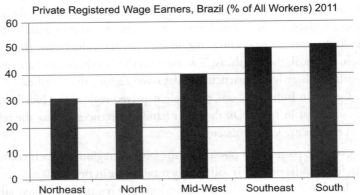

Source: Unit level data, PNAD (Brazil) and NSS (India).

Graph 5.2.2. Casual or Unregistered Wages by Region, 2011–2012

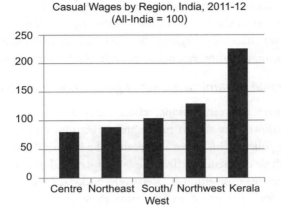

Casual Wages by Region, India, 2011-12
(All-India = 100)

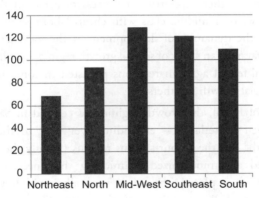

Wages of Unregistered Workers by Region, Brazil
2011 (Brazil = 100)

Source: Unit-level data, PNAD (Brazil) and NSS (India).

The relatively low proportion of regular or registered workers in these poorer regions in both countries (Graph 5.2.1) suggests that labour market structures play an important role in these regional differences, as they match the existing productive structures and also reflect the extent of labour surplus. The poorer regions have greater informality in the labour market and so less effective protection of work and workers. Logically, wages are also relatively low in these regions (Graph 5.2.2), while there is mostly little difference among advanced regions.

However, there are also distinctive patterns in the two countries. In India, Kerala has exceptionally high wages, which can be traced to its historical and political situation and high levels of organization of labour, while there is less difference among other regions, reflecting a national labour market for casual labour that is integrated through large migration flows. In Brazil, on the other hand, casual wages in the Northeast are particularly low, lower than the North, and much lower than other regions. So, there are specific factors, different in both countries, that modify regional patterns in the labour market.

5.2.3 Regional dynamics, growth regimes, and inequality

These differences between regions reflect many factors, such as differences in resource endowments and in productive structures, and in the quality and nature of state policies. But above all, because of a historical process of economic polarization, these differences reflect the overall national growth regime and the role of different regions within it. Relatively backward regions may serve as a labour reserve for a process of accumulation elsewhere, as did the Northeast of Brazil vis-à-vis the Southeast during the period of rapid growth prior to 1980. In India today, the central region provides richer regions with millions of casual migrant workers – either supporting a process of accumulation or providing an increasingly well-off middle class with cheap labour services. But in these large countries, the dynamics of development at the local level is sufficiently differentiated that one can speak of several growth regimes. For instance, in India, exploitative semi-feudal agrarian relations persisted in some regions alongside capitalist industrial growth in others.

In the case of Brazil, the growth regime was centred in São Paulo, Rio de Janeiro, and their hinterlands – expanding over time to the Southeast and also to the South. But the labour-surplus regions (mainly the Northeast) were also transformed and modernized, mimicking the unequal and dependent development already in place in the richest areas, albeit with fewer compensating mechanisms, through interventions of the state. This was highlighted by economist Celso Furtado (1981) when, returning from exile, he noticed how the development pattern of the Northeast was quite different from the one he had devised through SUDENE – the federal agency in charge of promoting the region's development, created in 1959.

In India, the available evidence suggests that there was a degree of convergence between states in output and income per capita after independence and up to the 1980s, but this was subsequently reversed (Ramaswamy, 2007; Ahluwalia, 2000). We can see this divergence since the 1980s in Graph 5.2.3. The highest growth rates of Net State Domestic Product (NSDP) throughout the period since the early 1980s were in the better-off Northwest and South/West regions, which increased the gap between these regions and the rest. The more backward Centre region had the slowest growth rate, especially up to 2004-05, and lagged further behind. After 2004-05, growth picked up in the Centre region, benefitting from the spillover effects of high growth of the national economy, but despite very high growth in one backward state (Bihar) the average for the region was still lower than the all-India level. The other lower-income region, the Northeast, did about as well as the average until the 2000s, but failed to benefit from the spurt in growth at the national level after 2004-05.

Graph 5.2.3.A. Regional Output Growth Rates, India, 1982/83–2011/12 (% per annum)

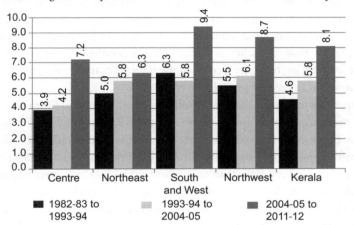

Source: Calculated from RBI database. Output measured by Net State Domestic Product.

Graph 5.2.3.B. Regional Output Growth Rates, Brazil, 1980–2011 (% per annum)

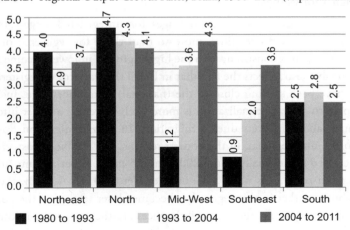

Source: Calculated from IBGE System of National Accounts.

Brazil presents almost the opposite story. During the period of rapid industrialization, divergence increased up to 1970, while a slow process of convergence – measured by GDP per capita – started in the 1970s, the last decade of high growth, and continued in recent decades: during the crisis of the 1980s, the low growth 1990s, and the growth recovery period from 2004 to 2010. Output grew faster than the national average in the North and the Northeast during these periods, as depicted in Graph 5.2.3. The Mid-West also started to grow at a much higher rate than the average from the 1990s onwards. In the 2000s, pulled by the dynamism of the internal market and also boosted by exports, these three regions had a rate of economic growth above the national average of 4 per cent per annum. However, the growth was more evenly spread across regions than in earlier periods, with the Southeast close to the national average, benefitting from the growth of the internal market. Only the South grew more slowly in the recent period.

Disparities in growth patterns can be expected to translate into disparities in labour market outcomes and poverty reduction. Ramaswamy (2007) finds that, in India, employment growth was faster in states that had initially more diversified economies. Low-income states like Bihar, Uttar Pradesh, and Madhya Pradesh in the central region (and Rajasthan in the Northwest) had less diversified structures to begin with, and their labour markets changed at a much slower pace. It is less certain that increasing regional inequality in output has been associated with an increasing inequality in wages. Chavan and Bedamatta (2006) find that the coefficient of variation of wage earnings of agricultural labourers (across states) was much the same in 1999-2000 as in 1977-78 or 1964-65 for men, although it was higher for women.

In Brazil, regional disparities in wages for unregistered wage-earners are becoming less marked over time, more so than those for registered or regular wage-earners. This is consistent with the higher growth in lower-income regions. But it probably also reflects the fact that in Brazil the wages of unregistered wage workers have been settling close to the (national) minimum wage. In India, a similar pattern of wage equalization is more likely to reflect a wider integration of regional labour markets due to migration. In Brazil, migration flows have been mostly intra-regional. In the poorest regions, like the Northeast, registered work increased substantially in the 2000s, at 5.5 per cent per annum, attracting workers from rural areas nearby (Guimarães Neto, 2014). Actually, the profile of the labour market in this region has become closer to that of the Southeast, and the most important remaining differences are the size of the informal and agricultural sectors. However, the convergence in terms of wages is less marked.

In terms of poverty reduction, in India the outcomes tend to mirror the disparities in growth rates. Poverty has been declining in all regions since the 1980s, as can be seen in Table 5.2.5. But the poorest, central region, has done less well. Graph 5.2.4 shows that the ratio of the poverty rate in the Centre to the all-India level has been rising steadily (the drop between the two poverty estimates for 2004-05 merely reflects the new method of calculation). The other poor region, the Northeast, did relatively well in terms of poverty reduction up to 2004-05, a period when the region's growth was close to the all-India average. After 2004-05, this was reversed; growth rose less than in other regions and poverty declined more slowly. The faster growing Northwest and South/West show some relative improvement in poverty, but it is Kerala that did best despite lower output growth, partly no doubt because of remittances from migrants (not counted in NSDP), but probably also because of more effective state redistribution and minimum wage policies.

The Brazilian scenario is different, in that the regional picture in terms of poverty reduction does not match the regional pattern of output growth. In the period from 1993 to 2011 – but especially from 2005 to 2011 – the Mid-West had the largest fall in the percentage of households living below the poverty line. The South and Southeast came next, despite the lower rates of economic growth. The Northeast and the North had the weakest performance in terms of poverty reduction despite relatively high growth. But the 60-per-cent decline in the poverty rate in the Northeast between 1993 and 2011 was in fact not much less than the national average; so, like in India, all regions shared in the decline in poverty. In 2011, 3.4 million households were below the poverty line in the Northeast, 43 per cent of the total number of poor households in the country (7.9 million); while the Southeast, the most populous region, had 36 per cent of all poor households.

These outcomes are summarized in Graph 5.2.4. The ratio of the poverty rate in the Northeast and North to the Brazilian average rose between 1993 and 2011. At the same time, the corresponding ratio for the South was considerably reduced although this region was the least dynamic in terms of output growth.

This regional pattern can be explained if we consider that labour market dynamism (the increase in the minimum wage included) was the main driver of social improvement in Brazil. Regions with a wider and more inclusive labour market, with fewer people outside the scope or implementation of labour law – notably the South and Southeast – benefited more than the others. On the other hand, higher growth in the poorest regions may have led to an increase in income differentials in regional labour markets, especially in the large metropolitan areas, due to the need for more skilled workers in better-paid high-productivity economic activities. At the same time, at the bottom of the scale, incomes are below the minimum wage, and workers are occupied mainly in informal activities. In fact, Fortaleza, Salvador, and Recife – major metropolitan areas in the Northeast – have the highest levels of inequality in the country (Barbosa et al., 2013).

One consequence of these patterns is that cash transfer programmes, such as the PBF, contributed most effectively to the reduction of inequality in the rural Northeast, as in the other areas labour income still represents over two-thirds of total family income.

Table 5.2.5.A. Poverty by Region, India, 1983–2011/12 (% of Households below Poverty Line)

Region	1983	1993-94	2004-05	2004-05 Revised*	2011-12
Northeast	50.2	37.0	22.9	33.5	22.8
Centre	53.5	45.8	37.7	47.2	32.0
Northwest	28.0	24.2	17.1	26.3	11.8
South/West	39.4	30.7	22.9	32.8	14.8
Kerala	40.4	25.4	15.0	19.6	7.1
All India	44.5	36.0	27.5	37.2	21.9

Source: Government of India, Planning Commission; India Human Development Report, 2011.
Note: *A committee chaired by Suresh Tendulkar developed a new method of calculation of poverty that was applied after 2009-10. For 2004-05 the calculation using the old and new methods are both presented. The new method gave poverty estimates about 10 percentage points higher than the previous method for India as a whole. The estimate for 2011-12 uses the new method, estimates prior to 2004-05 the old method.

Table 5.2.5.B. Poverty by Region, Brazil, 1993 to 2011 (% below Poverty Line)

Region	1993	2005	2011
Northeast	53.8	34.8	22.0
North	39.0	22.3	17.7
Mid-West	40.0	25.5	12.2
Southeast	30.2	19.0	11.2
South	19.0	9.3	4.5
Brazil	35.5	22.2	13.5

Source: PNAD/IBGE data using Sonia Rocha's poverty line (Rocha, 2003).

Graph 5.2.4.A. Poverty Level (% of Households) by Region as a Ratio to the National Average, India, 1983–2011/12

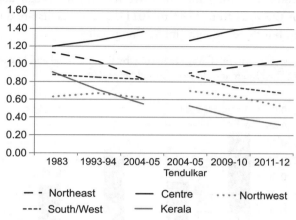

Source: Table 5.2.5.A.

Note: For the two estimates for 2004-05 see the note to Table 5.2.5.A.

Graph 5.2.4.B. Poverty Level (% of Households) by Region as a Ratio to the National Average, Brazil, 1993 to 2011

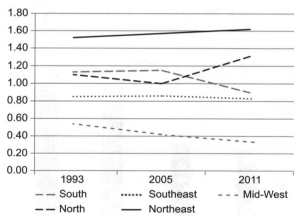

Source: Table 5.2.5.B.

5.2.4   *Regional factors in the decomposition of wage inequality*

Another way to examine the contribution of regional differences to inequality is by decomposing the overall (Theil) inequality index into inequality within and between regions, as discussed in Section 4.3. Graphs 5.2.5 and 5.2.6 give the results of the decomposition of the Theil index of wage inequality by region in the two countries, using the same five regions, for urban and rural areas separately, for the years from 1983 to 2011-12. The results are different in the two countries, but there are some interesting parallels.

Graph 5.2.5. Decomposition of Wage Inequality by Region, Rural and Urban, India, 1983–2011/12. Theil Index and Between Group Share (%)

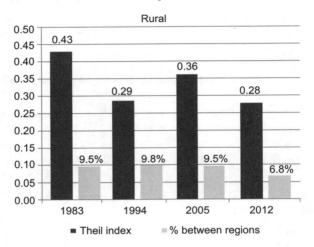

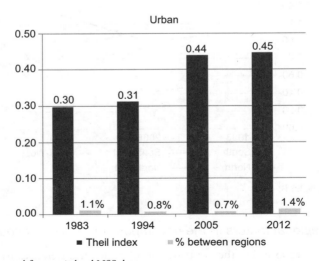

Source: Computed from unit-level NSS data.

Graph 5.2.6. Decomposition of Wage Inequality by Region, Rural and Urban, Brazil, 1983–2011. Theil Index and Between Group Share (%)

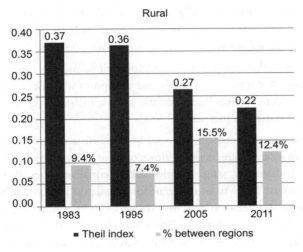

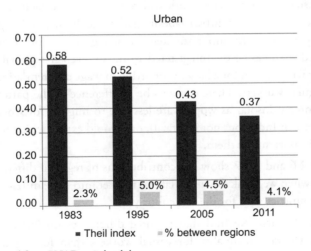

Source: Computed from PNAD unit-level data.

First, the contribution of regional differences to overall inequality is significant in both countries in rural areas. It accounts for close to 10 per cent of the Theil index in India until 2004-05 and declines to 7 per cent in the most recent data; and 12 per cent in Brazil in the most recent year, after fluctuating over time.

The relative importance of regional inequality has increased in Brazil compared with the 1980s and 1990s but, since overall inequality has been declining (the left-hand column for each year gives the Theil index), its absolute contribution has declined. In India, there has been some decline in both absolute and relative importance of regional inequality in rural areas after 2004-05.

In urban areas, the contribution of regional differences is much less than in rural areas in both countries, but it is more important in Brazil, where it has shown some tendency to decline since the 1990s. In India, the contribution is smaller, but has started to increase.

To interpret these differences, we need to take into account the segmentation of the labour market. There are large flows of migrant workers between regions, at least in the Indian case, which would tend to equalize wages. But these flows and their impact are likely to be different for casual and regular workers, in rural and urban areas, and between men and women. There is some expectation that the labour markets for regular or registered work would be better integrated at the national level than those for casual or unregistered work, because wages for regular or registered work are likely to be more standardized and regulated while those for casual or unregistered work will respond to local factors. For similar reasons, one would expect urban labour markets to be better integrated than rural. But, perhaps more important, regular or registered work is much more differentiated than casual or unregistered work; so, even if regional factors are similar, they will account for a larger proportion of wage differentiation for casual than for regular workers. There can also be a difference in the pattern between men and women; insofar as women are less free to migrate for work (which is largely the case in India, but not in Brazil), one would expect regional differences to be more important for them.

Tables 5.2.6 and 5.2.7 show the contributions of regional differences to the Theil index when we break down the labour market into these different segments in the two countries, and for the same four years.

Taking India first, we find that regional differences do indeed contribute much more to wage inequality for casual workers than for regular workers, in both urban and rural areas; and, among both casual and regular workers, the contribution is distinctly greater in rural areas than in urban areas. These differences are sustained over time but, for casual workers in both urban and rural areas, there is a tendency for the contribution of region to rise until 2004-05, and then fall somewhat. For regular workers, the pattern is less consistent, but there is a slight tendency for the regional contribution to increase in the most recent data.

Table 5.2.6. Percentage Contribution of Regional Differences to Decomposition of Theil Index by Work Type and Sex, Rural and Urban, India, 1983–2011/12

		1983	1993-94	2004-05	2011-12
Rural regular	All	4	1	4	5
	Female	7	3	5	5
	Male	4	1	4	6
Rural casual	All	14	24	28	24
	Female	18	18	22	11
	Male	11	25	31	30
Urban regular	All	1	0	1	2
	Female	4	3	3	4
	Male	1	0	1	2
Urban casual	All	7	10	18	14
	Female	12	8	13	9
	Male	6	10	23	18

Source: Computed from NSS unit-level data.

Table 5.2.7. Percentage Contribution of Regional Differences to Decomposition of Theil Index by Work Type and Sex, Rural and Urban, Brazil, 1995–2011

Area	Work Status	Sex	1995	2005	2011
Rural	Registered	Total	1.1	7.9	6.9
		Male	0.3	9.1	8.0
		Female	7.9	5.9	6.5
	Non-registered	Total	10.9	14.7	9.4
		Male	8.8	15.1	10.1
		Female	24.2	14.0	12.0
Urban	Registered	Total	2.7	2.6	2.6
		Male	2.7	3.0	3.2
		Female	2.8	2.1	2.0
	Non-registered	Total	5.8	5.3	5.4
		Male	5.9	6.3	6.6
		Female	5.9	3.8	3.7

Source: Prepared by authors based on PNAD/IBGE micro-data.

There is also a tendency for regional factors to be somewhat less important for women than for men, except in urban regular work. This is contrary to expectations if constraints on migration are playing an important role, and suggests that patterns of gender inequality across the country mainly reflect other factors.

In Brazil, for which we have data from 1995, we find the same pattern as for India when we compare registered and unregistered workers (which we treat as comparable with regular and casual workers). The contribution of region is much higher for unregistered workers in both rural and urban areas. And, like in India, the contribution of region is greater in rural areas than in urban areas. The patterns in Brazil and India are fairly similar for regular workers in both urban and rural areas, but there is a bigger gap for casual workers. Taking the most recent data (2011 in Brazil and 2011-12 in India), the contribution of region is as follows

- Rural regular wages: 5 per cent in India and 7 per cent in Brazil;
- Urban regular wages: respectively, 2 per cent and 3 per cent;
- Rural casual wages: 24 per cent and 9 per cent; and
- Urban casual wages: 14 per cent and 5 per cent.

The pattern for female versus male workers is also somewhat similar in the two countries. In general, regional differences account for a larger share of inequality for men than for women, the main exception being unregistered work in rural areas in Brazil and regular work in urban areas in India.

How do these results relate to the broad picture we presented above? On the whole, in India, the contribution of regional inequality to overall wage inequality has risen since the 1980s for most segments of the labour market, with the clearest growth in inequality between 1993-94 and 2004-05. This is in line with the conclusions based on output, expenditure, and poverty. On the other hand, the trend seems to have been reversed after 2004-05. In Brazil, the contribution of regional differences to overall inequality has been small and quite stable in urban areas (the majority of the population), but the absolute contribution of region has declined along with other factors. In rural areas, regional differences are somewhat more important, with a tendency to first rise and then decline after 2005.

5.2.5   Final remarks

The importance of regional inequality lies not only in the regional differentials themselves but also in the relationship with other forms of inequality. The distribution of the population by race, caste, or community varies between regions in both countries and generates a connection between racial/caste inequality and regional inequality that may reinforce both. In the case of India, the more backward central and northeastern regions have a relatively high tribal population, and while Muslims are found throughout India they constitute a larger share of the population in the poorer Centre region. In Brazil, the tribal populations are concentrated in the North, but they are few in number, and there are large differences between regions in the proportion of the population described as 'white', 'black', or 'mixed'. The proportion of 'white' varies from almost 80 per cent in the South to less than a quarter in the North and, in this situation, racial and regional differences overlap, interact, and assume different configurations.

The same is true of gender inequalities, which vary from region to region, and even more so in rural or urban areas within each region. In India, wage differentials by sex are larger in rural areas than in urban areas, and discrimination against women is greater in the North of the country than in the South or the Northeast. The difference in literacy rates between men and women is only 4 points in Kerala but 20 in the Centre region. Looking at the disparities in terms of schooling in Brazil, a college degree means something totally different in a small town in the Northeast as compared to large metropolitan areas like Salvador or Recife in the same region. And to be a black person with a diploma in these cities, in which the bulk of the population consists of black and mixed people, is different than for someone living in the capital city of a southern state, like Porto Alegre. We will be able to say a little more about these connections between different aspects of inequality when we look at multivariate decompositions in Section 5.5.

How do the regional patterns we describe above relate to the overall growth regimes in the two countries? It seems plausible that the growth observed in regional inequality in India is in part due to liberalization since the 1980s. During the state-led period prior to 1980, mechanisms were in place to equalize opportunities between states, for instance in the pricing of rail transport, and some large-scale public investment was located in relatively backward states such as Bihar. The partial deregulation of industrial licensing after the 1980s and the reduction of the role of the state in investment facilitated a process of polarization. Private investment became concentrated in areas with the easiest access to markets, friendly state governments, higher levels of education, and good infrastructure. States with political instability, such as Punjab, and especially Bihar or Uttar Pradesh, were not favoured, and investment tended to concentrate in states such as Gujarat and Tamil Nadu, and cities such as Delhi, Mumbai, and Bangalore. Mining was the main exception, but the benefits of large-scale mining tend to be captured by national rather than local interests.

This process of polarization continues today. Large states in the poor Centre region such as Bihar and Uttar Pradesh continue to serve as labour reserves, and provide migrant workers on a large scale to industrial and service sector development elsewhere. Growth in Bihar has accelerated recently, but it is on a rather tenuous base of construction and trade, and output per capita in the state remains far below the all-India average. Social policy could in principle partly compensate for regional differences (Section 4.4), but in practice some of the most important such policies – notably the PDS that provides subsidized food and the MGNREGA in rural areas – are least effectively implemented in the poorest regions (Dutta et al., 2012). Meanwhile, remittances from migrants lead to consumption differentials between regions that are lower than production differentials, and so alleviate (but do not reverse) the trend towards greater regional inequality in living standards.

In Brazil, the liberalization in the 1990s occurred in an economy that was already highly polarized. Further, it generated neither a large increase in productive investment nor a substantial rate of growth. So it is not surprising that there was little change in the pattern of regional inequality either. It is true that the poorest regions did better in terms of economic performance, but this was because the more diversified industrial base of the Southeast had shrunk due to economic liberalization. The real change occurred with the new growth regime put in place after the turn of the twenty-first century. This regime, however incomplete it might have been, was one in which a substantial effort was made to redistribute the benefits of higher growth, with increasing formalization, higher minimum wages, and a wider set of social policies. The result was a shift in the pattern of growth in favour not only of lower-income groups but also of relatively disadvantaged regions, which also benefited from public investment and were able to attract private investment – even in capital-intensive industries aiming to supply the internal market. Levels of output, income, and employment rose faster in these regions, and made them much more important than in the past as internal engines of growth. However, inequalities became more deeply embedded within these regions, and poverty fell less rapidly than in the richest regions. In the Northeast, for instance, this can be observed not only in the levels of income but also in terms of access to social policies like health, education, housing, and basic infrastructure, which affected rural areas as well as the poor living in metropolitan regions. In these respects, the gap with the Southeast is still enormous, and even larger than in terms of incomes (Cacciamali and Barbosa, 2014).

The experience of the two countries is, therefore, different. But both show the association of growing regional inequality with higher growth rates – in India in the last three decades, and in Brazil during its high growth period before 1980. Both countries also show how the overall growth regime shapes the pattern of regional inequality; therefore, regional variations have to be interpreted within the larger picture. This is particularly so because increasingly integrated markets for labour, capital, and goods – but to a different extent in the two countries – mean that regional growth patterns are inter-related. In the case of India, flows of labour from backward regions tend to discourage private investment in those regions and concentrate industrial growth in higher-income areas, as was the case for Brazil in the 1950s. In Brazil, in the recent period, there has been some diversification of investment decisions, which has benefited the poorest states, and especially their metropolitan areas. This may, in turn, yield positive effects for the richest regions, as they have broader economic structures that can respond to the growing demand from poorer regions. On the other hand, the recent Brazilian experience suggests that national social policies to reduce poverty or create social infrastructure – even if effective in reducing poverty in the relatively backward areas of the poorest regions – may not be enough to change the embedded patterns of inequality.

Annex: Regional Clusters in India

As noted above, for purposes of comparison with Brazil, five regions were identified in India, based on geographical clusters of states. Regional patterns in India are complex, and it is easy to make the case for six, eight, or ten regions rather than five. The choice of five was dictated by the desire to facilitate comparison with Brazil, but there is significant heterogeneity within each of the five regions identified. Moreover, state boundaries are not always a good basis for defining regions – for example, western and eastern Uttar Pradesh are very different from each other, and many states contain both 'advanced' and 'backward' areas.

We have also neglected some small states and territories that have their own characteristics. So, this exercise does not pretend to fully depict the detail of regional disparities in India; rather, it presents a broad overall picture, built upon certain key differences between different parts of the country. This being said, we consider that the regional structure proposed here does capture some of the most important aspects of regional differentiation, and is a legitimate basis for the comparison with Brazil.

Annex Table 5.2.1 gives some social and economic indicators for major Indian states. The states were clustered on the basis of the first six variables in the table, covering expenditure per capita, poverty, output per capita, and its growth and urbanization, all of which share the same broad regional pattern, along with a criterion of geographical contiguity. The Centre region is perhaps the most sharply distinguished from the others, with high poverty and low expenditure, per capita product, growth, and urbanization. The Northwest has, on average, low poverty and high expenditure, output, and urbanization. There is some variation between states, and Rajasthan is a particular outlier here – it is really intermediate between the Northwest and the Centre regions. The other state with really high expenditure and low poverty is Kerala, which is so much of an outlier that it is placed in a region on its own. Kerala has the highest educational levels and wages by some margin, but a low share of manufacturing.

The South/West region combines several states with a high reliance on manufacturing and high growth, all quite urbanized, which nevertheless does not give them the highest household expenditures per capita or the lowest poverty. This group includes Gujarat and Maharashtra in the West and Karnataka, Andhra Pradesh (including what is now Telangana), and Tamil Nadu in the South. It is not usual to group Tamil Nadu with the regions around Mumbai and Ahmedabad, for it has a completely different history and culture, but on the basis of the indicators used here it fits this cluster, rather than grouping it with Kerala, which would be a more conventional approach.

Finally, the Northeast is extremely heterogeneous. Its indicators for output, expenditure, and poverty are better than the central region, and its economic structures are different. In India, the 'Northeast', as the term is usually understood, does not include West Bengal or its capital Kolkata, but in terms of these indicators, the whole northeastern region is best taken together.

Annex Table 5.2.1. Regional Inequality Indicators for India

	Per Capita Expenditure 2011-12		Poverty % of Households	Per Capita Net State Domestic Product 2010-11 at 2004-05 Prices	Urbanization 2011(%)	Agriculture Share of Output 2008-09	Manufacturing Share of Output 2008-09	Male Casual Wage 2011-12	Regular Workers % 2011-12	Literacy % 2011 Female
	Rural	Urban								
Northwest	**1879**	**2772**	**10.5**	**51246**	**37.5**	**22.3**	**13.8**	**200**	**26.2**	**68.1**
Delhi	2690	3161	9.9	108876	97.5	0.5	8.8	265	62.9	80.9
Haryana	1926	3346	11.1	59221	34.8	23.1	20	204	23.9	66.8
Himachal	1801	3173	8.1	47106	10	19	13.6	173	18.2	76.6
Jammu/ Kashmir	1601	2320	10.4	27607	27.2	28.6	8.1	211	20.5	58.0
Punjab	2136	2743	8.3	44752	37.5	32.6	16.1	203	27.5	71.3
Uttarakhand	1551	2452	11.3	44723	30.6	28.4	14.1	177	17.5	70.7
Rajasthan	1445	2207	14.7	26436	24.9	24	15.6	167	13	52.7
Centre	**965**	**1780**	**34.1**	**21327**	**20.9**	**23.2**	**16.7**	**124**	**9.7**	**59.0**
Bihar	970	1397	33.7	13632	11.3	31.6	2.5	132	5.8	53.3
Chhattisgarh	904	1776	39.9	27156	23.2	18.3	21.9	96	9.7	60.6
Jharkhand	916	1894	37.0	21734	24.1	15.5	32	141	10.2	56.2
Madhya Pradesh	1024	1842	31.7	22382	27.6	26.2	12.7	113	11.3	60.0
Odisha	905	1830	32.6	25708	16.7	19.2	17	127	10.6	64.4
Uttar Pradesh	1073	1942	29.4	17349	22.3	28.4	14	137	10.6	59.3

Cont.

Cont.

	Per Capita Expenditure 2011-12		Poverty % of Households	Per Capita Net State Domestic Product 2010-11 at 2004-05 Prices	Urbanization 2011(%)	Agriculture Share of Output 2008-09	Manufacturing Share of Output 2008-09	Male Casual Wage 2011-12	Regular Workers % 2011-12	Literacy % 2011 Female
	Rural	Urban								
Northeast	**1213**	**2251**	**24.2**	**30221**	**25.0**	**22.5**	**10.4**	**137**	**16.4**	**71.5**
West Bengal	1170	2490	20.0	32228	31.9	20.7	16.4	128	16.8	71.2
Assam	1057	2090	32.0	21406	14.1	23.9	10.7	145	14.2	67.3
Other NE	1412	2174	20.7	37029	29.1	22.9	4			76.0
South/West	**1481**	**2680**	**15.1**	**49406**	**41.7**	**15.3**	**21.7**	**161**	**23.4**	**69.6**
Gujarat	1430	2472	16.6	52708	42.6	16	29.9	123	24.7	70.7
Maharashtra	1446	2937	17.4	62729	45.2	13.4	23.4	142	26.5	75.5
Andhra Pradesh	1563	2559	9.2	40366	33.5	22.2	12	168	17.9	59.7
Karnataka	1395	2899	20.9	39301	38.6	13.8	19.9	170	22.5	68.1
Tamil Nadu	1571	2534	11.3	51928	48.6	11	23.3	204	25.5	73.9
Kerala	**2355**	**3044**	**7.1**	**49873**	**47.7**	**15.7**	**10**	**350**	**22.5**	**92.0**
India	**1287**	**2477**	**21.9**	**35993**	**31.2**	**16.2**	**17**	**155**	**17.9**	**65.5**

Source: First three columns, Planning Commission (2013); fourth column, Government of India, Ministry of Statistics and Plan Implementation; fifth column, Census of India (2011); sixth and seventh columns, Government of India, MOSPI; eighth and ninth columns, IHD (2014); tenth column, Census of India (2011).

5.3 Inequalities across Race and Caste

As we have seen, labour markets are deeply segmented in both India and Brazil. Different social groups face disparities in employment opportunities and wages, which reflect unequal access to segmented production structures, patterns of power and control in the labour market, as well as attitudes of employers towards different categories of workers. This often takes the form of overt or hidden discrimination against some groups on the basis of social attributes such as caste, ethnicity, religion, language and, of course – as we saw in Section 5.1 – gender. Discrimination in the labour market can be found in barriers to entry in the labour market, restricted occupational mobility within internal labour markets, and differing returns for equivalent work.

The forces driving segmentation are pervasive, for it is generally the case that overall wage costs are lower where employers are able to differentiate between workers and pay lower wages to those who are less well endowed or organized. But the factors of segmentation vary across time and space. In this section, we consider caste, ethnicity, and religion in India, and race or colour in Brazil. These heterogeneities have different historical origins and social meanings, but there are some parallels in the role they play in the labour market. Of course, these are all social constructs, rather than fundamental differences between populations. So we do not equate caste in India with race/colour in Brazil, but rather examine and contrast the roles they play in differently segmented labour markets.

In Brazil, we consider race, which is usually identified with skin colour. For our purpose, it should be noted that in the last Demographic Census (2010), five skin colour/racial groups were available for respondents: white, yellow, mixed, black, and indigenous. Even though the government introduced this classification in the Census, the respondent self-identifies her or his skin colour, which is a matter of individual and social identity.

In India, caste has a more formal status, since it is both officially and socially recognized, but its deep historical roots do not make it any less arbitrary. Tribal populations are also recognized in both countries, populations that may predate later invasions and colonizations and that either live on the margins of these societies, or are integrated, but usually in a subordinated fashion.

We first consider these dimensions of labour market inequality in India and Brazil separately, before comparing them.

5.3.1   India

The overall pattern

In India, caste, tribe, and religion are all sources of discrimination and differentiation – through social and economic inclusion and exclusion, segregation in housing, differences in access to public and private services, and differences in employment opportunities, including traditionally prescribed occupational segregations.

Caste is an ascriptive, hereditary, and hierarchic system of social grouping. The system in its traditional form categorized individuals into four *Varnas* – *Brahmin* (priests and scholars), *Kshatriya* (warriors and rulers), *Vaishya* (merchants and traders), and *Shudra* (service and artisanal occupations, labour). In principle, each caste had a fixed hereditary occupation by birth, resulting in a clearly defined pattern of inclusions and exclusions in society. Those who did not belong to any of the four *Varnas* were historically untouchable, relegated to stigmatized 'impure' occupations (like tanning, scavenging, sweeping, and cleaning), and denied access to society and to alternative employment opportunities. The majority of these 'low' caste workers or Dalits are today landless manual or agricultural labourers (Thorat and Umakant, 2004).

The reality of caste, how it has evolved, and its role in today's society constitute a large subject. Caste and class appear to belong to two different domains, but there is a long tradition of debate on their intersection and on how this intersection has changed (Srinivas, 1962; Beteille, 1966; Sharma, 1980; Pankaj, 2004; among many others). Here, we confine ourselves to some of the practical consequences. The caste system widens options for some and limits them for others, and so creates a complex pattern of social stratification. Dalits have been particularly disadvantaged in social, economic, and political spheres; the prohibitions placed on them are multiple, and these have been enforced by both state and non-state actors. This group was officially recognized by the Constitution (Scheduled Castes) Order, 1950. The word 'Scheduled' refers to the fact that these castes have been listed in a schedule, and are entitled to benefit from certain forms of affirmative action, including reservations in the political sphere and in public sector employment. More recently, there has been official recognition of caste groups located in the middle of the caste hierarchy, known as the Other Backward Classes (OBCs), which have often claimed 'disadvantaged' status and have also been considered for affirmative government policies (Section 4.4). There is a bewildering variety of OBC categories in different parts of the country, but they often dominate particular occupations, which tends to fragment the labour market. In reality, many OBCs are better organized and economically well off than notionally higher status social groups and in some areas are dominant, both economically and politically.

A second source of differentiation concerns certain ethnic groups known as Scheduled Tribes (STs). Cultural and spatial isolation, among other factors, have led to their exclusion from the mainstream social, economic, and political spheres. They constitute about 9 per cent of India's population and are mostly concentrated in the Northeast and the hilly and dry regions of eastern and central India. They also have low access to economic resources, education, and income and employment opportunities; and their socio-economic status is often even lower than that of SCs. Like the SCs, their position is officially recognized in the Constitution (Scheduled Tribes) Order, 1950.

Religion acts as another basis for social and economic differentiation in India. Different religious communities have different socio-economic characteristics and levels of living. Among the various religious communities present in India, Muslims and Christians are often found to be relatively deprived, though there are also well-off groups within both communities. There is a significant regional dimension to this religious differentiation (Basant, 2012). For instance, in terms of access to employment, control over economic resources, income and standard of living, Muslims in eastern and northern India are less well off than their counterparts in southern and western India.

Some aspects of the system of caste hierarchy present in Hindu society are also found in Muslim and Christian communities in India, though the system of occupational divisions is less rigid (Ahmed, 1978). In any event, the OBC categorization has been extended to a number of Muslim groups, and some Christian groups are considered as Dalits.

Thus, Indian society is quite fragmented. It was widely expected that these caste divisions would disappear gradually with urbanization, education, and rising incomes. But they have continued in practice, in part because of endogamy and a strong sense of caste identity, especially in rural areas, but which carries over in attenuated fashion in urban areas too. Upper castes are distinctly over-represented among the urban middle class (Rao, 1992). The role of caste evolves, helping to legitimize inequality and playing a role in Indian society comparable to that played by racial distinctions in some other countries (Deshpande, 2011; Jodhka, 2014). Of course, the Constitution of India prohibits caste-based discrimination, but it persists despite the variety of policies that have attempted to overcome this form of inequality over the years since independence.

Differential ownership of and access to productive assets is one fundamental cause of inequality and exclusion. Caste-based unequal access to land has been a root cause of structural inequality in rural society. The ownership of land has largely been concentrated among upper-caste Hindus, a minority of Muslims, and some OBC groups. The majority of SCs, and many Hindu and Muslim OBCs, are landless, and work as tenant farmers or agricultural labourers. STs have greater access to land, sometimes through community ownership; however, this land is generally forest, hilly, or dry land, often unsuitable for agriculture. Table 5.3.1 shows how the pattern of landholding and landlessness is differentiated among these groups. There is comparable inequality in the ownership of private enterprises. In 2004-05, SCs accounted for ownership of only 10 per cent of enterprises against a 21 per cent share in population, and these were disproportionately small household enterprises; there was a similar pattern for STs (Thorat et al., 2010).

Table 5.3.1. Land Ownership and Landlessness by Caste in Rural Areas (% of Households), India, 2011–2013

Year	Scheduled Caste	Scheduled Tribe	Other Backward Classes	Other (upper) Castes	All Households
Landlessness (%), 2011-12	61.2	38.7	43.3	n.a.	47.4
Average land holding (ha.), 2013	0.27	0.65	0.60	0.82	0.59

Source: Landlessness, NSS unit level data, 68th round, 2011-12. Landholding, Government of India, National Sample Survey Office (2015).

The close nexus between land and caste permeates class relations in rural India, though the patterns and mechanisms vary from one part of India to another. It also provides the basis for diversification away from agriculture, so that rural hierarchies are reproduced in urban areas. For instance, caste groups like the Reddys in Andhra Pradesh and Kammas in Karnataka have been successful in converting the surplus from agriculture into investment in modern entrepreneurship (Benbabaali, 2013). Access to education and modern employment was first gained by the landed castes because they were in a position to invest in the education of their children, a pattern that has been replicated in other parts of the country.

In urban areas, access to education, financial resources, and high-end occupations constitute important bases for class differentiation. With higher levels of education and greater access to finance, upper castes dominate modern occupations and have greater ownership of industrial and service capital.

Caste-based division of occupations has been another basis for inequality. For instance, business and trade were socially earmarked for the Vaishyas, one of the four major caste groups. Modern business families like the Ambanis, Mittals, Birlas among others, belong to this community. Dalits have been relegated mostly to the lowest ranks of employment. Recently, there has been some growth in the numbers of Dalit businessmen and entrepreneurs in the form of petty shopkeepers, businessmen, and traders, and the Dalit Chamber of Commerce and Industries has been established to promote the cause of this group. But this growth of small businesses among Dalits and lower castes mainly follows traditional occupational patterns, with cobblers becoming shoemakers and barbers opening salons.

Access to modern employment is greatly dependent on educational qualifications and skill, so inequality in education is an important source of inequality in the labour market. Modern educational institutions from both before and after independence mainly served the elite and social biases persisted. Children belonging to backward classes and low castes, and girls in particular, had little access to education. These biases are still present, although their impact has declined. Instances of denial of education to SC and ST children still occur. Differential levels of school enrolment and high drop-out rates among lower-caste children, especially girls, is a direct consequence of this discrimination. Some children from the Muslim community continue to attend religious institutions of elementary education, the *madrasas*, which have been slow to adopt a modern curriculum (Alam, 2013). Today, primary school enrolment has risen substantially, but children belonging to these groups still have a lower rate of completion of secondary or higher education. This can be seen in the overall pattern of years of schooling across social and religious groups. In 2007-08, upper social groups reported an average of 5.7 years of schooling, double that of STs (2.8 years), and almost double that of SCs (3.2 years). Muslims had distinctly less schooling (3.3 years) than Hindus (4.3 years), on average (Government of India, 2011).

Nevertheless, the gaps in literacy rates between SCs, STs, and others have declined substantially (Table 5.3.2), especially after 1980. Compared with the average for the population as a whole, the difference in 2011 was less than 10 percentage points for both men and women among SCs, a little higher for

STs. But this progress in literacy has been accompanied by a shift in educational inequality further up the system, for it is now secondary and tertiary education that provide the credentials required for access to good jobs, and at this level caste inequalities persist, as we discuss further below.

Table 5.3.2. Male and Female Literacy Rates (%) Among SCs, STs, and Total Population, India, 1961–2011

	Total Population			Scheduled Castes			Scheduled Tribes		
Year	Persons	Male	Female	Persons	Male	Female	Persons	Male	Female
1961	28	40	15	10	17	3	9	14	3
1971	34	46	22	15	22	6	11	18	5
1981	44	56	30	21	31	11	16	22	8
1991	52	64	39	37	50	24	30	41	18
2001	65	75	55	55	67	42	47	59	35
2011 (P)	74	82	65	66	75	57	59	69	49

Source: Census Reports of various years.

The labour market

The distribution of some of the most important groups in the population as a whole and in different employment statuses is summarized in Table 5.3.3.

Table 5.3.3. Percentage Distribution of Workers (UPSS) by Social Group and Work Status, India, 2011-12

Socio-Religious Group	Share in Total Population	Share of Workforce	Self-Employed	Regular Wage Workers	Casual Wage Workers
STs	8.7	10.2	10.4	5.0	12.8
SCs	18.8	19.3	13.6	16.5	30.4
OBCs	44.0	43.5	46.1	38.5	42.0
Upper Hindus	20.1	19.4	21.4	31.7	8.6
Upper Muslims	6.6	5.9	6.5	5.5	5.1
Others	1.7	1.8	2.1	2.8	0.7
Total	100	100	100	100	100

Source: IHD (2014). Computed from unit-level data of NSSO, 68th Round. Muslim OBCs are included with other OBCs in this table, so that 'Upper Muslims' refers to the remaining, generally better-off, Muslim groups.

In the labour market, SCs and STs are disproportionately found in low-wage employment or low-productivity activities. This is not necessarily or even principally due to direct discrimination, since it also reflects the skewed distribution of assets and of educational qualifications. But the result is that casual wage workers come disproportionately from the SC and ST communities. On the other hand, regular employment in both public and private sectors is dominated by the upper castes. Lower-caste workers, if at all employed in regular and salaried jobs, are generally found in menial and lower-grade occupations. The proportion of STs, SCs, and OBCs is higher in low-paid agricultural work and in other labour-intensive sectors like construction. Many caste and community groups show a concentration in specific occupations; for instance, upper-class Muslims have a larger presence in manufacturing and trade activities in urban areas (IHD, 2014).

Tables 5.3.4 and 5.3.5 give the broad pattern in 1983 and in 2011-12. It can be seen that in 1983 half of SCs were in casual work, as against only 22 per cent of 'others' (i.e., middle and upper castes), who were more likely than average to be in regular work or self-employment. STs were mostly self-employed, but mainly in low-productivity agriculture, with few regular jobs. This difference in employment status was then compounded by differences in wages within each employment category. For all categories of wage work – whether regular or casual, rural or urban – SCs and STs received wages below the average, and in the case of regular work 20–30 per cent below the average. Differences were less for casual work, where the labour market was more homogenous, but even here STs received 13 per cent less than average in urban areas.

In the following three decades, the improvements were small (Table 5.3.5). In 2011-12, the OBC category can be separated out in the statistics. It can be seen that the employment status pattern for this group was not much different from the overall average, with slightly more self-employment. OBCs were much less likely to be in casual employment than STs and, especially, SCs. But, in regular work, their wages were lower than the average, and much lower than for 'other', mainly upper-caste, groups. As for SCs and STs, their employment pattern had hardly changed since 1983. SCs obtained a little more regular employment, but their wages remained low – for example SC wages in regular work were still 15–25 per cent below the average. STs showed some improvement in regular wages, but little gain in regular employment, and they still seemed to be disadvantaged in the casual labour market. The upper-caste category was much more likely to be in regular work – 26 per cent against 15 per cent for SCs and OBCs and 9 per cent for STs – and in that work they had wages 20–25 per cent higher than average.

The policy of job reservations for SCs and STs in the public sector (Section 4.4) has clearly had some impact, because the share of these groups employed (in regular work) is higher in the public sector than in the private sector, and this higher share may in part account for the rise in regular work among SCs. Nevertheless, public sector workers from lower castes tend to be concentrated in lower level jobs, such as peon, cleaner, sweeper, driver, and assistant. It has also been observed that posts reserved in the public sector for SCs and STs have often been left vacant.

Table 5.3.4. Employment Status and Wages by Social Group, India, 1983

	SC	ST	Other	All
Employment status (%)				
Self-Employed	37.9	55.5	62.6	57.3
Regular	11.4	7.9	14.8	13.4
Casual workers	50.1	36.3	22.4	28.9
Wage (2011–12 rupees per day)				
Regular urban	139	155	196	188
Regular rural	72	66	111	99
Casual urban	74	66	77	76
Casual rural	44	43	46	45
Wage ratio to average				
Regular urban	74%	82%	104%	
Regular rural	73%	67%	112%	
Casual urban	97%	87%	101%	
Casual rural	98%	96%	102%	

Source: Computed from NSSO unit level data.

Over the period as a whole, it could be said that there is no great change in the overall pattern of caste differentiation. Upper castes are still most likely to be in regular work and least likely to be in casual work; SCs shared in the (rather small) increase in regular work, but remained concentrated in casual employment; and STs experienced very little change over the period as a whole. So, over the thirty years during which the Indian economy was transformed, there was very little impact on the social hierarchy in the labour market.

With respect to wages, STs did relatively well in regular work – but there were few regular ST workers. In casual work, they gained less than average, and had the lowest daily wages of any group. The wages of SCs in casual work were close to the overall average throughout the period. But, of course, since SCs and STs were concentrated in lower-paying casual work, the overall wage differentials between social groups remained large. Moreover, upper castes did much better than SCs and STs in regular urban work, which was the important and expanding category, and paid wages almost three times those in casual work.

Taking into account both type of work and wage, it can be said that SCs broadly maintained their relative position over 30 years; STs clearly did the least well overall; and upper castes gained both in wages and in the type of work.

Table 5.3.5. Employment Status and Wages by Social Group, India, 2011-12

	SC	ST	OBC	Other	All
Employment status (%)					
Self-employed	36.7	53.6	55.3	57.7	52.2
Regular	15.3	8.7	15.8	26.4	17.9
Casual workers	48.0	37.6	28.9	15.9	29.9
Wage (2011–12 rupees per day)					
Regular urban	324	423	360	558	445
Regular rural	249	288	272	348	294
Casual urban	165	141	175	153	166
Casual rural	137	114	140	139	135
Wage ratio to average					
Regular urban	73%	95%	81%	125%	
Regular rural	85%	98%	93%	118%	
Casual urban	99%	85%	105%	92%	
Casual rural	101%	84%	104%	103%	

Source: Computed from NSSO unit-level data.
Note: OBC as a social category was only introduced in the 1999-2000 survey.

How far the relatively poor showing of STs and SCs is due to direct discrimination is unclear. Madheswaran and Attewell (2007) argue that caste is still a determining factor in how individuals are remunerated in the wage labour market. In their analysis, belonging to a socially backward group such as SC or ST, or being a Muslim, is associated with significantly lower wages. The wage differences are more evident for regular than for casual workers.

Part of the difference in wages is certainly a reflection of lower educational qualifications and low skill levels among these groups; in other words, the discrimination occurs prior to labour market entry. Table 5.3.6 shows that the educational levels of SC and ST workers rose substantially between 1983 and 2011-12, but remained lower than those of other groups. Moreover, the educational credentials required for access to good jobs had also risen.

Table 5.3.6. Workforce by Education and Social Group: Distribution of Workers and Wage Ratios, India, 1983 and 2011-12 (%)

	Level of Education	1983	2011-12
Scheduled Castes and Scheduled Tribes	Not literate	73.8	39.1
	Literate less than primary completed	12.8	19.5
	Primary completed	7.5	14.9
	Middle school completed	4.0	12.9
	Secondary and higher secondary completed	1.7	10.9
	Graduates and above	0.3	2.9
All others	Not literate	54.9	28.9
	Literate less than primary completed	16.0	17.5
	Primary completed	12.8	13.5
	Middle school completed	8.6	14.1
	Secondary and higher secondary completed	5.9	18.0
	Graduates and above	1.8	8.0
Wage ratio, Others to SC/ST	Not literate	1.07	1.07
	Literate less than primary completed	1.15	1.12
	Primary completed	1.14	1.09
	Middle school completed	1.28	1.14
	Secondary and higher secondary completed	1.34	1.08
	Graduates and above	1.27	1.30
	All education levels	1.70	1.55

Source: Computed from NSSO unit-level data.

One way to assess the overall effect is to look at wage differentials between all others and SCs/STs. We see in the table that the overall wage differential between these two groups had fallen to some extent between 1983 and 2011-12, from 1.70 to 1.55. But this ratio was much higher for the workforce as a whole than for each educational category separately, because there is a concentration of SCs/STs at lower educational levels and lower wages. So, a considerable part of the overall wage differential was driven by differences in schooling. Nevertheless, if we look at the wage ratio within each educational category, the story is more complex. In 1983, these differentials rose fairly steadily with increasing education level, suggesting that wage discrimination was greater at middle and higher levels of schooling. In 2011-12, however, the pattern had changed – the wage ratio was around 1.1 for all categories up to secondary schooling, having declined substantially for all the higher groups. The one exception is the top level, graduates and above, where the wage differential had if anything slightly increased, and this is the category that grew most in the period. So it seems that wage discrimination against SC/ST, while present at all levels, has declined at middle and secondary levels, and is now more concentrated at the top of the educational ladder.

5.3.2 Brazil

In Brazil, there is no social hierarchy comparable to caste in India; the nearest analogy takes the form of racial inequality. But it is important to start by pointing out that we cannot talk about races as defined by biological factors – they do not exist as such. On the other hand, what can be done is to treat race as a 'social construct', reflecting the need to consider that discrimination and disparities related to skin colour are not only class-based. From this perspective, racial relations should not be regarded as a given, but investigated historically and empirically (Guimarães, 2002). It is, thus, essential to take into account the historical transformation of racial relations and disparities during the industrialization process (1930 to 1980), which brought about a new social stratification in which race (or skin colour) did matter, and also to examine whether they changed – and if so how – in the recent period.

Historical background

Racial cleavages and inequalities are a striking fact in Brazil's social reality even today. Part of the reason lies in the very history of the country, which had slavery as a basic institution for more than three centuries. But that is just a part of the reason.

During the colonial period, slavery was the backbone of society. This could be depicted as a 'social body made out of a double structure' (Mattoso, 2001). Even though (black) slaves were the ones who worked and the white population held the means of production, which included the slaves themselves, there was a growing population that did not fit into either of these two categories, especially in the nineteenth century, that is, before the abolition of slavery in 1888. They were made up of the white or mixed-colour 'poor free men', depending on personal relations with their 'masters' in rural areas, and of an increasing mixed-colour population performing a variety of non-slave tasks in cities. They were socially declassified in a slave-based society and – as skin colour mirrored a process of social stratification – some even held important positions when their 'whitening' could not be symbolically doubted (Prado Jr., 1942). This is related to the emergence of more skilled functions in a growing slave-based economy.

In addition, the security apparatus – in order to contain slave unrest – was quite strong. Mixed-colour people found a place, although very unstable, in this peculiar society (Alencastro, 2000).

Actually, there was no legal or fixed barrier, but rather a cultural and political one, against the social mobility of non-slave blacks and mixed-colour workers even in the colonial period. Also, their lack of skills and assets proved to be an important impediment (Hasenbalg, 2005). The idea of racial democracy – a myth developed in the mid-twentieth century in Brazil and very useful for white elites – was that there were no barriers between blacks and whites but only different endowments. The cultural and skin colour blending of most of the population was used to support this classist-racist viewpoint. The eugenics movement, especially during the late nineteenth century and the first decades of the past century, also helped to reinforce the belief in the inferiority of black people. These myths supported white privilege and black subordination, a configuration that would change once the labour market grew, receiving new entrants and leading to a process of social mobility.

In the 1960s, the idea of a racial democracy was highly contested. In his masterpiece of a study, which focused on the city of São Paulo, Fernandes (1964) showed how after slavery, blacks and mixed-colour groups were mostly excluded from the growing labour market in urban areas as they became increasingly restricted to menial jobs, precarious self-employment, or forced inactivity. The main reason could be found in the inheritance of slavery, which made them unable to psychologically and culturally fight for social positions in the upcoming capitalist society. So this was a type of exclusion from the labour market, or a partial incorporation into its borders and weaker links. However, after industrialization gained momentum, from the 1950s, black and mixed-colour people were increasingly incorporated as workers – although less skilled and lower paid – and even a black middle-class emerged. This proves that they were not incapable or inferior, as the white elites believed, but rather that they had been excluded from the core labour market. This exclusion was due especially to the labour surplus fed by the immigration of Europeans up to 1930, at least in the case of São Paulo, which was the cradle of the industrialization process.

After 1950, the work of blacks and mixed-colour groups was valued and trusted, and helped to hold labour costs down. This process benefited also from internal migration from the Northeast, with a preponderance of black and mixed-colour workers. They were now within the realm of the labour market, although at the bottom of the social pyramid. This optimistic approach even led Fernandes to call this new phase the 'second abolition' (of slavery).

Other authors were critical of this perspective, even if helped by Fernandes' research and hypotheses, and tried to show the coexistence of racism and capitalism in Brazil. This could be seen not only in the differentiation of labour status and wages between white and non-white workers, but also in a peculiar social stratification within both groups. This stratification created among blacks – especially black women – underclass positions not typical of a purely capitalist society, but essential to this new pattern of inequality, which should not be seen as an inheritance from slavery (Hasenbalg and Valle Silva, 1988).

After this brief account of race relations over time in Brazilian society, it should be stressed that they vary a great deal across different regions, as the racial composition of the population is not the same across the country. Also, the data used below distinguish non-white (black, mixed-colour, and indigenous populations, the latter a very small group) from white (including those of Asian origin). 'Non-white' is not a sociological category, but just a way of putting together 'racial' groups that have in common a distance from the other group, the whites. In socio-economic terms, mixed-colour people are between blacks and whites, but much closer to blacks. Actually, during the 1991 Census, a campaign was launched asking for the population to 'declare its colour', that is, to stress its racial identity. This campaign led to the grouping of the mixed-colour population and blacks in a single category (dos Anjos, 2013).

The indigenous population should also be mentioned here. Estimates suggest that they were five million in 1500 and had declined to one million in 1980, due to imported diseases, slavery, and other causes (Ribeiro, 1995). We can break them down into two basic groups: the indigenous in more isolated tribes, and the generic indigenous, the latter acculturated by the relationship with the market and the overall society. Today, like the other categories (blacks, whites, mixed, and yellow), the indigenous population is self-identified in the Demographic Census and the National Sample Survey (PNAD). This self-identification explains the rising figures for the indigenous population, especially those living in urban areas, who increasingly classify themselves as 'indigenous'. The so-called indigenous population jumped to around 800,000 (0.4 per cent of the total population) in the last Census (2010) from 300,000 in 1991. Most of the growth was concentrated in urban areas. However, 60 per cent of the total indigenous population lives in rural areas under a myriad of different cultural, social, and economic forms. The point about the changing size of the self-identified indigenous population also carries over to other groups. The data analysed here come from PNAD/IBGE and the Demographic Censuses. The percentage of population considered black and mixed-colour (our category of 'non-whites', which also includes the indigenous population) increased over the period. This was due to the method of self-identification, along with a political battle led by the black movement and social scientists around asserting one's blackness. In 1980, the percentage of mixed-colour and blacks together constituted 'only' 45 per cent of the total population, against 54.2 per cent of whites. In 2010, the percentage of the mixed-colour population was 43.1 per cent, and of blacks 7.6 per cent; that is, the sum of the two categories was a little over half the population. So, skin colour/race in Brazil has become a contentious issue, which has affected its very definition.

Situation in 1980

The Census data show that historical colour/race inequalities still persisted in the early 1980s but, as pointed out above, non-whites were now within the labour market, instead of being excluded from it. A higher proportion of white workers were wage employees and employers, whereas non-whites were over-represented among the self-employed (Table 5.3.7). Actually, the figures in the table underestimate the inequalities, as non-white workers were more often found in unregistered wage jobs and in forms of self-employment that required fewer assets and skills, apart from being less autonomous and more subject to exploitation.

Table 5.3.7. Work Status by Race for Workers Aged 15–65 Years, Brazil, 1980 (% Distribution)

	Non-white	White	Total
Unpaid	4.0	3.9	4.0
Employee	65.2	69.6	67.7
Employer	1.1	3.8	2.6
Self-employed	29.7	22.6	25.7
Total	100.0	100.0	100.0

Source: 1980 Census.

It is worth noting that, at this time, the rather low unemployment rate did not appear as an indicator of inequality between whites and non-whites, since it was 1.4 per cent for non-whites and 1.3 per cent for whites, according to the 1980 Demographic Census.

Disparities in wage levels between white and non-white workers for the same work were quite significant, as can be seen from Table 5.3.8.

Table 5.3.8. Average Monthly Labour Income for Non-white and White Workers Aged 15–65 by Work Status, Brazil, 1980 (in Brazilian Reais of September 2012)

	Employee	Employer	Self-employed	Total
Non-white	408	1705	373	412
White	780	2838	812	869
Wage ratio White: Non-white	1.91	1.66	2.18	2.11

Source: 1980 Census.

On average, white workers earned incomes 2.1 times those of non-whites. The gap was larger among the self-employed (2.2 times higher). The reason probably lies in the greater diversity of incomes among the self-employed, a category including people near the subsistence level and also quasi-entrepreneurs. Non-whites were more likely to be found in the former group.

In short, the 1980 Census portrays a still racially-unequal Brazilian labour market at the end of the industrialization process. Black and mixed-colour workers were over-represented in the most precarious forms of employment, in addition to earning lower average labour incomes, even within similar work status categories.

Situation from 1995 to 2011

Racial segmentation in the distribution of workers across employment status categories remained a distinctive feature of the Brazilian labour market throughout the 1990s and 2000s, as shown by the data from PNAD in Table 5.3.9 and Graph 5.3.1. Data here are not directly comparable with Census data for 1980, as methodologies for capturing employment status differ. However, for the recent period, the distribution of workers from the two racial groups by employment status covers more categories, permitting a more in-depth analysis.

Between 1995 and 2011, there was a decrease in the total proportion of self-employed workers and unpaid workers in the Brazilian labour market and an increase in the proportion of registered wage workers. Racial segmentation in the labour market persisted, but did not intensify: as in 1980, the non-whites continued to be over-represented among the unpaid workers and the self-employed. There was a decrease in the share of these employment status categories among non-whites, but this followed the overall trend for the labour market. If we add unpaid workers, unregistered wage workers, and self-employed workers, they together accounted for 52 per cent of non-white workers in 2011; for whites the share of these categories was 41 per cent. Nonetheless, it is worth highlighting the large increase in the share of registered employment among blacks and mixed-colour workers, from 34 per cent in 1995 to 46 per cent in 2011. The increase for whites was almost as large, from 44 per cent in 1995 to 54 per cent in 2011. On the other hand, the percentage of employers was still more than twice as high for whites as for non-whites.

Table 5.3.9. Occupied Population by Race and Employment Status for Workers Aged 15–65 Years, Brazil, 1995, 2001, 2005, and 2011 (% Distribution)

		Employment Status					
		Registered Employee	Unregistered Employee	Self-employed	Employer	Unpaid	Total (%)
1995	Non-white	33.8	27.3	24.4	2.1	12.4	100
	White	43.9	17.7	22.4	5.7	10.3	100
	Total (%)	39.5	21.9	23.3	4.1	11.2	100
2001	Non-white	34.9	29.2	23.3	2.2	10.4	100
	White	44.6	20.3	21.5	5.9	7.8	100
	Total (%)	40.3	24.3	22.3	4.2	8.9	100
2005	Non-white	36.4	27.8	22.7	2.4	10.8	100
	White	46.3	19.8	20.5	6.0	7.4	100
	Total (%)	41.5	23.7	21.6	4.2	9.0	100
2011	Non-white	45.9	23.4	21.3	1.9	7.5	100
	White	54.4	16.2	19.9	4.8	4.7	100
	Total (%)	50.1	19.9	20.6	3.4	6.1	100

Source: PNAD for the corresponding years.

As regards unemployment rates, these rose more rapidly for non-whites as joblessness increased (1995 to 2001) and dropped more slowly as unemployment declined (2001 to 2011). In this last year, the unemployment rate of non-white workers (7.6 per cent) was almost one-third higher than that of whites (5.8 per cent). It is also worth noting that over the entire period the participation rate rose for whites but fell for non-whites.

While inequality in employment status did not change much, this is not true of wage inequality, for which we observe a downward trend across race/colour groups, especially after 2001. The ratio of average income for whites to non-whites – which was 2.11 in 1980 in the Census data – fell from 2.05 in 1995 to 1.66 in 2011 in the PNAD data (Table 5.3.10). The greatest drop occurred between 2005 and 2011, when there was a strong recovery in average labour income, led by the rising minimum wage.

Graph 5.3.1. Employment Status of Non-white and White Workers Aged 15–65 Years, Brazil, 1995, 2001, 2005, and 2011 (% Distribution)

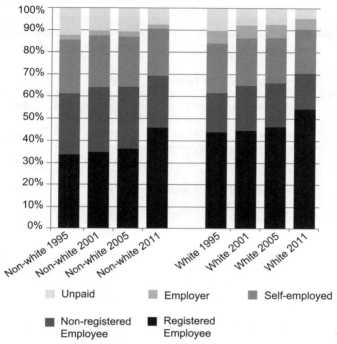

Legend:
- Unpaid
- Employer
- Self-employed
- Non-registered Employee
- Registered Employee

Source: PNAD for the years concerned.

Table 5.3.10. Average Monthly Labour Income for White and Non-white Workers Aged 15–65 Years, Brazil 1995, 2001, 2005, and 2011 (in Brazilian Reais of September 2012)

	1995	2001	2005	2011
Non-white	811	763	761	1043
White	1662	1516	1425	1727
Wage ratio White: Non-white	2.05	1.99	1.87	1.66

Source: PNAD for the years concerned.

However, the downward trend in the income ratio between whites and non-whites varies across labour status categories (Table 5.3.11). Wages of whites were always higher than those of non-whites, but the ratio fell between 1995 and 2011 for every employment category, by around 15 per cent for all categories except employers. However, for the recent period (2001 to 2011), the ratio fell less for registered wage-earners, so that in 2011 this group had the highest ratio, except for the self-employed.

Table 5.3.11. Average Monthly Labour Income for White and Non-white Workers Aged 15–65 Years by Employment Status, Brazil, 1995, 2001, 2005 and 2011 (in Brazilian Reais of September 2012)

	Employment Status	1995	2001	2005	2011
	Registered Wage Earner	1012	979	975	1197
	Non-registered Wage Earner	448	471	473	665
Non-white	Self-employed	738	654	604	931
	Employer	3157	2367	2308	3318
	Registered Wage Earner	1716	1579	1490	1765
	Non-registered Wage Earner	775	815	763	967
White	Self-employed	1479	1334	1199	1584
	Employer	4773	4212	3918	4563
	Registered Wage Earner	1.70	1.61	1.53	1.47
Wage ratio White:	Non-registered Wage Earner	1.73	1.73	1.61	1.45
Non-white	Self-employed	2.00	2.04	1.98	1.70
	Employer	1.51	1.78	1.70	1.38

Source: PNAD for the years concerned.

A tentative explanation for these outcomes is the following. The minimum wage was an important driver of the reduction in race/colour inequality for registered wage-earners, implying that the bottom income level was the same for white and non-white workers. As more non-whites received the minimum wage – which increased faster than the average – inequality declined, but not as much as might have been expected, as whites were more successful in climbing the wage scale above the minimum wage. Many unregistered wage-earners were previously earning an income below the minimum wage, and as their average income approached the minimum wage level, the white/non-white ratio fell more steeply. The fall of the ratio for the self-employed and employers suggests that, in these categories, the less skilled and those holding fewer assets either moved out into wage employment or did better by taking advantage of the increasing aggregate demand, especially due to the rise of labour incomes in general.

Despite the different dynamics across the various types of workers, these findings corroborate recent analyses that suggest a decrease in racial (and other dimensions of) inequality in the distribution of labour income (Barros et al., 2006, 2010; Barros et al., 2007).

In short, the results for the 1995–2011 period suggests that racial inequality is still a salient aspect of the Brazilian labour market. A higher proportion of black and mixed-colour workers were found among the self-employed and unregistered workers, in addition to higher unemployment rates and lower average income levels for these racial groups, even among individuals in the same labour status category. At the same time, there was an important reduction in income inequality between whites and non-whites, especially for the most precarious and low-paid jobs.

There was also a reduction in white to non-white differences in terms of educational attainment (Table 5.3.12). The proportion of non-white workers with less than complete primary education decreased from 78 per cent in 1995 to 44 per cent in 2011, although the latter was still very high; for white workers, this percentage declined from 58 per cent in 1995 to 29 per cent in 2011.

By the same token, the proportion of non-white workers with complete primary schooling and more jumped faster than the corresponding proportions of white workers. But while 38 per cent of non-white workers had at least secondary education in 2011, this was true for 55 per cent of whites. The gap of 17 percentage points was almost the same in 2011 as in 1995. And while the proportion of non-white workers with higher education rose from 1.8 per cent to 6.3 per cent over the period, for whites it was already 8.8 per cent in 1995, jumping to 17.2 per cent in 2011. So, at higher education levels, the gap remains quite large. Out of every ten people with a college degree in Brazil, seven are whites, whereas the great majority of people without schooling are non-white.

The bottom part of the table shows interesting changes in the wage patterns by educational level. The white/non-white wage differentials have been reduced over time, and more strongly after 2001, for each educational level except those located at the extremes, that is, without schooling and with higher education. These latter categories now have the highest ratios. This can be explained by the very factors we mentioned above. For very low-skilled jobs, those who are getting paid a little better are whites, even if they hold 'black jobs'. On the contrary, at the top of the educational ladder, blacks need to fight for a position in careers made up mostly of 'white jobs'.

In sum, we can see how racial discrimination in Brazil shows remarkable strength, and how it appears under new forms, despite the advances made in terms of labour statuses, educational attainment, and income disparities.

Table 5.3.12. White and Non-white Occupied Workers by Level of Education and White/Non-white Wage Ratios, Brazil, 1995, 2001, 2005, and 2011 (% Distribution)

		1995	2001	2005	2011
		%	%	%	%
Non-whites	No schooling	23.7	18.1	14.2	12.7
	Incomplete primary	54.2	49.1	44.4	31.2
	Complete primary	10.4	14.6	16.1	18.3
	Secondary	9.8	15.7	22.0	31.4
	Higher education	1.8	2.5	3.3	6.3
Whites	No schooling	9.0	6.6	5.6	5.7
	Incomplete primary	48.8	38.7	33.2	22.9
	Complete primary	14.9	17.2	16.6	16.2
	Secondary	18.5	26.7	32.1	38.1
	Higher education	8.8	10.9	12.6	17.2
Wage ratio White: Non-white	No schooling	1.50	1.35	1.27	1.42
	Incomplete primary	1.50	1.46	1.43	1.31
	Complete primary	1.39	1.39	1.34	1.27
	Secondary	1.52	1.47	1.41	1.31
	Higher education	1.42	1.44	1.45	1.44

Source: PNAD for the years concerned.

So, the Brazilian labour market is characterized by persistent racial wage differentials, just as it is by persistent gender differentials (Section 5.1). Graph 5.3.2, which brings these two dimensions together, suggests that differentials in terms of race are more marked than gender differentials. As we have seen, only a part of the difference can be explained by educational attainment, because wage differences still exist at the same level of education. Hence, other factors are also at play, in particular mechanisms of occupational segregation with direct and indirect discrimination (Abramo, 2006). However, Graph 5.3.2 suggests that the influence of these factors was declining from the 1990s up to 2005, since there was a significant improvement in the average hourly wages of black women and men relative to those of white men.

Graph 5.3.2. Average Hourly Wage of White and Black Women and Black Men as a Percentage of that of White Men, Brazil, 1992–2005

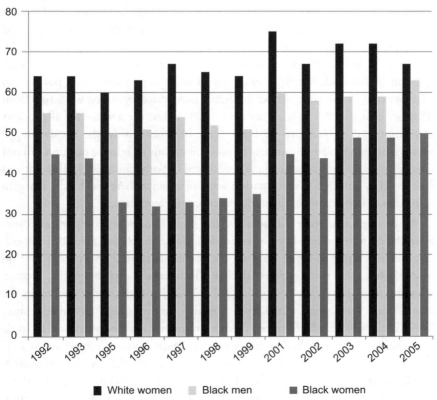

■ White women   ■ Black men   ■ Black women

Source: ILO (2007). Based on IBGE data.

5.3.3 Comparing Brazil and India

Inequality between social groups plays a powerful role in labour market segmentation in both India and Brazil. In both countries, historical inequalities among population groups, with different origins but with similar effects, give rise to unequal labour market opportunities, and these are reflected in labour market structures.

Because these inequalities are embedded in quite different social frameworks, it is obviously difficult to compare them. However, some parallels can be drawn in terms of changes in employment structures and wage ratios between different groups. In addition, we can examine the contribution of race in Brazil and caste in India to the overall decomposition of wage inequality.

The most basic divide in India is that between SCs/STs on the one hand and all other groups; in Brazil between non-white and white. In terms of employment structure, if we consider the proportion of regular or registered wage employment as an indicator of labour market status, in both countries the relatively deprived group progressed, but so did other groups of workers, so that the gap was hardly changed. In India, SC regular work rose from 11.4 per cent in 1983 to 15.3 per cent in 2011-12, but the average for all workers rose from 13.4 per cent to 17.9 per cent in the same period. In Brazil, non-white registered work rose from 33.8 per cent in 1995 to 45.9 per cent in 2011, but the average for all workers rose from 39.5 per cent to 50.1 per cent. In other words, the disadvantaged group shared in the labour market improvement, but its relative position did not change, and labour market inequality persisted in both countries. In India, it was true for SCs, but for STs the situation was worse, since there was hardly any gain in regular employment; so their relative situation deteriorated.

With respect to wage differentials, the most interesting comparison comes from the pattern broken down by education (Tables 5.3.6 and 5.3.12). In Brazil, the overall white/non-white wage ratio came down from 2.05 in 1995 to 1.66 in 2011, but there was much less decline within educational categories, broadly speaking from 1.4–1.5 in 1995 to 1.3–1.4 in 2011. Most of the decline in the overall wage ratio, then, came from a relative improvement in the education level of non-whites, which moved them up to higher wage occupations. In India also, there was some decline in the overall wage ratio between others and SC/ST, though less than in Brazil, from 1.7 to 1.55. Here too, the decline was smaller within most educational categories, but there was a significant decline for those with middle and secondary schooling. So there was some sign of reduction of wage discrimination in both countries, in addition to an improvement in education. However, one common pattern was that wage ratios were maintained, or even rose slightly, for graduates. In other words, the wage gap between white and non-whites in Brazil, and between SC/ST and others in India, was rising for those at the top of the educational system. Wage discrimination was, therefore, shifting upwards as average educational levels increased.

Another interesting comparison concerns the decomposition of the Theil index for wage inequality. Graph 5.3.3 gives the pattern for Brazil. It can be seen that the difference between whites and non-whites contributed significantly to inequality in 1995, when over 7 per cent of the Theil index was accounted for by the difference between these two groups, but this contribution has declined in both rural areas (to 2.8 per cent) and urban areas (to 5.6 per cent).

Graph 5.3.3. Decomposition of Theil Index of Wages by Race, Brazil, 1995–2011

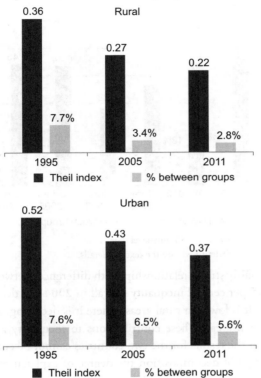

Source: Computed on the basis of PNAD/IBGE micro-data.

Note: The left hand bar for each year gives the overall Theil wage inequality index and the right hand bar gives the percentage of the index that reflects wage differences between whites and non-whites. See the discussion of decomposition in Section 4.3.

To compare these patterns directly with India, we can, as above, break down the Indian population into SC/ST and all others. A decomposition in these terms accounts for only 3 per cent of wage inequality since 1983 in both urban and rural areas, and 2 per cent in the most recent period. This would suggest at first sight that the caste factor in India is less important in wage inequality than race in Brazil.

However, given the fragmentation of the Indian labour market, it is interesting to break down social groups into a larger number of categories. A more detailed breakdown is available for 2004-05 and 2011-12 in India, which identifies seven groups: STs, SCs, Hindu OBCs, Hindu others (upper castes), Muslim OBCs, Muslim others (upper), and other religions. The results of the Theil decomposition are given in Graph 5.3.4.

Graph 5.3.4. Decomposition of Wage Inequality across Social Groups, India, 2004-05 and 2011-12, Urban and Rural

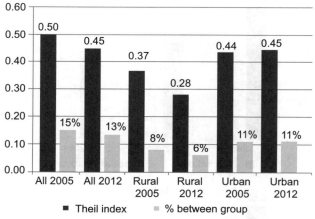

Source: Computed on the basis of NSS unit-level data.
Note: Seven social groups identified. See the text for details.

Here we see a fairly strong relationship, with differences between social groups accounting for 15 per cent of inequality overall in 2004-05, declining to 13 per cent in 2011-12. It is lower in rural areas, where it is declining, but is stable and quite high in urban areas. These contributions to inequality are much higher than in Brazil, but the results for the two countries cannot be compared directly, because in this type of decomposition the degree of explanation increases with the number of groups defined.

However, even Graph 5.3.4 understates the contribution of social group to inequality in India, because the patterns vary greatly from one part of the country to another. In Bihar, the impact of caste is large and rising. In Punjab, it is low and stable. In rural Tamil Nadu, it is high and stable. Different castes dominate in different parts of the country. These factors are lost in a national analysis. It seems quite reasonable to conclude that caste and community differences play a distinctly greater role in wage inequality in India compared to race in Brazil.

5.3.4   Some conclusions

In India, caste, tribe, and community have a deep and pervasive effect on labour market access. Lower castes are disproportionately found in the more precarious jobs, with lower wages and incomes. Decades of policies to change this situation have had relatively little impact: the caste differentials in the labour market today are little different from what they were thirty years ago. In particular, STs seem to be falling further behind. The policies that have been used in an attempt to overcome this situation – legal instruments to ban discrimination and reservations of jobs in the public sector and places in educational institutions – are clearly insufficient. Indeed, job reservation has had the effect of further fragmenting the labour market, as groups further up the social hierarchy demand their share.

In Brazil there is also a striking differentiation in opportunities available to whites and non-whites, but the mechanisms seem to be weaker. In the most recent data, 54 per cent of whites were in registered wage employment against 46 per cent of non-whites. In India, if we use regular work as the corresponding type of employment, 26 per cent of upper castes were in regular work as against 15 per cent of SCs and only 9 per cent of STs.

But while racial distinctions in Brazil seem to be less powerful as a way of rationing labour market opportunities than caste and community in India, this is not the end of the story. The wage differentials between non-white and white workers in Brazil are as large as the wage differentials in India between SCs and STs on the one hand, and all other social groups, with an overall ratio of between 1.5 and 1.6 in both countries. Indeed, until recently, they were significantly larger in Brazil, where they have fallen from over 2.0 in 1980 (1.7 in India in 1983). We also saw that the distinction between SCs/STs and the rest accounted for a smaller share of wage inequality in India than does the white/non-white distinction in Brazil.

However, the wage differential between the bottom and top of the caste hierarchy has been rising over time in India, and when a larger number of caste groups are distinguished, the contribution to wage inequality is much more important. Meanwhile, in Brazil, the ratio of unregistered to registered workers' wages has been increasing. Since non-white workers are more likely to be in unregistered work in Brazil, this implies a gain in their relative income. In India, lower-caste workers are concentrated in casual work, and have not seen the same relative gain in wages. And the largest contribution of caste to wage inequality is found in the most sought-after type of work, notably regular employment in urban areas.

So, the overall picture on wages is mixed. And there are so many diverse mechanisms at work in India that it is unrealistic to seek a uniform pattern. But it could be concluded, at least as a plausible hypothesis, that in India the primary mechanism of inequality is one of exclusion of lower castes from good jobs, and only to a secondary extent one of lower remunerations for those who gain access. In Brazil, there are signs that it may be the reverse – more open job access, but larger wage differentials within labour market segments, which might for instance reflect more limited career progression for non-whites. In other words, in Brazil the main mechanism may be discrimination within the market, while in India the dominant factor may be institutional constraints prior to the market, and which therefore affect labour market access. But in Brazil there are signs that at least some aspects of racial inequality are declining; in India, caste and community differences are very persistent, even in the urban labour markets where they were once expected to disappear.

5.4 The Role of Education

5.4.1 Introduction

In the analysis of inequality, education needs to be considered from at least three different angles.

First, there is inequality with respect to education itself, seen as a human goal and a source of capability and personal development. Unequal access to schooling and learning is, therefore, an important dimension of inequality in its own right.

Second, education is associated with other forms of inequality, notably in the labour market – education provides or denies access to occupations and incomes, and is associated with differentials in productivity, wages, and other benefits.

Third, education is often seen as a powerful policy instrument for reducing inequality, precisely because of its potential for raising skills and widening access to opportunities.

It is, therefore, rather different in kind from the three dimensions of inequality discussed in previous sections. Nevertheless, there are some elements in common. In particular, once people leave the schooling system, education levels are quasi-fixed, like race or gender, and this opens possibilities for labour market segmentation and differentiation. In addition, like race or region, there is a degree of transmission of characteristics from one generation to the next – in the case of schooling, because better educated parents transmit higher levels of education to their children.

This issue merits a book rather than a short section. Here, we consider mainly two issues: first, the long-term trends in education levels in Brazil and India, and how this has played out in terms of the education differentials between different groups; and second, the roles played by education and educational qualifications in the labour markets of the two countries.

5.4.2 The expansion of education

India

The divide between the literate and the illiterate is a fundamental dimension of inequality. In India, at the time of independence, more than 80 per cent of the population was illiterate (Table 5.4.1). In the decades after independence, while education was considered an important component of national development planning, in practice the pursuit of industrialization was placed ahead of all other goals, and expansion of education was slow. The low levels of existing infrastructure, availability of teachers, and limited resources at the time of independence were barriers to its growth. Literacy rates rose slowly, and overall literacy was still well below 50 per cent in 1981. In rural areas, only one-third of the population was literate by that date, and improvement was much slower than in urban areas.

Table 5.4.1. Literacy Rates by Sex and Urban-Rural Residence, India, 1951–2011 (%)

Census Years	Rural			Urban			All-India		
	Male	Female	Total	Male	Female	Total	Male	Female	Total
1951	19.0	4.9	12.1	45.5	22.3	34.6	27.1	8.9	18.3
1961	34.3	10.1	22.5	66.0	40.5	54.4	40.4	15.4	28.3
1971	48.7	15.5	27.9	69.6	48.5	60.2	46.0	22.0	34.5
1981	49.5	21.7	36.0	76.7	56.3	67.2	56.4	29.8	43.6
1991	57.9	30.4	44.7	81.1	64.0	73.1	64.1	39.3	52.2
2001	71.4	46.7	59.4	86.7	73.2	80.3	75.9	54.2	65.4
2011	78.6	58.8	68.8	89.7	79.9	84.1	82.1	65.5	74.0

Source: Decennial Census of India, various years.

Note: Literacy rates for 1951, 1961 and 1971 relate to population aged 5 years and above whereas literacy rates for 1981, 1991, 2001, and 2011 relate to population aged 7 years and above. Also, the 1981 literacy rate excludes Assam, where the 1981 census could not be conducted.

During this period, it was higher education that expanded the fastest, although absolute numbers were small. Enrolment in higher education rose by fourteen times between 1950 and 1980, in secondary education by seven times, and in primary education by less than four times (Government of India, Ministry of Human Resources Development, 2004; University Grants Commission, 2003). The focus on higher education further reinforced existing inequalities as only social groups whose levels of education were already high, such as the higher castes and the well-off, were able to access it.

From the late 1960s onwards, there was a renewed emphasis on primary education as well as literacy. But initiatives in education take a long time to deliver results. Even in 2011, a quarter of the population was illiterate. Enrolment in primary schooling was approaching universality by that date, but there remained a large adult population that had not had access to schooling as children.

By the 1980s, the fraction of the population that had completed secondary school or more was still small (Table 5.4.2), but it rose rapidly thereafter, from 6 per cent in 1983 to 23 per cent in 2011-12. At the latter date, almost half of young people aged 15–20 had had at least some secondary schooling, and there was a growing group with tertiary qualifications.

Table 5.4.2. Population (All Ages) by Level of Education, India, 1983–2011/12 (%)

	1983*			1999-2000**			2011-12		
	Male	Female	Total	Male	Female	Total	Male	Female	Total
No schooling/ illiterate	51.1	72.6	61.6	37.4	55.6	46.2	25.3	39.6	32.3
Below primary	16.0	10.3	13.2	18.8	15.4	17.2	18.2	16.7	17.5
Primary	14.0	8.7	11.4	13.3	10.6	12.0	14.6	13.2	13.9
Middle	10.0	4.8	7.5	13.4	9.0	11.3	15.3	12.1	13.7
Secondary	6.9	2.9	4.9	8.4	4.9	6.7	11.5	8.1	9.9
Higher secondary	-	-	-	4.4	2.4	3.4	7.1	5.3	6.2
Diploma and above	-	-	-	-	-	-	1.2	0.5	0.9
Graduate and above	2.1	0.8	1.5	4.3	2.2	3.3	6.9	4.5	5.7
Total	100	100	100	100	100	100	100	100	100

Source: NSS 38th, 55th, and 68th rounds.

Note: *Secondary education includes Higher Secondary in 1983.

**Higher Secondary includes Diploma and above in 1999–2000.

Nevertheless, inequalities in access to education remained large. The gap between men and women is evident in the above tables. The gender gap in literacy, after widening until 1981, is only recently starting to close. A third of women were still illiterate in 2011, twice as many as men. And, despite some improvement, rates of secondary and tertiary education also remain significantly lower for women than for men (Table 5.4.2), and this is clearly visible in the educational distribution of the labour force (Graph 5.1.2, Section 5.1).

Differences between social groups in educational attainment have, likewise, persisted (Section 5.3). In 1983, almost 80 per cent of STs and 74 per cent of SCs were illiterate, compared with 57 per cent among all other groups combined. About 6 per cent among 'others' (mainly upper castes) had secondary education, compared with less than 2 per cent among STs and SCs (Jodhka, 2010). In 1999-2000, almost 63 per cent of STs, 60 per cent of SCs, 53 per cent of OBCs, and

50 per cent of 'others' were illiterate in rural areas. By 2011-12, this percentage had dropped in all groups, to 44 per cent and 42 per cent among STs and SCs; and to 37 per cent and 28 per cent among OBCs and others. But the decline was greatest among the 'others', mainly the upper caste category. Studies of the period between 1983 and 1999-2000 found that inequalities in access to both primary and secondary education had declined, but this was not true for higher education (Desai and Kulkarni, 2008); so inequalities had become concentrated at higher levels.

Regional variations in education levels are also large and persistent (Section 5.2). In 1983, literacy in Kerala already exceeded 70 per cent, compared with 30 per cent in the Centre region (following the regional breakdown used in Section 5.2). By 2011-12, more than 18 per cent of the population of Kerala had higher secondary education or above, followed by the South/West and Northwest at about 16 per cent. The Northeast and Centre regions lagged behind with 10 per cent. Taking middle school and secondary school together, Kerala again topped at 40 per cent, the South/West followed at about 26 per cent, and the Centre region performed the worst, at less than 20 per cent.

While progress has been made in equalizing access to lower levels of education, wide differences in the quality of education exist, offsetting to a significant degree the gains made from the increase in access. There are differences in the quality of teaching between government schools and private schools, and the latter have been expanding. In addition, if children belonging to upper social groups move to private schools, the pressure on government schools to perform is reduced. At the same time, private education is providing opportunities and filling a vacuum: for instance, private colleges and technical institutes are catering to those who may have had no other avenue for gaining qualifications.

So the overall picture is one of steady expansion of educational levels, accelerating after the turn of the century. But the inequalities in access that were earlier visible in primary education are still present, having shifted to the higher levels of the educational system, and as we see below these higher qualifications are increasingly required for access to the formal labour market.

Brazil

Education levels in Brazil have been higher than those in India over the whole period considered. But the expansion of formal schooling in Brazil was slow, especially if compared with developed countries rather than with India. Illiteracy rates remained high for most of the twentieth century, as can be seen from Table 5.4.3.

Table 5.4.3. Illiteracy Rate, Population Aged 15 or More, Brazil, 1900–2010

Year	Population Aged 15 Years-Plus (million)	% Illiterate
1900	9.7	65.3
1920	17.6	65.0
1940	23.6	56.1
1950	30.2	50.6
1960	40.2	39.7
1970	53.6	33.7
1980	74.6	25.9
1991	94.9	19.7
2000	119.5	13.6
2010	145.1	9.6

Source: Demographic censuses.

These data show that more than half of the Brazilian adult population was illiterate until 1950. By the 1960 Demographic Census, adult illiteracy had fallen to 40 per cent, and thereafter it declined steadily to 26 per cent in 1980 and under 20 per cent in 1991. But it was only after 1980 that the absolute number of illiterate people in Brazil began to decrease. Illiteracy rates were higher for women than for men at least up to the mid-1990s, when the gap was closed. From 2000 onwards, they were lower for women. This convergence did not occur for differences by colour/race, however, and illiteracy rates are still almost 2.3 times higher for non-whites than for whites.

In terms of expansion of the education system, Brazil followed a different pattern from that of developed countries, where, after a fast increase in enrolment at the lowest levels, growth stabilized, paving the way for another increase in enrolment rates at the next level, and so forth. In Brazil, although fundamental education was still far from reaching universality in the 1970s, the annual rate of expansion was much lower (3.6 per cent) than for secondary education (11.4 per cent) and tertiary education (11.6 per cent) (Castro, 1986). Moreover, during this period, only 3.5 per cent of children entering fundamental education continued on to secondary education and 1 per cent on to tertiary education (Luna and Klein, 2007).

During the 1990s, the expansion of basic levels of schooling accelerated, a process that was consolidated in the 2000s. This concentration of efforts on universal access to elementary education was one of the main features of the Brazilian educational system over the two last decades, and resulted in a significant drop in illiteracy levels. As measured by the Demographic Census, adult illiteracy in Brazil had fallen to 9.6 per cent in 2010, amounting to approximately 14 million people.

Prior to this move towards universal basic schooling, education was still highly concentrated at the elementary school level, and illiteracy was widespread. Table 5.4.4, which gives the educational breakdown of the economically active adult population, shows that in 1980 those with no more than four years of education comprised more than 75 per cent of the workforce in Brazil. Only 24 per cent of the workforce had completed fundamental education; 10 per cent of all workers had completed middle school and workers with complete higher education accounted for around 4 per cent of the labour force.[14]

Table 5.4.4. Occupied Population Aged 15–65 Years by Schooling Level, Brazil, 1980 to 2011 (% Distribution)

Schooling Level	1980	1995	2001	2005	2011
No schooling	20.8	11.8	8.6	6.3	7.1
Incomplete fundamental	54.9	48.8	41.1	35.7	24.8
Complete fundamental	10.4	14.7	16.8	16.9	17.4
Complete high school	10.2	17.2	25.0	31.1	36.8
Complete higher education	3.8	7.5	8.6	9.9	14.0
Total	100.0	100.0	100.0	100.0	100.0

Source: For 1980, Census of Brazil, 1980; For 1995 to 2011: PNAD/IBGE.
Note: For definitions of schooling levels, see the annex to this section.

By the mid-1990s (Table 5.4.4), the expansion of the educational system had significantly raised the educational levels of the workforce. The proportion of illiterates had dropped almost by half, and the proportion with middle school or higher education levels had almost doubled. Thereafter, the trend shown by the PNAD data is one of

- A steady reduction in the proportion of workers who were illiterate or had not finished fundamental school, from over 61 per cent in 1995 to 32 per cent in 2011

---

[14] The figures for Brazil in Tables 5.4.4 to 5.4.7 refer to the occupied population, and so are not directly comparable with the Indian figures in Table 5.4.2, which refer to the whole population.

- A rise in the proportion of workers with complete middle education from 25 per cent in 1995 to 37 per cent in 2011 and
- An increase in the share of workers with complete higher education from 8.6 per cent in 1995 to 14 per cent in 2011.

During the 2000s, enrolment in tertiary education in Brazil more than doubled. This increase was led by private universities, accounting in 2010 for 73 per cent of all students at this level of education (INEP, 2011). On the other hand, at fundamental and high school levels 90 per cent of students attended public schools.

It is important to notice that the education system in Brazil is extremely unequal in the sense that public universities, which are usually of better quality than private ones, are still dominated by students from private schools, although this share went down in the 2000s. On the other hand, centres of excellence are found mainly in private schools for elementary and middle levels of education, while public schools have expanded their enrolment at the expense of quality, which is much lower than their private counterparts.

In 2011, for the first time, the country's workforce was made up mostly of workers who had achieved at least the middle schooling level. The period from 1995 to 2011 therefore marks a turning point, with a shift from an overwhelmingly poorly educated workforce to one that was increasingly made up of educated workers, that is, those having at least completed high school. However, almost universal access to education (especially for the younger cohorts in the case of fundamental school and, increasingly, for high school) does not mean equally universal access to quality education. As in India, this is one of the ways inequality reappears in disguised forms.

Despite the rise in the educational level of workers, significant inequalities still remain between different groups of the population. Tables 5.4.5, 5.4.6, and 5.4.7 show the pattern by sex, rural-urban, and region. It can be seen that economically active women had higher education levels than men in both 1995 and 2011; 56 per cent of economically active women had completed middle school or higher, as compared with 43 per cent of men, a trend already discussed in Section 5.1.

On the other hand, the rural/urban cleavage persisted. In 1995, over 90 per cent of the rural workforce had no more than fundamental education, whereas this was true of only 55 per cent of urban workers. Educational levels rose in both urban and rural areas between 1995 and 2011, but the rural-urban gap rose for those with no schooling or incomplete fundamental education. There was faster growth of the share of workers with secondary and higher schooling in rural than in urban areas between 1995 and 2011, but this is probably explained by the fact that the shares of these workers were very low in the rural areas in 1995, allowing for a greater magnitude of growth.

Table 5.4.5. Distribution of the Occupied Population Aged 15–65 Years by Level of Education and Sex, Brazil, 1995 and 2011(%)

	1995		2011	
Level of Education	Male	Female	Male	Female
No schooling	13.9	11.6	9.3	5.8
Incomplete fundamental	53.1	47.9	29.4	22.1
Complete fundamental	14.1	13.7	18.9	15.7
Complete high school	13.3	18.7	32.4	39.0
Complete higher education	5.5	8.2	10.1	17.4
Total	100.0	100.0	100.0	100.0

Source: PNAD/IBGE.

Table 5.4.6. Distribution of Occupied Population Aged 15–65 Years by Schooling Level, by Rural-Urban Domicile, Brazil, 1995 and 2011(%)

	1995		2011	
Level of Education	Rural	Urban	Rural	Urban
No schooling	30.1	8.2	17.7	5.7
Incomplete fundamental	57.8	47.0	46.5	22.1
Complete fundamental	5.9	16.4	15.3	17.6
Complete high school	5.1	19.6	17.3	39.3
Complete higher education	0.9	8.8	3.2	15.3
Total	100.0	100.0	100.0	100.0

Source: PNAD/IBGE.

Educational levels were also unequal across Brazilian regions. The difference between the educational level of workers in Brazil's Northeast and Southeast, in particular, gives us an idea of the regional gap, as shown in Table 5.4.7. The gap is narrowing, but is still very large at the top and at the very bottom. For instance, 41 per cent of workers in the Northeast had not completed elementary school in 2011, against 27 per cent for the Southeast. At the other extreme, the percentage of workers with higher education was almost twice as high for the Southeast (16.7 per cent) as for the Northeast (9.4 per cent).

Table 5.4.7. Occupied Population Aged 15–65 Years by Educational Level in the Northeast (NE) and Southeast (SE) Regions, Brazil, 1995 and 2011 (%)

	1995		2011	
	NE	SE	NE	SE
No schooling	25.7	6.7	13.0	4.5
Incomplete fundamental	45.8	48.4	27.9	22.3
Complete fundamental	9.6	16.9	15.7	17.5
Complete high school	14.8	18.4	34.0	39.1
Complete higher education	4.1	9.6	9.4	16.7
Total	100.0	100.0	100.0	100.0

Source: PNAD/IBGE.

The pattern of education by race (colour) was discussed in the last section. Broadly, it was found that non-whites do worse than whites at all levels of the educational system. At lower and middle levels, the gap, especially in the latter, has been reduced since 1995. At the upper (tertiary) level also, the gap has fallen, even though it is larger than for the other education levels, almost reaching a factor of 2.8, as 6.3 per cent of non-white workers have higher school education, against 17.2 per cent of whites (Table 5.3.12). So, it can be concluded that regional, racial, and rural-urban differences persist at the top of the education system, where the narrowing has been quite limited.

Comparing Brazil and India

In 1950, the literacy rate was 20 per cent in India and 50 per cent in Brazil. By 1980-81, literacy had risen to 44 per cent in India but 74 per cent in Brazil, so the gap had not changed in percentage point terms. By 2010-11, literacy had climbed to 73 per cent in India and to 90 per cent in Brazil, so the gap had come down. But a large differential between the two countries remained higher up the education system. If we compare the population who had at least completed middle school in India with those who had at least completed fundamental school in Brazil – these being broadly equivalent in terms of years of schooling (see the annex to this section) – the percentage rose in India from 13.8 per cent in 1983 to 36.3 per cent in 2011-12, but in Brazil from 24.4 per cent in 1980 to 68.2 per cent in 2011; so the gap had widened.[15]

At the top of the educational system, the gap also widened in terms of the percentage share of the population with tertiary education. In India, this share

---

[15] As noted above, the Brazilian figures refer to the occupied population, and the Indian figures to the whole population; so these are not directly comparable, but it seems likely that this conclusion will hold with comparable data.

increased from 1.5 per cent in 1983 to 6.5 per cent in 2011, while in Brazil there was a larger increase from 3.8 per cent in 1983 to 14 per cent in 2011.

Another key difference between the two countries lies in the gender gap. In India, literacy rates for women have been generally 20–25 percentage points lower than for men, though the gap narrowed in the most recent census. Data on the occupied population between 1995 and 2011 in Brazil show that literacy rates are higher for women than for men – around 3 percentage points more, or 10 percentage points more if we exclude all those who have not completed fundamental education.[16] This gender difference is found at all educational levels, with substantially more women than men reporting completed secondary or tertiary education. It follows that the gap between Brazil and India is much larger for women's education than for men's.

In both countries, there are also large regional differences in educational attainment. In 1983, illiteracy rates varied from 27 per cent to 70 per cent across the five Indian regions considered in Section 5.2. These gaps had been considerably reduced by 2011, when illiteracy varied from 8 per cent to 30 per cent for women and from 4 per cent to 21 per cent for men (Table 5.2.1). In 1981 the gap in literacy between urban and rural areas in India (33 per cent illiteracy in the former against 64 per cent in the latter) was almost as large as the differences between regions. This urban-rural difference was still large in 2011 (down to 16 per cent illiteracy in urban areas but still 31 per cent in rural). In Brazil too, the gap between urban and rural areas was substantial as late as 1995 (30 per cent illiterate in rural areas against 8 per cent in urban) but had declined by 2011 (18 per cent against 6 per cent). The gap between the Northeast and the Southeast region was almost as large: 26 per cent to 7 per cent in 1995 and 13 per cent to 4.5 per cent in 2011.

While these data are not strictly comparable, it seems that the order of magnitude of these regional and urban-rural differences is similar in the two countries, though the regional gap may be somewhat larger in India. However, as the two countries approach universal literacy, these differences naturally decline; so access to the higher echelons of the educational ladder becomes a better measure of the gap. In this respect, access to secondary and higher education continues to be regionally unbalanced in both countries. In Brazil, 16.7 per cent had completed higher education in the Southeast in 2011 against only 9.4 per cent in the Northeast region. Similarly, in India, 16–18 per cent had completed

---

[16] However, these data refer to workers, and illiterate women are less likely to be in the labour force, so female illiteracy may not be much lower than male illiteracy in the population as a whole.

higher secondary education in Kerala, the South/West and the Northwest, but only 10 per cent in the central region. Rural-urban differences persist in both countries. In 1983, those in India who had completed middle school and above constituted 9 per cent of the population in rural areas but 30 per cent in urban areas; these numbers had increased to, respectively, 18 per cent and 42 per cent in 1999-2000; and to 30 per cent and 53 per cent in 2011-12. In Brazil, those who had completed fundamental school or above constituted 11 per cent of workers in rural areas and about 45 per cent in urban areas in 1995, rising to respectively, about 36 per cent and 72 per cent in 2011.

So, with the notable exception of gender differences, there are some similarities in patterns between the two countries and how they are changing. But in India, the average education levels are still much lower.

5.4.3 Education and the labour market

Education patterns interact with the labour market in several different ways.
- First, education can affect economic activity rates.
- Secondly, it is an important determinant of access to different occupations.
- Thirdly, it is likely to affect unemployment rates insofar as the patterns of supply and demand of labour differ across educational levels.
- Fourthly, it can of course have a direct impact on wages, even within the same occupation, because of the criteria for wage setting or the relationship between education, skills, and productivity.

Labour force participation and occupation

In both countries, education has relatively little impact on male labour force participation except, of course, at the younger ages when people are likely to be studying rather than working. However, in Brazil male labour force participation tends to be lower for those with lower educational levels (no schooling and incomplete fundamental), a pattern that has become stronger over time. For women, this pattern is even more striking (Table 5.4.9).

On the other hand, there is a substantial impact of education on female labour supply, and it is different in the two countries. Table 5.4.8 shows that since at least the 1980s there has been a U-shaped curve in India, with high female labour force participation at both low and high levels of education. The minimum was at the middle-school level until 2004-05, and at the secondary level in the most recent data. In Brazil, on the other hand, there is a steady rise in female labour force participation with education, lowest among the illiterate (43.4 per cent in 2011) and highest among those with higher education. Among the latter, it fluctuates around 84 per cent over the period (Table 5.4.9).

Table 5.4.8. Labour Force Participation Rates (25 to 64 Years) by Sex and Level of Schooling (%), India, 1983 and 2011-12

	1983		2011-12	
	Male	Female	Male	Female
No schooling/illiterate	95.5	54.6	95.1	44.0
Below primary	96.6	36.3	96.4	35.8
Primary	96.8	33.9	97.1	35.9
Middle	97.4	25.4	97.6	30.9
Secondary	96.5	32.1	95.4	25.7
Higher secondary	-	-	95.5	21.0
Diploma/Certificate	-	-	94.7	54.5
Graduates and above	96.3	41.4	93.5	35.1
Total	96.2	49.9	95.8	37.5

Source: NSS.

Table 5.4.9. Labour Force Participation Rates (15–65 Years) by Sex and Level of Schooling (%), Brazil, 1995 and 2011

Level of Schooling	1995		2011	
	Male	Female	Male	Female
No schooling	87.6	50.4	78.1	43.5
Incomplete fundamental	87.7	53.6	81.2	50.9
Complete fundamental	86.4	53.5	85.8	65.5
Complete high school	86.9	66.2	84.7	75.7
Complete higher education	93.9	84.0	92.4	83.7
Total	87.7	57.3	83.5	60.8

Source: PNAD.

With respect to the relationship between education and the type of employment, we need to consider the segmentation of the labour market. In 1999-2000, almost 90 per cent of the Indian workforce was in the unorganized sector, but this was true for more than 97 per cent of illiterate workers. The figure was 70 per cent among those with higher secondary education, and was only 54 per cent among those with tertiary qualifications. Moreover, the concentration of the less educated in the unorganized sector has been increasing. Between 1999-2000 and 2011-12, there was a decline of less than 5 percentage points in the percentage of illiterates in the unorganized sector but of about 10 percentage points among those with a graduate degree or above.

The segmentation can be seen most clearly in terms of work status. Table 5.4.10 shows the employment profiles, in terms of self-employment and of regular and casual wage work, for different education levels in rural and urban areas in 2011-12. There is a very large difference between these three work status categories in their relationship with education. Those with low educational levels are much more likely to be engaged in casual work; this pattern is very strong in both rural and urban areas. Those with higher education levels are, in contrast, much more likely to be in regular work. In rural areas, virtually no one with primary schooling or less is in regular work, compared with around 50 per cent at the highest educational levels. In urban areas, a larger share of those with low levels of education are in regular work, but the positive relationship between regular work and education is similar to that in rural areas. For the self-employed, in contrast, there is much less variation with education level, and the highest share is found at intermediate education levels. These patterns are persistent over time – the relationship was very similar in 1999-2000.

So, education clearly plays an important role in labour market segmentation, by providing the credentials required for access to regular work. This also explains the pattern of female labour force participation – high participation at low education levels is participation in casual work, and high participation at high education levels is participation in regular work. And, of course, the segmentation goes beyond whether the work is casual or regular, because there is a much wider range of occupations in regular work – many of them with better working conditions and higher incomes. On the other hand, the weak relationship between self-employment and education no doubt reflects the heterogeneity of self-employment, which ranges from low-productivity informal production or small-scale cultivation at the bottom to, at the top, well-off farmers, independent professionals, and larger businesses. This is not just a question of larger and smaller farmers, because the pattern is found in urban areas as well. Overall, those with the least schooling have less access to self-employment, while the returns to tertiary education may well be higher in regular wage employment.

In Brazil, the relationship between employment status and education in 2011 was quite different from that in India in the more recent data (Table 5.4.11). Wage employees (registered, unregistered, and public) are the largest group in the occupational structure for all educational levels except the illiterate.

Moreover, the share of employees increases as the educational levels of workers rise, from less than 50 per cent among the illiterate to 85 per cent for those who have completed high school. The percentage of self-employed and unpaid workers (the latter usually working in family businesses without employees) falls

Table 5.4.10. Distribution of Labour Status by Education Level (%), by Urban-Rural Residence, India, 2011-12

Educational Level	Rural			Urban			Total		
	Self-employed	Regular	Casual	Self-employed	Regular	Casual	Self-employed	Regular	Casual
No schooling/illiterate	51.5	2.8	45.7	39.9	26.7	33.4	49.9	6.1	44.0
Below primary	50.8	5.3	43.9	44.5	28.1	27.4	49.6	9.7	40.7
Primary	52.7	6.7	40.6	42.3	34.1	23.6	50.3	13.1	36.6
Middle	57.3	10.1	32.5	44.1	37.3	18.5	53.7	17.5	28.7
Secondary	62.3	14.2	23.5	47.5	42.8	9.6	57.2	24.1	18.7
Higher secondary	61.6	21.9	16.5	46.7	48.8	4.6	55.3	33.2	11.5
Diploma/Certificate	32.4	55.8	11.9	23.8	72.8	3.5	27.8	64.8	7.4
Graduate and above	48.1	47.0	4.9	31.5	67.6	0.9	37.0	60.8	2.2
Total	54.0	9.6	36.5	40.7	44.5	14.8	50.3	19.3	30.5

Source: NSS, 68th round.

Table 5.4.11. Occupied Population Aged 15-Plus by Employment Status and Schooling Level, Brazil, 2011

Schooling level		Employment Status					
	Unpaid	Private Employee		PublicEmployee	Employer	Self-employed	Total
		Registered	Unregistered				
No schooling	18.5	20.2	25.5	1.5	1.5	32.8	100.0
Incomplete fundamental	10.2	33.7	24.1	2.2	2.6	27.3	100.0
Complete fundamental	3.3	53.5	17.3	6.2	3.5	16.2	100.0
Complete high school	1.9	51.6	18.4	14.1	4.3	9.8	100.0
Complete higher education	1.0	41.6	10.5	25.4	7.3	14.2	100.0
Total	6.9	41.5	19.8	7.0	3.4	21.3	100.0

Source: PNAD 2011.

from 50 per cent of the illiterate group to 15 per cent at the top. For those with higher education, public employees account for 25 per cent of the jobs, private wage earners around 50 per cent (25 per cent of them unregistered), employers 7 per cent (twice the average), and the self-employed another 14 per cent.

So, in fact, as in the Indian case, the relationship with labour market segmentation is clear in Brazil, but it takes a different shape. For instance, the share of self-employment in the more educated groups is below the average. For lower educational groups, this consists more of poorly paid services, while for the higher education group high-productivity and more skilled activities predominate. It is also quite impressive to observe how the importance of public jobs increases for higher levels of schooling.

Unemployment

As discussed in earlier sections, the interpretation of unemployment is different in the Brazilian and Indian labour markets, and open unemployment has historically been higher in Brazil and more sensitive to economic fluctuations. This difference in the role of unemployment in the labour market carries over to the relationship with education. It can be seen in Table 5.4.12 that in India open unemployment is negligible at lower education levels, but rises steeply at the tertiary education level, especially for women. This is the well-known phenomenon of educated unemployment, reflecting the gap between aspirations generated by higher education and the availability of jobs to meet the goals of young people in the labour market, particularly young women (which we have discussed in previous sections).

Table 5.4.13 shows that the pattern for Brazil is entirely different. The overall unemployment rate is higher, and like in India it is higher for women than for men. But, here, the highest unemployment rates are found at middle levels of schooling, notably complete fundamental and complete middle school, for which the labour supply has increased quite significantly, especially the latter group. The problems of labour market access faced by those with tertiary education in India are less prominent in Brazil. Here, the problem for graduates is more one of finding a well paid job rather than just finding a job, as sometimes they displace workers with lower education, even though the latter might be better suited to the occupations available.

One possible interpretation is as follows: the returns to high educational qualifications are higher in India than Brazil, making it worthwhile for young people with tertiary education to hold out for a better job, while in Brazil the issue is more a question of scarcity of jobs – at least for some occupations – that call for tertiary qualifications. But there is also another possible interpretation: the market is more segmented in India and access more difficult than in Brazil, so that only those with the right networks (or from the right social groups) are able to make their qualifications pay in the Indian labour market, while the Brazilian labour market is more open. That would be consistent with the analysis in Section 4.3. In that case, unemployment is more social-structural in nature in India, and more a question of mismatch of supply and demand for different skills (and conjunctural factors) in Brazil.

Table 5.4.12. Unemployment Rate by Sex and Education (%), India, 2011-12

Education Level	Male	Female	Total
No schooling/Illiterate	0.6	0.8	0.7
Below primary	1.4	1.6	1.4
Primary	1.7	1.2	1.6
Middle	2.2	4.4	2.5
Secondary	2.5	8.7	3.3
Higher secondary	4.5	12.7	5.6
Diploma/Certificate	8.0	18.3	9.7
Graduate and above	6.5	16.6	8.4
Total	2.4	3.7	2.7

Source: NSS 68th round.

Table 5.4.13. Unemployment Rate by Sex and Level of Schooling (%), Brazil, 2011

Level of Schooling	Male	Female	Total
No schooling	3.5	6.8	4.6
Incomplete fundamental	4.8	8.8	6.3
Complete fundamental	5.9	11.9	8.7
Complete high school	6.2	7.8	7.1
Complete higher education	2.3	4.2	3.4
Total	4.9	9.1	6.7

Source: PNAD.

Wages

In India and Brazil, as elsewhere, wage patterns show very considerable returns to education. Graphs 5.4.1 and 5.4.2 show the wage ratios between different educational levels in the two countries, and how they have changed over time.

For India, we used the following classification for these graphs:
- Illiterate (no schooling) (32 per cent);
- Below primary or literate without schooling (18 per cent);
- Primary completed (14 per cent);
- Middle-school completed (14 per cent);
- Secondary or higher secondary completed (16 per cent); and
- Graduates and other tertiary education (7 per cent).

Figures in brackets are the percentages of the population in each category in 2011-12, according to NSS data.

Graph 5.4.1 shows the wage ratios between these different educational categories for four NSS survey years – 1983, 1993-94, 2004-05, and 2011-12. There is an interesting and very clear pattern. The premium to education everywhere is above 1, indicating that more education is reflected in higher wages. The overall ratio between the top and the bottom has fallen in rural areas from 4.7 to 3.7, and risen in urban areas from 3.7 to 4.4. But the premium for all schooling levels below middle school has fallen over time in rural areas, and not changed much in urban areas. Thus, the wage premium for minimal schooling or literacy, as compared with illiteracy, has fallen in rural areas from 29 per cent to 11 per cent and in urban areas from 36 per cent to 13 per cent, and there is now little additional gain from completing primary or middle school. In contrast, the premium to secondary and college education (and above) is higher, though declining in the most recent data. Meanwhile, the returns to tertiary education are increasing rapidly. Over the thirty-year period, the premium to college education over secondary/higher secondary education has risen in rural areas from 39 per cent to 111 per cent and in urban areas from 49 per cent to 118 per cent. This shows the upward shift in the educational credentials demanded by the labour market. Secondary schooling is no longer sufficient to deliver a substantial wage premium; it is necessary to move up the scale. Even at the bottom of the scale, primary education conveys very little labour market advantage any more.

In Brazil, we used the following educational categories:
- No schooling (7.1 per cent);
- Incomplete primary (24.8 per cent);,
- Complete primary (17.4 per cent);
- Secondary (36.8 per cent), and
- Tertiary (14 per cent).

Figures in brackets refer to the percentage share of each category in the workforce in 2011.

Graph 5.4.1. Wage Ratios across Different Education Categories, Rural and Urban, India, 1983–2011/12

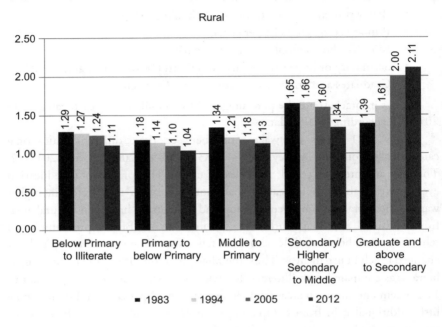

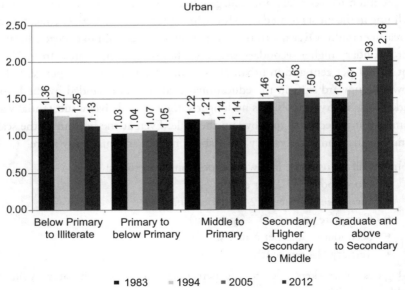

Graph 5.4.2. Wage Ratios across Different Education Categories, Rural and Urban, Brazil, 1995–2011

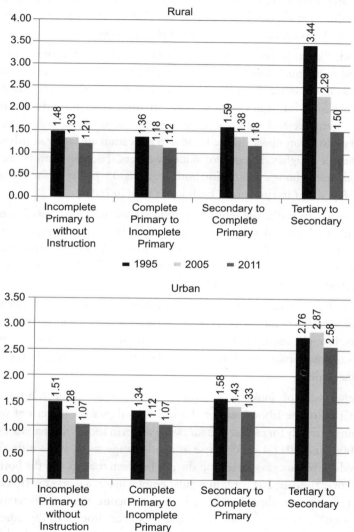

The wage ratios in Graph 5.4.2 give a picture that is in some respects similar to India's.

First, the returns to education are substantial, and similar in order of magnitude to those in India. At the same time, the income gap between poorly educated workers and better educated workers has declined. In 1995, illiterate workers earned, on average, 10.3 per cent of the average income of a worker with a higher education degree. In 2011, this had risen to 20.8 per cent. Most of the gain for poorly educated workers occurred after 2005.

Second, like in India, the returns to lower levels of education have fallen. They tend to be much lower for urban areas than for rural areas up to complete primary, as in the latter the still-large share of workers with incomplete primary education allows for segmentation. Also, in rural areas minimum wages are less easy to enforce and there are more unregistered workers. In contrast, from secondary education upwards, the returns to education are larger in urban areas, where there is a higher demand for skilled workers. The premium to secondary education, even though falling for both areas, is 33 per cent for urban areas against 18 per cent in rural areas, both lower than in India.

But, unlike in India, the returns to tertiary education have also fallen, more sharply in rural areas than in urban areas. The fall in rural areas is probably related to the scarcity of high-quality jobs. The wage ratio between tertiary and secondary education was significantly higher in urban Brazil than in urban India (2.58 against 2.18), but the gap was falling.

The decline in wage differentials by educational level in Brazil between 1995 and 2011 was largely due to an increase in the wage floor for more poorly skilled segments, brought about by the rise in the minimum wage. This is certainly one of the factors explaining the difference between the two countries in the trend of overall inequality.

Another way of looking at returns to education is in relation to the segmentation of the labour market. Table 5.4.14 shows the pattern of wages by education separately for regular and for casual wages in India for three years – 1983, 1999-2000, and 2011-12. For those in regular wage work, wage differences by level of education are very large, and the gap between the top and the bottom has widened over time. In 2011-12, in regular employment, a worker with secondary schooling had wages almost twice as high as someone who was illiterate. With a tertiary qualification, the difference was over four times. On the other hand, while there is some increase in casual wages with education level, this is far smaller than for regular work. And these differences across educational levels in casual work seem to have been narrowing. So the influence of education is quite different in the regular and casual segments of the labour market.

There is some difference in these patterns between urban and rural areas (not shown in the table). The returns to education were lower in rural areas than in urban areas for both regular and casual work – indeed, for the latter, differences across education levels were negligible in rural areas. In urban areas, casual wages do tend to rise with increasing education levels, but still much less than for regular wages.

Table 5.4.14. Regular and Casual Daily Wages by Level of Education, India, 1983, 1999-2000 and 2011-12, in Rs. (in 2011-12 Prices)

	Regular Wage			Casual Wage		
	1983	1999-2000	2011-12	1983	1999-2000	2011-12
No schooling/illiterate	108	152	171	68	99	145
Below primary	124	178	195	82	119	159
Primary	134	183	205	83	131	168
Middle	158	225	233	90	129	183
Secondary	225	315	322	100	146	188
Higher secondary	-	397	389	-	141	181
Diploma and above	-	-	498	-	-	240
Graduate and above	325	560	760	135	171	210
Total	188	336	445	76	117	166

Source: NSS 38th, 55th, and 68th Rounds.
Note: Secondary education includes Higher Secondary in 1983. Higher Secondary includes Diploma and above in 1999-2000.

Table 5.4.15. Monthly Wages of Registered and Unregistered Workers by Level of Education, Brazil, 1995 and 2011 (Reais)

Level of schooling	Registered Workers		Unregistered Workers		Self-employed	
	1995	2011	1995	2011	1995	2011
No schooling	626.1	901.1	343.6	571.8	452.4	664.6
Incomplete fundamental	892.8	988.8	510.3	655.2	905.0	924.6
Complete fundamental	1,174.9	1,142.2	739.8	851.2	1,425.1	1,349.2
Complete high school	1,604.5	1,629.6	970.8	1,067.2	1,837.4	1,894.6
Complete higher education	4,774.3	3,254.5	3,465.3	2,477.7	4,746.1	3,455.0
Total	1,389.1	1,379.8	633.7	877.6	1,105.5	1,219.0

Source: PNAD.

In Brazil, we can also see the behaviour of wage differentials across education levels for registered and unregistered workers in Table 5.4.15. It is interesting to note that in 2011 the wage ratios across education levels for registered workers were very close to those for regular workers in India - a ratio of 3.6 between workers with tertiary education and those without schooling and 1.8 between secondary education and without schooling. However, the trend is quite different from India, for these ratios had fallen quite abruptly since 1995, when they were 7.6 and 2.6 respectively.

Another difference with India was found in the wage differentials for unregistered workers in Brazil, which we can compare to casual workers in India. Here, the differentials across education levels in 2011 were even higher than for regular workers, 4.3 and 1.9 times for tertiary and secondary education respectively. Also, the fall was even sharper when compared with 1995. This can be explained by the fact that the average wage of the illiterate unregistered workers is closer to the minimum wage than the average wage of illiterate registered workers; so the rising minimum wage had a greater impact on the average wages of illiterate unregistered workers.

An interesting point can be made about self-employed workers in Brazil. Even though their income sources are quite different, the disparities across education levels have followed more or less the same trends as those of wage workers, falling over time. This group also showed the highest income ratio between tertiary and illiterate workers in 2011, at 5.2 times. Even though wages of registered workers were 13 per cent higher than self-employed incomes on average in 2011, for those with tertiary education the income of registered workers was 6 per cent lower than that of the self-employed.

In both Brazil and India, these changes in the returns to education have to be analysed in the light of the changing educational composition of the population. In both countries, the share of the higher educational groups has risen substantially. The fact that wage differentials nevertheless continued to rise in India suggests either an even faster increase in demand for highly qualified workers, or a capturing of the gains from growth by a relatively small category of workers, or both. In Brazil, on the other hand, educational improvements did not lead to a more than proportional income rise for the more educated segments. This is, in all likelihood, due to the occupational profile of the jobs occupied by each educational segment, and also because in some segments (like middle school, but also higher education to a lesser extent), the rise in the labour supply was quite substantial, probably not matched by the demand, especially for those with an university degree.

What was the overall contribution of education to wage inequality? A partial answer is provided by a decomposition of wage inequality (the Theil index) by education level, as has been done for other factors in previous sections. This uses the same educational categories as in Graphs 5.4.1 and 5.4.2 above. Graphs 5.4.3 and 5.4.4 give the decomposition separately for rural and urban areas for India and Brazil, respectively.

Graph 5.4.3. Decomposition of Theil Index of Wage Inequality across Education Categories, India, Rural and Urban, 1983–2011/12

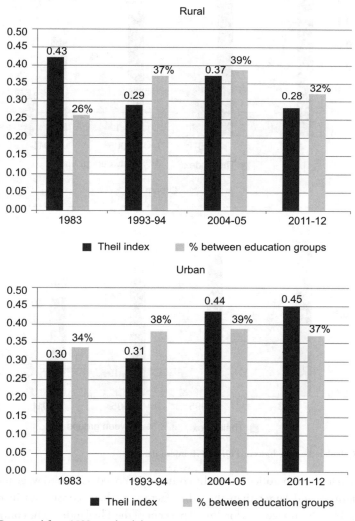

Source: Computed from NSS unit-level data.

Note: Level of Theil Index (left hand column in each year) and percentage explained by differences between education groups (right hand column).

Graph 5.4.4. Decomposition of Theil Index of Wage Inequality across Education
Categories, Rural and Urban, Brazil, 1983–2011

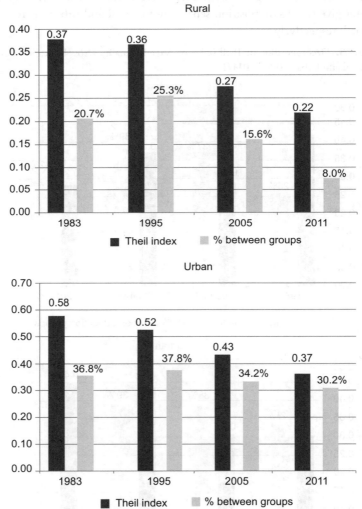

Source: Calculated on the basis of POF/IBGE micro-data.

The first point to notice is that the contribution of education to wage inequality
is substantial, and larger than the other factors we have considered in previous
sections. In India, it accounts for 25–40 per cent of the Theil index. The contribution
of education is generally higher in urban areas, although the difference between
urban and rural areas is not large. Over time, in both rural and urban areas, the

percentage contribution of education to inequality first rose (until 2004-05) and then fell. But the fall is small in urban areas. In addition, there has been a long-term tendency for inequality to rise in urban areas. So, the absolute contribution of education to wage inequality rose until 2004-05, and then stabilized up to 2011-12, while falling in rural areas. It seems that wage compression in the lower part of the education hierarchy compensated for the growing gap at the top.

In Brazil, there are some similarities, in that the contribution of education to the Theil index is of a similar order of magnitude as in India until 1995, although it is much higher in urban areas than in rural areas. Like in India, it first rises, and then falls. But the time pattern is different – the peak was reached in 1995 in Brazil but in 2005 in India. Moreover, after 1995, there is a much sharper decline than in India in both urban and rural areas, especially in rural areas. Compared with the 1980s, in India education is playing a larger role in wage inequality today, while in Brazil its impact has been reduced.

It is also instructive to break down the decomposition by work type and sex (Tables 5.4.16 and 5.4.17). This confirms that the contribution of education to inequality is very different in different segments of the labour market, but the gap is much larger in India than in Brazil. In India, education accounts for around 30 per cent of the Theil index, on average, in regular work, but only around 5 per cent in casual work. The similar difference in Brazil between registered and unregistered work is much weaker, and declining over time. By 2011, there was very little difference between the registered and unregistered segments of the labour market. There is also a difference between men and women in India, with the contribution of education greater for women, except in rural casual work. In Brazil, education is more important for women in rural areas, but less in urban areas, where there is not much difference between men and women for either registered or unregistered work.

5.4.4   Conclusions

It is often argued that investment in education is the most effective way to reduce inequality. For instance, recent studies of declining inequality in Latin America (Cornia, 2014; López-Calva and Lustig, 2010) have suggested that rising education levels have played an important role in this trend; see also Dreze and Sen's (2013) discussion of education in India. This view is often based on human capital models in which investment in education produces a return; so expanding education to all should also widen income opportunities and reduce inequality.

Table 5.4.16. Contribution of Education to Theil Index of Wages by Employment Status, Sex and Rural-Urban Residence, India, 1983–2011/12 (%)*

Employment status		1983	1993-94	2004-05	2011-12
Rural regular	All	21	32	23	20
	Female	20	43	31	26
	Male	21	30	22	20
Rural casual	All	4	7	9	4
	Female	1	2	1	1
	Male	2	4	5	2
Urban regular	All	28	29	33	24
	Female	45	37	31	24
	Male	27	29	32	33
Urban casual	All	4	5	7	4
	Female	6	2	7	5
	Male	1	2	4	3

Source: Computed on the basis of NSS data (38th, 50th, 61st, and 68th rounds).
Note: *Percentage of the overall Theil wage inequality index that reflects wage differences between different educational groups. See the discussion of decomposition in Section 4.3.

Table 5.4.17. Contribution of Education to Theil Index of Wages by Employment Status, Sex, and Rural-Urban Residence, Brazil, 1995–2011 (%)

Area	Employment Status	Sex	1995	2005	2011
Rural	Registered	Total	28.1	15.0	5.9
		Male	36.2	15.8	8.8
		Female	26.8	29.4	16.8
	Unregistered	Total	10.2	10.3	6.0
		Male	10.7	9.3	7.8
		Female	30.5	26.5	9.7
Urban	Registered	Total	37.2	34.8	30.5
		Male	45.1	39.8	36.0
		Female	35.6	38.6	32.4
	Unregistered	Total	31.4	30.1	26.8
		Male	37.7	32.9	32.4
		Female	32.7	35.4	28.9

Source: Computed on the basis of POF/IBGE micro-data.

We have seen that education levels have been rising steadily in both India and Brazil, but that substantial inequalities persist. These education patterns interact with an unequal labour market in both countries. These structural factors tend to undermine the human capital argument. In particular, inequalities in access to education are transmitted from generation to generation; this is true in both India and Brazil, but is particularly clear in India. An analysis of the determinants of education in India (see Rodgers and Soundararajan, 2016) shows pronounced caste, community, regional, and gender effects. The rise in average educational levels, then, confronts a labour market in which the qualifications required for access to different types of occupation also rise. In both Brazil and India, the result is a decline in the returns to education. The main exception concerns the highest, tertiary education levels in India, where wage differentials have widened. But access to tertiary education in India remains confined to a minority, and the high wages contribute to growing inequality.

In India, education strongly affects employment status. The less educated are much more likely to be in casual employment, and the more educated in regular employment; education is not strongly related to self-employment. In Brazil, the pattern is more complex: while registered work predominates for all education levels with the exception of the illiterate, there is some tendency for the less educated to be found in unregistered wage work or low-paid registered work, and especially as self-employed in less-skilled and lower-income activities. So, education stratifies the labour market – and also adapts to an already stratified labour market – in both countries, but in different ways.

The relationship between education and wages is strong, but quite different in the two countries. In the early 1980s, wage differentials by education were much higher in Brazil than in India. In India, the wage ratio between those with tertiary education and illiterates was between 3 and 4 in 1983. In Brazil, the corresponding ratio was over 10. And when comparing those who had completed middle school in India and the broadly equivalent fundamental education in Brazil with illiterates, we find a wage ratio of about 2 in India, but 3 in Brazil. This sharp difference between the two countries in the wage scales was certainly an important reason why overall inequality was so much higher in Brazil than in India at the time.

These patterns had changed by 2011, but much more in Brazil than in India. In India, the wage ratio between graduates and illiterates had risen to between 4 and 5 in urban areas, while that between completed middle school and illiterates had fallen slightly to less than 1.4. But, in Brazil, these ratios had fallen sharply, approximately halved, by 2011; they were down to 5 for tertiary graduates and 1.5 for fundamental school graduates – approaching the figures for India. It is important to note that a large part of this fall occurred after 1995. So a considerable process of wage compression across education levels was occurring in Brazil, especially in the last decade, which certainly is connected with the declining level of inequality overall. At the same time, no such compression was occurring at the top of the educational pyramid in India – if anything, gaps were widening slightly, although they were narrowing in the middle. And this in turn surely helps to explain the increase in inequality in India.

The question of inequality in education is not only one of the schooling level completed, but also of the quality of education received. In both Brazil and India, the same problem can be identified – rapid expansion of education, with a view to its universalization, can easily be to the detriment of its quality. Both cases illustrate how the expansion of private education can strengthen inequality precisely by providing education of higher quality to those who can pay. This, in turn, influences access to the labour market, since employers may rate qualifications from private institutions more highly than public. This may also hinder access to public universities, as in the Brazilian case, where quota systems have been introduced not only for disadvantaged groups, such as indigenous populations and blacks, but also for students from public schools.

All of these factors show that education plays an important role in inequality in both countries, but has different patterns and impacts. Education is closely connected with labour market segmentation, as educational qualifications provide or deny access to particular types of jobs, especially the more desirable jobs, and this interacts with racial and gender inequality. Since access to education is restricted, especially at the top of the education ladder, wage differentials between the top and the bottom widen in periods of higher growth. That has been visible in India in recent years, and such mechanisms were certainly important in the high-growth period in Brazil before 1980. It is only in the past two decades that wage ratios between the top and the bottom have declined towards Indian levels. But these ratios take place in differently segmented labour markets. Also, the fall in Brazil is far from spontaneous, closely related to the minimum wage policy, and also to the faster growth of supply of workers with higher education levels in a context of stagnant productivity levels – the opposite of the Indian case.

So, the view that expansion of education is the route to declining inequality has to be considered in social and economic context. There is surely an important potential here. But at the same time we see that as access to one level of education is equalized or universalizes, inequality shifts to the next level up. And it is the better-off and better-educated who are in a better position to invest in their offspring, so education also serves to transmit inequality across generations. Expanding education is of course desirable in its own right, but it is not a panacea for growing inequality.

Annex to Section 5.4. Schooling Systems in Brazil and India

Brazil	India
System 9+3 since 2010 (previously 8+3)	**System 8+2+2**
Fundamental education I = Grades I – V 5 years (from age 6)	Primary school = Classes I–V – 5 years (6 to 10 years of age)
Fundamental education II = Grades VI – IX 4 years	Middle school = Classes VI–VIII – 3 years (11 to 13 years of age)
Middle school (Ensino Médio – Secondary or high school) = 3 years (15 to 17 years of age)	Secondary school = Classes IX–X – 2 years (14 and 15 years of age)
	Higher secondary school = Classes XI–XII – 2 years (16 and 17 years of age)

Note: In India, there are some regional variations around this basic model.

5.5 Some Multivariate Results

In this book, we have avoided taking too statistical or econometric a view of the determinants of inequality, believing that greater insight can be gained from examining different aspects of inequality in their social and historical context. Nevertheless, in the preceding sections we have explored the statistical contribution to wage inequality of different factors – the type of employment, gender differences, regional variations, differentiation by race or caste, and in the last section, the role of education. For some of these we have looked at several factors together – for instance, in the last section, the joint effects of sex, education, and type of employment. In this section, we take the multivariate approach to its logical conclusion, by examining the joint effects of the different variables examined above, along with others. We use the decomposition method developed by Fields (2002). A simple ordinary least squares regression of the determinants of log wages is conducted on various worker characteristics like age, education, social group, industry of work, etc. The coefficients obtained from this regression are used to calculate the contribution of each of these characteristics to the overall observed wage inequality. The base of this approach is therefore the standard earnings functions which are common in the labour economics literature. The method is explained in more detail in Cacciamali et al. (2015).

For this decomposition we used the following characteristics of the individuals concerned in the two countries:

- Age;
- Sex;
- Type of wage work (regular or casual in India and registered or unregistered in Brazil);
- Education (the six categories used in Section 5.4 for the education decomposition for India and the five categories for Brazil);
- Region (the five regions identified in each country as in Section 5.2);
- Socio-religious group (the basic breakdown in India was SCs, STs, Muslim, other; in Brazil, white and non-white were distinguished);
- Industry (standard classification, 1-digit);
- Occupation (standard classification, 1-digit); and
- Rural-urban residence.

With the exception of age, industry, and occupation, these are the variables which were used in previous sections. Age was added because it is generally included in earnings functions of this type as a proxy for experience. There is an expectation that productivity is a positive function of experience, so this should appear as a positive relation of wages with age. Industry and occupation were added because of the expectation that these are important influences on wages, which are not captured by the other variables.

For Brazil we report the decomposition for 1995, 2005, and 2011 using unit-level data from the PNAD. For India we report 1993-94, 2004-05, and 2011-12 using unit-level data from the NSS.

More detailed results are presented in Cacciamali et al. (2015). Here we summarize the main findings for wage inequality.

When all of these variables are included in the decomposition, the level of statistical explanation of (log) wages overall is quite similar in the two countries: 50.1 per cent in Brazil in 2011 and 52 per cent in India in 2011-12. These degrees of explanation can be considered high, since there are always important interpersonal variations between individuals that cannot be captured by these standardized models. There are also unknown but probably significant errors of measurement that introduce random variation into the data. In discussing the results below, we report the relative contribution of each variable to the share of the variance that is explained by the decomposition.

In both countries, the largest contribution comes from education – over 30 per cent – while there is a downward tendency over time in Brazil (Graph 5.5.1) and slight upward tendency in India (Graph 5.5.2). The second-largest factor since 2005 is occupation. In both countries the contribution of occupation is rising, as the labour market diversifies, while at the same time the contribution of industrial sector is much less important than occupation, and is decreasing.

The influence of labour market segmentation (employment status) is significant but not preponderant. It accounted for about 10 per cent of inequality in 2012, down from a maximum of 16 per cent in 1993-94, and rather more in Brazil, where it is also in slight decline. In fact, it should be considered in conjunction with occupation, since many occupations typically fall within one or other of these labour categories (white-collar workers are mostly regular; unskilled labour is casual). Occupation and work type together account for over 30 per cent of wage inequality in India, and almost 40 per cent in Brazil in the most recent data. Actually, if taken together, their importance for overall inequality is greater than that of education in Brazil, and it has increased since 1995. In India, the joint contribution of occupation and work type to inequality is still less than that of education, but it too is increasing.

Graph 5.5.1. Fields Decomposition of Wages, Brazil, 1995 to 2011

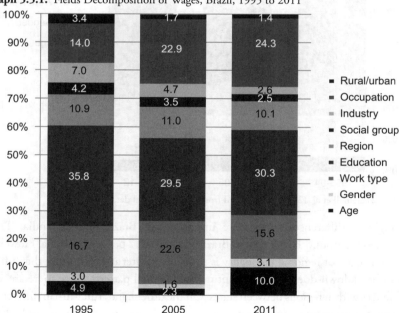

Source: Cacciamali et al. (2015); based on PNAD/IBGE micro-data.

Note: The sequence of items in the legend, from top to bottom, corresponds to the sequence of the elements in the bars of the graph.

Gender is much more important in India than in Brazil. In India, it accounted for almost 10 per cent in 2011-12 (though down from 13 per cent in 1993-94). In Brazil, it was under 4 per cent (though increasing). Thus there is more discrimination or differentiation to the disadvantage of women in India. Age is also a significant factor in both, but its contribution has grown in Brazil and stagnated in India. This may reflect a labour market that favours career progression in the former, if we are considering age as a proxy for experience.

Graph 5.5.2. Fields Decomposition of Wages, India, 1993/94–2011/12

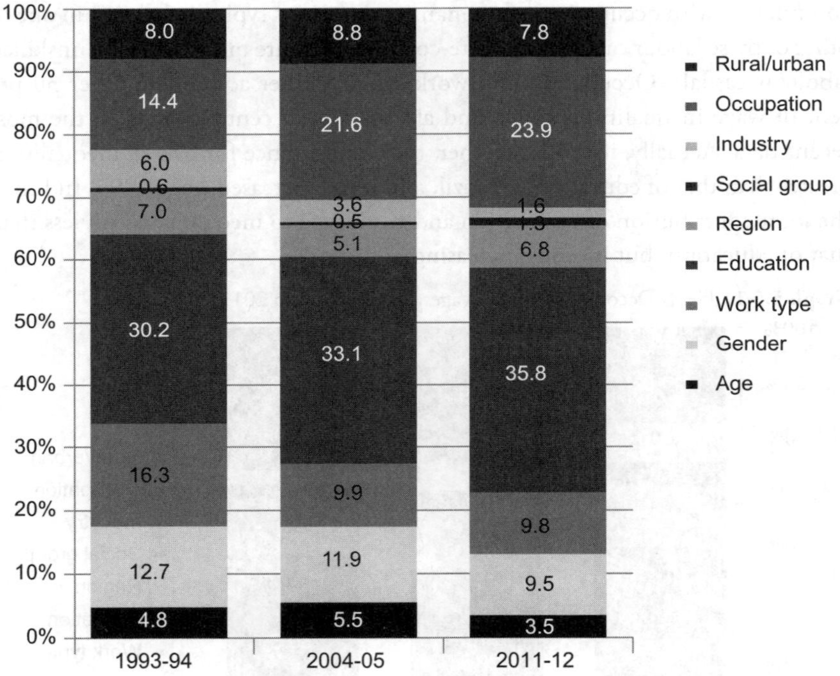

Source: Cacciamali et al. (2015). Computed from NSS unit-level data.

Regional differences were more important in Brazil than in India. They accounted for around 10 per cent in Brazil and around 7 per cent in India. However, the real impact of regional inequality is probably greater if we consider that a five-region breakdown does not fully capture the regional pattern, since there are also differences within regions between states. On the other hand, rural-urban differences were more important in India, around 8 per cent in recent years against only 2 per cent in Brazil. If we take region and rural-urban together as an overall indicator of regional disparity, there is not a large difference between the two countries.

The largest surprise in these charts comes in the contribution of social differences (race and caste) to wage inequality – quite small in both countries, but especially in India. The breakdown in India is quite limited (SC, ST, Muslims, and others) but the small contribution to inequality is still contrary to expectations. It is nevertheless consistent with the finding in Section 5.3 that discrimination against social groups in India operates more at the point of entry to employment than in wage differences among those in work.

The results for gender and social groups also indicate that inequality within population sub-groups is becoming more significant than inequality between groups, even among those socially vulnerable.

Some caution is required in comparing these results between the two countries, because the explanatory power of each variable in the decomposition depends not only on the differences in wages between categories, but also on the sizes of those categories. So, the contribution of urban-rural differences in Brazil is relatively small, but only a small part of the Brazilian labour market is rural today, while the Indian labour market is more evenly balanced. And the declining contribution in India of gender differences to inequality, and its increase in Brazil, may be due in part to the declining share of women in the Indian labour force and an increasing share in Brazil. Nevertheless, these results give us some interesting hypotheses or provide additional evidence to support or contradict findings from the more qualitative analysis above.

On the whole, the results of the multivariate analysis are consistent with the bivariate analysis in preceding sections. In other words, the inter-dependence between these variables does not seem to undermine the conclusions based on bivariate relationships. The weak effect of social group in India is perhaps the main exception to this conclusion. It suggests that the influence of social group on wage inequality comes not directly as wage discrimination but through discrimination in access to education and occupation (which was documented in the last two sections). On the other hand, the substantial and persistent influence of gender in this analysis suggests that women are subject to significant direct wage discrimination, and that this is an important factor in wage inequality overall.

6

Inequality in Social and Economic Context

6.1 A Summing Up

Inequality is treated by some economists as a technical issue – the consequence of a particular production technology and of differing returns to production factors as a result of market forces; from this perspective, large differences in wages are seen merely to reflect returns to human capital. Other economists may see inequality as a straightforward reflection of production relations, a consequence of the model of growth and the degree of exploitation associated with the process of capital accumulation. Both views may capture a part of the whole, for these relationships are usually present, but the history of Brazil and India suggests that a broader perspective is needed. We have tried above to analyse the pattern of inequality within the context of growth regimes – understood as a set of macroeconomic, social, and institutional factors that play out in markets and production relations, and take particular shapes because of the national and global context, the nature of the state, and the social interests that it represents.

These growth regimes vary over time, and of course differ between the two countries, but similar forces can be observed within each, and some outcomes are similar. Over the past seventy years, both countries have seen periods when inequality increased, stabilized, or declined, though generally not at the same time in both, for their histories have been different. This is partly because they have been subordinated to, and interacted with, global markets in different ways, but also because their political settings and production structures have followed different trajectories. Brazil industrialized successfully, especially during the authoritarian regime before 1980, when the state subsidized private capital accumulation, especially in the most dynamic sectors, paving the way for the internationalization of its internal market. India's autarkic industrialization stalled, but eventually, and much later than Brazil, it generated increasing capital accumulation and high growth, based more on services than on industry, and in a democratic framework. In contrast, economic growth was meagre in Brazil from 1980 to 2010, and the share of manufacturing in GDP went down. These different trajectories led to quite different patterns of inequality, for many years much greater in Brazil than in India. But as India's growth accelerated around the turn of the twenty-first century and inequality started to increase, in Brazil a reaction set in to the extremes of inequality, and led to effective state action to change the trend.

So, the pattern of inequality has to be understood in the broader historical context, and is the result of a number of overlapping forces:

- The distribution of wealth, which is inherited and changes only slowly
- The nature of economic relations, and the power of capital and labour
- The form of integration in the global economy
- The pattern and organization of production
- The role played by the state and
- A variety of specific institutions and cleavages embedded in each society.

What, then, are some of the key ideas and observations that emerge from the comparison of the two countries?

◆ It used to be widely thought that Brazil was more unequal than India, and this was certainly the case thirty years ago. But, since then, inequality has declined in Brazil and risen in India, so that today, the levels of inequality in the two countries may not be much different; which country is more unequal varies from one aspect of inequality to another.

◆ In both countries, periods of high growth were usually associated with declining absolute poverty but increasing inequality; so relative poverty increased in those periods, notably in Brazil before 1980 and India more recently.

◆ The sectoral pattern of growth, and its consequences for employment, played a key role in differentiating the labour force. Brazil created an industrial workforce by the 1970s and a growing middle class, but also a considerable urban labour surplus. India's recent economic growth, led by services and construction, has resulted in a heterogeneous urban workforce with an emerging middle class, while the large agricultural sector serves as a labour reserve even today. These patterns provide the foundations of class interests and identity and, thus the basic structure of inequality.

♦ In Brazil, an increase in GDP growth after 2000 was associated with a more-than-proportionate increase in formal job creation. In India, the opposite occurred, to the point where there was much concern with 'jobless growth'.

♦ The difference in the recent growth paths also reflects the role of the internal market. Brazil relied on rising wages and public expenditure to drive growth, with only a small recovery in the rate of investment after 2000, while India was more dependent on increasing exports, middle-class consumption, and private investment at much higher levels than in Brazil.

♦ The distribution of income between wages and profits shows different trends in India and Brazil. In India, after the 1980s, there was a sharp shift away from wages to capital incomes, which seems to have been a significant factor in the increase in overall inequality. In contrast, there was a recovery in the wage share in Brazil in the 2000s, though from very low levels if compared to developed countries.

♦ Rising wages can be associated with both rising and falling inequality. In India, real wages have been rising for all categories of wage workers since the 1980s. This was one reason for a substantial fall in poverty, despite an increase in inequality. In Brazil, the fall in inequality was associated with a rise in real labour income after 2003, although the latter was not much higher in 2012 than in the mid-1990s or in the late 1970s.

♦ Labour market segregations and segmentations play an important role in inequality in both countries. The largest divide is between formal and informal employment. But informal work accounts for a much larger share of employment in India than in Brazil, and this generates a pattern of labour market inequality in which a much larger proportion of Indian workers are insecure and unprotected. In both countries, formal production systems use informal workers through outsourcing and other means, and there are large variations in wages, employment security, protection, and vulnerability in both formal and informal work.

♦ The precise factors of labour market segmentation are different in the two countries, but some of the mechanisms are similar. Labour markets are segmented by sex, caste/race, and other cleavages, which gives rise to complex patterns of inequality and exclusion.

◆ There have been reductions in income differences in Brazil in the 2000s between formal workers, on the one hand, and informal workers and the self-employed, on the other. Inequality also has fallen within each group. This is true for casual workers in India as well, suggesting that unskilled labour markets are becoming more integrated in both countries. Wage differences between casual and regular workers in India widened in the wake of liberalization in the early 1990s, but the trend has been reversed in recent years.

◆ But in India, gaps have continued to widen between skilled and white-collar occupations, on the one hand, and casual or production workers, on the other. In Brazil, the opposite has occurred, due to the rapid increase in the minimum wage.

◆ While both countries have an extensive labour code, it plays a more important role in Brazil than in India, where it is effective only for a minority of workers. In Brazil, the framework of labour regulation was reinforced after 2002, with a growth in the share of formal work. This contributed to the decline in labour market inequality.

◆ Trade unions are more powerful in Brazil than in India, and influenced the political agenda after 2002. However, in neither country have trade unions been able to adequately represent the interests of informal workers.

◆ Minimum wage regulation in Brazil worked as an engine of inequality reduction in recent years because it sets an effective national floor for the income of unskilled workers. Minimum wages in India do not play the same role because they are complex, varying from region to region and from one category of workers to another, and subject to widespread violation and non-compliance.

◆ Regional inequality is large in both countries, but there is a clear difference in the trends. Regional differences in wages and employment have widened in India and narrowed in Brazil in the past two decades. However, at least in Brazil, inequality has fallen less rapidly within the poorest states, due to the importance of self-employment and other non-wage work in these regions, which are not directly affected by minimum wages.

◆ Education is associated with large wage differentials in both countries. But rising average education levels have not reduced these differentials. Instead, they have led to lower returns to each level of education, as the supply of educated workers increases, while the differentials are reproduced at higher levels of education than before. However, in Brazil the wage differential between the top and bottom education levels has been reduced in the past decade.

◆ With respect to gender equality, Brazil has moved faster than India in terms of fertility reduction, urban job opportunities, and education, but women workers in both Brazil and India continue to face similar challenges: labour market segmentation, social norms, and how to reconcile work and family responsibilities. A disproportionate number of women workers are found in precarious and low-quality employment in both countries. Gender wage differentials have declined in both countries, but there is still both a 'sticky floor' and a 'glass ceiling' – the former stronger in India, the latter stronger in Brazil.

◆ Discrimination and differentiation by caste and community in India and by race or colour in Brazil are persistent, although there has been some progress in both countries. There is some sign that in India differences in access to employment for different castes and communities are more important than wage discrimination, while in Brazil it is the reverse. In both countries, wage discrimination between social groups appears to be greatest for those with the most education. Job reservation policies in India have been insufficient to deal with this issue, and tend to fragment the labour market as many social groups – not all disadvantaged – demand their own share in reservations.

◆ In Brazil, social policy accounts for a much larger share of GDP than in India, and Brazil has progressed towards a near-universal social safety net (especially through non-contributory pensions and cash transfer mechanisms), which contributed to the reduction of inequality. In India, social policies have been more targeted and less comprehensive, while conventional social security has mainly been limited to the formal sector. However, innovative social policies in India seem to have slowed the rise in inequality.

These outcomes reflect overall regimes of growth and capital accumulation, which themselves change over time. A number of factors in these regimes are common to Brazil and India. Globalization plays an important role in both countries. Depending on the pattern of integration in the world economy, it limits policy options, strengthens competitive forces in the labour market, and makes national economies more vulnerable to international economic fluctuations. The state always plays a central role in both production and distribution, partly conditioned by its alliances with powerful economic actors – whether business, finance, trade unions, landed elites, nationalist forces, international creditors, or others. It also plays a crucial role with respect to some key determinants of inequality – education, discrimination, and social protection. And beyond the state there are deeper, embedded patterns of organization of society that are reflected in labour market institutions, in the extent of gender inequality, the exclusion of particular groups, patterns of participation and representation, the sense of community, and the extent of solidarity. Above all, the distribution of wealth – on which data are scarce – sets the basic parameters for the distribution of income.

The corollary is that inequality needs to be understood as the overall outcome of a system rather than being determined by some specific factors in each country. These specific factors may help us to describe the features of inequality – for instance, between castes in India – but do not really explain it.

We must not use the word 'inequality' as if its content were obvious. It takes different forms. We have focused on wages, incomes, and consumption levels, but this is only part of the story, for there is inequality in wealth, security, capability, prestige, and power. Nor is it simple to characterize inequality. Although we reduce it to summary measures, such as the Gini or Theil coefficients, in fact we are also interested in specific questions such as how well people do at the bottom or the top compared with the rest. For instance, it may be, and often is, argued that the primary concern should be to ensure that everyone reaches a certain standard of economic welfare, without regard to what happens at the top of the distribution. However, what happens at each extreme is inter-related, depending on the nature of growth regimes and the policies that are adopted. So, reducing inequality is not a matter of simple redistribution, but also of change in the underlying social and economic structures.

Measures of inequality are not easy to interpret, as inequality reflects individual choices as well as societal structures. And there are inevitably moral or ethical considerations. How much inequality is acceptable? This question is at the heart of politics, and the history of India and Brazil shows that there have been different answers at different times. In today's world, widening gaps between the rich and the rest have become central to economic debate. This is a concern at the global level among those who fear that growing inequality may, for various reasons, be a cause of global stagnation. But it is also a concern among the many who find the gaps between rich and poor to be morally intolerable.

In this debate, the contrasts between Brazil and India help to show what is specific and what is general. The divergences help to identify proximate causes and correlates. The similarities may point to more systematic, wider influences that are felt beyond these two countries.

6.2 Growth Regime and Inclusive Growth

Inequality, then, is the outcome of a wide variety of forces, which we try to capture through the analytical device of growth regimes. And since inequality is embedded in the different institutional components of each growth regime, and their interaction, it follows that to reduce inequality there is no silver bullet. Multiple factors are involved.

The state is only one of these factors, but it is a central one, since it is both endogenous and exogenous. Endogenous, because the state reflects the prevailing economic and social forces, and so is one of the mechanisms by which particular patterns of inequality emerge. Exogenous, because we expect the state to intervene with a view to achieving particular goals. Reducing inequality may be among these goals, but this is just one among a set of objectives which may contradict each other, depending on the social forces underpinning the state and its room for manoeuvre. So the endogeneity of the state comes back to the fore. Its ability to move forward and reshape its political foundations is also to some extent related to the nature of the growth regime itself.

The experience of Brazil and India shows clearly that in order to modify the pattern of inequality a comprehensive approach is required. Single-dimension solutions, whether they consist of focused policies such as cash transfers or employment creation programmes, or broader strategies built around industrialization or liberalization, give unbalanced results. In both Brazil and India there have been periods when a push for growth has led to concentration of income and wealth. But in both countries democratic institutions have led, sooner or later, to pressure for complementary social policies and even for a change of growth regime, in order to offset or compensate for the tendencies to exclusion or exploitation. This is what happened in Brazil after 2002. But while there was a major change of political direction at that time, the growth regime that emerged was unstable and after some time a backlash against redistribution developed. In India this dialectic was weaker, but a similar interpretation is possible. Growing inequality around the turn of the century was one factor in the change of government in 2004, and the new government expanded social policy, but without fundamental change in the pattern of growth. So the relationship between growth and distribution is complex and cannot be summed up in equations in which the political forces are absent.

The mirror image metaphor is useful here. In the period before 1980, Brazil was the archetype of a disequalizing high-growth economy, and with weak democratic forces there was little countervailing pressure on the state to redistribute. In India, in a much more democratic and egalitarian framework, growth was low in this period, which sharply limited the capacity to redistribute. The immediate result was declining poverty in Brazil and stagnant poverty levels in India. But the intensification of class differentiation in the former, along with increasing tensions within the growth regime, led to a period of deep economic crisis in the 1980s; in contrast, India was able to build accelerating growth from the 1980s on. The more recent period from the early 2000s until 2014 is also instructive, since it shows that a broad based policy framework, as in Brazil, can generate a clearly declining trend in inequality in a context in which growth was lower than before 1980 and if compared to India. Meanwhile, the more fragmented attempts in India to deal with deficits in employment and income security during a period of high growth at least slowed the upward trend in inequality.

That is, the metaphor is just a way to express the contrasts between the two countries in the underlying forces leading to particular growth regimes and their impacts on inequality, at different points of time.

One of the underlying forces is the tendency for wealth to concentrate, whether as a result of Piketty-type mechanisms where the rate of return on capital exceeds the rate of growth, or because of more overtly political means. This is hardly visible in the statistics, which are quite insufficient when it comes to measuring wealth, although it may be visible in an explosion of urban construction or a conspicuously different life-style among the elites in both countries. In India, it is surely connected with the increasing share of capital in value added in recent years, and with the apparently large financial flows into tax havens. In Brazil, even though the wage share recovered after 2000, the rate of profit remained very high, especially for some fractions of capital, notably in the financial sector, non-financial TNCs and the largest national enterprises. In any event, in the absence of effective taxation of wealth, this is a powerful force for the persistence of inequality.

However, in contrast to Piketty's model – in which the rate of return on capital and the rate of growth are considered independent variables – for both Brazil and India the potential rate of growth is still very high, due to the availability of underutilized labour and the possible gains in capital and labour productivity, if new sectors and productive niches are opened for capital accumulation. But this requires a new set of economic policies and a different pattern of international integration.

Another powerful mechanism for the transmission of inequality is the educational system. Of course, education can also be an equalizing force, if there is universal access. But in practice, investment in education helps to ensure that differentials in income and wealth are also transmitted from one generation to the next. When one level of the education system universalizes, the mechanism for differentiation shifts to the next level. And both countries have failed to adequately equip young people, especially from low-income households, with skills and capabilities on which to build their lives, since these too are concentrated among a fraction of the population.

A persistent force for inequality lies in labour market segmentations, often connected with particular identities. Caste continues to play a surprisingly important role in India, race in Brazil, and gender in both. These identities interact with others and may lead to persistent deprivation. Nonetheless, wage differentials by race and gender in Brazil have been reduced by labour and social policies during a period of internal market-led growth during the 2000s. The new growth regime in Brazil was unable to do away with the segmentations of the past, but altered the way they worked and reduced their impact.

The combination of these different factors within broader growth regimes underlines the need for a comprehensive strategy, in which distribution is a central concern, if inequality is to be reduced. Yet in both countries it can be seen that different policy instruments affect different parts of the income distribution. Cash transfers, wage policies, education policies, employment policies, and effective labour market regulation do not reach the same populations, nor deal with the same mechanisms of inequality. A package of complementary measures is required.

In higher income countries redistribution through taxes and transfers account for a fairly substantial proportion of GDP, though varying greatly from one country to another. This plays a much more significant role in Brazil than in India, since social policies account for a much higher share of GDP in the former. A rising share of direct taxation is also an important aspect of a redistributive strategy, since it tends to be more progressive than indirect taxes. Wealth taxes face considerable political and practical obstacles; indeed, the existing rather limited tax has just been abolished in India. In the case of Brazil, wealth taxes are quite low and regressive by international standards.

Within the labour market, the experience of India and Brazil suggests that some combination of wage policy and skill development can have a substantial impact, either to reduce inequality or to increase it. Minimum wage policy has played an important equalizing role in Brazil in recent years, but under the military regime before 1980 it served to keep a cap on wages and to widen differentials. In India too, wage policy seems to be a force for differentiation rather than equalization. Meanwhile, skill gaps legitimize wage differentials. Differences in wages between white collar and other occupations also help to drive a wedge between different groups of workers and reinforce the growth of the middle class.

The Indian state has over the years done little to reform labour market institutions. However, there is a strong argument that more effective labour institutions, which can reduce insecurity and vulnerability in the labour market, are an important part of any effort to reduce inequalities. That, at least, is one of the lessons of Brazil's recent experience.

Policies to compensate for specific disadvantages and vulnerabilities in the labour market, or to reduce the exclusion of particular groups, interact with these broader factors. Affirmative action is particularly important in India, but has not resulted in fundamental change. In Brazil, it has been strengthened, but remains mainly focused on access to university education. It is often politically feasible to redistribute to disadvantaged groups, regions, or sectors, up to a limit set by the presence of countervailing forces.

This is about the state. But as the experience of both countries shows, democratic forces, representation and mobilization beyond the state play a critical role. The trade union movement (more in Brazil) and NGO activism (more in India) have had significant consequences for the rights of workers and the political priorities of the state. And in India, recent developments in social policy such as MGNREGA and the extension of a rights-based approach (in education and other fields) owe a great deal to social mobilization over a long period of time.

These are some of the major policy issues that impact inequality. But there is also the wider issue of the future of the growth regime as a whole in both countries. Growth regimes come to an end, in the sense that they face a crisis and are transformed, as a result of internal or external forces. The global financial crisis set in motion a process that exposed the weaknesses of the redistributive growth regime in Brazil; and it also raises questions about the future path of growth in India. The next chapter reflects on the current situation in both countries in the light of the analysis of their growth regimes set forth in this book.

7

Post-Script

This is a long-term study, and our original intention was to address the period from the 1940s to 2010 or 2012. But we cannot end a book that compares Brazil and India without considering the divergent paths taken by the two countries since the start of the global financial crisis in 2008, and especially after 2014 – though this is an ongoing story, which has not yet fully worked itself out in either country.

The growth of the global economy remained obstinately low after the crisis. After the initial shock, world GDP fell by close to 2 per cent in 2009, but recovered to a 4.3 per cent growth rate in 2010, and growth in both India and Brazil recovered as well. But the so-called 'double-dip' was stronger and longer than expected. World GDP growth dropped to 2.3 per cent in 2013, and after another weak recovery it came down to 2.3 per cent again in 2016. At the same time, the gap between developed and developing countries narrowed, contrary to the idea that there would be some decoupling of their fortunes. So, while in the first stage of the crisis (2008–2011), the growth of the latter countries was three times as fast as the former, in 2015–2016 it was only twice as fast. But there is also great diversity among developing countries, and at present India and Brazil are at the extremes. India is doing the best among large national economies, with growth at around 7 per cent, and Brazil is doing the worst – its GDP fell 3.8 per cent in 2015, and another 3.6 per cent in 2016, in what can be considered its deepest recession in the last century (United Nations, 2015, 2017).

Initially, in both countries, the growth regimes seemed to have survived the global financial crisis unscathed. But as the crisis continued, the social and economic effects were felt in both countries, more sharply in Brazil than in India. It is therefore paradoxical that in the elections of 2014, the government in India fell while that in Brazil just survived. But this respite in Brazil was temporary, for the president was impeached and the PT removed from power in 2016, in what has been described as an 'institutional coup'. At the same time, the deep economic recession in Brazil has partially reversed some of the earlier achievements in terms of formalization of the labour market and reduction of unemployment. Meanwhile, India has returned to higher growth, though not at the pace of the 2000s. How can we characterize and interpret these changes in terms of our framework of analysis? And what might be the longer-term consequences in the two countries?

In India, the fall of the Congress-led UPA government in the 2014 general election was less about the failure of its economic policies than about corruption scandals and weak leadership. It is true that economic growth, after a fairly rapid recovery from the global financial crisis, had dropped again, to 4–5 per cent per year over 2012–2014. But poverty had clearly declined, formal employment and wages had risen, and there were signs that the increase in inequality had at least abated. Moreover, while the new BJP government had a different social agenda, its economic model maintained and strengthened the liberal strategy of the previous government. Orthodox economic policies aimed at the control of inflation and a reduction in the fiscal deficit. Engagement with the global economy was continued and strengthened, at least in terms of rhetoric, and restrictions on FDI were further eased (and there was some increase in FDI, though it remained rather small as a proportion of all investment). Coordination with business was pursued, and lower corporate tax rates were promised, with a view to strengthening investment incentives. The deregulation agenda initiated by previous governments was continued, including reform of taxation (where some progress was made) and of the labour code (which met significant opposition from organized labour, but advanced in some states). The abolition of the Planning Commission was an important symbolic step away from a state-managed economy. This was to some degree offset by an increase in the power of the Finance Ministry, but there was a general predisposition to reduce state intervention in the economy and promote market forces, which can be seen in the language of the 2015-16 Economic Survey:

> India has moved away from being reflexively anti-markets and uncritically pro-state to being pro-entrepreneurship and sceptical about the state. But being pro-industry must evolve into being genuinely pro-competition …

(Government of India, 2016, p. 3).

This also provides the framework for major initiatives such as 'Make in India' and 'Smart Cities'.

With respect to social policy, the initial orientation was to de-emphasize important existing programmes such as the MGNREGA and the public distribution system, and focus on the efficiency of delivery mechanisms and the reduction of unwarranted subsidies. Allocations to some social programmes were cut in favour of investment in physical infrastructure within a public sector budget that was declining as a percentage of GDP (Chandrasekhar, 2016; Drèze, 2016a). For instance, there were reductions in the budget for child development (the ICDS), and while initiatives on education, training, and health were launched, there was little fiscal space for large investments, and a stress on public-private partnerships. On the other hand, the budget allocation to the MGNREGA was subsequently increased again and its share in GDP was maintained at a little over 0.3 per cent (though this may not have been enough to meet the legal obligation to satisfy demand for employment). This compared with 0.6 per cent in 2009-10, though most of the decline occurred under the previous government. It has been argued that allocations to social policy have also been cut by underspending budgets (so the figures in annual budgets are misleading; Ghosh, 2015), or that more responsibilities for implementing social policies have been decentralized to states than can be covered by the increased transfers of resources foreseen by the Fourteenth Finance Commission. But in reality, three years into the term of the new government, the evidence is still insufficient to judge the size and reality of these changes and even less so their impacts.

In fact, the main concern in social policy has been to find ways to reduce leakages and misallocations, and to deal with social shortfalls through deeper integration in the market economy. A major initiative aims at financial inclusion, by universalizing access to bank accounts and promoting the digital economy. And in the 2016-17 Economic Survey there is analysis of the possibility (but as an idea for discussion rather than a firm proposal) of a universal basic income to replace the plethora of targeted social programmes with (electronic) cash payments. The latter has been met with some scepticism, for even the calculations in the Economic Survey assume that it would not in reality be universal, and it is far from clear that it could be a substitute for other social programmes (Ghosh, 2017). It can be argued that making pensions and the public distribution system for foodgrains truly universal would be a more realistic goal.

The broader question is whether there will be a return to the pattern of the last NDA government (1999–2004), when economic growth was high, but real wages hardly rose, and inequalities grew. Certainly a part of that equation seems to be repeated. There was virtually no increase in real agricultural and unskilled construction wages between April 2014 and September 2016, a period during which total growth of real GDP was around 19 per cent.[1] And while wage data for urban areas are very incomplete, real wages of unskilled workers in cotton mills in Mumbai grew only either 1 or 4 per cent during the same period (depending on which price index is used) and in Ahmedabad only 3 or 6 per cent. This suggests either that increases in national income were mainly captured by white-collar and skilled workers, or that the profit share had started to rise again. Meanwhile, as commented in Chapter 4, in addition to union opposition to labour reform, there was unrest among a number of social groups in different parts of the country demanding reservations in government jobs. In this it is the most vocal who receive attention, and as a result other important, relatively deprived groups, including Muslims and Scheduled Tribes, may well find themselves at the back of the queue.

There is also the possibility that GDP growth rates have been over-estimated. It is no mean achievement for the Indian economy to have grown at over 7 per cent per year in a depressed world economy. But changes in the method of estimation of some components of national accounts increased the measured rate of growth in 2015-16, notably for the manufacturing sector, and there have been large differences between consumer price indices, wholesale prices, and the GDP deflator. There is an ongoing debate about what biases might have been introduced (see, for instance, Nagaraj, 2015). Whatever the outcome of this debate, high growth may be difficult to sustain with the current pattern of demand, for exports have hardly increased and private investment is also weak. Most of the growth is coming from private consumption and government expenditure, and the latter will be constrained by increasingly tight fiscal targets. At the beginning of 2017 there are signs that growth is slowing, though the official government forecast is for it to continue in the vicinity of 7 per cent (Government of India, 2017).

The situation was complicated by the shock to the economy delivered by the demonetization of high value currency notes in November 2016 without their immediate replacement, and the chaos that resulted from the consequent shortage of cash. Much could be (and has been) said on this policy, but most economists anticipated an adverse effect on growth, with the judgement varying from small, short term effects on the government side to several percentage points

---

[1] Wage and price series from Government of India, Labour Bureau, *Indian Labour Journal*, various issues, 2014 to 2016. Real wages for construction work were virtually unchanged; for ploughing they were down by 3 per cent, for general agricultural work up by 3 per cent.

of GDP among some academic economists (including former Prime Minister Manmohan Singh, who foresaw a two percentage point drop in the growth rate (Singh, 2016)). At the time of writing insufficient national data are available to back up one or other of these points of view. For our study, the most interesting question is the impact on inequality, a subject which is entirely neglected in the chapter on demonetization in the 2016-17 Economic Survey. On that the evidence is largely anecdotal, but it is fairly obvious that the adverse impact of demonetization was greatest on the part of the economy most dependent on cash, namely the informal economy, small scale production, and casual wage labour (Kannan, 2016; Krishnan and Siegal, 2017). And there were indeed many reports of small businesses at a standstill and unpaid casual migrant workers, returning to their villages for lack of work (Harriss-White, 2017, among others). These are, of course, mainly low income groups, mostly without the reserves to face up to a shock of this sort. The better off, apart from those dependent on black money, were much better able to protect themselves. In other words, this policy certainly had an adverse impact on inequality and poverty, at least in the short term.

So, there are tensions within this economic model. India has maintained rapid growth on the basis of its domestic market, despite the failure of the global economy to recover from the financial crisis of 2008. It has also benefitted from low commodity prices – the opposite of Brazil, which suffered from the same cause. But it is not certain that the growth of consumer demand can be sustained if wages do not grow and inequality continues to rise. And the growth regime could be disrupted by social strains, including conflict between communities, religious intolerance, atrocities against Dalits, continuing pressure on the land rights of Scheduled Tribes, increasing regional inequality, and failure to meet the expectations of young people for decent jobs. There are clearly dangers ahead. There is in particular a risk that social policy, instead of playing an important structural role by supporting accumulation and growth and ensuring that there is widespread participation in the benefits, will increasingly be seen as an add-on, targeting particular groups or issues, and failing to address the key social dimensions of the growth regime.

In Brazil, the election of Dilma Rousseff as president in 2010 implied the continuation of the PT-led government, but in a much less favourable international economic environment than before. Initially, restrictive policies to control inflation led to high interest rates and overvaluation of the currency, and undermined the competitiveness of manufacturing exports at a time when commodity export prices were falling. Growth dropped. But in 2012, when expansionary policies were adopted instead – tax breaks, reduction in interest rates, subsidised credit and a small devaluation of the currency – this did not lead to sustained higher growth either. Even though inflation was limited to around 6 per cent and GDP growth reached 3 per cent in 2013, interest rates were raised once again. In 2014, GDP growth was 0.5 per cent as investment expectations deteriorated, affecting domestic demand. Both manufacturing and overall investment fell by 4.4 per cent in 2014. Moreover, despite the stagnation, the current account deficit jumped to 4.2 per cent of GDP. Rising government expenditure with stagnant GDP, compounded by the rising interest rates, led to a fiscal deficit and to a substantial increase in the debt-to-GDP ratio.

Dilma was re-elected in 2014, by a very small margin, but the economy was rapidly going into recession. The growth regime was visibly falling apart. High inflation, prompted by increases in fuel, electricity and other administered prices, led to even higher interest rates, and the commitment to achieve a fiscal surplus had become an almost impossible task in the context of falling government revenues. Already in early 2015 the forecasts for that year indicated a fall of 1–1.5 per cent of GDP, but it fell 3.8 per cent in reality. From 2014 to 2016 GDP per capita in Brazil dropped by close to 10 per cent.

In Dilma's first term, up to 2014, the decelerating economic growth did not much affect the labour market (Cacciamali and Tatei, 2016). After 2014, however, all data point to a rapid rise in unemployment, a fall in average wages, and growth of precariousness in the labour market. In 2015, the unemployment rate in major metropolitan areas rose from 4.8 per cent to 6.8 per cent.[2] Employment fell by 1.6 per cent in these areas, and average income fell by 4 per cent; 1.6 million formal (registered) jobs were lost in 2015, more than unregistered ones, while self-employment increased (Cacciamali and Tatei, 2016).

PNAD data covering the whole country available at the time of writing (IBGE, 2016) allow for a comparison between the second quarter of 2016 and the same period of the previous year. These data show that wages for registered workers fell 4 per cent in real terms, and that self-employed income was even more negatively affected, falling by almost 5 per cent. In contrast, the wages of unregistered workers increased by 5 per cent, probably because they displaced some registered workers with higher income levels. This points to an increasingly informalized labour market. It is too early to say whether this pattern will

---

[2] Source: IBGE/PME (*Pesquisa mensal de emprego*).

continue once the crisis is over, for this will depend on the duration of the crisis itself and on the nature of a new emerging growth regime.

According to the PNAD, unemployment went up from 8.3 per cent in the second quarter of 2015 to 11.3 per cent in the second quarter of 2016, and to 13.7 per cent in the first quarter of 2017, affecting more than 14 million people. This latter figure is almost twice as high as the rate of unemployment in the first quarter of 2014, 7.2 per cent – which was the lowest level reached after a long period of declining unemployment.[3]

This economic scenario was quite tragic and unexpected, but the political scenario was even more so. Corruption scandals are widespread in Brazilian political life (as in India, although their manifestation is different), but these shifted to a higher plane with 'Operation Car Wash' (*Operação Lava Jato*). Starting in 2014, an investigation by the federal police and federal prosecutors unveiled a massive corruption scheme at Petrobras, the giant oil company owned by the Brazilian state. As it proceeded, the largest national construction companies were also found to be heavily involved. Illicit transfers of all kinds funded electoral campaigns, benefiting almost all the political parties, including the ruling party PT and its main ally PMDB – which held the presidency of both the Senate and the House of Representatives – and even PSDB, the main opposition party. Ultimately, it seemed as if the entire political elite was involved, and political debate moved away from how to promote growth and social justice and towards fierce accusations in all directions of personal and institutional corruption. Moreover, the political context played a significant role in the economic downturn, by negatively affecting economic expectations.

These political and economic scenarios fed a third factor, an emerging middle class backlash against the redistribution promoted by the PT governments. As long as there was growth, the social policies of the government retained widespread support, but in a situation of recession, fiscal deficit, and widespread corruption, there was increasing opposition to redistributive macroeconomic and social policies. A political realignment in Congress led to the necessary two-thirds majority for Dilma's impeachment in August 2016, on the rather thin ground that she had artificially manipulated the public sector accounts. In reality, her impeachment reflected the shift in Brazilian politics away from the attempt to reconcile stronger social policies with economic development towards a more orthodox programme of austerity and renewed liberalization.

---

[3] PNAD started a new series with a different methodology in 2012, named PNAD Contínua, which is not comparable to the data presented elsewhere in the book.

The realignment of forces was marked by a clear-cut class cleavage. Private business representatives, including FIESP, the industrial association of the State of São Paulo, and especially financial groups, all backed by conservative segments of society, supported the impeachment. However, the new group in power is not coherent. Internal frictions arise as many of its political leaders face corruption charges, and they represent a heterogeneous group of specific interests.

Overall, the social and economic progress achieved between 2002 and 2014 did not give rise to a comprehensive growth regime which could have changed Brazil's position in the world economy by producing more high-value goods. Instead, the political process threw up a government committed to social goals, but captured in the machine of traditional politics. All in all, there seems to be little doubt that this growth regime has come to an end. It is not possible to predict the features of a new growth regime, as they depend on political, economic and social factors. However, it does not look likely that the same kind of redistributive growth can be replicated in the next decade, regardless of how far the new government goes in its liberalization policies.

It should be pointed out that, even during the crisis, the minimum wage has still played an important role, as the gap between the minimum and the average income continues to fall. The problem now, however, is the fall in the proportion of workers who can find a job that actually pays the minimum wage, compounded by the approval, in March 2017, of a law allowing outsourcing not only of support services, but also of core production activities. This is a setback for union power and labour rights. If the labour reform, expected to be voted in the first semester of 2017 in the Senate, is passed, this will mean that agreements could be reached between workers and individual companies, weakening the role of unions, and flexibilizing further the use of the workforce.

The major aim of the new president, Michel Temer, and his economic team was to satisfy the demands of the business sector and bring about 'economic stabilization'. The basic argument was the following: the crisis was caused by overspending by the government, leading to a hike in the gross debt-to-output ratio, which reached close to 70 per cent at the end of 2016. With a sufficient conservative majority in both houses of Congress to approve constitutional amendments, he started with a proposal – which became law in December 2016 – to put a cap on primary government expenditures (i.e. excluding interest payments) in real terms for 20 years with the possibility of revision after 10 years. This is expected to have an impact in the medium term, and in particular to lead to lower interest rates, which are considered to be high due to the size of the public debt. PEC 55, as the constitutional amendment was labelled, will ensure that the primary expenditures are reduced as a percentage of GDP, once growth resumes. As a consequence, expenditures on social security, health and education, for instance, can only increase above the cap at the expense of cuts in other parts of the budget. So the constitutional obligation to maintain health and education at fixed percentages of total primary expenditures is unlikely to be kept, thus jeopardizing the redistributive effects of such policies. Programmes at risk include PBF (Bolsa Familia), which may be downsized in terms of the number of beneficiaries or the amounts they receive in order to conform to PEC 55.

A proposal for social security reform, also a constitutional amendment, was sent to Congress on December 2016. It sets a minimum age of retirement and increases the duration of contributions required in order to receive a full pension. Even though some of the most controversial items of this proposal have been changed due to political and societal pressure, the ratio of pensions to the previous wage is likely to fall for large segments of the workforce.

The other part of this equation is political. The forces that brought the PT to power, and in particular the trade unions, have been relatively subdued through the crisis. However, as the recession reached its peak at the end of April 2017, a general strike was called, which had not happened in the previous 20 years. It was organized by trade unions and social movements against the labour, outsourcing and social security reforms proposed by the Temer government. Moreover, many social movements are counting on a victory for Lula in the presidential elections of 2018. However, as the ex-president is under investigation in the corruption scandals, there is a possibility that he will not be able to run. At the time of writing, the political situation is quite unclear as there are also allegations of corruption against president Temer.

So, it seems that we can still use the mirror image metaphor when contrasting Brazil and India. But this is a mirror with many facets. On the one hand, Brazil has plunged into social and economic crisis, and the political turmoil has a potential to affect the very nature of its democratic institutions; on the other, India's economy has recovered and continues to grow despite social strains. But there are tensions and contradictions within both countries, and no one can say how they will be managed.

This is essentially a political issue, although the potential ways out of the crucible depend on the interaction of institutional forms that have shaped, are shaping or will shape the growth regimes. The Brazilian economy will surely start to grow again in the future, because of its idle capacity and the power of its internal market, but attempts to return to a liberal model in which inequality increases once again are likely to revive conflict, since a substantial fraction of the population has benefitted from the social policies and redistributive growth path of the last decade and a half. Meanwhile, India's macroeconomic performance has been good, and here too many groups have benefitted, but the mechanisms of the economy and of the labour market concentrate the gains from growth and perpetuate diverse forms of exclusion. Ultimately, if inequality grows further, there are dangers for the sustainability of growth. In reality, the mirror is cracked and distorted, and each country faces different challenges and finds its own responses.

If there is a single message of this book, it is that social and economic inequality has to be considered as a whole. The Brazilian crisis illustrates that well, showing how inequality is one element in the interplay of social, political, and economic forces. The decline in inequality in Brazil that was observed in the 2000s reflected economic change, but also resulted from the workings of a variety of social institutions and policies in the labour market and elsewhere. India's pattern of inequality is different, but like that in Brazil, it has economic and social dimensions which interact and often reinforce each other. A greater and more coherent investment in social policy would make for a less disequalizing growth regime.

A move towards greater equality is possible, and in the chapters of this book there are illustrations of the situations and relationships where progress has been or can be made. But a sustained reduction in inequality requires action on a broad front, in which equality and growth are considered two sides of the same coin. That would imply a change of trajectory in both countries.

Bibliography

Abramo, Lais. 2006. 'A Desigualdades de Gênero e Raça no Mercado de Trabalho Brasileiro.' *Ciência e Cultura* 58 (4): 40–42. São Paulo.

Acemoglu, Daron, and James Robinson. 2012. *Why Nations Fail: The Origins of Power, Prosperity, and Poverty.* New York: Crown Business.

Acharya, Sarathi. 1990. 'The Maharashtra Employment Guarantee Scheme: A Study of Labour Market Intervention.' *ARTEP Working Paper.* New Delhi: Asian Regional Team for Employment Promotion, International Labour Office.

Agénor, P-R., and O. Canuto. 2013. 'Gender Equality and Economic Growth in Brazil: A Long-Run Analysis.' *Policy Research Working Paper WP/6348.* Washington, D. C.: World Bank.

Aggarwal, A., and N. Kumar. 2012. 'Structural Change, Industrialization and Poverty Reduction: The Case of India.' *ESCAP Development Papers 1206.* Bangkok: UN-ESCAP.

Aglietta, M. 1982. *Régulation et Crises du Capitalisme.* Paris: Calmann-Lévy.

Ahluwalia, Montek Singh. 2000. 'Economic Performance of States in the Post Reforms Period.' *Economic and Political Weekly* 35 (19): 1637.

———. 2002. 'Economic Reforms in India since 1991: Has Gradualism Worked?' *Journal of Economic Perspectives* 16 (3): 67–88.

———. 2011. 'Prospects and Policy Challenges in the Twelfth Plan.' *Economic and Political Weekly* 46 (21): 88–105.

———. 2016. 'The 1991 Reforms: How Home-Grown Were They?' *Economic and Political Weekly* 51 (29): 39–46.

Ahmed, Imtiaz. 1978. *Caste and Social Stratification among Muslims in India.* Delhi: Manohar Book Services.

Ahn, Pong-Sul. 2010. *The Growth and Decline of Political Unionism in India: The Need for a Paradigm Shift.* Bangkok: International Labour Office, Decent Work Team for East and South-East Asia and the Pacific.

Alam, Arshad. 2013. 'Madrasas and Educational Conditions of Muslims'. In Council for Social Development, *India, Social Development Report, 2012: Minorities at the Margins,* edited by Zoya Hasan and Mushirul Hasan. New Delhi: Oxford University Press.

Albert, Michel. 1993. *Capitalism vs. Capitalism.* New York: Four Walls Eight Windows.

Aldrighi, D., and R. P. Colistete. 2013. 'Industrial Growth and Structural Change: Brazil in a Long-Run Perspective.' *Working Paper WP 2013–10, FEA/USP.* São Paulo: Economics Department, University of São Paulo.

Alencastro, L. F. de. 2000. *O Trato dos Viventes: Formação do Brasil no Atlântico Sul.* São Paulo: Companhia das Letras.

Amable, Bruno. 2005. *Les Cinq Capitalismes: Diversité des Systèmes Économiques et Sociaux dans la Mondialisation.* Paris: Seuil.

Anand, Ishan, and Anjana Thampi. 2016. 'Recent Trends in Wealth Inequality in India.' *Economic and Political Weekly* 51 (50): 59–67.

Arbache, J. 2012. 'Is Brazilian Manufacturing Losing its Drive?' *SSRN,* 13 October. Accessed 15 November 2016. Available at: http://ssrn.com/abstract=2150684.

Arulampalam, W., A. L. Booth., and M. L. Bryan. 2007. 'Is there a Glass Ceiling Over Europe? Exploring the Gender Pay Gap across the Wage Distribution.' *Industrial and Labor Relations Review* 60 (2): 163–186.

Atkinson, Anthony. ed. 1973. *Wealth, Income and Inequality.* Harmondsworth: Penguin.

———. 1983. *The Economics of Inequality.* Oxford: Clarendon Press.

———. 2015. *Inequality: What Can be Done?* Cambridge, Ma: Harvard University Press.

Atkinson, Anthony, and Thomas Piketty. 2010. *Top Incomes: A Global Perspective.* Oxford: Oxford University Press.

Baer, Werner. 2014. *The Brazilian Economy: Growth and Development,* Seventh edition. London: Lynne Rienner Publishers.

Banerjee, Abhijit, and Thomas Piketty. 2005. 'Top Indian Incomes, 1922–2000.' *The World Bank Economic Review* 19 (1): 1–20.

Barbosa, Alexandre de Freitas. 2013. 'Os Avanços da Era Lula.' *Interesse Nacional,* year 5 (20), January–March.

Barbosa, Alexandre de Freitas, Maria Cristina Cacciamali, Ashok Pankaj, Gerry Rodgers, and Vidhya Soundararajan. 2014a. 'Data Sources for the Analysis of Labour Market Inequality in Brazil and India.' *CEBRAP-IHD Working Paper WP/03/2014.* New Delhi: Institute for Human Development.

———. 2014b. 'Labour Market Inequality in Brazil and India: Concepts and Methods.' *CEBRAP-IHD Working Paper WP/04/2014.* New Delhi: Institute for Human Development.

Barbosa, Alexandre de Freitas, Maria Cristina Cacciamali, Ian Prates, and Fabio Tatei. 2013. 'Desigualdades Econômicas e Sociais do Nordeste.' In *Estudos Prospectivos sobre o Desenvolvimento do Nordeste.* Fortaleza: BNB, Relatório Técnico.

———. 2015. 'Minimum Wage in Brazil: A Useful Policy Tool to Reduce Wage Inequality?' In *Global Wage Debates: Politics or Economics,* edited by Gregory Randolph and Knut Panknin. Washington: Just Jobs Network.

Barbosa, Alexandre de Freitas, Maria Cristina Cacciamali, Nandita Gupta, Ian Prates, Gerry Rodgers, and Priscila Vieira. 2015. 'Vocational Education and Training and the Inequality Challenge in Brazil and India: A Policy Review.' *CEBRAP-IHD Working Paper WP/04/2015.* New Delhi: Institute for Human Development.

Barbosa, A. L. N. de H. 2014. 'Participação Feminina no Mercado de Trabalho Brasileiro.' *Boletim Mercado de Trabalho-Conjuntura e Análise* 57: 31–41. Brasília: Instituto de Pesquisa Econômica Aplicada (IPEA).

Bardhan, Pranab. 1989. 'Poverty and Employment Characteristics of Urban Households in West Bengal, India: An Analysis of the Results of the National Sample Survey, 1977–78.' In *Urban Poverty and the Labour Market,* edited by Gerry Rodgers. Geneva: International Institute for Labour Studies/ International Labour Office.

Barros, Ricardo Paes de, Mirela de Carvalho, Samuel Franco, and Rosane Mendonça. 2006. 'Uma Análise das Principais Causas da Queda Recente na Desigualdade de Renda Brasileira.' *Econômica* 8: 117–147. Niterói.

———. 2010. 'Determinantes da Queda na Desigualdade de Renda no Brasil.' *Texto para Discussão 1460.* Rio de Janeiro: IPEA.

Barros, Ricardo Paes de, R. Henrique, and R. S. P. Mendonça. 2001. 'A Estabilidade Inaceitável: Desigualdade e Pobreza no Brasil.' *Texto para Discussão 800.* Rio de Janeiro: IPEA.

Barros, Ricardo Paes de, M. N. Foguel, and G. Ulyssea. 2007. *Desigualdade de Renda no Brasil: Uma Análise da Queda Recente*. Brasília: IPEA.

Basant, Rakesh. 2012. 'Education and Employment among Muslims in India: An Analysis of Patterns and Trends.' *WP 2012-09-03*. Ahmedabad: Indian Institute of Management Ahmedabad.

Belser, Patrick, and Uma Rani. 2011. 'Review of Labour: Extending the Coverage of Minimum Wages in India: Simulations from Household Data.' *Economic and Political Weekly* 46 (22): 47–55.

Benbabaali, Dalel. 2013. *Caste Dominante et Territoire en Inde du Sud: Migration et Ascension Sociale des Kamma d'Andhra Côtier*. PhD thesis submitted to the Université de Paris Ouest Nanterre La Défense, Paris.

Berquó, E. S., and S. M. Cavenaghi. 2005. 'Brazilian Fertility Regimes: Profiles of Women Below and Above Replacement Levels.' Paper presented at the 25th Conference of the International Union for the Scientific Study of Population (IUSSP), Tours, 18–23 July.

———. 2014. 'Perfil Socioeconômico e Demográfico da Fecundidade no Brasil de 2000 a 2010.' Paper presented at the 6th Congreso de la Associación Latinoamericana de Población, Lima, 12–15 August.

Beteille, André. 1966. *Caste, Class, and Power*. Berkeley: University of California Press.

Bhadhuri, Amit. 1973. 'A Study of Agricultural Backwardness under Conditions of Semi-Feudalism.' *Economic Journal*, 86: 120–137.

Bhalla, G. S., and Gurmail Singh. 2012. *Economic Liberalization and Indian Agriculture: A District Level Study*. New Delhi: Sage.

Bhattacherjee, Debashish. 1989. 'Evolution of Unionism and Labour Market Structure–Case of Bombay Textile Mills, 1947–1985.' *Economic and Political Weekly* 24 (21): 67–76.

———. 1999. 'Organized Labour and Economic Liberalization, India: Past, Present and Future.' *Discussion Paper 105*. Geneva: International Institute for Labour Studies/ILO.

Bhowmik, Sharit K. 2012. *Industry, Labour, and Society*. New Delhi: Orient Blackswan.

———. 2013. 'The Labour Movement in India: Fractured Trade Unions and Vulnerable Workers.' *Rethinking Development and Inequality* 2 (Special Issue): 84–96.

Biavaschi, Magda. 2016. 'O Processo de Construção e Desconstrução da Tela de Proteção Social do Trabalho: Tempos de Regresso.' *Revista do IEA* 30 (87): 75–87, March–August.

Biles, J. J. 2009. 'Informal Work in Latin America: Competing Perspectives and Recent Debates.' *Geography Compass* 3 (1): 214–236.

BNDES. 2001. 'Carga Tributária, Evolução Histórica: Uma Tendência Crescente.' *Informese* (29). Rio de Janeiro.

Bolt, J., and J. L. van Zanden. 2013. 'The First Update of the Maddison Project, Re-estimating Growth before 1820.' *Maddison Project Working Paper WP 4*. Accessed 15 November 2016. Available at: www.ggdc.net/maddison/maddison-project/publications/wp4.pdf.

Bonnelli, R., and S. Pessoa. 2010. 'Desindustrialização no Brasil: Um Resumo da Evidência.' *Texto para Discussão 7*. Rio de Janeiro: Centro de Desenvolvimento Econômico, Instituto Brasileiro de Economia-Fundação Getulio Vargas.

Boyer, Robert. 1990. *The Regulation School: A Critical Introduction*. New York: Columbia University Press.

———. 1994. 'Do Labour Institutions Matter for Economic Development? A "Regulation" Approach for the OECD and Latin America with an Extension to Asia.' In *Workers, Institutions and Economic Growth in Asia*, edited by Gerry Rodgers. Geneva: International Institute for Labour Studies.

Boyer, Robert, and J. Rogers Hollingsworth. 1997. 'From National Embeddedness to Spatial and Institutional Nestedness.' In *Contemporary Capitalism: The Embeddedness of Institutions*, edited by J. Rogers Hollingsworth and Robert Boyer. Cambridge: Cambridge University Press.

Bresser-Pereira, Luiz Carlos. 1998. *Economia Brasileira: Uma Introdução Crítica*. São Paulo: Editora 34, Third edition.

Bresser-Pereira, L. C., and N. Marconi. 2010. 'Existe Doença Holandesa no Brasil?' In *Doença Holandesa e Industria*, edited by L. C. Bresser-Pereira and N. Marconi, 207–230. Rio de Janeiro: Editora FGV.

Bruschini, M. C. 2007. 'Trabalho e Gênero no Brasil nos Últimos Dez Anos.' Paper presented at the International Seminar on Work and Gender, 2–12 April. São Paulo and Rio de Janeiro: Fundação Carlos Chagas. Accessed 15 November 2016. Available at: http://www.scielo.br/pdf/cp/v37n132/a0337132.pdf.

Cacciamali, Maria Cristina. 1988. *Mudanças Estruturas no Produto e no Emprego no Brasil, 1950–1985.* São Paulo: Tese de Livre Docência/USP. (Doctoral thesis, University of São Paulo).

Cacciamali, Maria-Cristina, and André Britto. 2002. 'A Flexibilização Restrita e Descentralizada das Relações de Trabalho no Brasil.' *Revista da ABET* 2 (1): 92–120.

Cacciamali, Maria-Cristina, and J. W. Rosalino. 2008. 'Estreitamento dos Diferenciais de Salários, Diminuição do Grau de Discriminação?' In *A Construção da Igualdade de Gênero e Raça na America Latina do Século 221: O Caso do Brasil,* edited by Maria-Cristina Cacciamali and M. de F. José-Silva, 27–52. São Carlos, Brazil: Suprema Gráfica e Editora.

Cacciamali, Maria-Cristina, Fabio Tatei, and J. W. Rosalino. 2009. 'Estreitamento dos Diferenciais de Salários e Aumento do Grau de Discriminação: Limitaçõe da Mensuração Padrão?' *Planejamento e Políticas Públicas* 33. Brasilia: IPEA.

Cacciamali, Maria-Cristina, and Alexandre de Freitas Barbosa. 2014. 'Desigualdades Econômicas e Sociais do Nordeste.' *Estudos Prospectivos para o Desenvolvimento do Nordeste.* Fortaleza: BNB.

Cacciamali, Maria-Cristina, Fabio Tatei, Gerry Rodgers, and Taniya Chakrabarty. 2015. 'Minimum Wage Policy in Brazil and India and its Impact on Labour Market Inequality.' *CEBRAP-IHD Working Paper WP 02/2015.* New Delhi: Institute for Human Development.

Cacciamali, Maria-Cristina, Fabio Tatei, Gerry Rodgers, and Vidhya Soundarajan. 2015. 'Wage Inequality in Brazil and India: A Quantitative Comparative Analysis.' *CEBRAP-IHD Working Paper WP 03/2015.* New Delhi, Institute for Human Development.

Cacciamali, Maria-Cristina, and Fabio Tatei. 2016. 'Mercado de Trabalho: Da Euforia do Ciclo Expansivo e de Inclusão Social à Frustração da Recessão Econômica.' *Revista do IEA* 30 (87), March–August.

Campos, André. 2014. 'Sindicatos no Brasil Hoje: Dilemas Apresentados Pela Sindicalização.' *Boletim Mercado de Trabalho—Conjuntura e Análise.* Brasília: IPEA, February.

Cano, Wilson. 1998. *Desequilíbrios Regionais e Concentração Industrial no Brasil. 1930–1995.* Campinas: Instituto de Economia/Unicamp.

Cardoso, Adalberto. 2010. *A Construção da Sociedade do Trabalho no Brasil.* Rio de Janeiro: Editora FGV.

Cardoso de Mello, João Manuel. 1990. *O Capitalismo Tardio*, Eighth edition. São Paulo: Brasiliense.

Castro, Antônio Barros de. 1971. *Sete Ensaios Sobre a Economia Brasileira 2*. Rio de Janeiro: Forense.

———. 1999. 'O Lado Real do Real: O Debate e Algumas Surpresas.' In *Vinte Anos de Política Econômica*, edited by J. P. Almeida Magalhães. Rio de Janeiro: Contraponto.

Castro, Antônio Barros, and Francisco Eduardo Pires de Souza. 2004. *A Economia Brasileira em Marcha Forçada*. São Paulo: Paz e Terra, Third edition.

Castro, Cláudio de Moura. 1986. 'O Que Está Acontecendo com a Educação no Brasil?' In *Transição Incompleta: Brasil desde 1945, Volume 2*, edited by Edmar Bacha and Herbert Klein. Rio de Janeiro: Paz e Terra.

Chandrasekhar, C. P. 2016. 'Budget 2016–17: Signs of Paralysis.' *Frontline*, 1 April.

Chandrashekar, C. P., and J. Ghosh. 2011. 'Latest Employment Trends from the NSSO.' *Business Line (The Hindu)*, 12 July.

Chari, M. 2014. 'Economists Fear Changes to NREGA but Fund Squeeze is already Curtailing its Operations.' *Scroll.in*, 15 October. Accessed on 15 November 2016. Available at: http://scroll.in/article/683705/economists-fear-changes-to-nrega-but-fund-squeeze-is-already-curtailing-its-operations.

Chatterjee, E., S. Desai, and R. Vanneman. 2013. 'Rising Education, Declining Female Employment: An Indian Paradox.' Paper Presented at the Annual Meeting of the Population Association of America, New Orleans, 11–13 April.

Chatterjee, U., R. Murgai, and M. Rama. 2015. 'Job Opportunities along the Rural–Urban Gradation, and Female Labor Force Participation in India'. *Policy Research Working Paper WP/7412*. Washington D. C.: World Bank.

Chaudhuri, Pramit. 1978. *The Indian Economy: Poverty and Development*. London: Crosby Lockwood Staples.

Chavan, Pallavi, and Rajshree Bedamatta. 2006. 'Trends in Agricultural Wages in India.' *Economic and Political Weekly* 41 (38): 4041–51.

Chibber, Vivek. 2012. 'Organised Interests, Development Strategies, and Social Policies.' In *Growth, Inequality, and Social Development in India: Is Inclusive Growth Possible?* edited by R. Nagaraj. Basingstoke: Palgrave Macmillan.

Chopra, Saloni, and Jessica Pudussery. 2014. 'Social Security Pensions in India: An Assessment.' *Economic and Political Weekly* 49 (19): 68–74. Reprinted: Drèze, Jean. ed. 2016, *Social Policy*. New Delhi: Orient Blackswan.

Cornia, Giovanni Andrea. ed. 2014. *Falling Inequality in Latin America: Policy Changes and Lessons.* Oxford: WIDER Studies in Development Economics, Oxford University Press.

Crouch, Colin, and Wolfgang Streeck. 1997. 'Introduction: The Future of Capitalist Diversity.' In *Political Economy of Modern Capitalism: Mapping Convergence and Diversity,* edited by C. Crouch. and W. Streeck. London: Sage.

Dandekar, V. M., and N. Rath. 1970. *Poverty in India.* New Delhi: Ford Foundation. Also in *Economic and Political Weekly* 6 (1 and 2): 25–48 and 106–46, 1971.

Datt, Gaurav, and Martin Ravallion. 2010. 'Shining for the Poor Too?' *Economic and Political Weekly* 45 (7): 55–60.

De, Rahul, and Vamsi Vakulabharanam. 2013. *Growth and Distribution Regimes in India after Independence.* Paper presented to the World Economics Association Conference on Inequalities in Asia, 12 May–8 June.

Dedecca, Cláudio Salvadori. 2005. 'Notas Sobre a Evolução do Mercado de Trabalho no Brasil.' *Revista de Economia Política* 25 (1): 94–111.

De Negri, Fernanda, and Luiz Ricardo Cavalcante. eds. 2014. *Produtividade no Brasil: Desempenho e Determinantes, Volume 1.* Brasília: IPEA.

Departamento Intersindical de Estadísticas e Estudos Socioeconómicos (DIEESE). 2012. *A Situação do Trabalho no Brasil na Primeira Década dos Anos 2000.* São Paulo.

Desai, S., and V. Kulkarni. 2008. 'Changing Educational Inequalities in India in the Context of Affirmative Action.' *Demography* 45 (2): 245–270.

Deshpande, Ashwini. 2011. *The Grammar of Caste: Economic Discrimination in Contemporary India.* New Delhi: Oxford University Press.

Deshpande, Ashwini, Deepti Goel, and Shantanu Khanna. 2015. 'Bad Karma or Discrimination? Male-female Wage Gaps among Salaried Workers in India.' *IZA Discussion Paper 9485.* Bonn: Institute for the Study of Labor.

Deshpande, S., and L. K. Deshpande. 1985. 'Census of 1981, and the Structure of Employment.' *Economic and Political Weekly* 20 (22): 969–973.

Dos Anjos, Gabriele. 2013. 'A Questão 'Cor' ou 'Raça' nos Censos Nacionais.' *Indicadores Econômicos FEE* 41 (1): 103–117.

Drèze, Jean. 2004. 'Democracy and Right to Food.' *Economic and Political Weekly* 39 (17): 1723–1731. Reprinted: Drèze, Jean. ed. 2016. *Social Policy*. New Delhi: Orient Blackswan.

———. 2016a. 'Introduction.' In *Social Policy*, edited by Jean Drèze. New Delhi: Orient Blackswan.

———. 2016b. 'Dark Clouds over the PDS.' *The Hindu*, 10 September.

Drèze, Jean, and M. Murthi. 2001. 'Fertility, Education, and Development: Evidence from India.' *Population and Development Review* 27 (1): 33–63.

Drèze, Jean, and Amartya Sen. 2013. *An Uncertain Glory, India and its Contradictions*. London: Allen Lane.

Duggal, Ravi. 2001. *Evolution of Health Policy in India*. Mumbai: Centre for Enquiry into Health and Allied Themes (CEHAT). Accessed 15 November 2016. Available at: http://www.cehat.org/go/uploads/Publications/a147.pdf.

Dutta, Puja, Rinku Murgai, Martin Ravallion, and Dominique van de Walle. 2012. 'Does India's Employment Guarantee Scheme Guarantee Employment?' *Economic and Political Weekly* 47 (16): 55–64. Reprinted: Drèze, Jean. ed. 2016. *Social Policy*. New Delhi: Orient Blackswan.

Evans, Peter. 1979. *Dependent Development: The Alliance of Multinational, State, and Local Capital in Brazil*. Princeton: Princeton University Press.

———. 1995. *Embedded Autonomy: States and Industrial Transformation*. Princeton: Princeton University Press.

Fagnani, Eduardo. 1997. 'Política social e Pactos Conservadores no Brasil: 1964–92.' *Revista Economia e Sociedade 8*. Campinas: IE/Unicamp.

———. 2005. *Política Social no Brasil 1964–2002: Entre a Cidadania e a Caridade*. Doctoral Thesis in Economics. Campinas: Instituto de Economia da Unicamp.

Fernandes, F. 1964. *A Integração do Negro à Sociedade de Classes*. São Paulo: Dominus Editora.

Ferreira, Jorge. 2005. *O Imaginário Trabalhista*. Rio de Janeiro: Civilização Brasileira.

Fields, Gary S. 2002. 'Accounting for Income Inequality and its Change: A New Method, with Application to the Distribution of Earnings in the United States.' Ithaca: Cornell University, School of Industrial and Labor Relations. Accessed 15 November 2016. Available at: http://digitalcommons.ilr.cornell.edu/articles/265.

Foguel, M. N. 2016. 'Salário Mínimo, Emprego e Desigualdade de Renda no Brasil.' In *CPP Debate – Salário Mínimo: Vantagens e Desvantagens*. São Paulo: Insper. Accessed 15 November 2016. Available at: http://www.insper.edu.br/cpp/cpp-debates/cpp-debate-salario-minimo-vantagens-e-desvantagens.

Franco, Gustavo. 1999. *O Desafio Brasileiro: Ensaios Sobre Desenvolvimento, Globalização e Moeda*. São Paulo: Editora 34.

Furtado, Celso. 1959. *Formação Econômica do Brasil*. Rio de Janeiro: Fundo de Cultura.

———. 1974. *O Mito do Desenvolvimento Econômico*. Rio de Janeiro: Paz e Terra.

———. 1981. 'Uma Política de Desenvolvimento Para o Nordeste.' *Novos Estudos, CEBRAP* 1 (1): 13–19.

Gerschenkron, Alexander. 1962. 'On the Concept of Continuity in History.' *Proceedings of the American Philosophical Society* 106 (3), June.

Ghose, Ajit. 2016. *India Employment Report 2016*. Delhi: Oxford University Press.

Ghosh, Jayati. 2002. *Social Policy in Indian Development*. Paper Prepared for the UNRISD Project on Social Policy in a Development Context, Geneva, UNRISD.

———. 2009. *Never Done and Poorly Paid*. (Feminist Fine Print Series), 185. New Delhi: Women Unlimited.

———. 2014. 'MGNREGA: The Impact.' Paper presented at the International Seminar on Development from the Perspective of Labour – Experiences, Challenges, and Options, Lucknow, 21–23 February.

———. 2015. 'Lost between Intent and Belief.' *Livemint*, 2 March.

———. 2017. 'A Universal Basic Income for India.' *Frontline* 34 (3), 17 February.

Goldani, A. M. 2001. *Rethinking Brazilian Fertility Decline*. Paper presented at the 24th General Conference of the International Union for the Scientific Study of Population (IUSSP), Salvador de Bahia, 18–24 August.

Goodman, David. 1986. 'Economia e Sociedade Rurais a Partir de 1945.' In *A Transição Incompleta. Volume. 1,* edited by Edmar Bacha and Herbert Kleint. Rio de Janeiro: Paz e Terra.

Gopalan, Suresh T. 2016. 'Withering Regulation? An Interim Review of Modi Government's Labour Reforms.' *Journal of Asian Public Policy* 9 (2): 170–184.

Government of Brazil, Ministry of Labour and Employment. Various years. *Relação Anual de Informações Sociais (RAIS)*. Brasilia.

Government of India. 1969. *Fourth Five Year Plan 1969–74*. Draft. New Delhi: Planning Commission.

———. 1980. *Report of the Backward Classes Commission. Mandal Commission Report*. New Delhi.

———. 1987. *Economic Survey 1986–87*. New Delhi: Ministry of Finance.

———. 2002. *National Human Development Report 2001*. New Delhi: Planning Commission.

———. 2004. *Selected Educational Statistics 2001–02*. New Delhi: Ministry of Human Resources Development.

———. 2006. *Social, Economic and Educational Status of the Muslim Community of India. Sachar Committee Report*. New Delhi: Prime Minister's High Level Committee.

———. 2011. *Economic Survey 2010–11*. New Delhi: Ministry of Finance.

———. 2011. *India Human Development Report 2011*. New Delhi: Planning Commission and Oxford University Press.

———. 2013. *Poverty Estimates for 2011–12*. New Delhi: Planning Commission.

———. 2015. *Ajeevika Skills Program Status: Overall Achievement in the Country.* New Delhi: Ministry of Rural Development (MORD). Accessed on 15 November 2016. Available at: http://www.nrlmskills.in/ProgramStatus.aspx.

———. 2015. *Indian Public Finance Statistics 2014–2015*. New Delhi: Ministry of Finance. Available at: http://finmin.nic.in/reports/ipfstat.asp.

———. 2016. *Economic Survey 2015–16*. New Delhi: Ministry of Finance.

———. 2017. *Economic Survey 2016–17*. New Delhi: Ministry of Finance.

Government of India, Central Statistical Office. 1983. *Basic Statistics Relating to the Indian Economy 1950 to 1981*. New Delhi.

Government of India, Labour Bureau. Various years. *Indian Labour Journal.* Simla.

Government of India, Ministry of Rural Development. 2016. *Mahatma Gandhi National Rural Employment Guarantee Act: The Journey of a Decade. Report to the People*. New Delhi. Accessed on 15 November 2016. Available at: http://nrega.nic.in/netnrega/home.aspx.

Government of India, National Sample Survey Office. 2014. *Employment and Unemployment Situation in India 2011–12, NSS Report 554*. New Delhi: Ministry of Statistics and Programme Implementation.

————. 2015. *Household Ownership and Operational Holdings in India, NSS 70th Round, 2013*. New Delhi: Ministry of Statistics and Programme Implementation.

————. (Various years). *National Sample Survey Data and Survey Reports*. New Delhi: Ministry of Statistics and Programme Implementation.

Government of India, National Sample Survey Organisation. 1997. *Employment and Unemployment in India, 1993–94*. New Delhi.

Government of India, University Grants Commission. 2003. *Annual Report 2002–03*. New Delhi.

Guerra, Alexandre, Marcio Pochmann, and Ronnie Aldrin Silva. 2015. *Atlas da Exclusão Social no Brasil: Dinâmica da Exclusão Social na Primeira Década do Século 21*. São Paulo: Cortez.

Guimarães Neto, L. 2014. 'Mercado de Trabalho no Nordeste 2000–2010: Avanços e Desafios.' In *Um Olhar Territorial Para o Desenvolvimento: Nordeste*, edited by P. F. Guimarães, et al. Rio de Janeiro: BNDES.

Guimarães, Antônio Sérgio. 2002. *Classes, Raças e Democracia*. São Paulo: Editora 34.

Hall, David. 2010. *The Past, Present and Future of Public Spending*. Draft Paper, Public Services International Research Unit. Accessed on 15 November 2016. Available at: http://www.global-labour-university.org/fileadmin/ GLU_conference_2010/papers/59._The_past_present_and_future_of_ public_spending.pdf.

Hall, Peter A., and David Soskice. 2001. *Varieties of Capitalism: The Institutional Foundations of Comparative Advantage*. Oxford: Oxford University Press.

Harriss, John. 1989. 'Vulnerable Workers in the Indian Labour Market.' In *Urban Poverty and the Labour Market*, edited by Gerry Rodgers. Geneva: International Institute for Labour Studies/ILO.

Harriss-White, Barbara. 2003. 'Inequality at Work in the Informal Economy: Key Issues and Illustrations.' *International Labour Review* 142 (4): 459–469, December.

————. 2017. Interview in *Madras Courier*, 13 January. Accessed on 20 February 2017. Available at: www.madrascourier.com/barbara-harriss-white-on-demo netisation-part-1/ and -part-2/.

Hasenbalg, Carlos, and Nelson do Valle Silva. 1988. *Estrutura Social, Mobilidade e Raça*. Rio de Janeiro: IUPERJ.

Hasenbalg, Carlos. 2005. *Discriminação e Desigualdades Raciais no Brasil.* Belo Horizonte: Editora UFMG, Second Edition.

Heston, A. 1982. 'National Income.' In *The Cambridge Economic History of India, Volume. 2,* edited by Dharma Kumar. New Delhi: Orient Longman.

Higgins, S. 2012. 'The Impact of Bolsa Familia on Poverty: Does Brazil's Conditional Cash Transfer Program Have a Rural Bias?' *The Journal of Politics and Society* 23 (1): 88–125, January.

Himanshu, and Abhijit Sen. 2013. 'In-kind Food Transfers – I.' *Economic and Political Weekly* 48 (45): 46–54.

Himanshu. 2011. 'Employment Trends in India: A Re-Examination.' *Economic and Political Weekly* 46 (37): 43–59.

Hirway, Indira. 2012. 'Missing Labour Force: An Explanation.' *Economic and Political Weekly* 47 (37): 72.

Hoffmann, Rodolfo. 1975. 'Tendências da Distribuição da Renda no Brasil e Suas Relações com o Desenvolvimento Econômico.' In *A Controvérsia Sobre Distribuição de Renda e Desenvolvimento,* edited by Ricardo Tolipan and Arthur Carlos Tinelli. Rio de Janeiro: Zahar.

Hudson, R. A. ed. 1997. *Brazil: A Country Study.* Washington: GPO for the Library of Congress.

Ianni, Octavio. 1971. *Estado e Planejamento Econômico no Brasil. 1930–1970.* Rio de Janeiro: Civilização Brasileira.

Instituto Brasileiro de Geografia e Estatística (IBGE). 2006. *Estatísticas do Século XX.* Rio de Janeiro: IBGE.

———. 2010. *Síntese de Indicadores Sociais 2010.* Rio de Janeiro: IBGE.

———. 2016. *PNAD Contínua (Pesquisa Nacional Por Amostra de Domicílios). Divulgação Mensal.* Rio de Janeiro: IBGE, March–June.

———. Various years. *Pesquisa Nacional Por Amostra de Domicílios (PNAD).* Unit level data and reports. Rio de Janeiro: IBGE.

INEP (National Institute of Educational Studies and Research from Portuguese *Instituto Nacional de Estudos e Pesquisas Educacionais*). 2011. *Censo da Educação Superior 2010.* Brasília : INEP.

Institute for Human Development. 2014. *India Labour and Employment Report 2014.* New Delhi: IHD and Academic Foundation.

International Labour Office. 1958. 'Record of Proceedings.' *Fourth Asian Regional Conference, New Delhi,* November 1957. Geneva: ILO.

————. 2007. *Equality at Work: Tackling the Challenges*. Geneva: ILO.

————. 2012. *Trade Unions and Special Economic Zones in India*. Geneva: ILO Bureau for Workers Activities.

————. 2015. *Key Indicators of the Labour Market (KILM)*, Eighth and Ninth Editions. Geneva: ILO. Accessed on 17 February 2017. Available at: www.ilo.org/kilm.

Jagannath, R. 2014. 'The Rs. 2,66,000 Crores NREGA Boondoggle, for Every Rs. 5 Spent, the Poor get Re. 1.' *First Post,* 25 October. Accessed on 7 February 2017. Available at: http://www.firstpost.com/business/economy/the-rs-266000-crore-nrega-boondoggle-for-every-rs-5-spent-the-poor-get-re-1–1994617.html.

Jha, Shikha, and P. V. Srinivasan. 2001. 'Taking the PDS to the Poor: Directions for Further Reform.' *Economic and Political Weekly* 36 (39): 3779–86.

Jodhka, Surinder S. 2010. 'Engaging with Caste: Academic Discourses, Identity Politics and State Policy.' *Working Paper Series*. New Delhi: Indian Institute of Dalit Studies and UNICEF.

————. 2014. *Caste in Contemporary India*. New Delhi: Routledge.

Jose, A. V. 1974. 'Trends in Real Wage Rates of Agricultural Labourers.' *Economic and Political Weekly* 9 (13): A25–A30.

————. 1988. 'Agricultural Wages in India.' *Economic and Political Weekly* 23 (26): A-46–A-58.

————. 1994. 'Earnings, Employment and Productivity Trends in the Organised Industries of India.' In *The Indian Labour Market and Economic Structural Change*, edited by L. K. Deshpande and Gerry Rodgers. New Delhi: B. R. Publishing Corporation.

Joshi, Seema. 2006. 'Impact of Economic Reforms on Social Sector Expenditure in India.' *Economic and Political Weekly* 41 (4): 358–65.

Kannan, K. P. 2014. 'The Long Road to Social Security.' In *Interrogating Inclusive Growth*. New Delhi: Routledge.

————. 2016. 'Livelihoods in peril.' *Frontline* 33 (25), 23 December.

Kannan, K. P., and G. Raveendran. 2012. 'Counting and Profiling the Missing Labour Force.' *Economic and Political Weekly* 47 (6): 43–59.

Kaur, H. 2000. 'Impact of Income and Education on Fertility.' *Journal of Family Welfare* 46 (1): 70–76.

Kerstenetzky, C. L. 2012. *O Estado do Bem-Estar Social na Idade da Razão: a Reinvenção do Estado Social no Mundo Contemporâneo*. Rio de Janeiro: Elsevier.

Khera, Reetika. 2011. 'The Revival of the Public Distribution System: Evidence and Explanations.' *Economic and Political Weekly* (46): 44–45. Reprinted: Drèze, Jean. ed. 2016. *Social Policy*. New Delhi: Orient Blackswan.

Klasen, S., and J. Pieters. 2012. 'Push or Pull? Drivers of Female Labor Force Participation During India's Economic Boom.' *IZA Discussion Paper 6395*. Bonn: Institute for the Study of Labor.

———. 2013. 'What Explains the Stagnation of Female Labor Force Participation in Urban India?' *IZA Discussion Paper 7597*. Bonn: Institute for the Study of Labor.

Kohli, Atul. 2012a. *Poverty amid Plenty in the New India*. Cambridge: Cambridge University Press.

———. 2012b. 'State and Redistributive Development in India.' In *Growth, Inequality and Social Development in India: Is Inclusive Growth Possible?* edited by R. Nagaraj. Basingstoke: Palgrave Macmillan.

Krein, José Dary. 2007. *Tendências Recentes nas Relações de Emprego no Brasil: 1990–2005*. PhD thesis. Campinas: IE/UNICAMP.

Krishnamurty, J. 1983. 'The Occupational Structure.' In *The Cambridge Economic History of India, Volume 2*, edited by Dharma Kumar. Cambridge: Cambridge University Press.

Krishnan, Deepa, and Stephen Siegal. 2017. 'Survey of the Effects of Demonetisation on 28 Slum Neighbourhoods in Mumbai.' *Economic and Political Weekly* 52 (3).

Kulkarni, P. M. 2011. 'Towards an Explanation of India's Fertility Transition.' *George Simmons Memorial Lecture*. Lucknow: 33rd Annual Conference of the Indian Association for the Study of Population, 11-13 November.

Kundu, A. 2012. 'Migration and Exclusionary Urbanisation in India.' *Economic and Political Weekly* 47 (26–27): 219–27.

Kupfer, David. 2005. 'Tecnologia e Emprego São Realmente Antagônicos?' In *Novo-Desenvolvimentismo: Um Projeto Nacional de Crescimento com Eqüidade Social*, edited by J. Sicsú, L. F. de Paula and R. Michel. Rio De Janeiro: Manole.

Kuznets, S. 1955. 'Economic Growth and Income Inequality.' *The American Economic Review* 45 (1): 1–28, March.

Lafer, Celso. 2002. *JK e o Programa de Metas, 1956–1961: Processo de Planejamento e Sistema Político no Brasil*. Rio de Janeiro: Editora FGV.

Lavinas, Lena, and S. Garson. 2004. 'O Gasto Social no Brasil: Transparência, Sim, Parti-pris, Não.' *Econômica* 5 (1). Rio de Janeiro.

Lerche, Jens. 2015. 'Making India? The Labour Law Reforms of Narendra Modi's Government.' *Assessing Modi's Track Record Eighteen Months on*. Presentation at London University, SOAS South Asia Institute Panel Discussion. Accessed on 19 November 2015. Available at: https://www.soas. ac.uk/south-asia-institute/events/19nov2015-assessing-modis-track-record-eighteen-months-on.html.

López-Calva, L. F., and N. Lustig. eds. 2010. *Declining Inequality in Latin America: A Decade of Progress?* Washington D. C.: Brookings Institution Press.

Luna, Francisco, and Herbert Klein. 2007. *O Brasil Desde 1980*. São Paulo: A Girafa.

Madalozzo, R. 2010. 'Occupational Segregation and the Gender Wage Gap in Brazil: An Empirical Analysis.' *Economia Aplicada* 14 (2): 147–168.

Madalozzo, R., and S. R. Martins. 2007. 'Gender Wage Gaps: Comparing the 80s, 90s and 00s in Brazil.' *Revista de Economia e Administração* 6 (2): 141–156.

Maddison Database. 2013. *Statistics on World Population, GDP and Per Capita GDP. 1–2010AD* (1990 International Dollars). 2013 version available at: http://www.ggdc.net/maddison/maddison-project/home.htm.

Madheswaran, S., and P. Attewell. 2007. 'Caste Discrimination in the Indian Urban Labour Market: Evidence from the National Sample Survey.' *Economic and Political Weekly* 42 (41): 4146–53.

Margin, Stephen, and Juliet Schor. eds. 1990. *The Golden Age of Capitalism: Reinterpreting the Postwar Experience*. Oxford: Clarendon Press.

Marques-Pereira, Jaime. 1998. 'Trabalho, Cidadania e Eficiência da Regulação Econômica: Uma Comparação Europa/América Latina.' In *Regulação Econômica e Globalização,* edited by Bruno Thére, and José Carlos de Souza Braga. Campinas: Instituto de Economia/Unicamp.

Martine, G. 1996. 'Brazil's Fertility Decline, 1965–95: A Fresh Look at Key Factors.' *Population and Development Review* 22 (1): 47–75.

Martine, G., and G. McGranahan. 2010. *Brazil's Early Urban Transition: What Can it Teach Urbanizing Countries?* London and New York: International Institute for Environment and Development (IIED), and United Nations Population Fund (UNFPA).

Mattoso, Kátia Queiroz. 2001. *Ser Escravo No Brasil*. Trans. James Amado. São Paulo: Brasiliense.

Mazumdar, Dipak, and Sandip Sarkar. 2009. 'The Employment Problem in India and the Phenomenon of the Missing Middle.' *The Indian Journal of Labour Economics* 52 (1): 43–55.

Medeiros, Marcelo, Pedro Souza, and Fabio Ávila Castro. 2014. *A Estabilidade da Desigualdade de Renda no Brasil, 2006 a 2012*. Brasília: UNB.

Medici, A., F. E. B. Oliveira and K. Beltrão. 1993. 'Subsídios Para Reforma Constitucional no Campo da Seguridade Social: Uma Visão Histórica e Perspectivas.' *Planejamento e Políticas Públicas* (9). Brasília: IPEA.

Mehtabul, Azam. 2012. 'The Impact of Indian Job Guarantee Scheme on Labor Market Outcomes: Evidence from a Natural Experiment.' *Discussion Paper 6548*. Bonn: IZA. Available at: http://www.econstor.eu/bitstream/10419/58685/1/716016915.pdf.

Menezes-Filho, N., and L. Scorzafave. 2009. *Employment and Inequality Outcomes in Brazil*. Paris: OECD.

Milanovic, Branko. 2005. *Worlds Apart: Measuring International and Global Inequality*. Princeton: Oxford University Press.

———. 2016. *Global Inequality: A New Approach for the Age of Globalization*. Cambridge, Ma: Harvard University Press.

Mitra, Asok. 1978. *India's Population: Aspects of Quality and Control*. New Delhi: Abhinav Publications.

Mitra, S. 2006. 'Pattern of Women Employment in Urban India.' *Economic and Political Weekly* 41 (48): 5000–08.

Morris, Morris David. 1965. *The Emergence of an Industrial Labor Force in India: A Study of the Bombay Cotton Mills, 1854–1947*. Berkeley: University of California Press.

Motiram, Sripad, and Vamsi Vakulabharanam. 2011. 'Indian Inequality: Patterns and Changes, 1993–2010.' In *India Development Report 2011*, edited by D. M. Nachane. Delhi and Mumbai: Oxford University Press and IGIDR.

Müller, Geraldo. 1986. *O Não Direito do Não Cidadão*. Novos Estudos, 15. São Paulo: CEBRAP.

Nagaraj, R. 2012. 'Development Strategies and Poverty Reduction.' In *Growth, Inequality and Social Development in India: Is Inclusive Growth Possible?* edited by R. Nagaraj. Basingstoke: Palgrave Macmillan.

———. 2015. 'Growth in GVA of Indian Manufacturing.' *Economic and Political Weekly* 50 (24): 117–120.

Nassif, A., C. Feijó, and E. Araújo. 2013. 'Structural Change and Economic Development: Is Brazil Catching Up or Falling Behind?' *Discussion Paper 211*. Geneva: UNCTAD.

Nassif, André. 2008. 'Há Evidência de Desindustrialização no Brasil?' *Brazilian Journal of Political Economy* 28 (1): 109, January–March.

National Commission for Enterprises in the Unorganised Sector (NCEUS). 2008. *Report on Conditions of Work and Promotion of Livelihoods in the Unorganised Sector*. New Delhi: NCEUS.

———. 2009. *Main Report: The Challenge of Employment in India: An Informal Economy Perspective*. New Delhi: NCEUS.

Nayyar, G. 2012. *The Service Sector in India's Development*. Cambridge: Cambridge University Press (Kindle Edition).

Neetha N. 2009. 'Women's work in the Post Reform Period: An Exploration of Macro Data.' *Occasional Paper 52*. New Delhi: Centre for Women's Development Studies.

Nölke, Andreas. 2012. 'The Rise of the B(R)IC Variety of Capitalism: Towards a New Phase of Organized Capitalism?' In *Neoliberalism in Crisis*, edited by H. Overbeek and B. Van Apeldoorn. New York: Palgrave Macmillan.

OECD. 2010. *Tackling Inequalities in Brazil, China, India and South Africa: The Role of Labour Market and Social Policies*. Paris: OECD.

Oliveira, Fabrício Augusto. 1999. 'Evolução, Determinantes e Dinâmica do Gasto Social no Brasil: 1980/1996.' *Texto Para Discussão 649*. Brasília: IPEA.

Oliveira, Francisco de. 2003. *Crítica à Razão Dualista: O Ornitorrinco*. São Paulo: Boitempo editorial.

Oliveira, Ivan T. M. 2013. *BRICS and the Global Economy: International Trade in Services in Focus*. Accessed on 7 February 2017. Available at: http://www. dhet.gov.za/brics/Content/Papers%20for%20publication/Brazil/Paper_ OLIVEIRA_BRICS_AF_2013.pdf.

Pais, Jesim. 2014. 'Growth and Structure of the Services Sector in India.' *Working Paper WP 160*. New Delhi: Institute for Studies in Industrial Development.

Palriwala, Rajni, and Neetha N. 2011. 'Stratified Familialism: The Care Regime in India Through the Lens of Childcare.' *Development and Change* 42 (4): 1049–78.

Pankaj, Ashok K. 2004. 'Engaging with Discourse on Caste, Class and Politics in India.' *South Asia Research* 27 (3): 333–53.

———. 2012. 'Guaranteeing Right to Work in Rural India: Context, Issues and Policies.' In *Right to Work and Rural India,* edited by Ashok Pankaj. New Delhi: Sage.

Papola, T. S. 1992. 'Labour Institutions and Economic Development: The Case of Indian Industrialization.' In *Labour Institutions and Economic Development in India,* IILS Research Series 97, edited by T. S. Papola and Gerry Rodgers. Geneva: International Institute for Labour Studies/ILO.

———. 2013a. 'Economic Growth and Employment Linkages, the Indian Experience.' *Working Paper WP 2013/01.* New Delhi: Institute for Studies in Industrial Development.

———. 2013b. 'Role of Labour Regulation and Reforms in India: Country Case Study on Labour Market Segmentation.' *Employment Working Paper WP/147.* Geneva: ILO.

Papola, T. S., and Partha Pratim Sahu. 2012. 'Growth and Structure of Employment in India: Long-Term and Post-Reform Performance and the Emerging Challenge.' *Working Paper WP.* New Delhi: Institute for Studies in Industrial Development.

Paukert, Felix. 1973. 'Income Distribution at Different Levels of Development.' *International Labour Review* 108: 97–125, August-September.

Piketty, Thomas. 2014. *Capital in the Twenty-First Century.* Cambridge, Ma: Harvard University Press.

Piketty, Thomas, and Emmanuel Saez. 2012. 'Top Incomes and the Great Recession: Recent Evolutions and Policy implications.' *IMF Economic Review* 61 (3): 456–78.

Pires, Julio Manuel. 1995. *A Política Social no Período Populista.* São Paulo: IPE/USP.

Polanyi, Karl. 1944. *The Great Transformation: The Political and Economic Origins of Our Time.* Boston: Beacon.

Pomeranz, Kenneth. 2000. *The Great Divergence: China, Europe, and the Making of the Modern World Economy.* Princeton: Princeton University Press.

Prado Jr., C. 1942. *Formação do Brasil Contemporâneo.* São Paulo: Brasiliense.

Prasad, Pradhan H. 1987. 'Towards a Theory of Transformation of Semi-Feudal Agriculture.' *Economic and Political Weekly* 22 (31): 1287–90.

Ramaswamy, K. V. 2007. 'Regional Dimension of Growth and Employment.' *Economic and Political Weekly* 42 (49): 47–56.

Rangel, Ignacio. 1986. *A Inflação Brasileira*. São Paulo: Bienal, Fifth edition.

Rao, M. S. A. 1992. *Urban Sociology in India*. Hyderabad: Orient Longman.

Ravallion, Martin. 2011. 'A Comparative Perspective on Poverty Reduction in Brazil, China, and India.' *World Bank Research Observer* 26 (1): 71–104.

Razavi, S. 2007. 'The Political and Social Economy of Care in a Development Context: Conceptual Issues, Research Questions and Policy Options.' *Gender and Development Programme Paper 3*. Geneva: United Nations Research Institute for Social Development.

Ribeiro, D. 1995. *O Povo Brasileiro: a Formação e o Sentido do Brasil*. São Paulo: Companhia das Letras.

Rocha, Sônia. 1997. 'Do Consumo Observado à Linha de Pobreza.' *Pesquisa e Planejamento Econômico* 27 (2). Brasília: IPEA.

———. 2003. *Pobreza no Brasil: Afinal, de Que Se Trata?* Rio de Janeiro: Editora FGV.

Rodgers, Gerry. 1972. *Poverty and Policy: The Impact of Rural Public Works in the Kosi Area of Bihar, India*. DPhil thesis, Brighton, University of Sussex.

———. ed. 1989. *Urban Poverty and the Labour Market*. Geneva: International Institute for Labour Studies/ILO.

Rodgers, Gerry, and Vidhya Soundarajan. 2016. *Patterns of Inequality in the Indian Labour Market, 1983–2012*. New Delhi: Academic Foundation.

Rodrik, Dani, and Arvind Subramanian. 2004. 'From 'Hindu Growth' to Productivity Surge: The Mystery of the Indian Growth Transition.' *IMF Working Paper WP/04/77. Washington*.

Roy, Tirthankar. 2007. 'Globalisation, Factor Prices and Poverty in Colonial India.' *Australian Economic History Review* 47 (1): 86, March.

Rustagi, P. 2010. 'Employment Trends for Women in India.' *ILO Asia-Pacific Working Paper Series*, June. New Delhi: ILO Subregional Office for South Asia.

Sabóia, João. 1985. 'A Controvérsia Sobre o Salário Mínimo e a Taxa de Salários na Economia Brasileira: Novas Evidências.' *Revista de Economia Política* 5 (2).

Sadgopal, Anil. 2016. '"Skill India" or Deskilling India: An Agenda of Exclusion.' *Economic and Political Weekly* 51 (35): 33–37.

Salardi, P. 2012. *An Analysis of Pay and Occupational Differences by Gender and Race in Brazil – 1987 to 2006.* DPhil Thesis. Brighton: University of Sussex. Accessed on 7 February 2017. Available at: http://sro.sussex.ac.uk/45204/1/Salardi,_Paola.pdf.

Sankaran, Kamala. 2007. *Labour Laws in South Asia: The Need for an Inclusive Approach.* Geneva: International Institute for Labour Studies/ILO.

_____. 2012. 'Making Labour Laws Work, the Challenges Ahead.' *The Long Road to Social Security,* 7. The Hague: Hivos Knowledge Programme.

Sankaran, K., and Madhav, R. 2011. 'Gender Equality and Social Dialogue in India.' *Bureau for Gender Equality Working Paper WP/1/2011.* Geneva: International Labour Office.

Santos, L. M. V. V. 2010. *Bolsa Familia Programme: Economic and Social Impacts Under the Perspective of the Capabilities Approach.* Paper presented to the 13th Bien Conference, University of London, June.

Santos, W. G. Dos. 1979. *Cidadania e Justiça: a Política Social na Ordem Brasileira.* Rio de Janeiro: Campus.

Sen, Amartya. 1982. *On Economic Inequality.* Oxford: Oxford University Press.

_____. 2001. 'Many Faces of Gender Inequality.' *Frontline,* 18 (22), 27 October–09 November.

Shah, Mihir. 2015. 'Should India do Away with the MGNREGA?' *Keynote Paper,* 10–12 October, Srinagar: Indian Society of Labour Economics 57th Annual Conference.

Shariff, Abusaleh, Prabir Ghosh, and S. K. Mondal. 2002. 'State-Adjusted Public Expenditure on Social Sector and Poverty Alleviation Programmes.' *Economic and Political Weekly* 36 (8): 767–87.

Sharma, K. L. 1980. *Essays on Social Stratification.* Jaipur: Rawat.

Singer, Paul. 1977. *A Crise do 'Milagre': Interpretação Crítica da Economia Brasileira.* São Paulo: Paz e Terra.

_____. 1981. *Dominação e Desigualdade: Estrutura de Classes e Repartição da Renda no Brasil.* Rio de Janeiro: Paz e Terra.

Singh, A. 2008. 'The Past, Present, and Future of Industrial Policy in India: Adapting to the Changing Domestic, and International Environment.' *Working Paper WP 376.* Cambridge: Centre for Business Research, University of Cambridge.

Singh, Manmohan. 2016. 'Speech to the Rajya Sabha, 24 November.' *The Indian Express*, 24 November. Accessed on 20 February 2017. Available at: http://indianexpress.com/article/india/india-news-india/demonetisation-manmohan-singhs-full-speech-in-rajya-sabha-4392829/.

Soares, S. 2012. 'Bolsa Familia: A Summary of its Impacts.' *IPC-UNDP One Pager*. Accessed on 7 February 2017. Available at: http://www.ipc-undp.org/pub/IPCOnePager137.pdf.

Sood, Atul, Paaritosh Nath, and Sangeeta Ghosh. 2014. 'Deregulating Capital, Regulating Labour.' *Economic and Political Weekly* 49 (26 and 27): 58–68.

Sorj, B., and Fontes. A. 2009. 'Les Politiques Publiques au Brésil et l'articulation Entre Travail et Famille: Une Comparaison Interrégionale.' *Cahiers du Genre* 46: 155–176.

Souza, Paulo Renato Costa. 1999. *Salário e Emprego em Economias Atrasadas*. Campinas: Instituto de Economia/Unicamp.

Srinivas, M. N. 1962. *Caste in Modern India and Other Essays*. Bombay: Asia Publishing House.

Srivastava, Ravi. 2013. *A Social Protection Floor for India*. New Delhi: International Labour Office.

_____. 2015. 'Myth and Reality of Labour Flexibility in India and What is to be Done.' *Presidential Lecture,* 10 October. Srinagar: Indian Society of Labour Economics Conference.

Stallings, Barbara et al., 1998. *Impact of the Asian Crisis on Latin America,* 58. Santiago de Chile: United Nations Economic Commission for Latin America and the Caribbean (ECLAC). Accessed on 7 February 2017. Available at: http://repositorio.cepal.org/bitstream/handle/11362/34845/1/S9800515_en.pdf.

Stiglitz, Joseph. 2012. *The Price of Inequality.* London: Allen Lane.

Subramanian, K. N. 1977. *Wages in India.* New Delhi: Tata McGraw-Hill.

Sundar, Shyam K. R. 2011. 'Non-Regular Workers in India: Social Dialogue and Organizational and Bargaining Strategies and Practices.' *Industrial and Employment Relations Department Working Paper WP/30.* Geneva: International Labour Office.

_____. 2015. 'Industrial Conflict in India in the Post-Reform Period: Who said All is quiet on the Industrial Front?' *Economic and Political Weekly* 50 (3): 43–53.

Suzigan, Wilson. 1976. 'As Empresas do Governo e o Papel do Estado na Economia Brasileira.' In *Aspectos da Participação do Governo na Economia,* edited by Fernando Rezende et al. Rio de Janeiro: IPEA/INPES.

Thakur, B., R. Gupta, and R. Singh. 2012. 'Changing Face of India's Industrial Policy: A Look.' *International Journal of Scientific and Research Publications* 2 (12): 1–7.

Thakurdas, Purushottamdas. ed. 1945. *A Brief Memorandum Outlining a Plan of Economic Development for India,* Two Volumes. London: Penguin.

Thomas, J. J. 2012. 'India's Labour Market during the 2000s: Surveying the Changes.' *Economic and Political Weekly* 47 (51): 39–51.

Thorat, Sukhadeo, and Umakant. 2004. *Caste, Race, and Discrimination: Discourses in International Context.* Jaipur: Rawat Publications.

Thorat, Sukhadeo, Debolina Kundu, and Nidhi Sadana. 2010. 'Caste and Ownership of Private Enterprises: Consequences of Denial of Property Rights.' In *Blocked by Caste: Economic Discrimination in Modern India,* edited by Sukhadeo Thorat and Katherine Newman. New Delhi: Oxford University Press.

Tilly, C., R. Agarwala, S. Mosoetsa, P. Ngai, C. Salas, and H. Sheikh. 2013. *Final Report: Informal Worker Organizing as a Strategy for Improving Subcontracted Work in the Textile and Apparel Industries of Brazil, South Africa, India, and China, Los Angeles.* University of California: Institute for Research on Labor and Employment. Accessed 30 July 2014. Available at: http://www.irle.ucla.edu/publications/documents/Informalworkerorganizingintextilesandgarments-UCLAReport-9-2013.pdf.

United Nations. 1975. *Poverty, Unemployment and Development Policy: A Case Study of Selected Issues with Reference to Kerala.* New York: UN Department of Economic and Social Affairs.

_____. 2013. *World Population Prospects: The 2012 Revision.* New York: Department of Economic and Social Affairs, Population Division.

_____. 2014. *World Urbanization Prospects.* New York: Department of Economic and Social Affairs, Population Division.

_____. 2015. *World Economic Situation and Prospects 2015.* New York.

————. 2017. *World Economic Situation and Prospects 2017*. New York.

————. *Database: Demographic Yearbook, Population Census Datasets 1995–Present*. UN: Statistics Division. Accessed 22 December 2016. Available at: http://data.un.org/Data.aspx?d=POP&f=tableCode%3a22.

United Nations Development Programme (UNDP). 2015. *Human Development Report 2015*. New York.

————. *Human Development Reports Database*. Accessed on 7 February 2017. Available at: http://hdr.undp.org/en/content/database.

United Nations University, World Institute for Development Economics Research (UNU-WIDER). *World Income Inequality Database, Version 33*. Accessed on 7 February 2017. Available at: https://www.wider.unu.edu/project/wiid-world-income-inequality-database.

Vaidyanathan, A. 1982. 'The Indian Economy since Independence. 1947–1970.' In *Cambridge Economic History of India, 1757–1970, Volume 2*, edited by Dharma Kumar. New Delhi: Orient Longman.

Van Klaveren, M., K. Tijdens, M. Hughie-Williams, and N. Ramos Martin. 2009. 'An Overview of Women's Work and Employment in Brazil.' Wage Indicator Project. Amsterdam: Amsterdam Institute for Advanced Labour Studies.

Vargas da Cruz, M. J., G. Porcile, L. Nakabashi, and F. D. Scatolin. 2008. *Structural Change and the Service Sector in Brazil*. Accessed 15 November 2016. Available at: https://ideas.repec.org/p/fup/wpaper/0075.html.

Velho, Otávio Guilherme. 1976. *Capitalismo Autoritário e Campesinato*. São Paulo: Difel.

Venkataratnam, C. S. 2003. *Negotiated Change: Collective Bargaining, Liberalization, and Restructuring in India*. New Delhi: Sage Publications.

Verick, S. 2013. 'A Return to Stronger Employment Growth in India? Insights from the 68th NSS Round 2011–12.' *Asia-Pacific Research Brief Series 2*. New Delhi: ILO, Subregional Office for South Asia.

Verma, Satish, and Rahul Arora. 2010. 'Does the Indian Economy Support Wagner's Law? An Econometric Analysis.' *Eurasian Journal of Business and Economics* 3 (5): 77–91.

Vianna, Luiz Werneck. 1978. *Liberalismo e Sindicato no Brasil*. Rio de Janeiro: Paz e Terra, Third edition.

Vijay Shankar, P. S., and Mihir Shah. 2012. 'Rethinking Reforms: A New Vision for the Social Sector in India.' In *Growth, Inequality, and Social Development in India*, edited by R. Nagaraj. Basingstoke: Palgrave Macmillan.

Women in Informal Employment: Globalizing and Organizing (WIEGO) 2016. *Women's Economic Empowerment: WIEGO Position and Approach.* Accessed 15 November 2016. Available at: http://wiego.org/sites/wiego.org/files/resources/files/Chen_Economic%20Empowerment_WIEGO_Position.pdf.

World Bank. *World Development Indicators.* Accessed on 15 November 2016. Available at: http://databank.worldbank.org/data/home.aspx.

Index